The picture of Gwen carried by Harry throughout the war.

Being the unexpurgated letters, diaries and
other scribblings of an ordinary soldier

MY DARLING WIFE

By
HARRY BERRY

or
How I passed the time of day between
18th April 1940 and 5th November 1945

authors
On Line

Visit us online at www.authorsonline.co.uk

Published by Authors OnLine Ltd 2004

Copyright © Linda West 2004

Cover design by Siobhan Smith

ISBN 0 7552 0155 8

Authors OnLine Ltd
40 Castle Street
Hertford SG14 1HR
England

This book is also available in e-book format, details of which are available at
www.authorsonline.co.uk

Dedicated with eternal gratitude to the memory of all those who were not so lucky as my father, who did not come home from the Far East in 1945.

THE AUTHOR

Harry Berry was born in Islington, North London, of working-class parents on 1st December 1916.

At the local council Central School he learned shorthand, typing and other commercial subjects. His father taught him music and to play the piano.

By sheer luck he obtained a job as secretary/editorial assistant on a London evening paper, "The Star", and thus started a journalistic career. He also played piano in a semi-professional dance band in the evenings and at week-ends.

It was whilst on "The Star" that he met the lady cashier who was later to become his wife.

He was conscripted for National Service at the age of 23. After the war he returned to "The Star" for a few months but soon left to join a news agency covering Northolt and Heathrow Airports.

In 1953 he joined the Public Relations branch of British European Airways (later to become British Airways) and retired in 1979.

* * * *

NOTE FROM HIS DAUGHTER, LINDA WEST

After his retirement my father typed out this entire collection of letters and diaries. He wanted to get it published but conventional publishers requested it to be edited: the exciting, the dramatic and the brutal to be highlighted, the tedious to be cut out. Harry said, "No, that's how it was for me and is exactly what I wrote at the time. It's all or nothing!"

So there you are Pop. 60 years ago concluded the 2nd World War and we will not forget that many were still fighting, suffering and dying in the Far East when the war in Europe had finished. You always said you never forgot how lucky you were to be alive.

I have only put in an Appendix and some illustrations. But apart from that, it's unaltered as you wanted.

R.I.P. Loads of love, Linda.

Harry Berry as reporter at Northolt Airport with Brenard's Press in an old ex-WD caravan 1947.

INTRODUCTION

By no stretch of the imagination can this war story be called a literary masterpiece. It is just a factual report told mainly in the form of letters and diary notes of one young man's experience of World War II from the day he was 'called up' to the day he returned home almost five years later.

There are no heroics, no sex, and any drama is hidden between the lines. In other words, it has none of the attributes of the popular best-seller.

The letters to his wife are matter-of-fact, at times almost naïve, but often with a touch of humour. They were written in uncomfortable and sometimes primitive conditions from barrack rooms in England, India and Malaya, from the crowded decks of troopships and as censored postcards and letters from Japanese POW Camps in Singapore, Taiwan and Japan. They appear exactly as written. Nothing added, nothing taken away.

Parts of the Diary and other notes written during the first 19 months of captivity were confiscated by the Imperial Japanese Army in Tokyo. The remainder were hidden and brought safely home.

The published articles were written after the war.

When the author, now a far wiser and mature man, perused these letters and notes again some 50 years later, he found it hard to believe that this strange character was himself. How innocent he was. How weak. How strong. How on earth did he survive? An ordinary working-class snob who was never meant to be a soldier. Even less a prisoner-of-war.

But survive he did. And looking back to that so-different era he can now almost feel a sense of pride at the way he was able to 'take it'. How he learned such tasks as carrying 80 kilo sacks of soya beans on his back; how he successfully came through all the bullying and beating and the starvation diet.

My thanks to my wife Gwen, who not only never gave up hope even though it was 18 months from the fall of Singapore before she received news of me, but for also keeping all my letters, without which this small insignificant slice of 20th century history would never have been preserved for posterity!

CONTENTS

LETTERS:

STORY PUBLISHED IN 'WAR ILLUSTRATED':

THE DIARY AND LETTERS:

SONGS AND PUBLISHED ARTICLE:

APPENDIX:

PHOTOGRAPHS AND ILLUSTRATIONS

PART ONE

'CALL-UP'

and

TRAINING TO BE A SOLDIER

Gnr. Berry, H.W.
No. 974063
24 Squad.,
A. Bty.,
37th Sig. T
Reg.R.A.
Burniston Barracks,
Scarborough.

18th April 1940

Darling,

Well, darling, here I am. All safe and sound after a tiring and monotonous journey.

We arrived here about 4 o'clock and my feelings are, well - rather mixed. This is the first opportunity I have had to sit down (6.30 p.m.) and I think we have finished for the time being until we turn in. These are very large barracks and, on the whole, quite modern. Of course, our batch, being raw recruits, have the worst part of the building, but as the weeks slip by so we will get better quarters.

I was, at first, rather disappointed. The crowd here seems rather rough and it is the Royal Artillery - not the Signals. However, I mustn't pass judgement on the place too soon, but will bide my time. We have already collected our mugs, knife, fork and spoon and have had dinner – it wasn't bad but cold as we were late. We had steak and kidney pudding, potatoes and peas – our plates were piled high! I could eat only a quarter of mine. Then we had rice pudding – very tasty – for 'afters' and a mug of tea.

Since then we have filled large bags with straw – that's our mattress – and made our beds. We have quite good <u>spring</u> beds with four blankets. Darling, I must close now as I wish to catch the post. I hope this letter doesn't sound <u>too</u> cheerful. I am not very impressed with the place, but it is no good being miserable. I wish I were with you.

My darling,

Here I am mid-way through the second day of Army life! And things seem a little brighter.

The Sergeant Major came up to see us this morning. He is as much like a S.M. as a rabbit pie and is a splendid chap. He says he believes in "sympathetic" training – rather than bawling us about and swearing. Tomorrow we see the Major who asks all about us, and if you make an impression with him you're O.K. The Sergeant told me that money wasn't necessary now for a Commission – so just watch how your fiancé gets promoted. It's a cinch!

I have got my complete outfit today, including uniform. The only one so far. They tell me I look pretty smart. By the way, the S.M. said we were picked for R.A. Signals because of our education – although some of them here seem as if they don't know their ABC. However, I have found some decent chaps now and I feel a little better. Our training takes 21 weeks in which we learn Morse code, etc. and also learn to drive a car! I do not know yet whether they use teleprinters.

I may get a week-end off in about a fortnights time, when I shall come and see you. I can't come next week because we are to be inoculated – so Help me God.

I have written to you again today because we have a little spare time as we have not yet started training. But don't worry if you don't hear from me every day as we shall have more work to do shortly.

20th April 1940   Burniston Barracks,
                                                            Scarborough

My darling,

I have just received your letter and am sorry that you are not feeling too happy. I hope you're not feeling unhappy on my account. I can't say I'm happy exactly, but I am not too unhappy. (Rather complicated that!)

We are to be trained in very interesting subjects as I mentioned in my last letter. Motor-car driving, motor-bike driving, Morse code, wireless, etc. – in fact there is hardly any difference between the Signal Corps and us. We are very well treated – absolutely no 'bossing', and the food is not at all bad. Yesterday we had some fish and chips and I have never had such tasty f.a.c. And the quantity! I've never managed to eat more than half of my share yet. We saw the Major yesterday – a nice friendly chap and, of course, I told him <u>all</u> my good points. I wonder what will come of that? Our training lasts 21 weeks and we get odd week-ends off and 7 days every 3 months. We finished at 12.30 p.m. today and I could have had permission to come home, but my trousers are being altered and we are not really allowed outside the barracks without a uniform. I am now dressed in 'overalls' – a replica of the battledress, but in cloth-like material.

I have found about half-a-dozen chaps in our squad (23 in all) who are really decent and I think I shall now be all right. They do not drink!!!

I went out yesterday evening to view Scarborough. It is a marvellous place. I would like to see you here, darling. The girls here are very forward, cheap and common – so you won't have to worry that I shall stray from the straight and narrow.

I have been taking it easy this afternoon, resting and playing Solo with the 'decent' chaps. We have just moved into new quarters which are very fine and airy - with heating apparatus. But I have not felt too good today because my tooth – or rather late tooth – has been aching.

Darling, I have been thinking a lot of you today. I don't want you to be unhappy although I now realise it is worse for you than for me. I would, of course, much rather be at home, but I have got things to do which occupy my time and mind. Please don't worry. I shall come home on the first week available. Love to all.

21st April 1940   Burniston Barracks,
                                                               Scarborough

We have had a nice restful day today (Sunday) but we really start work tomorrow! I have spent this morning (did not get up till 8.30 a.m.) playing cards and lying on my bed thinking of you and I'm convinced that I adore you.

I was examined by the MO yesterday and as he tapped my back he said "Hm! You're very fit aren't you?" I also saw the dentist and my teeth only have to be scaled. So I shall be a superman when you see me. Went out yesterday with a chap from Ealing – Collins by name – very decent. We went to the local NAAFI where I played the piano for the first time here. Then we played billiards for the rest of the evening and got into barracks at 11.30 p.m. (We are allowed out until 12 o'clock).

As army life goes, I think we are very fortunate here. If I were only near you, darling, I should be quite happy and contented. Another battalion in the district, (the 39th), are told by their NCOs that we are 'cissies'. So you see we are not too badly off!!

I shall try and write tomorrow – unless we are worked too hard. Regards to all at 28. Love.
P.S. This is a Woolworth's fountain pen.

23rd April 1940   Burniston Barracks,
                                                               Scarborough

Darling,
I love you. I must apologise profoundly for not having written before, but honestly I have not been able to, and now I shall not be able to post this till tomorrow morning. I shall explain later in this letter. I received two letters today from you which I have been looking forward to. You ask such a lot of questions and there is so much to say that I have to leave a lot out; otherwise I should still be writing the first letter to you. I shall try and answer first, the questions in your first letter.

(a) I am sleeping much better now, darling, gradually getting used to our straw mattresses. In a few days time we are to get two sheets and a pillow to add to our four blankets. So we shall be quite comfortable.

(b) We have to be on the parade ground at 8.10 a.m. so, in order to have time to shave, wash, make our beds <u>tidy</u> and have breakfast, we should get up at about 6.15 a.m. Although this morning it was nearly 7 o'clock before we arose.

(c) There is a piano in the dining room, but it is not used except at dances. As it is a good piano and soldiers are usually careless, this is quite understandable. I have, however, applied for special permission and have to see a certain Bombardier tomorrow – I believe he's something to do with the Regimental Dance Band. (A bombardier, by the way, is a Corporal in the Royal Artillery)

(d) There are special tennis courts here and we have to get the Major's permission to play. There is no table tennis, but there are billiards and darts.

(e) We are on a cliff only a few yards from the sea.

You needn't be worried about guns, darling. We have one ancient howitzer here that doesn't fire and is used only for gun drill. (We have to do gun drill as we are in the R.A. and have to know something about everything including rifle shooting, drill, etc.)

Glad to hear you are taking such an interest in your garden. Perhaps I can have some of your home-grown potatoes when I get leave. I really love you darling and will try and get a STRIPE.

Thank you for all the news in your second letter. Please give my regards to everybody who asks after me. I will try and write to everyone I know sooner or later, but we don't seem to have much time lately. So I will explain why I haven't written before.

I believe I told you we started work on Monday – and we did with a vengeance. We had parade, drill, lecture and one hour's gym in the morning and another hour of gym in the afternoon, together with drill, etc. So you can guess how tired I felt yesterday evening. Even then I could have found time to write but the SM told me to have a hair-cut. (In fact, he told everyone in the squad). However, after doing fatigues while we were waiting he didn't have time to do all, so some of us had to go again this evening. However, yesterday evening another fellow and I thought it was a good chance to go to a private barber and perhaps get it done better. We washed and changed into our khaki uniforms (I have my trousers now!) and walked to Scarborough where we searched high and low for a barber's shop and found it – only it was shut! So we came "home" (?) tired out with aching feet and went straight to bed.

This morning I was up at 7 a.m. and had 2 hours gym again (climbing up ropes, etc. which I can't do and lots of other crazy things). The hard work and discipline made me a bit miserable yesterday and this morning, but some gun drill we had this afternoon was so comical (we made it comical with our mistakes) that it restored my good humour. The squad SM is a very decent fellow and even gives us a few minutes break in drill in which to smoke. I think I shall gradually settle down to this life of hardship. By the way, I can't even post this letter tonight as we are on fire-picket – which means we have to stay in barracks in case of fire: which we would have to put out – we hope!

The boys here are very decent (about 20 in this room) and at the moment they are singing "South American Joe" accompanied by an accordion which someone has borrowed. (It is now 8.10 p.m.).

Last night we all felt rather sentimental and homesick after "Lights Out" and (don't laugh) the boys started singing hymns. They sang very well and seemed to know the words. I felt rather out of it. Well, honestly, darling, my arm is aching terribly and I haven't written half I want to tell you.

I have just returned from the barbers and I look like a convict – I hope you still love me when you see me, darling.

Please write to me. We all rush for the post when the Sergeant brings it round. It is a great occasion to hear from the 'outside world'. Darling, I haven't smoked much, drunk much or spoken to a girl. Aren't I good? Au revoir my sweet.

P.S. The accordionist is now playing 'Sweet Mystery of Life'.
P.P.S. I still say 'Goodnight' every night, darling.

25th April 1940   Burniston Barracks,
                                                                                        Scarborough

This will be a short, sharp and snappy letter because I haven't much to say. I just want to tell you that I love you and am having an inoculation tomorrow – so if you don't hear from me until Monday or so, you will know why.

We are working very hard now and sometimes I feel thoroughly miserable, with P.T., drill, rifle drill, marching, etc., but it is a lovely feeling when 4.30 p.m. comes. Even then, by the time we've had a shower and changed our clothes, it is getting on, and, of course, we can't help wanting to get to bed early. However, in 3 weeks' time – there's a new squad today – we shall leave all this drilling and learn to drive. Also, leave, I believe, is pretty easy to get. By the way, I am having a 'trial' for the Regimental Dance Band on Tuesday.

Just one more thing. Couldn't it be arranged that I ring you somewhere after 7 p.m. for 1/- before the price goes up? What do you think? Well darling, I am now (it is 5.15 p.m.) going for a short walk to the sea-front before turning in. Please excuse writing, but all the drill today has made my hands shaky. The sergeant says I am more awkward than the rest of the squad put together – but he says similar things to everybody.

Fondest love.

P.S. It's been a marvellous day today. I have quite a colour.

28th April 1940   Burniston Barracks,
                                                                                        Scarborough

I am writing this letter in bed – the time is 9.30 a.m. As I told you, we had our inoculation on Friday evening and I am pleased to say I feel fine. Although several of the fellows were laid out, it had no effect on me whatsoever except a stiff arm – which has now practically returned to normal. We had 48 hours off duty (CB) and I am afraid I stayed in bed nearly all day yesterday and slept. That shows you how overworked I have been – sleeping all Friday night, Saturday and Saturday night. But I feel fine now – ready for the hardships of the forthcoming week.

I'm glad you have not 'tripped up' yet (literally and metaphorically) and are taking an interest in your garden. Thanks for the office news. Nothing more to report. I believe I told you that I have a trial with the Regimental Dance Band on Tuesday.

Your fiancé, Gunner Harry.

30th April 1940   Burniston Barracks,
Scarborough

My darling,

Thank you for your letter which I received today. I think you're right about the post. It is advisable, I think, to allow at least a day and a half for the letter to be delivered. That is the reason, of course, why I didn't phone you yesterday – and today I have the Dance Band trial at 7.15 p.m. I hope you don't hang about too long, darling. How about Friday – that should allow plenty of time for you to get this letter and let me know.

I'm improving at gym now and can climb half-way up the rope. We've only vaulted once and I <u>nearly</u> got across.

Thanks for the office news. A bloke who sleeps four beds away from me asked if I knew Roy Nash. He went to the same school. Isn't it a small world! Of course, I shall write to Roy and tell him.

Darling, I wish you wouldn't worry so. You know how I used to pull your leg about it! I have always been right up to now …… touch wood. I still love you very much and often sit and think about you. I imagine I'm sitting on your settee in front of that hot fire holding you in my arms. I am hoping to come and see you soon for 'tis rumoured that we are having a few days off at Whitsun, from

Friday lunchtime. If so, I shall be home like a shot about 7 o'clock the same day. But don't take it too much for granted darling. One can never promise anything in the army. I have not taken off your ring, darling. It slipped off once when I was washing, but that was the once and only. I often twist it around in bed, thinking of you. Darling, I want to get married to you. Will you?

I hope you don't think I am not phoning you tonight simply because of the dance band. I shall have to go to town (2d bus ride) to phone you and to do that I have to change into my walking-out battle dress (we're not allowed out in overalls) wash, shave, clean boots, etc. I wouldn't mind that, but I've got some terrific blisters on my feet and the sight of an Army boot sends cold shivers down my back! But I shall definitely be there Friday if that's OK for you. By the way, I've just been told I have to visit the dentist tomorrow at 10.30 a.m. for the scaling, I suppose – I hope!! I've fully recovered from the inoc. Now, I'm pleased to say I was the least affected of the lot.

I won't write much more now as a fellow is going to town and says he will post this letter for me. You will get it much quicker then, darling, because the last post at the barracks goes at 5.30 p.m. and it is now 6 o'clock.

I must tell you that we heard the Major tell our Sergeant that he thought we were the best squad they ever had for intelligence and smartness, etc. Perhaps we'll all get stripes! They are certainly a decent lot of fellows. We had a 'revolution' the other evening when I started preaching communism and all the other 'isms'. Only one other fellow supported me and the others grabbed their rifles; so we lay on my bed behind a kit-bag and popped them off. The rifles, by the way, are 'duds' – only used for drill purposes.

'Till Whitsun (?) my darling.

P.S. I've got a terrific cold.

1st May 1940   Burniston Barracks,
                                                           Scarborough

Just a short note to say I love you and that I received your
letter (the cheerful one) today. I am so glad you are feeling
better.

I did not have the trial for the dance band yesterday, after all.
I went along to the dining hall, but all the doors were locked, so
there appears to have been some misunderstanding. But I shall
have another try. There is plenty of time yet, of course, for me to
get on to the entertainment side. I have not even obtained
permission to play the piano here, but I must ask about that soon.

I'm getting a little used to Army life now. Last week it nearly
killed me and I was terribly fed up, but this week I seem much
better and the days seem to be going quicker. Did I tell you that
we do our Gym in a large hall with all windows open, dressed only in
shorts and slippers? It's a bit cold sometimes, but I'm even
getting used to that. Actually, our Sergeant is quite a decent
fellow, although a bit strict sometimes. He always gives us a few
minutes to smoke in the middle of drill (not P.T.).

I went to the dentist this morning and had my teeth scaled. He
scraped a lot of stuff off, but my teeth don't look much better I'm
afraid. He said it was calcium caused by the saliva and was making
my front teeth loose. He told me to go and see him again whenever
I liked – a nice bloke (officer).

Darling, whenever (if ever) you make some nice cakes, how about
sending me some?

Love.

5th May 1940   Burniston Baracks,
                                                           Scarborough

I was very thrilled to hear your voice once again – even if it was
only over the phone and you were so far away. I'm afraid I couldn't
think of much to say, but I don't think that mattered really. I

hope you did not think I was in a hurry to leave you, but the operator said 'Your time is up' and it did not occur to me until afterwards that you may not have heard him. I hope we can phone each other again soon, darling.

I am writing this letter sitting on a cliff and there is a marvellous view. Actually, I am in barrack boundaries as we are on fire picket today and not allowed out – but it is very nice here. There is a miniature railway below me which runs round the resort (It is not working yet) and just in front of that is the beach and sea. The sea is very blue and on my right is a cape which juts right out with an old castle on top. The scene is very reminiscent of the view from our hotel at Eze-sur-Mer and it reminds me of the good time we had together. I wish you were here with me, my sweet. Are you coming here for your holidays?

We have not heard anything about Whitsun yet, and probably will not know until about Thursday. So we just have to wait and see.

We have had quite a time lately. On Thursday evening we were inoculated for lockjaw (no ill effect), on Friday (when I phoned you) we were clearing our barrack room from 5 p.m. to 10.15 p.m. for kit inspection on Saturday (I had to wash and change just to get out of the barracks for a few minutes to phone you). On Saturday morning we had the kit inspection and a medical inspection (still O.K!), and in the afternoon we slept!

In the evening my friend and I went out and played billiards and we were in bed by 10 o'clock. Today we have been on fire picket and not allowed out, and, on top of that, we had to clean out the dining room. Next week, on Tuesday, we have our second inoculation for typhoid and shall probably all be dead by Thursday. Still, worse things happen at sea!

Actually, it is not quite so bad as it sounds and one soon gets used to a little hardship now and again. Our Sergeant reckons we are all on holiday compared with what he had to go through whilst training. I don't think he's kidding either.

With regard to this STRIPE – it is going to be very difficult to get as quite a number of the chaps in this squadron are Public school and secondary school fellows. But I shall do my best. In any case, we get paid no more for stripes whilst we are still in the Training Unit. By the way, you can say your fiancé is an R.A. Signaller. It's quite a good job – we get, I believe, 3/6d a day when we 'pass out'.

Will close now as I must write to the family and other people. I don't think I've written to anyone else except you. All my love.

8th May 1940   Burniston Barracks

Many thanks for your nice letter which I received about an hour ago. (It is now 9.30 a.m.). Through being 'sick' we don't have to wait until 11 a.m. for the post. I had my inoculation yesterday evening and feel all right this morning except for a rather stiff arm; but I did not have too good a night because of a cough which I seem to have developed. However, I'm O.K. now and quite pleased with the prospect of being off duty until Friday morning.

Darling, I'm afraid I know nothing about Whitsun yet. Whether we are having any time off, or not, or, if so, how long. The only thing I can do is to promise to send you a telegram directly I know saying 'King's Cross, Saturday, 1 o'clock', or something similar. I should know by Friday morning – of course I could 'phone the office, couldn't I? I don't know at all, my sweet, what to suggest about your going to Mary's. If I 'phone you Friday morning sometime, could you get in touch with her? Alternatively, you could go to Mary's and let me know her address so that I could go on to Staines to meet you. I don't mind in the least. I don't think it will be much fun for you to stay at home if I don't get leave.

I had a letter from Dad today. He is going to his sister's at Sudbury and Joyce might be there. He says "Should be pleased to see Gwen at Whitsun if you do not come up and she should want somewhere to go. My sister and her daughter would like to meet her. Please tell her that when you write." Please yourself what you do, darling, I'm afraid I'm not in a position to advise.

Darling, it is very sweet of you to knit me socks – I'm sure they will be very nice. I love you.

I'm so glad, my love, that you have decided to take your holidays here. I am looking forward to seeing you and showing you the sights. I think you would enjoy it.

Your devoted fiancé.

9th May 1940   Burniston Barracks
4.10 p.m.

My darling,

I suppose you have received my previous letter by now and have seen that I can't get leave. Isn't it a damn nuisance?

There seems to be something in the air up here – tonight at 5 p.m. (although it is our second day of inoculation) we are going on manoeuvres. On Monday at 10.45 p.m. we shall be on manoeuvres again – probably all night. Lord knows what the idea is and what we are supposed to do. The only thing to do is to grin and bear it.

However, most of us here are going to try hard for a short leave from next Saturday lunch time to 6 o'clock Monday morning, and if we don't get it there'll be a blinkin' revolution. It's not much of a break – we shall arrive at Kings Cross about 7 p.m. – but we all feel we want to get back to our homes and fiancées if only for a few hours.

STOP PRESS 4.40 P.M. Our bombardier has just been in to say we can skip the route march this evening as long as we keep in our barrack room out of sight – as we really are supposed to be on the manoeuvres. So we are stuck here from 5 p.m. until they return.

4.35 p.m. Just going to tea. Keep good, my love.

5 p.m. Just back from tea and a trip to the NAAFI for cigarettes. I am at rather a loose end now as there is nothing to do apart from writing. I suppose I had better take the chance of writing to the hundreds of people I promised to communicate with.

I can promise you that nothing much short of an earthquake will prevent my seeing you next week-end. So keep cheerful, my love.

P.S. By the way, darling, you mentioned in one of your letters that you had been invited to a dance. Why don't you go, my sweet? There is no reason why you shouldn't and I trust you implicitly. You must not hang about doing nothing in your spare time. Most of the fellows here go dancing on a Saturday night, but I don't fancy it. My Ealing friend – John – and I usually spend most of our money on pin-tables!!! But we have won quite a lot. Must end now in order to catch post.

All my love.

12th May 1940   Burniston Barracks,
                                                                                Scarborough

My darling,

Thank you very much for your letter which I received lunch time on Friday: fairly good going as you did not post it until 7.30 on Thursday. I think where the delay comes in, both ways, is here in the Barracks. Your letter might reach here by first post but I may not get it until the late afternoon. Alternatively, the Barracks post-box mail goes as early as 5.30 p.m. The next collection is 8 o'clock the following morning! So you see, if we are lucky, our letters reach each other fairly quickly. If not they take longer. Darling, you must try not to be sad. I like to think of you as cheerful, and although I know you love me and miss me, you must not become morbid. I am really always thinking of you, darling, and the only way I keep cheerful is by looking forward to the time when I see you again – and also when we are married. When you next walk through the Embankment gardens, please try and imagine I am with you.

Quite a lot has happened up here since my last letter. I told you something was in the wind, didn't I? They must have known Hitler was going to invade Holland or Belgium. Although we are continuing with our training as Signallers, we have also been formed into an infantry regiment. Our job is to defend

16

Scarborough and district from possible attack. We all have our full equipment now; steel helmets, etc., and yesterday we were issued with rifles (left over from the last war but still in working order). Every four days a platoon of us has to sleep in the gym fully dressed with equipment.

(3.30 p.m. Have just finished a game of solo and am now continuing with your letter, my sweet. I have also moved from our room to the reading room which is more convenient for writing.)

I believe our turn is next Tuesday night, so if any German paratroopers try to land here – God help Scarborough!

Since this affair started we have been confined to barracks and everybody is fed up as there is nothing to do. To crown it all, today's dinner was putrid, as well as being such a small portion. So everyone is half-starved. Consequently, the NAAFI has sold out of practically all edible things. If we don't get out tonight to get some decent food I shall stage a mutiny!! I haven't had a chance to use my organising ability yet!

I'm afraid that Mr. …… Hitler has temporarily messed up all chance of a few days leave. I know I said nothing short of an earthquake would stop me seeing you, darling, but I think we can safely call Hitler an earthquake. Still, my love, I will keep trying and may yet be lucky.

How are the family? Remember me to all. Keep cheerful and don't forget I love you with all my heart.

15th May 1940   Burniston Barracks
Scarborough

Thank you for your two nice letters which I received yesterday – one in the morning and one in the afternoon. I am very, very sorry my sweet that I have not written before but I am sure you will excuse me when I tell you what we have been doing.

Since last Thursday we have been confined to barracks and, as I told you before, have been formed into infantry companies to deal with these blasted paratroopers – should they come.

On Sunday evening we had to parade in full kit (Khaki suits, overcoats, gas masks and full pack; water bottle, blankets, ground sheet, gas capes, etc.) at 9.30 p.m. and hung about the parade ground until 10.45 p.m. (waiting for the Germans), when we went to bed. At <u>3.30 a.m.</u> we were up again waiting for them for over an hour, after which we again went to bed. Of course, we were up again, as usual, at about 7.15 a.m. for parade at 8.10 a.m. Up to now we have done this every night, so you can guess how we feel! Apparently, the idea is that these parachutists will most likely arrive at twilight or dawn – and so we have to be prepared at these times. While we are hanging about we are learning Charging (running – still in full kit) and falling on our tummies at a word of command. Last night we were taught street fighting and crept round the barracks popping off imaginary Germans with imaginary bullets. I think I must have been bumped off at least three times.

I don't know how long these arrangements will continue; I don't think we could stand it indefinitely, as, of course, we don't get more than four hours sleep at a time. However, I believe they are planning some new arrangements. So perhaps things will be easier soon.

But enough of my petty troubles. How are you keeping my sweet? I'm glad you went over to Sudbury on Sunday. It must have made a change for you.

I have not had an audition for the Dance Band yet, as I don't think this is exactly the time to think of dance bands. Last Saturday, however, after supper, I obtained permission to play the piano in the dining room. In no time the hall was practically full and a miniature concert was in progress. Several other people had a go at the piano, but personally I did not think much of them. However, that may be conceit! I'm afraid I don't get much chance to play here. None of the pubs have a piano and the only chance I get is at a NAAFI place in town. I'm afraid I shall lose a bit of my technique!

Darling, I'm very excited at the prospect of receiving a parcel from you. (The first of many I hope!!!) I hope there are a lot of nice things in it. In fact I know there are.

I'm glad you are feeling fit, my love. I love you with all my heart.

P.S. XXXXXXXXXXXX (more to follow in the next letter)

17th May 1940   Burniston Barracks
                                                                    Scarborough

It is now 8.55 p.m. and I am sitting on a bunk in the guard-room writing this letter. With three other fellows from our squad, I am on Guard tonight until 6 a.m. I was marching up and down the entrance to the barracks from 6 to 8 o'clock and my next period is from 12 to 2 a.m. Then I can try and get some sleep here until 6 a.m. when I shall have my breakfast and be on parade at 9.15 a.m.

I received your parcel yesterday and am very grateful for the contents. I was just going out for some razor blades when it arrived. I have the biscuits and cheese here with me now and will probably 'pile in' sometime during the early hours. I shall be thinking of you darling. We had a pleasant surprise yesterday. In the evening we were allowed out until 9.30 p.m. (first time for a week) and on top of that we did not have to get up at 3.15 a.m. I volunteered for guard tonight because I would rather have a sleep from 2 to 6 o'clock than be on parade for an hour at 3.15 a.m.

There does not seem to be much hope of getting leave now, my darling – unless of course this latest affair of Hitler blows over. You can be sure that I will dash to see you whenever it is possible, if only for a few hours.

Next week we leave 'A' Battery for 'B' Battery when we shall take our course in driving. That should be very exciting and they say it is almost a holiday. I hope it is – I could do with one.

This is only a short letter because I am sitting here in overcoat and gas-mask ready to be 'turned out' for inspection. I am very tired and you must forgive the scribble. I will write you a proper letter tomorrow (Half day tomorrow). Au revoir.

19th May 1940 Burniston Barracks
Scarborough

Once again this must be a short and snappy letter as I have at least 2 free hours - and I feel very thirsty as well as sleepy.

I told you in my last letter that I was on guard Friday night at the main gate; nothing eventful happened and I did not challenge or shoot anyone! We finished at 6 a.m. and were on parade as usual at 9.15 a.m. We had quite a good morning on Saturday. It was our last day in 'A' Battery and we bought the Sergeant some cigarettes and treated him to some beer. We also had a strenuous game of football during the gym period. At 6 p.m. Saturday all of us were on the Alert position for 24 hours. We slept in a building that used to be the old gym on straw mattresses on the floor in all our clothes.

Every day a platoon (about 60 men) have this job and the idea is that if any Germans arrive these men will be on the spot in a few minutes. There are lorries and cars waiting and we had three rehearsals. One at 10 p.m. Saturday, one at 4 o'clock this morning and another during the afternoon.

We have just finished now (at 6 p.m.) but at 9.20 we will be on parade again. Also we will be up for an hour at 3.30 a.m. tomorrow morning - so you see we are still getting our sleep in dribs and drabs. I believe there is talk (according to the newspapers) of a volunteer corps to deal with these parachutists. The quicker they do, the more pleased we shall be here.

I'll try and write you a real letter tomorrow and try and answer your two letters I have in my pocket.

As soon as this volunteer corps is formed I expect I shall be able to come and see you.

20th May 1940

Gunner Berry HW
No. 974063
24th Squad
"B" Battery
37th Sign. T. Reg.,
Burniston Barracks
Scarborough

It seems a long time since I heard from you, my darling (was it Friday?).

I know it isn't really, but it does seem rather a long time – I hope you haven't forgotten me.

I enjoyed the biscuits and cheese and thought of you while I munched. I have also used the toothpaste, shaving cream and am now using the writing paper. I have, of course, read 'Razzle' – although I hope you did not buy it specially for me; I'm not that kind of boy! Whatever made you think I was such a lowbrow? Of course it went all round the barracks room and it now seems to have disappeared. I shouldn't be surprised to know that the Major was reading it.

I'm still working overtime here. Tonight we are standing by and tomorrow I am on Main Guard. Since Friday, my programme has been:

Friday: 5.30 pm. to 6 am. Saturday. Main guard. Full kit (sleeping in coat, etc.). On 'alert' guard 6 – 8 pm., 12 – 2 am.

Saturday: 6 pm. to 6 pm. Sunday. Billeted with full equipment in old gym. Turned out several times during night.

Sunday: Parade at 9.15 pm. till 10.15 pm. Turned out at 4 am. to 5 am.

Monday: (tonight) same as Sunday.

Tuesday: Main Guard (Same as Friday).

So you see my darling I haven't had much opportunity lately to dream of you. I wouldn't mind missing sleep so much but we have semi-manoeuvres in the early hours of the morning and have to crawl on our tummies through mud. I'm afraid I shan't have a decent walking-out suit for long. However, worse things happen at sea.

You will notice that I have changed my Battery. We are now learning all about motors. This morning we had lessons and this afternoon we went out in cars. It only took me about 10 minutes to get the hang of the thing and I was soon careering along at 40 mph along the front. I'm glad I didn't spend three quid on learning to drive; it isn't worth it. But it's a grand sensation and I <u>must</u> buy a car when this war's over. I said when it's over ....

We are still all confined to barracks and everyone is a <u>little</u> fed-up. But we all do our best to keep cheerful and are fairly successful. I do want to get home and see you again my darling. (I haven't been out with any girls here yet!!!)

I don't know what to advise you about holidays. We never know what's going to happen from one day to another. The only thing you can do is to fix them up and chance to luck. I have 7 days leave to come in 2 months' time, but if you want to come here I expect I should be able to see you quite a lot. I have heard from Roy Nash ('Star' Editorial) who tells me he has been passed for the Air Force – so has Vern. The only flaw is that most of the fellows here were passed for the RAF!!

I'm afraid my hair is still short, darling. We have to have it cut twice a month, but I think I'll try and dodge that in future. I have just looked at your last letter and found it is dated last Tuesday. I believe you have forgotten me. I hope you are not ill or anything. Let me hear from you.

All my love.

37th Signal Training Regiment RA. (Harry Berry holding the rifle)

A great group of soldier lads! (Harry on the extreme right smoking!) .

Thank you for your letter which I received today. As in your case, I am afraid there is very little now I can tell you.

I had my first free evening for a week yesterday, so Johnny and I went out and played billiards and had 2 drinks. I also bought a peak cap (I look a twerp in a forage cap) and also some badges. Tonight we have had a pleasant surprise. We have just been told there is no parade tonight at 9.15 p.m. or 4 a.m., so we are all very delighted. We are confined to Barracks, but as we have to clean our room for inspection tomorrow that doesn't matter.

We moved from our old room on Saturday. This isn't quite such a good place, but there's nothing to grumble at.

I went driving again this afternoon and am getting quite good! We had rather an escape when one of the other chaps was driving. Coming down a steep hill we had a puncture and we nearly all went into the sea – but the instructor regained control just in time. Next week, I believe, we start on motor-bikes too. Actually it's quite a holiday now except for the 'standing to' at all hours.

I got my story back from 'Lilliput' with a letter saying it was not quite in their line – so I shall have to try some other paper.

Nobody in this squad has a stripe yet and I don't think any of us will get one for some weeks. It is going to be pretty difficult and there is plenty to learn. Every night now I have to swot mechanics and we shall have to learn Morse code, flag signalling, etc. too, soon. So to get a stripe one has to work damn hard – and you know how I like hard work!

I am gradually getting known as a pianist around here. We were on 'picket' in the gym Wednesday and I played quite a time during the afternoon, as they have a piano there. I played for you, darling. It seems years since I saw you last, and leave at the moment doesn't seem very hopeful. We are all due for a long week-end in three weeks time and unless we are invaded we should get it. So we must both look forward to then, with hope. All my love.

26th May 1940   Gunner Berry H.W.
                                                         'B' Battery

Sunday 2.30 p.m.

    About holidays, my sweet. I still don't know what actually to advise. I think we are going back to almost normality next week (no getting up in the middle of the night) and so we _might_ be more free and able to get leave. I should love to see you again but I don't really think it will be worth your while coming up here for a week-end only. It is a long and tiring journey and very expensive. On top of which I don't know whether or not I shall be confined to barracks. You could, of course, chance it darling, but I should hate you to come all this way and then not see me – or if you did only for a few minutes. The same applies to your holiday. I think, actually, if we could leave it over until the end of this week, I could advise you better. Then perhaps news may come through from France and things will be a little easier.

    I am having a look around the place here – what kind of 'billet' do you want? There is a nice hotel near the Barracks 9/- a day all in (£3.3.0 a week) but perhaps you would rather stay at a boarding house. Let me know in your next letter and then, I think, I could let you know definitely how things stand.

    I am writing this letter on my bed and it is a lovely day outside, so I must wash and change and get out (I wish I were meeting you). Some of us had to clean the floor of the hospital this morning – I don't mind really; it got me out of bed. I had a marvellous dream last night – about you. I also had toothache in the place where I had that tooth out – I can't understand that. I was rather annoyed as it interrupted my dream about you. I hope in a few more days we shall be able to make arrangements about seeing each other.

    Your fiancé.

29th May 1940   Burniston Barracks
                                                              Scarborough

Thank you for your letter and parcel. The cake looks very nice darling and although I have not tasted it yet, I am sure it will be delicious. I shall certainly save the tin and send it back when I want it refilled!!

Yesterday we started on motor-bikes. They are quite easy to drive but I think it will be better, darling, if we have a car. They are much more comfortable.

I heard nothing of the air-raid the other night, but there were dozens of planes flying around all night. However, we are used to them and take no notice - be they English or German.

It is interesting to hear about the refugees in Ealing. What type of people are they? People who had the money to flee from Belgium or genuine refugees?

I am glad you went to a dance, my sweet, although I hope you kept good. I have not been to one, but on Sunday, Johnny and I went to the pictures (first time since we've been here) and saw 'Remember'. Have you seen it? – it is very funny. (We went on our own by the way!) It seems funny to think that the office routine is carrying on as usual and that the same people are sitting down to lunch. It all seems a very long way from me.

I am sorry to hear about the socks going wrong, but I expect you will soon put them right. I still don't know what to fix up about holidays. At the moment we are confined to barracks every other day (allowed out on evenings off till 11 p.m.). On top of this we are liable to be called upon to (1) Be on picket in the Gym for 24 hours. (2) Be on main Guard. (3) Be on pier picket.

So you see, darling, if we fix anything up it will be a matter of luck whether we have much time together. I don't know what to suggest as I really do want to see you again. However, I'll leave it over till the end of the week in case there are any further developments due to this Belgium affair. I wish it were all over. Remember me to all. Love.

P.S. I am confined to Barracks tonight.

When we went down to learn to drive today only about half of us were required to ride the bikes down to the 'practice' road on the front. I was unlucky, but I was put in charge of the men walking down there. So it wasn't so bad – you know how I love giving orders!!!

29th May 1940   Burniston Barracks
                                                                                 Scarborough

Thank you for your letter which I read through very carefully in order not to miss any queries. Except for the week I had without sleep, I have always had your letter in front of me when answering. So I'm sorry I missed the bit about the socks, but I'm afraid I can't help you. I don't know what size I take. Whenever I buy a pair I always give my boot size (10).

My tooth is now O.K. and so are my feet. I have now got used to wearing these 'tanks'.

About your holiday, I must have a look around to see where you can put up. It isn't so easy really as I can't go round all the boarding houses (there are hundreds of them) asking to see rooms, so I think I'll buy the local rag and visit one or two likely-looking places. By the way, one of the fellow's fiancée is coming to Scarborough on June 29th. As she is coming on her own I wondered whether you would care to come at the same time – so that you can keep each other out of mischief whilst we are on duty! What do you think? Of course, you will realise it is a gamble whether or not I shall be able to see you much, but I expect I shall be able to get permission for a few extra hours now and again. Have I told you that we are confined within certain boundaries – so we shan't be able to walk far?

Went out driving cars again today and went all over the country. The instructor said I was very good!

4.15 p.m. Have just received your letter, thank you. You should have received a letter from me before you posted that. For goodness sake don't come and live here as I shall only be here for another 2 months for training, and then drafted to my unit. The cake was lovely, darling (it still is as we have not eaten much). I will pass it round again tonight. All my love.

2nd June 1940   Burniston Barracks
                                                                        Scarborough

   Many happy returns, my sweet, on the second anniversary of our engagement. I am writing this letter sitting with other fellows from my squad. On the cliff (excuse the pencil but the old pen has run out of ink and I want to catch the 5.30 p.m. post. It is now 5 p.m.). It is a lovely day and the scenery here always reminds me of the South of France and Cap Ferrat. There is not much to tell you except that we have gone back to the old system of getting up in the middle of the night and are working harder than ever. In future we are to work all day Saturday and probably Sunday morning. On Monday afternoons we will all do infantry training, and at other odd periods. Last night with 2 other fellows and a Bombardier I was stuck out in the country in a farmhouse on guard against parachutists. We were on from 10 pm. to 4 am. and our duty consisted of sitting on a chair in the hall by a telephone waiting for it to ring. We each did 2 hours and my period was from 2 – 4 am. I'm afraid I dropped off to sleep once or twice. I was lucky really - through doing this I had not much work to do this morning. My friend had to dig trenches and fill sandbags. I slept most of the time here on the cliffs. I hope you enjoyed your weekend at Mary's. Have you decided what you are doing about holidays yet? I'm longing to see you, darling. I am sorry this letter is not very long and must close now to catch the post. Au revoir.

3rd June 1940   Burniston Barracks
                                                        Scarborough

I have quite a lot to tell you as everything's gone topsy-turvy here this week. I told you that we were going to do more work – well, we have now been told that our training as Signallers has been postponed 'indefinitely' (whatever that may mean). We are now, in fact, (if not in name) just plain infantry. The only good point about this is that we shall probably be on Home Defence only. But we have much more tiring work to do. All day long today we have been digging trenches all over the countryside filling sandbags and putting barricades up on roads.

As you know, I have never fancied myself as a navvy and I am afraid the work does not agree with me! It was terribly hot and I often thought of shamming a faint so that I could get a breather for a few minutes. We got back to barracks at 6 p.m. (half-an-hour late) and were then told that we were on 'Inlying' (or 'Inline') picket for 24 hours from 7.10 pm. I am, therefore, writing this letter in the gym, and although I am lying on a straw mattress on the floor, it feels 'Very tasty, very sweet'. (I shall not be here for long as I am on guard for an hour from 9.20 pm. to 10.20 pm., which is better than having to get up in the middle of the night).

The idea of these 'Inlying Pickets' is, that should the enemy arrive we should be on them within a few minutes as we are all fully clothed with rifles and ammunition at the ready, and buses and lorries 'standing to' outside in the square. I hope they don't come tonight as I am very tired.

By the way, I didn't tell you in my last letter that I 'lost' ten shillings of my wages on Sunday. I don't know who took it although I am certain it was no-one in our squad. I am, therefore, completely broke until I can get out of barracks and draw a few bob out of the Post Office.

I have also got a nasty cut on my nose from last Saturday. I was standing behind someone who suddenly tipped his head back and the rim of his helmet caught my troublesome nose. However, I have still got it (the nose) so I suppose I must not grumble.

Well, my darling, I cannot post this letter tonight as I cannot leave the Gym (I am just being called out on guard).

11 pm. I have just come back from Guard and from half-an-hour's stand-to. I expect we shall be up at 3 am. again, so I will now turn in. Goodnight my darling.

7.30 am. Just got up and had some tea and biscuits. We were called out from 2.50 am. to 3.50 am. but I don't feel too bad. I shall play the piano after breakfast. I shall play for you, darling.

2.15 pm. Have just finished dinner and am reposing on my 'bed'. I have just received your letter. I wish I were with you. I am fed-up with Scarborough.

I am glad you are trying to fix up your holidays. I am afraid I can't promise you how often I can see you – if you do come, we will both have to trust to luck. I won't say wait until later because things will probably get worse. The same applies to leave. All leave everywhere has been cancelled as they are expecting Hitler to try to invade England. That is why we are all so busy here, and until things become more settled, nothing can be arranged. (I have just heard that 1,000 bombs have been dropped on Paris, so I probably shall get no leave until the war is ended!!!) So you see, darling, you will have to use your own judgement about when or whether you come here. I should love to see you. Please excuse the writing, but I am resting this paper on blankets and it is rather difficult.

Someone has just asked me to play the piano, so I will continue this letter in a few minutes.

4.30 pm. I didn't play the piano for long. We have just finished rifle drill and are now waiting for tea. We finish here in the Gym at 6 pm, but I shouldn't be at all surprised if we don't have guard on the pier or the roads all night. If I am, I shan't be in a fit condition to stop any Germans if, and when, they come. However, it is ten times better than being in France.

I will close now and try to get a stamp to post this letter. Don't forget, if you don't hear from me so often now, it is not my fault. Please write to me. Yours ever.

6th June 1940

Thank you for your letter which has just been handed to me. It is now 9 p.m. and I am very, very tired, so will not write much tonight. A couple of hours ago I finished 24 hours guarding the harbour – 2 hours on and 4 hours off. My guard times were 6 to 8 pm last night, midnight to 2 am, 6 to 8 am. and noon to 2 pm. this afternoon. We had a bit of excitement last night while I was on duty from 12 to 2 am. As you have probably read we had an air-raid and I had a wonderful view of it. There were dozens of searchlights reflected in the sea and I saw and heard the bombs being dropped. One of the German planes flew right over my head held by the searchlights but, luckily, took no notice of insignificant little me. After days and nights of hard and uninteresting work I was as thrilled as if I were at a show at the Palladium. Up to now I have had one night's complete sleep this week, but this evening we had some good news. Tonight from 10 pm. to 11 pm. is the last time we 'stand to' during the night and we do not have to get up in the morning (in the early hours, I mean). Also 'inlying picket' in the Gym is concluded and 'tis rumoured (very strongly) that we are continuing our usual training next week. We are also allowed out of barracks within certain boundaries. This makes life a bit brighter as I think any more nights without sleep would drive me potty.

Well, darling, I shall have to dry-up now as I have to get ready for 'stand in'. If there is any more news I will continue this letter tomorrow and then post it.

Friday: 1.30 pm. Hello, my love. We didn't get our night's sleep after all. About 1.30 am. the air-raid sirens went and we all had to dress and take cover for half-an-hour. This morning we have been digging trenches again and we have just heard that the present system is continuing and we are confined to barracks. Everybody's just about fed up and if the C.O. shows his face, I am sure he will get 'bumped off'. However, we must grin and bear it. We have ten minutes to go before parade, so I will close now and just have time to post this letter.

Au revoir, my love, and think of me stripped to the waist, digging for dear life.

11th June 1940   Burniston Barracks
Scarborough

12.45 p.m.

Thank you for your two letters. I am sorry I have not written since Friday, but you know the reason why.

It certainly looks as if we shall be permanently on Home Defence here for the duration unless any other arrangements are made, and I think it is very unlikely, especially now that Italy's joined in, that we shall ever get any leave. As you know, practically all leave in the Army has been cancelled, so it will be a long time before I see London again. I hope you do manage to get a holiday and come up here for a week to see me.

I did not find that ten shillings, and I am afraid I must admit that I have not yet succeeded in getting through the week on 14/-. However, I am really going to try now and shall ask the Pay Clerk to deduct 4/- a week for savings!! It will take a great deal of doing – for me. We were digging trenches all day Saturday and I think (on the quiet) it is doing me good. I feel as strong as a new-born bull. My Ealing friend, by the way, enjoys digging. He is a tough little fellow. (He would be annoyed if he read that.) There are two Ealing chaps in this Squad. Both public school boys, but as unlike Ealingites as it is possible to be.

I hope the blister on your heel has disappeared by now. My nose is back to its normal shape (unfortunately?!). Your bit about asking the C.O. about leave made me laugh – in fact it made us all laugh when I told the Squad. I expect the C.O. wants leave as much as we all do.

Glad to hear you went to a dance again. I don't mind where you go, darling, as long as you still love me.

You seemed to have a fine old time on Sunday, I wish I had been with you. We had an easy day for a change and it didn't rain. I was on the cliffs most of the day, but at 6 pm. I was on 'inlying picket' for 24 hours. I played the piano most of the day – my fingers weren't too bad.

This morning we have also had an easy time. We had a decent sergeant who was supposed to give us rifle drill, but took us out on the cliffs and told us to sit down. We sat down! This afternoon, however, we were digging again, and tonight we will be sleeping out in the open guarding trenches. We shall be doing this all the week. I think England's pretty safe against parachutists – and I'm not kidding.   I'm still practising throwing up my arms and saying 'Comrade' – just in case! Have you read that four people have been shot this week through ignoring a sentry? You can't be too careful, darling, as we have all got orders to shoot if a challenge is ignored – no matter who it is.

Well, darling, I must close now as dinner is ready (1.30 p.m.) and if I post this now you will get it tomorrow morning. I am taking care not to get sunburnt and am getting used to roughing it. It's only the lack of sleep that gets me down. All my love.

16th June 1940   Burniston Barracks
                                                                      Scarborough
Sunday, 9 p.m.

I now have a few spare minutes until we stand-to at 10 o'clock for an hour. Tonight, thank goodness, we are going to bed and I hope to feel much better in the morning than I feel now.

We were out on the cliffs last night from 10 o'clock to 5 this morning and it wasn't very comfortable. This morning at 9 o'clock several of us were detailed to clean out the hospital and dental rooms, but I dodged most of this as I went to see the doctor this morning. I woke up this morning with a tight pain across the chest – the doctor wasn't quite sure what was wrong but thought it was something to do with the muscles. It is a little better now, but I am going to be rubbed with oils twice a day until it disappears. Tomorrow, I believe we are on manoeuvres for the benefit of the

Brigadier-General and I am hoping I am not <u>quite</u> well enough to take part. But I shall have to wait and see!!

There have been rumours lately about normal training and leave being resumed, but it is advisable not to be too optimistic. However, even rumours are welcomed in these troubled times; and of course, we <u>are</u> entitled to a week's holiday after three months here. Nothing much has happened since I last wrote to you, but I was feeling very depressed and your letter did not seem too cheerful. I still love you darling and am longing to see you again. I think I had better finish now as I have my rifle and some buttons to clean. I will continue and post this letter tomorrow. Goodnight my darling and God bless you.

Tuesday 5.30 am.

Good morning my sweet. I am sitting in a trench on top of a cliff on Guard. I can't write any more now as it is very cold and I cannot write properly.

1.15 pm. Hello, darling. I am still sitting on top of a cliff near the trench and it is a marvellous day. We have certainly been having a stiff time lately. All yesterday afternoon we were in trenches. At 7.15 pm. we were rushed back to barracks, had half-an-hour in which to have 'tea' (one slice of bread and butter and cup of tea) and then drafted down here to the cliffs where we have been all night. All this, of course, due to the French affair. I don't mind roughing it in the least, but I do wish we could get some sleep and have some decent food. However, dinner is in half-an-hour's time and perhaps I can doze here in the grass during the afternoon. We finish here about 6 pm, but in future we shall have four consecutive days out of every eight manning these trenches. During the other four days we will be guarding the harbour, roads, etc. What a life!! Darling, I have just received your letter and was surprised to see that you had not received mine as I posted it on Saturday. I am sorry it is rather dismal, but I was terribly tired when I wrote it, and very down in the dumps. Please tear it up.

I am glad to hear that Herbert* has got a chance to get in the Air Force – I wish him the best of luck. But tell him not to be too optimistic as one can never be sure where one is going until the calling-up papers are received.

I am glad the stones said you were going to marry me sometime.

Darling, I do miss you so much and I want to have you near me always. If this war seems as if it is going on for years, and I am stuck up here, I would like to have you as my wife here in Scarborough. Would you mind? (That's not too plain darling. What I mean is, if we get married, would you come and live here?)

Just two minor items to tell you – I was inoculated again Sunday and I have also received a cheque from the 'Star' for £1.6.3d for syndication.

P.S. The chest pains have disappeared!

*My fiancée's brother.

14th June 1940   Burniston Barracks
                                                                  Scarborough

I am feeling very tired at the moment, as I have not been to bed since Monday, but I hope to get a good sleep tonight. The news has just come through that Paris has fallen, so what with one thing and another I am not feeling too happy. We have been on night guard all the week – on the beach, on the cliffs, on the pier – trying to sleep on concrete, grass and wooden seats. The reason, of course, if that we are actually on Active Service as much as the fellows in France, and the Government thinks invasion will come via the East Coast. So we should consider ourselves lucky that we have a bed to sleep in twice a week, instead of spending our whole time in the trenches.

I think our time as Royal Artillery men is finished and shortly we will be converted into an ordinary infantry regiment – but whether for home or overseas remains to be seen. (1.30 pm. Am just going to dinner.)

2 pm. Have finished dinner and have washed, etc., ready for Parade at 2.30 pm. The grub was terrible – bad potatoes, scraggy meat and leafy cabbage. The rice pudding we had for 'afters' (what there was of it) was the best.

This afternoon we are going on the ranges and firing our own rifles (first time). I'm not intending to be too good, in case they make me a sniper!!

Saturday 2 pm. I have just finished dinner and am getting ready for the afternoon's parade after a morning of digging. I am still very tired although we had a night in bed last night. We are on the cliffs again tonight – so that makes two nights of decent sleep a week!

I have just received your letter and am afraid it has not cheered me up much – after keeping me waiting all this time. You don't seem to appreciate, darling, how little spare time we actually have. If we are lucky enough to get a few hours off, we immediately drop off to sleep. I slept all day last Sunday on the cliffs and will sleep as much as I can tomorrow. We have to take every opportunity to get sleep in order to keep ourselves going. I particularly disliked your sentence about 'finding time to spend your money'. I spend most of it on grub as we don't get enough to eat – and there are always razor blades, soap, boot polish, metal polish, Lux, etc., that one has to buy. I think that remark was very unkind.

I enclose a photograph of myself with some of the Squad. The fellow in the gym vest is my friend and the other fellow on his right also comes from Ealing.

I think that's all for now, darling. If I post this now you should get it by Monday morning. Love.

P.S. No news about holidays yet?

18th June 1940   Burniston Barracks
                                                         Scarborough

Thank you for your letter which I have just received on returning to barracks this evening.

Darling, I am very, very sorry I misunderstood your letter and made you so unhappy. It was very silly of me and I deserve to be kicked. It was daft of me to think you would intentionally try to hurt me but I was so very tired, darling, and couldn't think straight. I am feeling fine now and honestly darling, I will always love you with all my heart. I hope you will forgive me.

We are free tonight (probably the last time for weeks) so Johnnie and I are going along to a beer-garden near here to have a drink. We won't have much as we haven't much money.

I am about the only chap in the Squad who hasn't been out with a girl. (There is one other - the fellow whose fiancée is coming here on the 29th). I shall always be faithful darling. All my love.

20th June 1940   Burniston Barracks
                                                         Scarborough

Thank you for your two letters. I'm glad you like the photo, darling, but that is not my real uniform I am in – only my workaday canvas suit.

At the moment I am having a nice rest. Since 2 o'clock yesterday I have been on 'Inlying Picket' in the Gym and have been sleeping and playing the piano most of the time. I finish this at 5.30 pm. tonight – if I am very lucky I will have the evening off. If not, I will probably be mixing cement until 10 pm.!! Yesterday morning I was digging holes in the road (Tank traps – sssh!) and am now quite an expert at heaving the pick. As you say, we do have a lot of planes over here and the air-raid warnings go. But most of the actual activity is further south down the coast. We take no notice of them.

I am glad to hear the old Victoria Embankment is the same. You certainly seem to be keeping in touch with the people at the office. They shouldn't forget me when the war's over – should they?

I hope you get your holidays, sweet. I hope we can see a lot of each other, although we must not be too optimistic. Being on Active Service means it would be just the same as your going to the front line to see me. So I don't suppose I shall get any special 'leave'. We must trust to luck, darling – the other fellow's fiancée is still coming. If you knew what time train you might catch you could meet each other at Kings Cross and travel up here together. It would relieve the monotony. I will still keep a look out for digs, darling, but they will be easy to get as holiday traffic has fallen off considerably up here.

I hope you have torn that letter up. I will write again soon. All my love.

23rd June 1940   Burniston Barracks
                                                         Scarborough

This is going to be a very short letter darling as we have just finished a terrible night and day in the open with rain pouring down most of the time. I am now very, very tired and want to get to bed as soon as possible.

First of all let me thank you for your letter and parcel – both containing very pleasant surprises. Darling, I am very happy that you are coming to see me and I shall count the days to next Sunday. My colleague's fiancée is stopping at a private house, so I shall make a few enquiries for you. The things you sent are just what I wanted - I am smoking one of the cigarettes now and am afraid I gobbled down most of the choc. Biscuits last night – you know how I like them!!

Now I have some news for you, darling. We were supposed to be on the cliffs for 4 days from yesterday afternoon, but the INFANTRY have arrived to relieve us. That means we go back to the luxury of living with the driving of cars and bikes tomorrow, and also get a full night's sleep. Much more important darling, it means that I shall be able to see a lot of you when you come – most probably every day for quite a long while. But we must not be too optimistic – just in case.

I will write you a much fuller letter tomorrow and tell you all the remaining news.

My love for always.

25th June 1940   Burniston Barracks
                                                                    Scarborough

I am sorry I did not write as promised, but we were suddenly put on 'Inlying Picket' for 15 hours (from 5 pm. to 8 am. this morning).

Darling, I'm sorry you won't be coming up until Wednesday next week, but perhaps, in a way, it might be better as we <u>may</u> get all one day (Sunday) together.   I don't think you will have any difficulty getting to Scarborough as there seems to be quite a few holiday-makers here.   There seems to be a lot of 'ifs and buts' about whether we shall see each other, but we must trust to providence. I don't think my good luck will desert me.

In answer to your numerous queries:-

1.   I really don't know how or why the triangle mark appeared on the envelope. It's nothing to do with the Army authorities as they don't handle the actual posting.   It's probably the 'Trade Mark' of the local head Post Office.

2.   Our Squad is expecting to get two or three stripes in a few weeks time.   Whether I shall get one or not, I don't know.   An ordinary bloke like me is at a disadvantage as we have people who have been in the Army before and expert drivers who are more likely, of course, to be favoured. However, I think I have a slight chance, although it is only a 'squad' stripe (unpaid).

3.   The 'pains' have completely disappeared.

4.   I haven't written to anybody for weeks except you and home, so don't know how Walt and Vern are.*

5.   In some ways, darling, it seems years since I last saw you, but in others it seems only yesterday I was holding you in my arms.

This morning we had a false alarm and had to parade in full kit and marched to the trenches. We really thought it was the real thing at last. This afternoon I have been driving (cars) and am almost perfect now.

I might go out tonight and get a photograph taken at a studio – I might!!! It all depends on how long I take to wash and change. Au revoir, my sweet. Try and let me know what time you expect to arrive here and I will also try and make arrangements to meet you. We still have odd guard duties to do, so once again we must trust to luck that I dodge most of them whilst you are here.

All my love.

* Old school friends of mine.

27th June 1940	Burniston Barracks

27th June 1940   Burniston Barracks

2.30 p.m.   Scarborough

Thank you for your letter. I am looking forward to Wednesday and hoping it won't take too long to arrive. When will you be letting me know what time train you are catching? If it is possible to get into Scarborough after 4.30 pm. I could meet you (as we should be finished work by then) and help you look for a place. I hope nothing happens to stop you coming.

You seem to have had your first air-raid warning for months. I shouldn't worry about getting up from bed as I don't think they would bomb London. Up here, like you, we don't even trouble to wake up – even if they are dropping bombs further down the coast.

Darling, you often say you wonder what I am doing when you write, so I will give you a rough idea of how our time-table goes.

7 am.	I get up (Sometimes a little earlier, sometimes a little later.) Then I wash and shave and make my bed.

7.30 – 8 am.	Breakfast. I usually hear the 'physical jerks' on the dining room wireless and sometimes stop to hear the news.
8 – 8.30 am.	General tidy up. Help sweep floor, etc. Smoke cigarette.
8.30 am.	Parade (A roll call and inspection to see if we keep ourselves nice clean boys).
8.45 – 9.30 am.	Usually a lecture on car engines or something similar.
9.30 – 12.30 am.	Motor-bikes.
12.30 – 2 pm.	Dinner and rest.
2 – 4.30 pm.	Cars; and then finished for the day if we are lucky.
9.45 pm.	Must be in barracks.
10.15 pm.	Lights out.
10........	Asleep.

There you are. That's my working day. What a change to what we have being doing during the last few weeks.

Do you see what time I am writing this? It is now nearly 3 pm. They have started a new system of having a room orderly every day (to keep the place tidy and see no strangers come in) and as I am first on the alphabetical list, I have first go. It is rather lonely sitting here all by myself, but it does give me a chance to do a few personal things. I'm sorry, though, that I have to miss a day's driving.

Remember me to all and give yourself all my love.

30th June 1940

I was rather disappointed at not hearing from you since Thursday, but I expect you have been busier than usual preparing for the 'great day'. Darling, do you realise it is also our 'anniversary'? There is just one spot of trouble on the horizon, my sweet, and it is slightly worrying me. There is a rumour about and it is a very strong one that we are moving further inland on Tuesday. That's all I know at the present and I don't know what to do about it. It is probably wrong, but if I hear anything further I will let you know directly either by telephone or telegram.

I enquired about a room today. The house is quite near the barracks and very nice. The landlady is also very decent and the terms she gave me were 4/6d a day, bed and breakfast, 7/6d full board, and 5/- if you wish to have the room only. Why bed and breakfast should be cheaper than just the room I don't know, unless the latter includes gas, etc. If everything is O.K. and you do come up here, shall I book you here or shall I try and find somewhere cheaper? In any case you can always leave it as I told her nothing could definitely be arranged until you actually arrive.

Last night I was on 'Inlying picket' and this morning I was on Church Parade – and went to Church! It was a very uninteresting and dull sermon.

It is now 9.10 pm. and I am sitting on the cliffs writing this. This afternoon I went for a walk with John and had a nice tea out. Tonight I am allowed out till 11 pm. but I shall be in bed before then.

1st July 1940   Burniston Barracks
                                                    Scarborough

5 pm.

I have just received your letters and am very disappointed that you were unable to get here. My friend's fiancée arrived here without any trouble, but she left King's Cross late Saturday night – that may have been the reason.

We have one slight consolation, darling, and that is, as I mentioned in my last letter, it is quite probable that we shall move one day this week. It is quite definite that we are evacuating this place and will probably land up at Wakefield. So perhaps it is all for the best.

By the way, news has just come in that we are all having 48 hours leave (in turn) starting from tomorrow. Everyone wanted to go so we drew out of a hat and I am afraid I wasn't the first lucky one. But never mind, darling, it is something to look forward to –

even if it is only for a few hours. I shall let you know how things develop and when you can expect me.

Everything is topsy-turvy at the moment – everybody shouting about leave, etc. – that I think I won't make this letter too long. I am longing to see you and hope I don't have to wait very long. It was a pity I didn't have a chance to see you whilst you are on holiday, but I am getting used to these disappointments now.

Goodbye for now. I am on main guard again tomorrow so will write you a long letter. All my love.

P.S. Sorry to hear about your brother Herbert not getting into the RAF. What section of the Army is he trying for?

3rd July 1940   Burniston Barracks
                                                    Scarborough

I have just finished main guard and am writing this letter in the early hours of the morning (6.30 am.).

Darling, I'm sorry if my last letter was not too cheerful, but I was feeling very miserable at not being able to see you after all and almost felt like crying. I expect you felt the same way. It was certainly a great disappointment for us both – I don't expect I shall feel too happy today as it was this afternoon I was originally expecting to see you. Our third 'anniversary' darling. Three months since you promised to be mine. I love you.

Yesterday we had another pick out of the hat for 48 hours leave commencing Saturday morning, and again I was unfortunate. My luck seems to have deserted me lately. However, I am going to suggest picking numbers so that we know roughly when we shall get our leave and then I will let you know when you can expect to see me. It now seems pretty certain that we are moving to Wakefield this week, and although I believe it is rather a dump, it will make a change and there is also a better train service to London. We may even, of course, get our week's leave that is due to us, as we will not then be in the first line of defence as we are now.

Yesterday I went for a nice drive in a car. I went up the local 'mountain' (Oliver's Mount) and the view from the top reminded me of the days in France. By the way, we pass out of 'B' Battery at the end of this week and I don't think I shall have any difficulty in passing my test. We shall then be in 'C' Battery learning signalling, wireless, etc., and that means more swotting of an evening.

It's just like being back at school! All my love.

5th July 1940   Burniston Barracks
                                                        Scarborough

Thank you for your letters. I am glad that you are doing your best to have a decent holiday and are getting in a bit of swimming. As you see, we have not moved yet, but are still expecting to do so any day. The trouble seems to be lack of billets. The officers have been touring the country trying to find a decent place, but so far have been unsuccessful. I am glad they are taking the trouble to find a decent spot. I expect we shall be very lucky if we can still get showers and hot baths.

This week finishes our 'B' Battery course and I have passed my exams and tests and am now a i/c driver – which means that I am an 'expert' driver of bikes and cars and also know all about the mechanism. Should a car break down, I am supposed to know how to repair it!!! I don't think I could, though.

I am writing this on 'Inlying Picket' and have just noticed that I have 5 minutes in which to catch the post, so will now close.

I enclose a photo which I don't think is very good but will do till I have a better one taken.

Au revoir, my love.

8th July 1940   Burniston Barracks
                                                    Scarborough
9.30 p.m.

I am writing this letter in bed and it is getting rather dark, so I don't know how long I will be able to write. We have just moved from our former barrack room and are now billeted in the old married quarters for a week. They are rather rough, but four of us who share this room have managed to pinch some bedsteads and so are not too badly off.

How are you keeping, darling? I have not heard from you since Friday. Are you getting tired of me? I hope not, because the only thing I have to look forward to is seeing you again. There is not much to tell you. All this week we are posted to 'Depot' Battery whilst we await for 25 Squad to pass out of 'B' Battery to join us in 'C' Battery. We are going to do elementary signal training and fatigues like barb-wiring all the week every other day. Today we were putting up barb wire in the morning and in the afternoon went on what they called manoeuvres. We hung about under trees and hedges in rain and sunshine from 3.30 pm. to 6.45 pm., all because some Big Noise came down to see 'how we were getting on'. Did we swear! The army seems to grow barmier every day.

I must close now as it is quite dark, so I will snuggle down and go to sleep. I will continue this letter in the morning. Goodnight, my sweet.

7.30 am. Good morning darling. I am up early this morning as this Battery has a Roll Call at 7 am. That shook us! I suppose you are just getting up.

As you have probably noticed, we have not moved yet. It has been postponed indefinitely until they find a suitable place. I hope we get away from here soon. Everybody is getting fed-up.

What did work seem like after a week of rest? I suppose quite a number of people asked you how I was. I do wish you had been here, darling. I like to pretend now that you were here last week – I'm always thinking of you.

We are getting no 48 hours leave this week, but they will recommence when we go into 'C' Battery. There is a rumour (ssh!) that the time will be extended to 72 hours – but nobody really knows.

I hope I hear from you today, my sweet. If not, I shall go to the nearest river – if there is one. I shouldn't be surprised though if I get two letters today – one in the morning and one in the afternoon; the delivery is very erratic.

In your letter of last Wednesday, you mentioned that you heard the 'Desert Song' selections on the wireless. I heard those too on the NAAFI radio during our morning 'break'.

Today we shall be doing elementary signalling and I shall be thinking of you and looking forward to seeing you again. All my love.

10th June 1940   Burniston Barracks
                                                           Scarborough

My darling fiancée,

Thank you for your letter which arrived just in time to save me from walking to the nearest river!!

We have had a terrific thunderstorm here since about noon – I don't remember ever seeing such a violent one. To cop it all we were out in it loading ammunition onto lorries and were soaked through. I am sitting in bed now clad in gym shorts and pullover and have hung my clothes up to dry in the scullery. What a life!

Glad you like my photo, darling, but I'm afraid I agree with your brother Frank. I shall have a good one taken one day; perhaps we'll have one taken together when I get home on leave.

I have been busy this week learning the Morse code, and other branches of signalling, ready for 'C' Battery next week. (I expect you know what this is ".. ._.. _ _ _ ..._ . _ . _ _ _ _ _ .._"

I know the Morse code already.

We aren't having too good a time this week being in Depot Battery as, in the ordinary way, it is composed of all the duffers of the regiment who do most of the fatigues. However, we have only three more days of it.

As you see, we have not moved yet. Information has just come from the Regimental Office that, unless we find new billets in a month, we will be disbanded and sent to other regiments. Of course, it may be only another rumour. We live on rumours here. Au revoir.

P.S. The Morse says 'I love you' and I mean it.

12th July 1940   Burniston Barracks
                                                                            Scarborough
8 a.m.

Thank you for your letter. As you say, it wasn't too cheerful, but I understand how you feel, darling. I often get very fed up but I'm afraid it doesn't help much in the long run.

I'm sorry I put you off trying to get here last week, but immediately I got your letter I went to the sergeant and asked him if it were possible to get a 'Special Permit' and he simply advised me to stop you coming as we were moving in a couple of days time. Darling, please be careful when you speak to my photo; I hope nobody catches you at it as you might then find people looking at you with some suspicion. Also, you make me feel very bashful showing my picture to everyone at the office. You'll have to be my publicity agent.

5.30 pm. I received another letter from you this afternoon and it is certainly a much brighter one. Please try and keep cheerful for me, darling.

You say that you are working late next week – does that mean permanently? I hope not, because I don't think late nights agree with you and I don't want to see you looking all sleepy when I do get home.

Am interested to hear about Herbert and hope Plymouth will not be too bad. Tell him the first week is usually the worst, but he will

47

soon get used to it and give the whole thing up as a bad job. If he tries to reason things out he will go mad. That's not too clear, but I can be no more explicit when trying to describe the Army.

We have all made enquiries here about sending letters with $1\frac{1}{2}$d stamps, but it can't be done. There is no reason, however, why you shouldn't try it out – I believe I have seen letters delivered here with $1\frac{1}{2}$d stamps.

The air raids have eased off here lately, but we usually have Heinkels over every night. We are so used to them that we take no notice at all. I don't think I'm good looking enough to get my picture shoved in 'War Illustrated'.

I didn't realise darling that it was a year ago we were on holiday together. I think about it so often that it seems like yesterday, although when I think of all that has happened since, then it seems years and years ago.

I am longing to see you again and I think I shall soon be able to let you know when you can expect me, as we shall be drawing out of the hat again tomorrow.

All my love for ever.

Author's note: Herbert was my future brother-in-law. He had risen to Lt.-Colonel by the end of the war!

On returning to Scarborough from 2 or 3 days leave.

18th July 1940   Burniston Barracks
                                               Scarborough

My darling little wife,

How are you today, darling? I expect you are feeling, as I am, rather tired and not too pleased at having to work till 10.30 p.m. I think it's an awful cheek!!

Darling, I love you. I have been thinking about you all day and even during lectures I kept falling asleep and dreaming you were with me. I am afraid I have fallen a long way behind the other fellows, but I shall get down to it during the next few days and will soon pull up. We had quite a comfortable journey up here and arrived here at 5.30 a.m. It was pouring with rain and has been raining ever since!

There's no news to tell you, of course, darling. I am still thinking of the marvellous time we had together – they were some of the happiest hours of my life. You are marvellous, darling, and I am more in love with you than ever. You will be the best wife in the world.

I am looking forward to hearing from you, darling and hope you will have found out something about getting married. I love you so much and I will always be faithful to you. I couldn't bear to make love to anyone else.

I am sorry you missed seeing Herbert off. I am afraid I was very selfish about you. Must close now as a fellow is going to town and promises to catch the post for me.

All my love for ever.

Your loving Husband.

20th July 1940   Burniston Barracks
                                                    Scarborough

Thank you for your letter which I received this morning. I'm glad you were happy, too, during those few hours together. It seems years ago already.

I have been to the MO for three days and three times a day have had olive oil put in my ears; they are to be syringed tomorrow morning – and won't I be glad! I can hardly hear anything at the moment. My cold hasn't been too good, but I think it is now mending.

Thank you for cutting my article out. You did not get two copies, I suppose, because I should like to see one if you have – just to make sure it is mine.

I hope you had a nice lie in bed this morning, darling, and that you will have a restful day tomorrow. As you say, I will feel much better next week knowing that you are on day duty.

We are still very busy here. We have piles of notes to write and I shall have to stay in tonight – as I did last night – to bring them up-to-date. Also, I have some letters to write and I think I'll have a shower.

Darling, I love you very much. I hope you don't think it's monotonous my keep telling you that. And I keep thinking of you. I shall imagine I am at Ealing tomorrow and remember those little walks we used to take which I pretended to hate!

All my love.

22nd July 1940   Burniston Barracks
                                                             Scarborough

My darling little wife,

Thank you for your note. Glad to hear that everything is O.K. and that you are gradually getting used to being without me again (!!)

I had my ears done Sunday morning and I can now hear splendidly. My cold is nearly better, but I still have to sniff a lot.

I dodged fatigues yesterday being 'sick' in the morning, and in the afternoon went for a walk with two of the fellows along the cliffs. We went down on the beach in order to shelter from the rain and nearly got cut off by the tide. We had to climb over rocks and paddle across a stretch of water to reach 'civilisation'. This afternoon we were on our usual weekly manoeuvres and the section I was in walked nearly five miles across country, finally climbing to the top of Oliver's Mount; only to be theoretically 'bumped off' when we reached the top. It was a sweltering hot day, too. Of course, one advantage we do have is that we are taken from the barracks to the 'battlefields' in cars and lorries and also brought home the same way – so we can't grumble too much.

Tonight I must stop in again to do some notes and must also write some letters to my sister Joyce and others. Also I must do some washing.

All my love for ever.

25th July 1940   Burniston Barracks
                                                            Scarborough

Thank you for your two letters to which I am sorry I have not replied before.

I was on main guard again last night (they do like me for that job) and I intended to write to you after my first two hours 'on' but I felt so tired that I slept during my hours 'off' and occasionally whilst actually on guard! It is now about 7.15 am. Thursday and I feel quite fit.

I am glad you are still going for walks. I used to pass Denham quite frequently when I cycled but I have forgotten what the place looks like now, although I remember it was very charming.

I am sorry you have to work on Sunday, but I hope you get your long week-end. By the way, have you found out anything about this marrying business yet – or have you changed your mind!? I'm getting fed up with being a single man and I want another leave! I don't know when I shall get 10 days, darling – I don't think they have heard of such a leave here. All my love, sweet. Keep good and beautiful.

28th July 1940   Burniston Barracks
                                                            Scarborough

Thank you very much for your letter. I am sorry I haven't written before, but we had an examination on Saturday (one of the many to come) and I spent my spare time swotting. We won't know the results until tomorrow (Monday). Up to yesterday I had not been out of barracks once since my leave, so you can guess how busy I have been. I shan't do it again though, as it began to make me feel rather depressed – like a convict not having seen any civilians for so long.

Last night I went out on a 'semi' pub crawl with two of the fellows (only a 'semi' as we cannot possibly afford much beer) and I felt a lot better when I got back. Also I slept like a log and had an easy and lazy day today. So I feel much better and ready for another week of work.

I am glad to have heard from Herbert; I shall write to him as soon as possible. It's surprising, by the way, how one's opinion of the army and surroundings changes as time goes by. I expect Herbert's opinion of the army and Plymouth will change several times before he has completed his training. He soon seems to have copped for potato peeling. Does he say what his companions are like?

I went to the cinema yesterday (before the 'semi') and saw 'Broadway Melody of 1940'. Have you seen it yet? It's very good.

About the $1\frac{1}{2}$d stamp business. It is on our regimental orders that the postage on letters is $2\frac{1}{2}$d and not $1\frac{1}{2}$d so that prevents us trying it. However, I should keep on until you are stopped.

Actually, I think somebody must have started the rumour that people can send letters to soldiers for $1\frac{1}{2}$d as there is definitely no law to that effect.

Another bit of news. A fellow in 26 Squad has his wife staying up here for a fortnight. She had no trouble getting here and he asked nobody's permission! So it seems as if a little bluff will get one through all right.

This morning we all gathered on the football field and saw various types of British aircraft fly overhead for instructional purposes. I am now going over to the café for a cup of coffee and will then probably go to the local YMCA for a game of billiards, darts or ping-pong.

Au revoir my love. I love you with all my heart and will always do so. I hope it's not too long before we are together again. I adore you.

Your faithful fiancé.

30th July 1940   Burniston Barracks
                                                      Scarborough
7 p.m.

Thank you darling for your two letters and the news contained therein. It seems as if to get married now is one of the cheapest things one can do – not like cigarettes, etc., going up and up and up. Thank you for finding out all about it.

I don't know exactly what we should do now. As you say, it would be better if we could see each other first to arrange things, but I am afraid, in the ordinary course of events, I will get no further leave until our training is finished, when we should get a week's leave. By the way, I forgot to tell you that the 48 hours leave was stopped in the Battery about a week ago, and they promise us the week's leave together when we finish here in about 6 weeks. Shall we arrange to get married then darling, or have you any better ideas or preferences? Let me know what you think.

I was amused to hear you nearly had a fire at the 'News Chronicle'. I wish the restaurant had been destroyed and they gave you all a week's holiday. Alternatively, I wish these blasted barracks would catch alight and give us all a break. We get regular sleep now. I am sorry that Herbert's nights are disturbed. I expect he will get used to it in time.

I am sorry you are working late again all this week. Is that right, darling, that you are working from 12 noon to 10.30 pm. or is that a mistake and do you mean 2 pm. to 10.30 p.m.? If you are right I think it's a damn cheek making you work $10\frac{1}{2}$ hours a day.

If they don't pay you any more, I think you ought to tell them off. I don't believe it is allowed.

During yesterday's manoeuvres we were in the old job of trench-digging again, and by the time you get this letter I shall have spent quite a few hours in them. Tonight at 12 o'clock we are on manoeuvres for at least 24 hours in a rehearsal of the defence of Scarborough. An infantry regiment is pretending to be German parachutists and is going to attack us. No-one knows actually how long it is going to last and how long we will be stuck in muddy trenches. We won't get much rest, so if you don't hear from me you know we are still on manoeuvres. I expect I shall find time to write but, of course, it is impossible to post letters. I shall be thinking of you, darling, whilst I am scrapping with imaginary Germans.

Don't forget I love you and let me know how soon you are going to marry me. Regards to the family and all my love to my darling wife. And please don't stop loving me.

2nd August 1940   Burniston Barracks
                                                   Scarborough

Thank you for your letter which I received yesterday. Darling, I am sorry you had not received a letter from me by Tuesday. Actually I posted one Sunday night and I can't understand why you did not receive it by Monday. I have sent you another since then – I wonder whether you have received them both by now?

1 pm. I had to break off the letter to polish the floor around my bed before I went on parade!! I will try and finish this letter before 2 pm. so that I can post it early and make sure you get it tomorrow.

I hope Ellen is back now and that you are having an easier time.

At 8.41 pm. on Wednesday we were just coming home from manoeuvres. It wasn't so bad except that I was almost covered with bites and was, of course, a bit tired yesterday. However, as you know, it was a lovely day and that put a better complexion on things. I did not do much except sit in a trench, although at about 5 a.m. I went on a patrol into enemy territory and returned safely!! The grub, of course, was a bit primitive – bread and cheese, and pineapple cubes for dinner! Darling, if you like open-air life, you should come up here and help me when I am digging. I wonder how many trenches we would dig …….. not many, I bet.

I am still in a dilemma as regards getting married to the sweetest girl in the world. The trouble is that nobody knows what is likely to happen in six weeks time – we may not get the leave.

But perhaps, as you say, it will be best if you take out a licence. It can't do any harm.

I can see you want to invite some people and have a reception. As you know I am very awkward at times with regard to questions like that, but I will leave it to you. As you say, it is very unsatisfactory to fix things up by letters, but, I am afraid, there is no other way. There are hundreds of things to think of, but we will leave them in abeyance for a few more days and see how events go. Darling, I have thought everything over carefully and have come to the conclusion that unless the price of cigarettes comes down I cannot possibly afford to get married!! But seriously darling I do love you and want you for my own. I shall try and be a good husband – I <u>know</u> that you will be the best wife in the world.

Well, darling, I will post this letter now and if you don't get it by tomorrow I'll write to Mr. Churchill. All my love to my future wife.

P.S. As you see, I received your letter this morning about 11 am., and so know that you have received my two letters.

5th August 1940   Burniston Barracks
                                                      Scarborough

I am writing this letter and it is just 10 pm. I am in bed and as 'Lights Out' is in a few minutes, I shan't be able to write much tonight.

However, darling, I just wanted to tell you before I go to sleep that I did not forget our 'anniversary' on Saturday. I certainly forgot to mention it in my last letter, but directly I posted it I realised I had forgotten to mention it. I hope you will believe me. I love you. We heard the result of our first exam yesterday and I was second in the squad. With 49 marks out of 50. Goodnight darling.

Monday 5.30 am. As you see the lights soon went out last night. I did not sleep very well (I think I had too many blankets on) but I feel all right now.

Thank you for your letter. It was a pleasant surprise to get one on a Monday morning. You seem very cheerful – are you still keeping fit? It sounds as if you are.

It would be nice if you could come here for a week-end; the restrictions certainly don't appear to be strict. If you are doubtful and it is no dearer, why not book through to York and then book separately from there to Scarborough? It should get over any difficulties if, as I say, it is not too expensive. I still think of you when I go to bed darling – I was thinking of you a lot last night. I love you very much. No, darling, the Prime Minister hasn't been here and I haven't had my picture in the paper.

Sorry to disappoint you.

There's not much more to tell you. We had a buzzer and lamp reading test on Saturday for which I got full marks, and this afternoon on manoeuvres I was laying telephone cable between trenches. It's quite an interesting job.

We have just started on wireless. They have marvellous sets here which both send and receive and are portable. I think my shorthand will come in handy now, as we are not allowed on air for longer than 20 seconds (In actual warfare the enemy would locate you if you were). So when taking messages I shall be able to get them down pretty quickly. Do you realise darling I have only 5 more weeks training before emerging a fully fledged signaller!! I expect I shall get more leave then. The last squad that left here was posted to Watford – lucky devils.

Have you heard any more from Herbert? All my love to my future wife.

7th August 1940 Burniston Barracks
Scarborough

Thank you for your letter. It was interesting to read your 'time-table' of the day's events – it reminds me very much of the sedate and luxurious existence which I used to lead of a week-end. I'm afraid I cannot give you an exact timetable of my daytime doings as it varies from day to day and is composed of lectures, buzzer and lamp reading, sending and receiving Morse and, for the first time today, wireless transmitting and receiving. We have to be careful on the former – no swearing, etc., as we never know who may pick it up. But it's great fun and quite thrilling to broadcast. We can, of course, tune in to ordinary broadcasts, but only when the sergeant isn't near!

I'm glad you are still getting around a bit, darling – although I hope you don't have too many parties and imagine someone else is me!! I wish someone would invite me to a party up here – the nearest I get to it is a game of solo in the barrack room. Do you still go dancing my sweet? You never describe them to me – where you go, etc. I sometimes wish I could dance so I could go dancing and get away from this military atmosphere, but I'm afraid I should be no good without my darling there to teach me.

I can't remember what I did Saturday night. Nothing very exciting though: the evenings are so much the same that I can't remember one from t'other. I'm sorry you had to have dinner alone on Sunday, but never mind darling. Let's hope it won't be long before we have dinner together every Sunday. I'm stopping in tonight to do some notes and also because I am broke.

But I have some handkerchiefs and vests to wash and then it will be time for bed. And then it will be one day less to go before I see you again.

Darling, I am still looking forward to the time when you will be my wife; I hope it won't be long. Have you decided what kind of wedding you would like yet? I will do anything you say. I love you and want to hold you in my arms again – I shall dream I am with you tonight. All my love for ever.

9th August 1940 Burniston Barracks
Scarborough

Thank you for your letter received today   I am still keeping very fit and am glad to hear that you are, darling. Keep fit and beautiful for me.

So Herbert doesn't find time to write many letters. I'm not surprised. It is difficult in the Army. Actually I seldom write to anyone but you and owe dozens of people letters. How Herbert finds time to write such a long single letter I don't know – but perhaps he doesn't have as many notes of an evening to do as I. He doesn't seem to be with very decent fellows (does he mention what they are like?). Theft is a rare occurrence here.

Darling I hope too that I get posted somewhere near you. I had a pleasant surprise this afternoon.   During the Parade the Sergeant Major asked all fellows who were qualified shorthand/typists to step out, and when several of us went up he asked if any had been in charge of an office. Of course I said I had been and he picked me and another fellow out and then asked us if we would prefer to stick to our trade in the Army. I said 'Yes' and he continued: 'If I recommend you for a commission in the Royal Pay Corps would you be interested?' You can guess what I said and so now I have to wait and see. It's no good getting too excited but I'm beginning to believe my luck hasn't deserted me after all! But what a jammy job if I get it – an officer in the Pay Corps. Whew!! Of course, I may still have to go abroad, but there would be a much better chance of getting back than if I were in the field.

I will let you know any further developments.

Well, sweet, I'll close now and try and catch the post so that you get this letter tomorrow. All my love for ever and ever.

P.S.   Darling I <u>do</u> send you kisses. I sent you some in my last letter and I don't think it silly. I love you. Xxxxxxxxxxx (for 300 pages)

11th August 1940
5.45 pm.

How are you sweet? Still fit and happy?

I am writing this sitting on my bed and directly I finish I shall have a shower. I have not been out yet today and I don't think I shall go out this evening. I shall probably have a game of 'solo' later.

Darling, I haven't felt too happy this week-end. I haven't heard from you since Thursday! I know, of course, that you probably posted one on Friday night and it hasn't reached me yet. I've never worried much before, but yesterday a fellow in the squad here told me that his girl had given him up after eight years (he hasn't had any leave at all since he's been here). He looked so miserable that it made me feel miserable too. And when I didn't get a letter from you on Saturday it made me think the worst. Very silly of me I know but you know how little things like that affect one sometimes. But don't ever leave me will you darling? I don't know what I should do without you.

There is not much news. On Saturday afternoon I had a test at typewriting and shorthand with some other fellows and think I got on all right. The only trouble now is that I don't know whether there's any catch in this business or not. I've started to imagine all sorts of things about being sent abroad, but I suppose this is the reaction after the little excitement I had on Friday. I haven't heard anything more about this commission business yet and don't suppose I will for some time. I will let you know at once if I hear anything.

I went to my first dance yesterday evening with six fellows from this squad. It wasn't bad – I danced a couple of waltzes – but I wished you were there darling to teach me how to dance properly. The dance ended at 10.30 pm. and Johnnie and I just managed to get home before 11 pm. (About a two mile walk).

This morning we were cleaning out the cookhouse – it took us about a couple of hours and since then I have been lazing on my bed. (We don't get much opportunity of doing that now!!)

A crowd of fellows are going to town so I'll give them this letter to post. I'm sorry it's not too cheerful, darling, but don't take any notice of that. I know you wouldn't leave me. Have you made any further arrangements about our getting married?

All my love.

P.S. I have just been told that the last post has gone even in town, so I will hold it over and post it there tomorrow morning at 7.45 am.

Monday 7.15 am. Good morning darling. How are you? I feel a lot brighter this morning so don't take too much notice of the depressing parts of this letter. I know I shall get a letter from you today.

14th August 1940   Burniston Barracks
Scarborough

Thanks for your letter which I received Tuesday morning and your parcel which arrived in the evening. I have just finished munching some of the crisps and chocolate biscuits and I feel very content. Darling, it was very nice of you to send me the parcel – I always imagine I am with you whenever I have chocolate biscuits or biscuits and cheese.

I was very, very miserable on Monday when I had no letter from you. You have never left it so long before writing to me and I thought you had forgotten me. I brightened up a bit when I received your parcel (well, not actually your parcel, but the letter inside it). I was quite happy again. It was more like my little Gwennie writing – although, of course, it must have been imagination thinking your first letter was different. Darling, I hope you still love me as much as ever. Promise me that if you grow tired of me you'll tell me at once and not keep me waiting days and then I shan't be so worried if I don't hear from you for some time.

I haven't heard anything about the commission or Pay Corps yet, but I'm not surprised. The regiment is asking for volunteers for going to Africa; several of the fellows in this squad say they are going and I would if you didn't love me any more. But I will never leave you darling, if you still love me. I couldn't possibly bear to be all those miles away.

I wrote to Dad on Monday (the first since my leave) and I heard from Aunt Bertha at West Drayton. She tells me that my brother Joe is now a lance-corporal and wishes to be remembered.

I hope you enjoyed your dance last Saturday. Why didn't you come to the one up here and teach me to dance? I'm sorry to hear you are on late duty this week. Just think, I am now going to bed and you haven't finished work yet!

Darling I must close now as 'Lights Out' is in a few minutes. I will continue this when I get up and catch the early morning post – I hope. Goodnight, darling. All my love and God Bless You.

I hope you get home all right – I shall be thinking of you catching your train. It is now 10.10 pm. and you must just be leaving the office. Goodnight sweet.

8 a.m. (19th August). Good morning darling. I feel very fit today. I'm afraid I've missed the first post, but I'll finish the letter before Parade and catch the 10.45 collection. There is not much more to tell you. We have to be in at 9.15 pm. now until further notice. So that cuts out cinemas and dances as we do not finish work till 6.30 pm. What a life we lead. It has not worried me much yet as the last two days I have slept from 6.30 pm. (directly work's finished) until the next morning. I think I have been a little run down – probably something to do with not hearing from you for a few days. That shows you how much I love you!! I wonder if there will be a letter for me today. All my love to my wife.

P.S. I'm not sure darling, but I don't think you've answered any of the questions I asked you in my last two letters – or perhaps I didn't ask any!!

16th August 1940   Burniston Barracks
                                                              Scarborough

Thank you very much for your letter which I received
yesterday. I feel very much happier in my mind now, although I
feel dreadfully tired all day long. I think we are all in need of a
change. If we could only stay in bed late one morning, it would do
us good, but we get very little, if any relaxation, and it's bound to
disagree with us after the comfortable lives we used to live as
'civvies'.

You remember I told you that they were asking for volunteers
for Africa? – well quite a number of people here want to go. There
are about eight in our squad alone (including Johnnie), so you can
see how fed up they are with Scarborough. I've got no inclination
at all to go darling – I prefer the sands of Scarborough to those of
Libya – so you needn't be afraid of my going. No, darling, one does
not have to have a private income now to get a commission. There
are plenty of 'poor' officers in war-time. I hope now I get that job
and am posted to London.

Darling, as you say, it is very difficult to arrange this marrying
business by letter, but I expect we shall get our week's leave in
about a month's time, so we had better start arranging things now
– if you still want to marry me then! Do you know whether you are
having another week off? Until you do we can't really arrange
where we are going to stay. I don't know whether you wish to go
away anywhere? What do you think about it all? I will leave it all
to you, darling and I don't mind really whether it is quiet or not.

Darling, I'm glad you still love me. I still love you with all my
heart and am longing to be with you for ever and ever.

We are allowed out to 11 pm. again now, so last night I went to
see 'North-West Passage' (on borrowed money). I remembered you
were reading the book. Wasn't it when I used to meet you in the
mornings and we went walking through Kensington Gardens?

All my love and don't stop loving me. Your loving 'husband'.

18th August 1940   Burniston Barracks
                                                   Scarborough
Sunday 7.30 pm.

Thank you very much for your letter which I received yesterday. Darling, it was very nice to hear from you again so soon and it made me, too, feel very happy. I think it was one of the nicest letters you have written to me and I love you very much.

As you say, it is probably the fact that we love each other so much that makes us feel run down sometimes. I wonder if we will always feel the same way together. I hope you are still quite fit. Darling, you know what you told me about husbands who feel out-of-sorts when their wives are!

I feel heavy-eyed this evening, darling, but hope that you are not. I think it is because I have been in all day (it's been raining). I shall probably, in a few minutes, take a walk to the post-office to post this letter – perhaps I shall feel better then.

I'm glad to hear Herbert's been 'recommended' and please give him my congratulations when you write. You will feel an important person if both Herbert and I get 'pips' – won't you darling? I haven't heard anything further yet, but neither have any of the other fellows who have also been recommended.

Darling, I don't mind so much now if I don't hear from you regularly – so long as you promise to let me know at once if you should fall out of love with me. I know how hard it is to write when there is no news and I also know how expensive it can be at $2\frac{1}{2}$d a time.

Have the firm given you a 'rise' yet in view of the higher cost of living?

I hope the tickling in your throat has disappeared entirely now darling and that you are still feeling happy. I know how depressing colds can be.

That fellow I told you about is gradually returning to normal, but it did upset me when he told me about it. I thought 'Been together for 8 years and then she gives him up – probably because she's grown tired of being alone. I hope Gwennie doesn't do that.' And when I didn't hear from you I nearly went frantic! He has volunteered for Africa now, but I don't want to go so please don't get too tired of being without me darling. I wouldn't be from your side at all darling if I could possibly help it. You know that don't you?

I had a letter from Dad and he wishes to be remembered to you. It looks as if it's going to pour with rain again, but I shall have to try and get to the post-office stamp machines as I haven't a stamp. All my love for ever and ever and don't forget you have promised to be my wife and I <u>don't</u> intend to let you get out of it – even if I have to sue you for breach of promise!!!

Au revoir my love and keep good and beautiful for me. Your loving 'husband'.

20th August 1940

Thank you for your two letters – one yesterday and one today! I love you very much.

I am glad you've had your photograph taken, darling – I should very much like to have a good picture of you. I know even that won't do justice to you, sweet, but it will be nice to have you inside my locker so that I will see you every time I get up, go to bed, and on every other occasion when I open it.

You certainly seem to be having lots of air-raids, darling; I hope they don't worry you too much. I don't think they will venture too near Pitshanger Lane (Ealing) because of the proximity of the balloon barrage. We had quite a decent air-raid last night – the explosions woke me up (the barracks literally rocked) – but none hit us and nobody troubled to go to the Air Raid Shelter. They didn't even trouble to sound the sirens!

I'm glad your throat is better. Yes, I feel very fit now and don't get so tired. We certainly do get the films earlier here than you do. I hope you liked 'Broadway Melody' – it wasn't bad, but I was a little disappointed. I don't go to the films much at all now. I don't enjoy them quite as much as I used to. I think it's because I miss holding my 'wife's' hand and taking her home afterwards. I always imagine when I come out of the pictures up here that I will find myself in the Uxbridge Road. One of the cinemas is very much like the 'Commodore'. I haven't played the piano for some weeks now. I don't get the opportunity.

But I shan't forget how to play!

I will now answer your second letter, sweet.

Darling, there seems to be so much that has to be arranged before we get married. I wish I only had to say "Will you be my wife?" and you say "Yes" and then it was all over. I shan't worry much if you don't get another week off when we get married – you must not risk losing your job as you won't be able to do much on Army allowance. Even then we shall have quite a lot of time together and can be quite happy. We must not be too selfish darling, although it's quite easy to forget everything and everybody else when people like us are in love.

I know how nervous you feel darling. I don't know what to suggest. I still think the Registry Office is the best idea for convenience, but I know how you feel about it. I have not told any of my people yet; I wanted to wait until things were more fixed, but I shall probably write to Do today and tell her about it.

I should very much like to see you up here but I must not encourage you too much. It is a lot of expense, the train will probably be crowded and we shall probably be in the middle of an air-raid when you arrive. But if you really want to come up here, I think you could do it quite easily. You could be here at 5 am. (!) on Saturday and would not have to leave until about 7 am. on Monday morning, reaching Kings Cross at 2 pm. That, of course, is taking the extremes; you could catch other trains. I should love to see you darling but it is a very difficult thing on which to advise. It is entirely up to you, my sweet. I shall quite understand if you decide not to come.

Well darling I think that answers all your questions.

We were on infantry training again today and have been out all the morning. I was trying to get to sleep (in a field) covered with my cape and the rain dripped down my neck. After about half-an-hour of that we moved to a semi-built house and stayed there till 2.30 pm., when we came home. We seem to have got the afternoon off as you notice by the time on this letter. It is now 4.15 pm. and we have to parade at 5.15 pm. again. I don't think we will have to go out. We had dinner, by the way, at 3.30 pm. You can see when I had it by the change in colour of the ink!

Darling, I love you with all my heart and am always recalling the little things we used to do. I didn't realise then how happy I was. But I have come to my senses since I've been away from you and know that I shall never fall in love with anyone else. You are always in my thoughts – so much that you are part of me and I couldn't bear to be without you. I love you with all my heart.

21st August 1940   Burniston Barracks
                                                     Scarborough
9.45 p.m.

As you see by the time, there is only half-an-hour before Lights Out, so I will not be able to write much tonight – just enough to tell you I love you.

Thank you for your second letter of yesterday. It arrived just as I was going out to post the letter I had written to you. Funnily enough (after telling you I did not go to the pictures very often) I went to see 'Typhoon' - by myself as John was out with his girl friend. It wasn't bad, but rather silly although amusing. I hope you have had a rest from air-raids in London now, darling: we have not been troubled for 2 or 3 days but I expect they will be over tonight now.

I'm feeling fine, darling and hope you are. It's been quite nice here but it's never actually hot now. There is always a cool breeze from the North Sea. Well darling, must close now and get undressed for bed (I wish you were with me!). I shall dream of when I see you again in about 3 weeks' time, I hope.

Thursday 7 pm. Hello darling; I'm sorry I didn't finish this letter this morning, but I was one of the 'cleaners-out' of the wash-house. I don't think there is much more to tell you. I have just thought that I might not get my leave in a few weeks' time. One reason is that I may not 'Pass Out' and have to do a few more weeks' training, and the other is that something may occur about this Commission business and it might interfere with leave.

I don't really know, of course. I shouldn't think it would, but it's best to remember these things.

Have you decided what you are doing this week-end? I have not heard from you yet, but I expect I shall get a letter tomorrow. I can soon fix you up with digs if you decide to come. All my love.

P.S. I haven't written to Do* yet! I shall not be able to write again until Friday evening as I am spending my last 2½d on a stamp now.

* the author's step-mother

23rd August 1940   Burniston Barracks
                                                         Scarborough
Friday 3 pm.

Thank you for your letter which I received this morning. I am very disappointed that I will not be seeing you this week-end, but I appreciate your point of view and quite agree that it is terribly expensive coming up here. But never mind darling, it won't be long before we see each other again now.

I am writing this out in a field by the side of the wireless set. It is very windy and I have my overcoat on. There are five of us here (we don't usually have so many to a set) and two fellows are working it while three of us take a rest! I shall have my turn in a minute, probably before I have finished this letter.

Darling you say I tell you nothing of what I do all day, but I am sure I have told you all about the wirelesses and Morse code and telephone, etc. There's nothing more to tell you as we are still on the same routine. In a fortnight's time we have our 'Passing Out' exam, then probably a week's special training and then LEAVE; after which I will be drafted to a training camp where there are <u>real</u> guns and then to a Regiment.

I don't know what else I can tell you sweet. I can do about 12 words a minute in Morse now (one of the fastest in the squad) and I think (strictly between ourselves) that there is a good chance of my getting a stripe. All this studying, etc., seems very silly if I am to get into the Pay Corps, but that's the way of the Army.

If I am a good signaller, they will say "Ah, this fellow's a good Signaller. He'll make a good officer in the Pay Corps." Crazy, but I expect that's what will happen.

It is now 4.15 pm. and we will be packing up in a very few minutes. I have had a go on the wireless, but am so used to being on the Air now that the thrill has gone!

Must close now. Will write a few lines when we get back and then catch the post so you will get this letter tomorrow. All my love.

6.15 p.m. Have just been paid, sweet, after having got back to barracks and had tea.

I <u>might</u> go to the pictures (again!) tonight and see 'Swiss Family Robinson' with Johnny. It's one of the cheapest forms of entertainment left now with the price of beer what it is. But I have been a bit lucky this week. John's got a horse-racing game like we've got at home and I, as bookmaker, won 2/3d. Quite a fortune in these troubled times. I have also won about a shilling playing cards. (I've never lost more than 2d or 3d). Well, darling, will 'cease fire' now, change and go to town to post this letter. All my love and may God look after you for me.

25th August 1940

Burniston Barracks
Scarborough

Sunday 5.15 p.m.

Thank you for your letter received yesterday. Thank you also darling very much for the stamps. You mustn't spoil me too much, I must learn to save enough to buy my own stamps – I expect I get as much actual 'pocket money' as you do. But it is very thoughtful of you, sweet.

I don't know what occupation you can put down for my father – you can say French Polisher or pianoforte craftsman or something. Isn't it a terrible lot of paraphernalia for two people in love who just want to get married? By the way, I haven't written to Do yet, I must try and do that as quickly as possible.

It was rather fortunate you didn't come up here this week-end as we had rather a bad air-raid last night. It lasted nearly all night from about 11 p.m. However, no sirens went so we didn't trouble to get up!

I hope the London raids don't worry you too much. I see you've had some more. Darling, I wish we were together in these troubled times. Would you get up in the night if we were? I wouldn't let you! Yesterday we had quite a nice afternoon passing messages all round Scarborough by Morse. There were parties of 3 or 4 of us and each was quite a distance from the other group. We passed the messages by means of lamps, telephones and flags. I was on top of the cliff where the castle stands reading a lamp about a mile away. It was very pleasant.

I haven't been out at all today. This morning at 8.20 am. I was on Church Parade. The sermon was awful tripe. I felt like shooting the preacher. When we go to church, by the way, we have to take rifles, steel helmets and ammunition. What a cock-eyed world!

Darling, I will now have a shower and then go out for a short walk and post this letter. All my love for ever.

P.S. I love you.

69

P.P.S. I didn't go to the pictures Friday after all, but went last night and saw 'Swiss Family Robinson'. It's not bad - have you seen it?

26th August 1940   Burniston Barracks
                                                                  Scarborough
6.15 pm.

Thank you for your letter which I received this morning.

I wish I were with you in London now, darling, that you keep having these air-raids. I believe you are on late duty at the office this week - I think they ought to do something about that. It's bad enough having to go home in the dark alone without air-raids probably interrupting your journey. How are the people down there reacting to the raids? Are they keeping cheerful and does life go on as usual? Please take care of yourself and please do not take any risks. You seem to have had quite an adventure Saturday night – I wish I could stay out to one o'clock in the morning.

We had the bombers over again last night and a couple of bombs landed in a golf course behind us. They seem to be getting nearer! It's a very uncomfortable feeling when you realise it's you they are trying to hit. I hope they give us a rest tonight – I'm just about tired of being woken up by bombs dropping around us. I think I will write to the local M.P. about it!

I've had quite an easy day today. Our sergeant's rather a lad and when he was giving us a lecture this afternoon I started to nod. He said "Feeling tired Berry?" I said "Yes Sarge," and he then said, "Then you had better go to bed." I couldn't believe my ears at first, but I thought I would take him at his word and left the lecture room – I was not called back! That was at 3 o'clock. I went to sleep till 4.30 p.m. He then said, "Clean my boots and you needn't go on Parade at 5.30." So that was another hour I had off!!

I haven't heard any more about the Commission yet. Several fellows from other squads have gone to the OTC - but that's for being trained as artillery officers. If I don't hear anything after I've passed out I shall make enquiries. I'm not going to let them get away with it.

Well, darling, will close now and try and find someone who is going to town to post this letter for me. All my love (My ring you bought me won't come off now. So you mustn't give me up).

Darling,

You will undoubtedly be surprised to receive a letter from me on this 'official' paper (Signal message forms) but when you pause to consider that today is Thursday and pay parade not till tomorrow night, you will realise that I have run out of notepaper and can't afford to buy any. I hope you don't mind, sweet, but I thought it would be better to write to you on this tonight than wait till tomorrow evening.

Thank you for your letter. I am very happy to see that you are keeping your chin up and still smiling. If God does take care of you for me, I will really believe in Him. I am longing to see you again.

I haven't written to 'Do' yet. I really must write tomorrow when I get some notepaper and tell her we are going to try and get married. I don't suppose she will be surprised.

Nothing much to tell you about myself. We had a stormy night last night, so were free from air-raids. Yesterday afternoon we were out on wireless sets. Today has been rather uninteresting with buzzer, lamp reading, lectures, etc.

These last few days I have had a bit of a cold, but it is getting better now. I know how I caught it – jumping out of bed in the middle of the night to watch bombs fall. I have learned my lesson now and stop in bed all the time. Sometimes I condescend to open my eyes and look at the searchlights out of the window.

I have stopped in every night this week and will be in again tonight. (I'll be glad when we get our extra 6d a day at the end of the month). Love.

30th August 1940   Burniston Barracks

My darling,

We have just been paid and now I am sitting on my bed writing this letter.

I hope you are still well and fit, darling. I read in the paper that London had a 7 hour raid Wednesday night but this morning there was no news at all about the raid. Does that mean you had an even longer one? I hope not, or if so, that it did not upset you too much. I shall breathe a sigh of relief next week when you are on early duty. I worry about your getting home of a night far more than the actual raids. I do wish I could meet you every night and take you home. I don't worry much about the bombs because the odds are very much against actually being hit by one. I believe I am still right in saying that it is far more dangerous crossing a main road.

I haven't felt too grand today – had a fit of coughing last night – but as soon as I finish this letter I will have a shower and probably feel better.

This morning there were only 8 letters for two squads (40 odd men) so presume that air-raids have delayed the post. I shan't worry too much, therefore, if I don't hear from you tomorrow. I shall just curse Hitler.

I am looking forward to when we are married. Love for ever.

1st September 1940   Burniston Barracks

As I half expected, I received no letter from you yesterday. I am, of course, a bit worried, but I know that the post from London is now very irregular. We never get the morning papers until about mid-day. I hope you are still well and cheerful. I do wish I were back home with you – it seems so silly hanging about here whilst London is being bombed. I expect you must be very tired, but I do

72

hope you will have more rest this week now that you are on early duty again. I have been going to ring you at the office, but it is almost impossible now to get a call through because of official calls. I hope I get a letter from you tomorrow, darling – I feel so lost when I don't hear from you.

I went to the pictures last night and saw 'Behind the Door' with Boris Karloff. Rather gruesome, but not too bad. Coming home we got caught in an air-raid. Luckily for us they did not seem to be keen on Scarborough and only dropped one or two on the outskirts. I think they were either heading further north or to the north-west coast. Of course, all during the night, they were coming back in dribs and drabs, but they left us alone.

I had quite a nice afternoon yesterday. We were out with the wireless and I was situated on the beach. It was a marvellously hot day – the only trouble being the sand which got into everything and the wet kids in bathing costumes who would crowd round us.

This morning I was cleaning out lecture rooms with the rest of the squad. We had a short parade and then it was dinner time. Some of the fellows have gone swimming this afternoon but I don't think I will. I don't feel too cheerful – silly of me I know darling, but you know how much I love you. All my love.

2nd September 1940   Burniston Barracks

Thank you for your letter. It was very nice to hear from you again darling – yes, I received both your letters last week. I wonder if you will get all my letters? I write to you every other day regularly now and always post a letter Friday night so that you will get it for the week-end.

Thank you for the proofs of your photographs. They are both very good, but, of course, don't do you justice. But I expect too much – I will not be really satisfied until I have YOU near me always – not just a photograph. It's very hard to choose which one I like best. I have looked at them over and over again. But although you look a bit stern in one, I think I like that best. It reminds me of your expression when you are a little annoyed with me. The other photo is also very nice, but your smile is much more attractive than that, although, as I keep looking at it, it reminds me of when I bought you a port and your eyes began to sparkle! Which do you like best sweet? Why not send me the one you think most like yourself? I don't mind really which one I have. It's very nice to see you again (if only an image). I'm still very much in love with you. I have been very faithful to you, sweet, and have not taken any girl out whilst I have been here.

I'm glad you've been having a bit more peace lately. I feel much happier this week knowing you are on day duty. Whenever Jerry wakes me up in the night I always wonder whether you have got home safely, and am always very relieved when I get a letter from you. I do get a bit tired of staying in sometimes, darling, but there's nothing else I can do. Our pocket money goes like lightning.

2nd September 1940

This week-end I did not go into a pub at all, but thought I would save money by going to the pictures Saturday and Sunday nights (one shilling seats). By the time I had bought soap, etc., I was broke Sunday night and today I had to go to the bank. Darling, you must marry me soon or I will spend all my money!

I've a lot more to tell you, but somebody is going to town and I want this letter posted tonight. Love for ever.

P.S. I hope that fellow who took you home is old enough to be your grandfather or I will be terribly jealous!

4th September 1940   Burniston Barracks
                                                          Scarborough
7.30 p.m.

Thank you for your two letters – one yesterday and one today. No darling, I didn't forget our 'anniversary' yesterday. I was going to mention it in my last letter, but had to finish abruptly in order to catch the post.

Herbert certainly seems to be getting on quickly. He is very fortunate – it is impossible for us to get any real promotion until we leave here. We seem to have to work devilishly hard here without hardly any compensation at all. Still, when we do get posted to our units, promotion should come quickly with the knowledge we have gained here. On Wednesday next we have our 'Passing Out' exam and then we have leave to look forward to – unless anything unexpected happens.

I'm glad you liked the snaps. I expect you have got your proofs back now with my letter. If you do intend to have them both printed I should, of course, like to have the two of them.

Thank you for all the news about the office. I expect the 'Star' personnel will have changed beyond recognition when I return.

I am feeling fine now and hope you are too. I know how one's eyes ache when one has not sufficient sleep, but don't let it get you down. The war can't last for ever. When things settle down a little I will give you a ring at the first opportunity. Let's hope it won't be long before you go to sleep in my arms. I <u>know</u> we shall always be very happy.

I don't think any of your letters have gone astray, darling. They were probably delayed and you have got my replies to them by now. I think I did miss the bit about your knitting something for me. I don't know really what I want – why not knit me something as a surprise? Khaki gloves, pullover, socks, balaclava – anything like that would be very useful.

Thank you for making excuses to everyone for my not writing. I do find it rather hard to write to everybody. As soon as I get a spare minute I like to write to you and then don't feel like writing to anyone else. I wrote to Dad a few days ago and told him we might get married. I have had a reply and he quite approves and wishes us all the best. Finsbury Park seems to have been let off pretty lightly in the raids. He went to Huntingdon and saw Do a few days ago. She and the children are all well.

They have just started football here and I have taken it up; we have had a couple of games and I think it has done me good. We have also started to go swimming in our gym periods. This morning we went for the second time this week and I enjoyed it. There is a marvellous open-air pool and the day was very hot. But I don't think I shall ever learn to swim properly! I don't know whether I shall catch the post tonight and nobody seems to be going to town – but I'll try. All my love.

6th September 1940   Burniston Barracks

Not much news to tell you. I can't reply to any of your letters as I have not received one since Tuesday. Air-raids again, I suppose. That bloke Hitler has certainly got something to answer for when we finally capture him. Delay letters from my love – how would he like it?

Have you had your photographs printed yet, darling? I am eagerly awaiting a copy to hang up in my locker.

How have you been keeping? I see London had its longest raid last night – I hope you weren't too much disturbed. We had them over again last night and they dropped 3 bombs somewhere in the district which woke me up. The first time they have taken a liking to this place for a week. I have been dreaming quite a lot about you this week, darling – I shall be happy when we are together again.

We have not been doing much out of the ordinary these last few days. We went swimming again this evening, but there was rather a chilly wind blowing – so I didn't go in until it was time to come out. But I wetted myself up to the waist!

We had another game of football last night. I am feeling much fitter and happier since I have taken it up – I think it's just what I need to relieve the monotony of everyday life here. Thank goodness we shall be able to take things pretty easy after next Wednesday - when (I hope) we shall have my 'flags' up. I don't think I shall experience much difficulty in 'Passing out'.

One more day is nearly finished and I am one more day nearer my leave and seeing you again. I have never looked forward so eagerly before in all my life.

All my love for ever and ever. Your faithful fiancé.

September 8th 1940   Burniston Barracks

I have been very worried today after the news of the raid on London came through this morning. I hope you are all right, sweet. I was glad that you didn't have to go to the office yesterday – they seemed to have copped it in East and Central London according to reports. I hope I'll get a letter from you tomorrow saying that you are all right. I wish you were up here with me now as it is comparatively quiet compared with the air raids you had yesterday.

We knew something was afoot yesterday afternoon when we were told to stay in our barrack room, but we were soon back to normal duties and went cable-laying. However, at 11.30 pm. at night we were roused from our beds and had to 'stand-to' till just gone 1 pm. We then went to bed (dressed in full equipment:- gas capes; masks; overcoats; packs, etc.) and tried to sleep until 3.30 am. when we were again called out. From then until 6 am. I was sleeping on a hard concrete floor in a garage. However, I don't feel too bad today as I didn't go out last night. I slept from about 5 to 8 pm. and it did me good.

Today we are only allowed out of barracks from 2 to 7 pm. and we have go out in gas capes, etc. At 7.30 pm. we have to 'stand-to' for an hour and also from 4 to 6 am. It all seems so silly and pointless as we could easily get dressed in a few minutes if there were an alarm. I wouldn't mind so much if we were in London, but none of us here has any inclination to defend this hole and we are praying that this arrangement is not carried on all the week. The Colonel of this Regiment is a complete fool. (I hope this letter won't be opened!)

Thank you for your letter which I received yesterday. Darling, please always tell me about the air-raids you have – I like to know what is happening back home. Do take care of yourself. My family still seems to be OK darling, as I believe I mentioned in a previous letter. I am going to write to 'Do' today. Thanks for the news about the office. Perhaps you will send me another 'Star' one day. I should like to see if there are any changes.

I shall be thinking a lot of you this week and shall be wondering whether you are home when I get up at 4 am. I wish you didn't have to work late, darling.

I shall not be able to go out this evening (I could for a little while until 7, but don't think it's worth it). So I will just stroll down to the barrack post-box and catch the 5.30 post; although I expect it will be delayed and you won't get it till Tuesday.

P.S. Don't forget the photographs, darling.

P.P.S. Darling, in some ways it doesn't seem as if we have been engaged 5 months in one way, but it seems ages and ages ago since I last saw you. I hope we can get married when I get my leave. I can't say exactly when we will get it, but it should not be longer than 3 weeks. I will let you know as soon as a definite day is fixed. All my love.

12th September 1940   Burniston Barracks

Thank you for your two letters. I wish you weren't in London. Since they have started raiding London we have had it fairly quiet up here and it doesn't seem fair that we, as soldiers, should be living peacefully while our families and sweethearts are being bombarded. Darling, I am very proud of you for keeping cheerful – you are the most wonderful girl in the world. But please don't take any risks. Do look after yourself. The raids can't last for ever and perhaps soon they will take more of an interest in Scarborough and leave London alone.

Darling, I don't expect so many letters from you in future as I know how full your spare time now must be. I shan't worry too much as long as you take care of yourself. I suppose, in a way, you are safer in the office shelter at night than being at home – but it can't be very nice not to be able to get home after being at the office all day. Every morning I rush to listen to the wireless or see a paper to find out what has happened at home. I can't express my thoughts very clearly, but I am always mentally praying for you and for the Germans to leave London alone. If we have to be apart I do wish we could change places. But I am really always with you in spirit and am always looking after you. Sometimes when I have a spare minute I sit and look at your ring on my finger and twist it round and round (it won't come off). I always seem to be much closer to you then.

I hope you are not on late duty when I get my leave - but, who knows perhaps they will have tired of bombing London by then. We must trust to our luck, darling and perhaps we won't be disappointed.

I suppose we will now experience greater difficulty in getting married. Do you still wish to marry me, darling, or would you prefer to postpone it for a little while now? I'll leave it all to you - I know you will decide on the right thing.

We are 'Passing Out' on Friday and Saturday and are looking forward to having a little easier time - for the time being. It will be nice to have a change from swotting, and I shall be able to write to you more often - I hope.

I will close now as I am very tired. (I have been swotting all the evening). I am afraid that I have missed the post and there is no late collection today. I don't know, therefore, when you will receive this letter, but I hope you don't worry too much. Have you had time to collect your photographs yet? Love for ever.

13th September 1940   Burniston Barracks
                                                                  Scarborough

Thank you for your letter which I received today.

This will be only a short letter as I want to catch the post this evening and you may get it sometime tomorrow. I am very sorry I have not written so frequently this week, but I did have a lot of swotting to do but I shall make up for it next week.

We had most of our 'exam' today and it was pretty easy – it will be finished off tomorrow morning. I am confident that I will pass and if I have time I shall probably buy my 'Flags' in town tonight.

We have just come back from Pay Parade with 21/-!! The extra 3.6d came into force last week and as we didn't get it then they gave us an extra 7/- this week. Tomorrow we are holding a little party in celebration of 'passing out' which the sergeants will attend and, we hope, an officer. It is a great relief to know that we shall have no more swotting to do.

I think you and other Londoners are really wonderful and I am very, very, proud of you. I pray God will still take care of you. We all feel very miserable up here and wish we were back in London. In comparison, being here is like being at a holiday camp. It's all wrong – although I expect our turn will come sooner or later.

I am glad you are fairly comfortable in the office shelter – it is surprising how one soon gets used to 'roughing it' a little. I am sorry Herbert isn't quite so enthusiastic, but we all get 'browned off' at times. I expect he is worried about you and the family and Hazel. I know how he feels. I am still fit and we are now getting a sleep every night. All my love for ever.

September 15th 1940   Burniston Barracks

How are you my sweet? I hope you are still fit and O.K. Is Ealing still being bombed? According to the newspapers the defence of London has been greatly improved and attacks are not quite so fierce. I hope this is true.

Well, darling, I 'Passed Out' yesterday and am now a Royal Artillery Signaller with flags on my sleeve! I got 246 marks out of 250, but as there were one or two fellows above me, I think I have just missed getting a stripe. Still never mind, there will be more opportunity and scope when I am posted. In any case the 6 months is not up until October 18th!

We had a little party yesterday evening which was quite enjoyable, and, as none of us has had much beer since being here, it did not take long to make us feel merry. It was a pleasant change, combined with the relief at having finished with swotting for the time being. We now have a fortnight's 'collective training' – that is working as if we were on actual active service – establishing communications between two Batteries while both advancing and retreating. Then, of course, we are due for our week's leave. It is cancelled at the moment, but, unless anything happens, will be resumed again in a few days time. I hope nothing else does happen darling. I am longing to see you again and hold you in my arms.

After leave we will move to 'Depot Battery' and do odd jobs such as 'Inlying picket' until we are required by some regiment or other. We shall probably be there quite a few weeks before being posted.

I hope I am lucky enough to be sent south. The last lot of southerners went to Watford! But it is purely luck as the Army doesn't worry about how far from home they send you. I think they should take it into consideration as it seems very silly to post Londoners to Scotland and Scots to London as they do.

Yesterday afternoon we were supposed to go cable laying, but we just jumped into the lorries and went for a ride round the local countryside, stopping at a pub for a drink on the way. The scenery round here is very beautiful and it almost reminded me of one of the conducted tours we used to go on at Eze-sur-Mer. I wish you could have been with me darling.

One of the fellows in the other squad has just gone on leave for 48 hours. His house has been smashed up by a bomb, but luckily his wife was not injured – being in an Anderson shelter. Still, it's tough luck.

Well darling, there's no more news. I will now clean my boots and dash to town to catch the 5.30 pm. post. I have spent this afternoon washing handkerchiefs, etc. I don't know what I shall do this evening, being on my own. John is out with his girl friend. I might go to the pictures, although I should do some sewing-on of buttons.

Au revoir darling.

18th September 1940   Burniston Barracks
                                                              Scarborough

Thank you for your letter which I received today. I'm sorry you hadn't heard from me for 2 days, but I expect you have had two letters from me since Friday.

I hope you have had more rest this week, darling, being on day duty.   Sometimes your letters are funny and difficult to understand. You said in your last one 'I arrived home at 7.45 a.m. this morning. Mr. Gamp was off duty and I had to walk to St. James' Park'. I had to think for a long time about that one. I couldn't see the connection between a certain Mr. Gamp being off duty and your walking to St. James's Park until it suddenly struck me that I suppose Mr. G. was the bloke at the office who gave you lifts home in the morning. Is that right?

How have the air-raids been lately darling? Are they easing off or worse than ever? Are you still keeping fit and cheerful? It won't be long now, darling, before I see you again. Keep beautiful for me. I think the Germans have a cheek to bomb 'our' first cinema. I shall get really aggressive if they continue to do things like that. A fellow in the squad has heard by letter that Finsbury Park Empire has been hit. I wonder how Finsbury Park has faired during the last week or so? Have you had any more bombs in Ealing?

We are having quite a hectic time now, darling. I thought we were going to 'ease off' a bit, but this special training is harder than ever. You would never believe the work there is in laying and keeping up communications between a battery of guns.

We went out today on 14 vehicles (the usual number in a battery without counting the actual guns which, of course, we didn't have). There are wireless vans, cable laying vans, motor-bikes – it looks like a Lord Mayor's Show. I was a wireless operator and had to keep communications going whilst the telephones were being laid.   Then we have to pack everything up, advance or retreat, and see how quickly we can lay it all out again. We did it on a small scale today – we were all in a decent sized field – but when we get going, we may cover an area of 10 square miles or more. I shall have to explain it all to you when I see you. We only had $\frac{3}{4}$ hour for lunch today because of it.

I went to the pictures last night and saw 'He Married his Wife' and on Sunday saw 'Night Train to Munich' which was very good.

I love you very much darling, and am hoping we can get married soon. Are you still willing to be my wife or have you decided not to risk it now? I shall try to make you very happy, darling, but don't really think I am good enough for you. But perhaps you will put up with me. All my love for ever.

19th September 1940   Burniston Barracks
                                                      Scarborough

Thank you for your letter. Darling I can't understand how you didn't receive a letter from me for a week. I have never left it so long as a week before writing to you and I can't think what could have happened. Either a letter has gone astray or they were delayed. Did you notice the dates on the two letters you received and the date of the previous letter? If the dates were more than 3 days apart then one must have gone astray. I don't think I have ever left it longer before writing to you. Darling, I'm very sorry this should have happened.

In answer to your letter, I think perhaps a postcard size photo of you would be best for me here and I should like very much for you to keep the mounted one for me. It will look nice in our sitting-room when we are married and the war is over.

Darling, you still seem to be having a lot of air-raids. I wish they would stop. I feel very worried.

Darling, if I get posted somewhere in England and it looks permanent and in a fairly quiet place, would you come and live near me if we get married? Or wouldn't you like leaving your family* on their own? On second thoughts, I don't suppose you could, unless Muriel and Frank also moved from London. I suppose, once again, we shall have to wait and see. If the raids continue and get worse,

I certainly don't like the idea of your staying in London. You must take care of yourself for me - I don't know what I should do without you.

As I have mentioned before darling I don't expect to hear from you so often now as I know how upset your life must be and how little spare time you must have. But don't stop loving me.

I'm sorry to hear Muriel is getting a little scared - I don't blame her really. I think you are very brave and I expect she is glad that she has you to comfort her. I only wish I were at home so I could comfort you too. Or, perhaps, you would have to comfort me!

We went out again this morning on the stunt I explained in my last letter. I expect we shall do it every day and the manoeuvres will probably last all day next week.

Tomorrow I am temporary NCO in charge of Signals - which means I am practically responsible for the whole thing - at least the telephone and cable laying. I shall have a motor-bike and this evening - as I hadn't ridden one since being in 'B' Battery - I went out on a practice run riding over rough country. It was very enjoyable and I got on all right.

I shall post this letter tonight so that you are almost certain to get it by Saturday. I hope it doesn't go astray as I know how worried I am when I can think of no reason why I haven't heard from you for a few days. Au revoir.

* Gwen's young brother and sister.

22nd September 1940   Burniston Barracks
                                                              Scarborough

My darling,

Thank you for your two letters. It was very nice to hear from you again - the first time since last Thursday. I know how difficult it must be for you to find time to write nowadays and I don't really mind not hearing from you so often, except that I get rather worried wondering if you are all right. Quite a number of fellows in our squad have had their homes bombed and have been granted a few days leave. It always makes us feel rather worried.

Herbert certainly seems to be having a rough time, but I don't suppose it will last long. The Army is always thinking of silly little orders like being confined to barracks, etc., but they usually change their minds three or four times a month. It's mainly due, I think, to the silly old fossils who 'run' the Army. Most of them have no idea of modern warfare.

You ask when you will see me again; I think I can promise you that it won't be long now. One of the fellows in the squad is going for 7 days today and, on Monday, I think they will be sending half-a-squad a week (about 12 men). We don't get much notice of leave, so I might arrive quite unannounced. I shall, of course, try to phone you or send you a telegram.

I think I mentioned that the Regiment is moving to somewhere near Manchester (nearer home!) but I don't think that will interfere with our leave. It will be marvellous to get away from the Army for 7 days and to see you again. I haven't heard from Dad lately. I wrote to Do about a week ago, but so far have had no reply (The postal delivery again, I suppose).

I am glad the bombs dropped on Sunday did not do much damage. I hope they leave us somewhere to take a walk when I see you again. I do not go swimming now, it is far too cold up here. I haven't played football much either; but we did have a little game this afternoon for about half-an-hour.

Darling I have asked you several questions in previous letters – important ones about whether we can still get married, but you never answer them. Please answer this question, darling, or else I shall really believe you don't love me any more. Do I answer your letters properly now, darling?

I discovered yesterday that the last post in town here is now 6.30 pm. so that makes my letters later. I can't catch that post, as we do not finish until that time.

All my love.

23rd September 1940   Burniston Barracks
                                                     Scarborough

My darling,

I'm sorry I have not written before, but I really could think of nothing much to tell you. I usually have a letter from you to reply to, but have not had one for some days. I know it is not your fault, darling, but I feel very lonely now that your letters aren't so frequent. Do you still love me? I wonder if any more of my letters have gone astray – I sent three last week. I wonder if you received them all. By the way, darling, I usually ask one or two questions in each letter but never seem to get any answers. Do you have the same trouble with me? I expect you do.

How are you keeping? Still fit and beautiful? According to reports, air-raids over London have diminished slightly. I hope it is true and that you are getting more sleep.

I have your last letter before me, darling (18th) and can't quite remember whether I have thanked you for it. By the way, your mention of Aldwych recalls that I read in the paper something about that Underground line being closed. I suppose you now have even more difficulty in getting to and from the office. I wish I were with you.

The same routine still goes on here, but definitely finishes on Saturday (Hurrah!). On Friday I had quite an enjoyable day riding about on a motor-bike, being, as I told you, NCO in charge of Signals. This morning we went on a rifle range and each shot 15 rounds. At a 100 yards range with 5 shots I got three bulls eyes and two inners, and at 200 yards with 10 shots, 4 bulls eyes, 5 inners and one miss! How the miss came in I do not know – probably because I was thinking of you instead of concentrating on what I was doing!

If all goes well, we should start our leave next week. But don't take this as all definite. There are several factors to be taken into consideration (a) Leave might again be temporarily cancelled (b) We might be posted first and then get our leave (c) There is a very strong rumour that the regiment is moving soon – either to

Manchester or Gloucester – and that, of course, could temporarily delay it (d) If leave is started, I might be one of the last to go as I have been lucky enough to get 48 hours leave before, which the majority have not.

However, darling, we should know something definite at the end of this week or beginning of next when, of course, I will immediately let you know. Actually I feel quite confident that it won't be long before we see each other again.

Nothing much more to tell you, darling. I have been to the pictures quite a lot lately (as it is about the cheapest pastime up here) and tomorrow evening I might go and see 'The case of the Frightened Lady'. Do you remember when we saw it at the Chiswick Empire with Sarah Churchill? I suppose the theatre is closed now.

I'll probably take a stroll down town to post this letter. Au revoir my sweet (for only a little while I hope). All my love.

26th September 1940   Burniston Barracks
                                                Scarborough

Thank you for your letter which I received this morning. It was quite a surprise as I see you did not post it until yesterday afternoon – the postal delivery seems to be improving.

I'll try not to worry about the air-raids but it is very difficult not to – I do wish you didn't have to stay in London. But I am glad you are still keeping fit and cheerful. I am very proud, darling, that I have a girl like you for my fiancée. I'll try and write more frequently in future than I have, but do not think I do not love you any more because you do not hear from me for 2 or 3 days. I often sit down to write but can think of nothing to say. But you are always in my thoughts and I love you very much. There seems to be a very good chance that I may get leave next week. Our training is now definitely finished and on Sunday we shall move to Depot Battery.

I had a letter from Do today and she is very pleased to hear that we might get married soon – I think she likes you very much. Dad has been invited to live at Huntingdon, but he refuses to leave home.

We went out on another stunt this morning and it was quite interesting. The Treasure Hunt the day before was also enjoyable and our squad won 100 cigarettes from the Major. All very nice and homely!

Tomorrow I am going to be 'under fire'. I am a telephonist at the firing butts and have to telephone back to the firing mark what they have scored. I will be in a trench behind the targets.

I will close now and take a walk to town to post this letter. I am looking forward to seeing you again very much, and hope it won't be long. I love you very much. Keep good and take care of yourself.

27th September 1940   Burniston Barracks
                                                          Scarborough

Thank you very much for your letter which I received this morning. It was certainly a great surprise to receive so many from you in one week – after getting used to waiting 4 days or so – and the post certainly seems to be getting back to normal.

Darling I still love you very much and will try and write more frequently in future. But you still don't answer my questions. I remember asking you one question as to whether or not you thought we could still get married during my leave and several others of less importance. If you look at my previous letters I am sure you will find dozens of questions which you have not answered. I began to think that you did not trouble to read my letters any more!!!

Darling I hope you still don't have to walk home of a morning. Things seem to be getting worse in London. I can't help worrying about you. Please take care.

I'm glad you have a new assistant at the office and hope she turns out to be O.K. I think the firm ought to treat you a lot better seeing the amount of work you have to do and what you have to put up with. Still I know you will come through it all smiling.

Thanks for all the news about the office. I hope they soon put Ealing Broadway station back into shape. The Jerries seem to be doing their utmost to make it difficult for you to get to and from the office. I do wish they would stop it. I think it is a shame that people should have to sleep in the Tubes – they should be provided with special shelters.

I don't like being pessimistic, but this war seems to be developing into a terrific muddle as I always thought it would. I wish a miracle would happen and put everything ship-shape again. I do so want to be back with you.

We went out for a nice ride in the cars this afternoon on a map-reading stunt. We drove through some very beautiful country which always reminds me of our 'day tours' together in France. I wish you could live up here with me. Everything now is so peaceful and quiet compared with London. But I will get my leave soon and I do hope we shall be able to spend a lot of time together. I will see if I can get my leave when you are on day duty – if it does not mean that I have to wait too long.

I am afraid I have missed the post, but will put this letter in the barrack post-box tonight and it will go first thing in the morning. All my love for ever.

29th September 1940

Depot Battery
Burniston Barracks
Scarborough

I am afraid I haven't much new to tell you but I thought I would write and tell you I still love you, as you suggested. I hope you are still fit, darling. Apparently you had an extra severe air raid the other day. I hope it did not inconvenience you too much. We still have it fairly quiet up here although we had several Germans overhead last night.

As you see, we have definitely finished our training now and are in Depot Battery. I have been very lucky as usually we have to do 'Inlying Picket' every other day, but I have been picked with some others as Regimental Signallers. So I miss it all – thank goodness. However, we still have to do 'fatigues' all day, but we will get used to it. In any case we won't be here for long we hope. There is still a chance that we may get our leave early next week. I will, of course, let you know as soon as I can. We are in quite a nice room now – a new 'bungalow' which has just been built. It is not as good as our old barrack room, but much better than the quarters we were last in.

Well, darling, nothing much more to tell you. It is now 5.15 pm. and I have been sleeping all the afternoon! I might go to the pictures tonight with a couple of fellows, but haven't really made up my mind yet. I feel too lazy to have a shave and clean my boots! But I must go out to post this letter to my love so that she doesn't worry too much. All my love.

30th September 1940   Burniston Barracks
                                                                              Scarborough

Thank you for your letter received today. I am sorry you were not feeling too well when you wrote your letter. I do hope you are feeling better now darling. I am also sorry that, on one of the rare occasions that you dream, you should have had such an unpleasant one. I hope I don't have to go abroad, darling. In any case it wouldn't make any difference in my writing to you. You would be bound to know before I went. I think you must have eaten something that disagreed with you, sweet!!! Or you are eating too much – as you mentioned!

I am glad to know that you are now taking air-raids in your stride and getting used to them. I only hope that they do not keep me from seeing a lot of you when I get my leave. We haven't actually heard anything yet, but are expecting to any day.

Talking about air raids … As I write this, bombers are flying overhead. But with one difference; they are going to Germany and not coming from there. It's rather satisfying in a way to know they are going to give Berlin a dose of what they give London.

You know best, darling, about whether or not you get another job. If it gets too dangerous travelling to town I should certainly advise you to. I don't want you to take any unnecessary risks. As usual darling, there's nothing much to tell you (We always say that in our letters to each other, don't we?). I am writing this in the light of a hurricane lamp. We have electric lights in the room but for some unknown reason the CO has turned them off at the main.

They do get crazy ideas. Actually it is lighter outside than in here for we have all the blackouts up. It is about 7.30 pm. now. This morning we had a fairly easy time – a little lamp and buzzer reading, drew another blanket and some long pants from the stores (the latter I certainly shan't wear) and had the rest of the morning off. In the afternoon "A" Battery had infantry training and, as I am a regimental signaller, was signaller with one of the platoons. It's really comical to watch the new recruits trying to be soldiers.

This evening we had gym and played rugger. By the way, we are now going to have gym every night – that will just about kill me! Tomorrow four of us are going to Catterick, a military town about 80 miles from here. We do not know why, but it will be a nice ride – four hours each way. I expect it's just unloading something or other. I hope it's not unpleasant anyway as we all volunteered for it. We jump at chances like this to get away from Scarborough. By the way, darling, when I moved from our old barrack room I had five tins full of your letters, and I was wondering how I could carry them when I am drafted. Also if anything should happen to me I should hate to think that other people might read them. So I really think the best thing I could do would be to burn them. What do you think darling? If, of course, I get my leave in a few days I will bring them home with me. That will solve the problem. I don't really want to burn them if I can possibly help it. I should like to read them again when we celebrate our Golden Wedding. I can't believe that I shall soon be seeing you again – it seems too good to be true. My love for always.

A WEEK'S LEAVE
(Hence no correspondence)

11th October 1940   Burniston Barracks
                                                Scarborough

    I arrived here quite safe and sound at 11.15 last night. It was terrible having to leave you again darling and I don't feel particularly cheerful. But we had a wonderful time together although it all went so quickly. I know darling that we shall be very happy when we are married and always together. I hope you are not feeling too unhappy darling.

    I shall be much nearer to you soon, sweet. On Tuesday I am being posted to WATFORD and I am hoping that I will be able to get home and see you as much as possible. It's a Reserve Regiment I am going to, so we probably won't be there indefinitely. But we are bound to be stationed there for some weeks. It will be nice to be only about 20 miles away from you, but don't forget, please don't get too optimistic as one can never tell what is going to happen in the Army. However, it all seems pretty definite. The only snag is that I shall still be In suspense wondering where I shall be posted next.

    I am very lucky in a way darling. Several fellows in my squad (including the one whose fiancée came to Scarborough) have been already posted and have had no leave. They all went to Salisbury Plain last Monday.

    There's not much news I can tell you (Same old cry!). I have had a pretty restful day today as I have been Room Orderly. It means quite an amount of work in the morning cleaning up the room, but after that is done there is nothing more to do except stay in and see no strangers enter.

I have felt very tired all day due, mainly I think, to day-dreaming about you. It was a wonderful week, darling. The bombers seem to have followed me back here. Just before I arrived they attacked the town. There are a couple of huge craters and about 10 people were killed. Everyone is talking about it here, but I was not very impressed after having seen London.

By the way I nearly missed my train at Kings Cross yesterday. I got to Finsbury Park Station at five minutes to five and then found I had left my kitbag at home. You should have seen me dashing back for it with my pack on – it was pouring with rain too. I know what you are thinking – I am hopeless, aren't I?

I think that's all for now. Keep cheerful darling – perhaps we shall see some more of each other in a few days time. It will be wonderful to be near London and you. Au revoir my darling. I will always remember our week together. I hope that we can get married soon and that you haven't made any arrangements about coming up here! All my love.

P.S. I nearly forgot.

6.45 am. Got up. 7 a.m. Parade and then had breakfast (fish cakes, marmalade and porridge). 7.30 a.m. Wash, shaved, etc. 8.30 a.m. Room Orderly. Swept up, etc. 1.30 pm. Dinner (mashed potatoes, beans and stewed steak), spotted dog (a few more spots today) and custard. 2 pm. Continued Room Orderly's duties (including writing this letter which I am now going to finish and post).

12th October 1940   Burniston Barracks
                                                                        Scarborough

It seems quite definite now that I am going to Watford on Tuesday – about 50 of us. I expect we shall go directly to Kings Cross first and then take a district train. The main line doesn't touch Watford.

I feel very happy and fit darling at the thought of being nearer home. Scarborough isn't such a bad place when one knows that one has only a couple more days there. It has been a lovely day today and the air is marvellous. My cold has almost disappeared. I am room orderly again today and so have not done any work. I am getting a really experienced 'old soldier' now and never do work unless I can possibly help it. This morning they gave us picks and shovels and we had to widen one of the barrack paths. I wasn't keen and suddenly remembered there was no-one looking after the room. I mentioned it hopefully to the NCO and he said "Well, you had better go back and look after it". The best of it is that we all cleaned up this morning for the weekly inspection, so there was absolutely no work to do. I also dodged 'Inlying Picket' by dodging out when I saw them coming round with a list. I have not done one yet in 'Depot' Battery, although they have one to do every 24 hours.

Continuing my 'daily account' from yesterday's letter:

4.30 pm. Tea: Bread & butter, two sausages and tea.

5.30 – 6.30   Room Orderly (no work). In the evening I had a wash, went for a short walk and then had supper in the café opposite the barracks. I then played the piano till about 9.15 p.m. Came in and went to bed.

Today (Saturday)

6.40 am. Got up. 7 am. Parade and then breakfast (2 sausages, bread and butter and tea). 7.30 am. Washed, shaved and then helped clean room for inspection. 9.30 am. Parade. Ten of us were detailed to widen the path, but I skipped it as I have already told you. I found an Edgar Wallace book and read most of the morning. By the way I met Johnny who arrived last night and we had a cup of tea in the NAAFI during break at 10.30 am. 12.30 pm. Dinner: stewed meat, potatoes and carrots. Rice pudding (of a kind) for dessert.

2 pm. – 4.30 pm. Room Orderly. Read book and lazed about (Also wrote this letter to you). It is now 4 p.m. Will close for time being as there is nothing more to tell you.

Sunday 3 pm. Well I didn't post this last night after all. I suddenly realised it was Saturday and that you would not yet this letter any earlier if I posted it then. So I thought I would leave it over and add further news – if any.

I didn't do anything in particular last night again. John was meeting his girl friend. I popped over to the café and had some supper and played the piano again. This morning I got up at 7.30 am., but didn't trouble to have any breakfast. We had a couple of parades in the morning - checking our kit, etc., as we are moving. For dinner there were baked potatoes, meat and greens, stewed plums for dessert. Believe it or not, it was quite enjoyable - perhaps because I was feeling rather hungry not having had any breakfast.

At 2 o'clock I was caught for fatigues in the cookhouse, but it was only for dishing out the jam for tea. I have to go back at 5 pm. however, and help wipe down the tables. It is rather a cheek really, but I don't mind too much as I have had it pretty easy since I have been back and had nothing particularly to do this evening (John is meeting girl friend again). I expect it will take only about half-an-hour.

How are the air-raids going? Not any worse, I hope. I shall soon know, however. Won't it be wonderful if I can pop home occasionally from Watford? Actually I think it's only about 10 miles from Ealing. Perhaps I can get my bike up there and cycle home!

I spoke to a fellow who works in the office about this Pay Corps business and he said it wouldn't make any difference my leaving here. The recommendation will follow me about. He added that it would probably be months before I heard anything. So there you are! I do really think that is all for now. I will pop out and post this letter catching the 5.30 pm. post. I hope you get it tomorrow. All my love for ever and ever.

PART TWO

AWAITING A POSTING

16th October 1940

Wednesday

Sig. Berry HW
974063
"P" Battery
3rd Medium
Reserve Regt. RA

As you see by the address, we have moved from Scarborough – at last. We left there at 5 o'clock yesterday (Tuesday) and arrived at Kings Cross at about 2.15. There was a coach waiting for us which took us to Euston and we caught an LMS electric "District" to Watford. It was very annoying darling to be so near you and yet not be able to see you. I thought I might have a chance to ring you, but we didn't have any spare time whilst going through Euston.

We got to Watford at about 4.15 p.m. (It took us about an hour and a half to get there) and we were marched hither and thither whilst they took particulars and issued us with bedding, etc. We had some dinner and it was very good – much better cooked and served than at Burniston. After hanging about some more, we were finally taken to our billet – an empty house but well equipped with spring beds. We then undid all our kit and made ourselves at home. John and I rested for about three quarters of an hour till 8 p.m., then took a short walk to the nearest pub and had a drink. The sirens go here at the usual time and planes fly overhead, but there is no din like there is in central London. We got 'home' again at 9.30 p.m. and went straight to bed as we were very, very tired after travelling all day. I slept like a log.

We got up at 7 a.m. this morning (by the way it is now 5.30 p.m. and the sirens have just gone) and washed and shaved in cold water (no hot).

We left here at about 7.45 a.m. and got to the Drill Hall where we had breakfast at 8 a.m. However, there was such a crowd around that we decided not to wait and went straight to the Parade Ground (a car park in the centre of the town). Most of the morning we hung about doing nothing much in particular. We found that they were drafting a party to Richmond, Yorkshire, and we prayed that we would not have to go back. You see this is a kind of sorting Depot from which men are sent to various units. And as they were short of men they were drafting people who had only just arrived! We were lucky in that respect however. I was hoping that I might be settled for a few weeks so that perhaps I could pop home and see you on Sunday. I was going to ring you this evening, but have now moved a few miles away.

This afternoon ten of us were told to pack up our kits again as we were going on a Special Guard for a week. Of course we all grumbled like anything. But here we are now, somewhere between Watford and Hatfield* guarding a building of some sorts miles from civilization! However, it is not too bad. The food, so far sampled, has been excellent, and although we are not allowed out any further than about 100 yards, I expect we shall be in worse places before the war has finished. We are here for either a week or ten days, but when you write, address your letters to Watford and they will bring them here.

Well darling that's all the news for now. I have not heard from you yet since I returned from leave. I hope you are still fit and still love me. How are the raids nowadays?

If, when we have finished here, we are still at Watford, I will try and pop home one Sunday, although we are really limited to a 4 mile boundary! It is a much better regiment than the 37th and they organise games. I have put my name down for cross-country running and table tennis, and might take up rugger. (If I am here long enough). I will now take a short walk to see if I can find a letter-box. I am told there is one fixed to a telegraph pole somewhere here. Au revoir darling. I will phone you as soon as I get a chance. All my love for ever.

P.S. I hope I get a letter forwarded from Scarborough from you tomorrow.

* Garston, Herts.

17th October 1940   Somewhere in Herts.

Thank you for your letter which I received today. It had been forwarded from Scarborough to Watford and from Watford to here. I hope you are still feeling fine and you did not worry too much at not hearing from me for a few days. I wrote at the very first opportunity as soon as I knew my address. I don't know for how long I shall be in Watford after we have finished our guard duties here. If ever I get the opportunity I shall come and see you – I will certainly phone as soon as I can.

I am glad to hear Herbert is progressing. I hope you get transferred to the Accounts Department darling. I really think it would be better for you if you can settle down to it. I think things will turn out for the best.

We are gradually settling down to our week's stay here. I start my guard duties tonight at 9 p.m. (it is now 8.15 p.m.) – the usual 2 hours on and 4 off. This continues until tomorrow morning when I get all day off. I then start again at 9 p.m. for 24 hours duty. What we really do is 12 hours on – 12 hours off; 24 hours on – 24 hours off. I started my stay here with the 24 hours off, so I now do not get another 24 hours off duty until Sunday.

We don't have too bad a time here. The principal disadvantage is being confined to such a small area. If we are not on duty we have light fatigues to do during the day and about a quarter of an hour's drill. The officer in charge is a very decent fellow and sees that we are made as comfortable as possible. The food is really marvellous. Only about a dozen of us are at meals and we can eat as much as we like.

There is also cocoa kept hot all night for when we come off guard. The cook really does his best to dish up a good meal. Scarborough cannot be compared to it.

Our sleeping accommodation is not too good. We are billeted in a barn loft and have to sleep on our mattresses on the floor. Not too good, but, as I said before, probably better than we shall get in the future.

We get very bad air-raids here. They are overhead now. Last night they dropped bombs all over the place. You hear more bombs than AA fire. There are so many military objectives around here – aerodromes, etc., and they seem to know it. We still don't know what we are guarding; this building is of a semi-manor, semi-farm type. There are several of them in the district and all are surrounded by barb wire (ssssh!). It all seems very secret.

Last night John and I took a walk to the only pub we are allowed to visit, and I was pleasantly surprised to find a piano. I played most of the time and got treated to 3 pints, which I shared with John. (Just my luck that I can't go along there every night). Coming back it was pouring with rain and bombs, but it didn't trouble us. I feel much happier and contended darling being near home. Everything seems more homely and cheerful despite the monotonous job we have got.

Must break off now as it is nearly 9 o'clock and I must get ready. I shall be on again from 3 – 5 a.m. Goodnight, my darling.

I will continue this letter tomorrow.

Friday 3 p.m. Hello darling. It was rather cold last night on guard, but I do not feel too bad today. I am off now until 9 p.m. when I am on for 24 hours. We had a much quieter night last night although one or two bombs were dropped. How are the air-raids in London now? Are they easing off?

Here is what I have been doing today.

9 a.m. Got up. Did not trouble to have breakfast. Washed, shaved, etc.

9.30 a.m. On usual morning fatigues. Today I was washing dishes, etc.

11.45 a.m. Finished fatigues. Had another wash and played cards with John till

12.30 p.m.

12.30 p.m. Dinner: mashed potatoes, carrots, swedes and meat. For dessert, rice pudding.

1 p.m. Had another wash and cleaned rifle.

2 p.m. Rifle inspection.

2.15 p.m. Resting. Tried to play the accordion and then settled down to finish this letter to my love.

There's nothing more to tell you, sweet, except that I love you very much. I think I will now take a walk to the letter-box and perhaps you will get this tomorrow morning. I shall be glad when I hear from you. All my love for ever.

P.S. Do you still wish to marry me, darling?

21st October 1940   Herts.

I'm sorry I did not write over the week-end, but I was hoping I would get a letter from you. It seems ages since I last heard from you – I hope you are all right. I expect, however, it is due to the post round here. They might keep letters for a day at Watford before they are forwarded here.

I have been trying to ring you, but I don't get much chance being confined to this small area. We have terrific air-raids here – it is just like an outpost in No Man's Land. It was particularly bad last night from about 8 p.m. to 3 a.m. I was on guard from 9 to 11 p.m. and they started dive bombing. Twice I had to throw myself flat on the ground when bombs fell a few yards away. (Today's post has just come in darling – no letter from you). They kept the game going for another two hours and as I couldn't get to sleep I watched them. Every time they dived they dropped parachute flares and then the bombs whistled down. Whew, what a night!! I hope we get a more peaceful night tonight. Jerry has also been pretty busy today. We saw one come over and watched it drop 6 bombs (we could actually see them fall) and then it machine-gunned the road. We are certainly having our share of excitement here after the quiet time at Scarborough. In a way, darling, I don't mind at all. I hated the peaceful existence at Scarborough whilst you were being bombed and I feel much nearer to you now. I hope I get a letter from you tomorrow, darling.

I don't expect we shall be here for many more days, thank goodness. I should like to be back in Watford with a bit more freedom.

On our night off (Saturday was the last one) Johnny and I go along to the pub. The 'locals' know us there now and always get me to play the piano. It makes a break, although life here is pretty monotonous now. However, as I said, the grub is really marvellous – as good as at home - so we mustn't grumble.

If we are lucky we will go back to Watford on Wednesday and I shall really try to pop home and see you if I get the slightest chance. But don't take too much for granted. If I don't get a letter from you tomorrow I shall feel really miserable.

All my love for ever.

23rd October 1940   Herts.

Thank you for your two letters which I received yesterday evening. They cheered me up considerably. If ever I move suddenly again you can always write to my previous address and they will be forwarded.

I am not feeling particularly happy at the moment. We were told that we were going back to Watford this afternoon, but, at the last moment, they phoned to say that we should have to stay here until Saturday afternoon. It would not have been so bad if we didn't expect to leave here until Saturday, but after having packed our kits and got everything ready, it came as a bitter disappointment. I will now answer your letters, darling.

You must not feel so miserable because you cannot see me often although we are not far apart. You must remember darling that I am still in the Army and cannot possibly get time off even to see you. You must try and forget that I am at Watford if it is going to make you unhappy. You see, darling, you must never anticipate things. It does not necessarily mean I should see more of you even if I were stationed at Ealing Common rather than say, Scotland. You suggest two things darling which are practically impossible. In

104

your first letter you say that if you had known (6.50 p.m. the sirens have just gone) I was off duty last Sunday you would have come to see me. But I am sure I mentioned that when I get this time off I am not allowed out (only to a pub around the corner). It is for resting purposes only after 36 hours guard duty and I am not actually off duty.

Also, darling, it would take you a great deal of time to get to such an outlandish place as this, apart from the fact that I cannot tell you where we are. You also suggest, darling, that you could come to Watford one morning and see me about 9 a.m., but unfortunately the whole British Army parades at 8.30 a.m. every morning and is kept hard at it all day until 4.30 p.m. (That is, of course, if one is not on guard duties when one gets hardly any time off).

So you see, my sweet, that you must not try and make these arrangements. It only makes you unhappy when you find you cannot see me and also makes me feel very discontented. As soon as I see another opportunity of our seeing each other at any time, whether by my going to London or your coming here, I will let you know. I want to see you as badly as you want to see me, but we must be patient and not get too excited because we are not so far apart. We might be able to see each other on Saturday or Sunday - it all depends on what time we leave here on Saturday. I shall try and give you a phone sometime this week – if I can find one. And if air-raids do not delay calls too long.

Darling, I am sure you don't read my letters carefully. You say 'Richmond is nice and near ......' but I'm sure I definitely wrote Richmond, <u>Yorkshire</u>, which is back near Scarborough. So you see, I don't want to go there. I don't suppose we shall be at Watford for long, darling. We were only shoved on this guard because they had no-one else available for it – it's not a signaller's job.

I don't know where I shall be going next – it might be Egypt, India, Scotland, Wales, Southend-on-Sea or Ealing Broadway. Nobody knows darling, so please don't hope for too much and please keep cheerful and optimistic. I love you very much.

Please give my love to the family. I am sorry Herbert is not too happy at his present station, but perhaps he will move to a better place. I shall be very glad when we get back to Watford. I feel very dirty as I have not had my clothes off since I have been here. It is only on rare occasions that I am allowed to take my boots off. As I told you before, we sleep in the loft of a barn and it gets very dirty. I am longing to see some tables and chairs again and get back to civilization.

I am sorry you have been having bad air-raids. I do wish they would stop bombing London. Monday night here wasn't too bad and last night was very quiet. Tonight has been rather noisy up to now – there's a Jerry overhead at the moment – but perhaps it will quieten down later. I am on guard tonight from 9 to 11 p.m. and then every four hours. I hope it's not like last Sunday night again. I don't feel like dodging bombs!!

Darling, it is now 8 p.m. and I don't think there is much more I can write. I'm afraid I've missed the post, but will add a few more lines in the morning and get somebody to post it.

By the way, this is how my programme works out – I know you are interested:-

Tuesday (yesterday):
8.45 a.m. Got up (On guard last night).
9 - 11 a.m. On guard.
11 - 12.30 Fatigues.
1 p.m. Dinner. 2 p.m. Rifle inspection & fatigues.
3 - 5 p.m. On guard. 5.30 p.m. Tea. Washed, etc.
8 p.m. Went to the pub with John and played piano. Got several free drinks as we told them we were going tomorrow. I did not spend a penny!
11 p.m. 'Bed'. Had a good sleep.
Today:
8.30 a.m. Got up and had breakfast. 9 - 12.30 Occasional fatigues.
1 p.m. Dinner. 1.30 p.m. Relieved a telephonist at H.Q. so he could have dinner.

106

2.30 p.m. Washed, shaved, etc.

3.30 p.m. Played cards and packed kit to 'go back'. 5 p.m. Tea.

6.30 p.m. The sergeant wants to go out so I offered to stay in Guard Room for a couple of hours, thus giving me an opportunity to write to you.

9.30 a.m. Thursday: Good morning, darling. We had a fairly quiet night but I feel rather tired today. Will close now as somebody is going to the post-box.

All my love. Your future husband.

27th October 1940   Watford
Sunday 3 p.m.

At long last I am back in Watford. We finally arrived here last night after being disappointed on Wednesday and then again on Friday. However, here we are at last in billets (an empty house, but not the same as previously).

How are you keeping, darling – I hope you are not feeling so miserable now. John and I tried to get home this morning by hitch-hiking, but we couldn't get a lift and could not come by train as we had not enough money. (We are paid on Wednesdays now). We walked for miles along the road leading to Harrow, but nobody would give us a lift and as I knew you would be leaving for the office at 2 p.m., we decided to return at about 12 o'clock as I would not get to Ealing in time to catch you. (If I got there at all). However, darling, I am going to try and phone you at about 4 p.m. today and perhaps we can make some arrangements to see each other. If you are off next week-end, perhaps I can get away then, or you, better still, could come here. You see we are not allowed out so far really, and, although that doesn't worry me a lot, I may have to go on Church Parade or fatigues in the morning. That means I would not get to Ealing till about late afternoon. But I will see what you think when I phone you. I hope I can get through.

We had rather a bad night on Friday at the Farm, and so did Watford. But last night was very quiet. I don't think I shall be kept awake here after my experience of being dive-bombed. I don't mind an ordinary, common, air-raid.

Has London been quieter lately? According to newspapers you have been having better nights, with one or two exceptions. I was very disappointed at not getting to Ealing today, darling. If I had known we were definitely coming back here last night I would have made arrangements, but as it was, there was no time to find out whether I should be missed at all. However, we should be here for quite a few weeks, so I hope we can see each other occasionally.

Watford is quite a nice place. There are plenty of canteens for soldiers and things are pretty cheap. Also, I believe, we have a fairly easy time of it here; the only trouble being numerous guard duties which have to be done by day and night; ammunition, etc. Still we mustn't expect too much. Our address is still the same, but for your information I am billeted at 34 Essex Street and sleep with 4 others on the ground floor in the 'parlour'. But don't address your letters here will you, darling? I would get the sack (I wish I could!). Well my love, I think I can pen no more. I was hoping I would hear from you on Saturday, but there was no post. I think maybe your letter is still hanging about here, but probably I won't get it till tomorrow. I hope I get through to you on the phone at 4 o'clock. All my love for ever.

28th October 1940   3rd Medium Reserve Regt.
                                                               Watford

I am writing this letter in the writing room of our canteen (paper and envelopes free!) and the time is about 6 p.m. I haven't heard from you for several days, darling, and I am rather worried. I hope you are still all right.

I tried to phone you yesterday and also several times today, but could not get through as there was an 'indefinite delay'. Isn't it annoying? It seems harder to get in touch with you now than when I was in Scarborough..

I am sorry the watch has gone wrong, darling, but the guarantee still holds – I think it was for 7 or 10 years. I can't remember exactly as the guarantee is in my desk at home. I shall have to try and pop home to Finsbury Park one day and get it. I wonder what we can arrange for this week-end? Would you rather pop up here on Sunday, or would you prefer my coming to Ealing? I'm afraid nothing definite can be arranged yet as I won't know until Friday whether I am on duty, but I do think we have an excellent chance of seeing each other this Sunday.

I have not felt too happy today. I lost the gloves you knitted for me. I think I left them on the table after breakfast, but I can't find who has got them. Darling, you must think me terribly careless to keep losing gloves – I am afraid I am. And I was going to mention to you how warm they kept my hands when I was on guard at the Farm. However, I may find them yet. I do hope so.

We've had a very uninteresting day today – marching practically all the morning. A short lecture in the afternoon and we were finished at 4 o'clock.

I am annoyed at being on that Special Guard last week for two reasons. One, they had asked for those with clerical experience to go in the office, and also a pianist had been wanted for the Regimental dance band. Two jobs which would have suited me down to the ground. However, I shall still have a shot for the band and they say there may be more vacancies for clerks soon. I hope so, for that would mean I would perhaps be here permanently and we could get married and live here. I think it's about time I had some good luck.

Two bits of news. We are all being or going to be vaccinated here and I am supposed to be in the cross-country race on Wednesday afternoon. Whether I am concerned with either remains to be seen.

Darling, I will still try and phone you, but not till Wednesday as I am now broke till we are paid. I do hope however that we can see each other on Sunday. All my love, darling.

31st October 1940   Watford
Thursday

I have felt miserable all day today and am absolutely down in the dumps. Darling I haven't heard from you for a week and I don't know whether or not you are all right. I have tried to phone you every day (several times a day) but have never been able to get through. Please write to me, sweet, and let me know you are safe.

Unless I hear to the contrary, I shall do my best to get home on Sunday if only for a few hours. I am longing to see you again. How have the air-raids been in Ealing lately? It is pretty quiet here, although last night a bomb dropped a few streets away. But that's only about once a week.

There is really quite a lot to tell you about what I have been doing and about life here, but I don't feel like describing things at the moment. I hope I hear from you tomorrow morning.

I had a rehearsal with the band Tuesday night, but the difficulty is that the present pianist is the leader! However, sometimes they have two pianists, and I know (not being modest for once) that I am a better _dance_ pianist than either.

I have been out on a stunt today – it has been pouring with rain all the time – I think I'm going to have another cold. Tonight I might go to a troop concert (free) at the Town Hall. As I told you before, there are plenty of canteens, etc., here for soldiers and it is possible to live quite cheaply. I don't feel like writing much more at the moment. Darling, let's get married soon. I miss you very much and am feeling very lonely. All my love for ever.

3rd November 1940   Watford

Have arrived back here quite safely – it is now 9.50 p.m. John and I got to Watford at 8.50 p.m. and went and had _one_ half-pint of beer in a pub. We then tried to get something to eat, but the cafes were either closed or sold out. None of the other three people are in yet, so it seems as if they had left it later. As you know, the 'all clear' went as I was walking up Kent Gardens, and we don't know whether or not the warning has gone since.

We booked through from Ealing Common to South Harrow (6d) and from there took a bus to Watford (10d). We had to wait 20 minutes for the bus but the journey was not too bad.

It was nice seeing you again, darling, even though it was only for a few hours. I will try and get home next Saturday if I am not on duty. John's father is coming to Watford on Saturday, so if we are lucky we may get a lift back to Ealing. But please don't get too hopeful; you know nothing short of duty will keep me from you and even that wouldn't if it were not compulsory.

Will close now, darling, as I feel rather tired. I will post this letter on my way to breakfast in the morning. All my love.

Monday 8.15 a.m. Have just got ready and have to be on Parade at 8.30 a.m. so must hurry. Good morning, darling. I love you. Will write again tonight.

5th November 1940   Watford
Tuesday 6.30 p.m.

I hoped I would get a letter from you today, but perhaps the deliveries are late again.

We had a very restful day today – I'm afraid we played 'truant' again. The other Battery, "Q" had a stunt on today and our NCOs and Officers were on it too, so we "P" Battery Signallers took the day off. Five of us went to the pictures in the afternoon.

There were only 4 Signallers on parade this afternoon and if anybody with any authority noticed it we should be in the 'soup'. We shall know however, in the morning. I had a thought of coming home, but I was persuaded not to risk it. I don't want to take too many risks and perhaps get guard duties or fatigues over the week-end.

I nearly lost my new gas-mask today, but luckily I found it in a café when we stopped to have a cup of tea during the morning. I am really getting very absent-minded, darling. This evening we have been invited to an 'At Home' by some people living nearby. They are quite well off and the 'old man' takes an interest in soldiers. He looks like a retired colonel and is very decent. They have billiards, darts, cards, etc., and supply us with cigarettes, tea and supper. I forgot to tell you that we went last week – it is really a nice, quiet, pleasant evening.

I have not been on guard yet, and am hoping I shall be before the week-end. I love you very much, darling and there is never anyone else but you. I shall always be faithful to you. All my love to my future wife.

P.S.   I had a pleasant surprise when I went to the bank. The clerk found out that the columns had been added up wrongly and I had two pounds more than I thought. I have also seen the Pay Clerk about my extra 3/6d proficiency pay, and I shall be getting it in about 3 weeks' time. But 3/6d a week will be put to my credit from October 18th (the sixth month). So that will be a bit more I shall have in hand.

6th November 1940   Watford

Just a very short note to let you know I received your letter this morning. I am glad you are feeling much better.

Darling, if you decide to come to Watford this week, don't come tomorrow (Thursday) as we shall be out on a stunt all day. I will look for you on Friday, if it is fine.

I hope you get this letter today in case you decide to come tomorrow. I won't write any more, but will post this letter right away and catch the post. All my love.

P.S. I don't know what's happening over the week-end yet.

10th November 1940   Watford

I arrived safely here at my billet at about 6.30 p.m. Johnny had just got back from Guard duty and there was a nice cheerful fire blazing away. I booked straight through to Watford from Charing Cross (2/7d!) but had to change at Harrow although I had only to wait a few minutes for the next train to come along for Watford.

Darling, it was a lovely week-end and I was very happy being with you all the time. I must try and get home next Saturday too. As far as Johnny knows, there has been no outcry about missing people. Three turned up for gym as instructed (out of about 15) so the bombardier (one of us) simply marched them round a corner and dismissed them.

I wonder if you are in the air-raid shelter now, darling. (It's about 7.30 p.m.). The sirens went off here about half-an-hour ago, but everything is still quiet, so I wondered whether it was a false alarm. Only the local siren seemed to go. It would be nice if you had another quiet night. (You always have quieter times when I come home).

Darling, I hope you were not feeling too miserable when I left. We must remember how lucky we are to be so near together. I love you very much darling and will try and save enough to get married soon. I hope we don't keep putting it off. I will also see the Sergeant-Major sometime this week and try to get an office job. We are out on a stunt again tomorrow. More chaos and inefficiency. I will post this tonight so that it will catch the earliest post in the morning. Thank you for the cigarettes and also for a marvellous time. I will let you know as soon as possible about next week-end. All my love.

12th November 1940   Watford

I was hoping to have a letter from you today, but have been disappointed. I hope I get one tomorrow.

113

How are you keeping, sweet? Have you been getting plenty of sleep? I went to see the Sergeant Major yesterday about an office job and gave him particulars. He told me he would bear me in mind but did not know whether I could be spared as I was a signaller. So, once again, I must wait and see.

Don't get too alarmed, darling, but there are two or three drafts of signallers going during the next week. But as about 150 new ones have or are coming in before the end of the week and I am, at the moment, a Regimental Signaller, the odds are that I shall not leave here yet awhile. However I thought I would warn you – just in case!! By the way I haven't been on Guard this week yet so, if I am unlucky, I will be on during the week-end. Also we have to be in our billets from 5 to 7 p.m. every evening 'standing to' and don't know whether this stunt will be over by the week-end. Altogether this is rather a critical week for me with one thing and another!

This morning and yesterday morning we have been out on 'stunts' and this afternoon Johnny and I played truant and spent the afternoon in a canteen playing billiards and table tennis. Unfortunately quite a number of other fellows had the same idea so there were not many signallers on parade! Whether anything will be said in the morning no one knows.

We had a very quiet night last night – no alarm at all. I expect it was the same in London. Tonight has been funny. It is marvellously clear and yet we have heard only one plane go over and there has been no gunfire. I think the wind must be keeping Jerry away.

I still love you darling and hope I can let you know soon about the week-end. Au revoir, my sweet and all my love for ever.

Please write to me.

14th November 1940   Watford

Thank you for your letter which I received yesterday. I am glad you are feeling fit and happy, sweet, and hope my last letter,

114

(in which I mentioned the possibility of being posted) did not upset you too much. The chances of my being drafted now appear to be very remote. Our NCO has told us that we shall probably be on the Staff for the next two months or so and that the new fellows (who came from Dover) will be first to go.

I think my chances of getting into an office have also considerably improved. They have been asking for clerks for the Regimental HQ and I have made my application. I expect I shall know one way or the other pretty soon.

We have been out again today on a stunt and most likely will be called out sometime tonight too. But we are all hoping that it will not occur. Johnny and I, however, have got quite an easy job being wireless operators.

The food is still pretty bad here, mainly, I think, because they have used more than the ration and now have to economise. If this is so it should improve sooner or later when the new ration arrives.

I don't know darling whether I say 'Goodnight' to you <u>every</u> night, but I honestly am always thinking of you and wishing I were with you. I hope you had a good sleep again last night, as I believe it was quite a quiet night. It was here, but extremely cold. All my love.

18th November 1940   Watford

I have made several attempts to write this letter but never before have I had to write a letter feeling so unhappy and knowing it will make the one who reads it very miserable.

I cannot even pretend to be cheerful darling, so please be brave when you read the next few lines and keep as cheerful as you possibly can.

As you know, I have often mentioned that there were chances that I might have to go abroad and now, I am afraid, the worst has happened. We are going to Woolwich on Wednesday and will be there only a fortnight or so before we leave for Egypt.

Darling, if I could I would say that perhaps even now I may not go, but that would be drugging you with false optimism. This time it is definite and not just a rumour that may not be true. I am very upset darling and still feel stunned. To be sent abroad after only eight months in the army – I wish I could wake up and find it was a nightmare.

There's nothing more I can add. It seems silly to say keep smiling; but what else can we do darling? However much we worry and think that fate should not have been so unkind to us, it won't make any difference. John's been very decent and has been trying to cheer me up. He wants to take me to the cinema or theatre this evening, but it seems such a puny antidote to this unfair and unjust thing that has happened to us.

Of course, darling, I shall get embarkation leave; if I'm lucky – 7 days. I would, darling, very much like you to be my wife before I go, but what do you think best?

I will agree to whatever you say because I know you will always love me and be faithful to me, and I promise darling that you can depend as much on me. Nothing can make our love stronger for each other and nothing can break it.

There's nothing much more to add, except of course, that I arrived here safely, but too late for parade. I was not missed. Thank you for a marvellous week-end, sweet. I shall always remember it and I meant everything I told you when you were in my arms.

Please write soon, darling and try and write a cheerful note. I expect we shall be seeing each other again soon. My love for ever.

20th to 26th November 1940
(No correspondence)

On the 20th November 1940, I, with the rest of the 'Scarborough Squad' of RA Signallers, was posted to Woolwich Barracks in south-east London.

Our time there was occupied mainly with marching and drilling, but we were expecting to be posted abroad at any time and were eagerly looking forward to what we all firmly believed would be a week's 'embarkation leave'.

I wrote no letters from Woolwich because I was able to 'phone my fiancée at her office more frequently (and cheaply!) now I was in London. I even sneaked back to Ealing taking 'French leave' whenever I could get away without the British Army noticing I was missing!

However, as will be seen in the following letter, instead of going abroad I, with my immediate chums, was posted back to, of all places, Watford!

I distinctly remember the Sergeant-Major who was on the platform to meet his new draft nearly throwing a fit when he was confronted with a gang of grinning familiar faces he thought he had finally got rid of a week ago.

27th November 1940

Gnr/Sig Berry, H.W.
974063
"Q" Battery
3rd Medium Reserve Regt. .
R.A.
Watford, Herts.

I am sorry I didn't phone you today, but, as you see by the above address, we have moved again – back to where we started from.

I told you that a rumour was going round that we were moving from Woolwich, but we didn't know until one o'clock this morning. The sergeant came round and woke us up and told us to get up early in the morning and be ready to move by 9 a.m. Eighty of us, he said, were being drafted to Watford. The funny part about it is that the majority of the 80 were ex-Watfordites, but apparently the authorities did not realise that. I'm fully convinced now that the Army is crazy, but we're not grumbling this time – we were only too glad to get out of the Woolwich dump.

John and I have still kept together and we are now in private billets at 37 King Street, Watford. We are very lucky for it is a very nice house and charming people. We have a marvellous bedroom with a spring bed, and I notice they have a piano in the sitting room. They have asked us to come into the dining room whenever we like. John and I are both writing letters in there now. I don't know, darling, why we have moved again, but I'm afraid we are still on draft for overseas service. It may mean, however, that we might still be here for Christmas. But it's no good speculating. I think actually that Woolwich was getting a little overcrowded.

I could not phone you from here, darling, as I had not enough money. I saved 2d to phone you today, but, of course, did not get the chance to ring you. I'm sorry this letter has only a 1½d stamp on, but I hope I get away with it and you do not have to pay any more. I will phone you as soon as I can on Friday morning (when we get paid) and I hope I get through all right. How are the arrangements going darling? I hope everything's going smoothly. I expect I will be home this week-end and will look for a nice ring – if you will let me have my bank book!! I have not been able to write to Do and Dad yet, but will try on Friday. I may pop home first on Saturday (if you are working) and see Dad.

Darling, it does not seem possible that we are to be married Saturday week – I wish it would hurry up and come. I hope you are not feeling too nervous, darling, I still love you very much. Well, darling, I don't think there's much more to add now. I am feeling very happy and contented now and hope you are. I also hope that you have a quiet night tonight even though I have left Woolwich! All my love to my wife.

28th November 1940 to 19th March 1941

Gwen and I were married on the morning of the 7th December 1940 at Haven Green Baptist Church, Ealing.

Because of the war, only a few friends were able to attend the ceremony and as the bride's parents were no longer alive and her brother was also in the army, the verger was persuaded to give the bride away.

My army friend, John Collins, also of Ealing, was best man, but failed to get me to the Church on time as I insisted on going to a barber and having a real shave with a 'cut-throat' razor for the first time in my life. Somebody took some photographs of the happy couple leaving the Church, but the snaps did not come out, so there was no pictorial record of this great occasion.

Our two day honeymoon (I was given 72 hours 'compassionate leave' for the wedding) was spent at Godmanchester, Huntingdonshire, where my stepmother 'Do' was looking after evacuated children.

Upon returning to Watford, Gwen joined me and stayed with me at various billets and we lived a fairly normal and happy married life.

Gwen went off to Fleet Street by train every morning and I reported for duty in the Regimental Office in a Police Station in King Street, where I did my best to make the Army more efficient! Except when I had guard duties or other army commitments, Gwen and I spent most evenings together during my three month stay in Watford.

About the beginning of March we were posted back to Woolwich again ready for Overseas Posting.

Despite the air-raids, which were now very bad, I used to take 'French leave' nearly every night and went home to Gwen who had returned to Ealing.

I had to leave Ealing in the early hours of the morning in order to get back to Woolwich in time for the morning parade and roll-call.

The journeys were 'hairy' as also was the task of getting back into the barracks undetected. On one occasion when stopped by an N.C.O. who wanted to know where I had been, I explained that I had just been out for breakfast as I couldn't stand Army food. I think he must have admired my cheek as he let me in with the remark that I was an effing liar.

On one occasion when I could not get to Ealing I entered a talent competition at the local cinema and gained second prize for my piano rendering of 'In the Mood'.

"See you again tonight," I said to Gwen one morning as I made my early start for Woolwich.

But this time I was wrong. It would be 4½ years before I returned to my wife in Ealing.

PART THREE

OVERSEAS POSTING

My darling wife,

I am writing this letter on a train. We are now at Leicester and the time is 3.10 p.m. We are on our way north – probably to Glasgow, but we don't know.

I returned safely back to Woolwich this morning in spite of there being hardly any trains because of the night's raids.

I finally got to barracks at 8.15 a.m. I had not been missed and was just in time to get packed up and ready to move off by 8.30 a.m. We left Woolwich finally about 10 a.m. and passed through Acton on the way. They had a terrible night at the barracks. Incendiaries and bombs all over the place. John had a narrow escape. The window was blown in on him, but he was saved from serious cuts by the black-out board. All the rooms are covered in glass and plaster from the ceiling.

I shall try and get this letter posted as soon as possible. We are not allowed to get off the train, so I must see if I can get someone to post it for me. There is a train full of evacuated children next to us at the moment – I may give it to one of them. Please excuse the scrawl, darling, but I want you to get this letter as soon as possible. I shall write to you again when we get to the port of embarkation.

All my love, darling. If I can get to a phone I will phone you as soon as possible. Your loving husband. Au revoir.

P.S. The train full of children has just moved off, so I will have to find someone else to post this.

21st March 1941   At Sea
Friday

My darling wife,

I am sitting on the deck in the sunshine writing this letter and it is now exactly 2 o'clock.

We arrived at this certain port at 6.30 a.m. after ------ hours travelling. However, it was not too bad and I slept through most of the night.

We came straight on board from the train, so I did not have a chance to phone or write to you before now. I don't know when you will get this letter as I shall have to post it - if that's possible - aboard ship; so goodness knows when it will be delivered.

It is quite a large liner and I suppose the conditions are not too bad. The only thing that annoys me is that we are herded together like cattle below decks, while the comparatively few officers seem to have most of the ship - including, of course, all the decent quarters - to themselves. However, we mustn't grumble. I should say this ship is almost twice as big as the 'Esperence Bay' on which I went for my cruise three years ago.

Here is what we have been doing since this morning.

6.30 a.m. Arrived at station. Managed to scrounge a cup of tea on the station kindly organised by some Women's voluntary service.

7.30 a.m. Boarded tender to take us to our particular ship. This was very similar to a cross-channel steamer. Whilst hanging about managed to get another cup of tea and a sandwich. Also bought some cigarettes.

8.15 a.m. Tender left dock and drew up alongside ship. Boarded and were shown to our 'room'. There are about 50 of us to each compartment in which there are rows of long tables for meals. At night we have to draw hammocks and rig them up over the tables. I am not looking forward to the time when I have to attempt this.

8.45 - 12 noon. Washed, etc., and unpacked kit.

12 noon. Dinner. This was very good and we had plenty. We had soup (in mugs), then meat (a good helping) potatoes (boiled in their skins) and beans. For sweet there was a kind of sultana and currant pudding which was very nice. I was completely satisfied after the meal - which is something to be grateful for!

After dinner, John and I explored the ship and finally found a nice warm spot in which to write these letters. It is a lovely day and the scenery around us is very pretty. We are not moving yet, but I don't think we will be here long. The other section from the barracks has not, however, arrived here yet.

Well, darling, I think that brings me right up-to-date in my 'diary'. As you can guess, these letters are censored so I cannot tell you too much.

How are you keeping darling? I hope you were not too worried when you did not hear from me yesterday morning, but I couldn't possibly get in touch with you. Please keep smiling and cheerful for me, darling. I shall come back as soon as I possibly can.

I will finish for now, darling, but will continue this letter later when, perhaps, I shall know something about the postal service.

All my love. I LOVE you, darling.

P.S. A bombardier has just come round for a fatigue party but by pretending to be busy, I think we have just missed it ..... Yes, we have!

7.30 p.m. John and I have just finished a stroll round the deck after tea. I'm afraid we are going to get very bored after a few days. There is nothing much to do and the two canteens (wet and dry) are far too crowded to be at all serviceable. We are not allowed out on deck after 'blackout' and 'bed-time' is 9.30 p.m. I think I shall be very glad when the voyage is over; although I don't suppose I shall mind the one back!

Well, that's all for now, darling. I shall write a few more lines before I go to bed. I haven't heard anything about the post yet.

8.30 p.m. Am just going to rig hammock up after wandering all over the ship to find the canteen only, when finally succeeding, to find it closed.

9 p.m. Am now going to try and settle down. Could not get any blankets, however. Goodnight, darling. I LOVE you.

Saturday 7 a.m.: Good morning, darling. I did not sleep too well owing to the cold. I did not undress. It's really disgraceful the way we are bundled together. When the hammocks are up, it is impossible to move (they are so close together) and when we are putting them up and taking them down, it is chaotic. We have nowhere to put our kit and there are only three wash-basins between about 100 men. I have not been able to wash yet, but will try again after breakfast – for which we are now waiting.

7.20 a.m. We are still waiting, so I thought I would write a few more lines. We heard last night that letters will be posted at 10 a.m. this morning, so I shall soon have to draw this letter to a close: I mustn't risk missing the post.

7.30 a.m. Still waiting – I think, darling I had better conclude this letter now in case we are kept busy for the rest of the morning. I shall add a postscript if anything interesting happens. I shall write to you every day, darling, and post them whenever it is possible. But don't worry if you don't hear from me for a long time. I haven't got a stamp, so I might have to post this letter without one – I hope you don't mind.

Au revoir, darling. All my love for ever.

Author's note: ------ means word or words censored.
The ship was the SS 'Strathmore' and the port of embarkation was
Gourock (Glasgow)

Date: Censored   At sea
Envelope postmarked Manchester 7th May 1941
Monday

My darling wife,
    I hope by now you have received my letter which I believe was posted sometime on Sunday. I am sorry I did not add a postscript, as promised, but just after I finished the letter the officer came round and asked for all the mail.
    How are you keeping, darling? I hope you are doing your best to keep fit and cheerful for me. I love you, my sweet.
    I actually started this letter on Saturday evening, but when I went to continue it today I found the page missing from my writing pad. It must be in my kit-bag somewhere, but I can't trace it at

126

the moment. Things are always disappearing here, but I can't see the point of anyone taking a written page from a notebook! My music seems to have been 'mislaid' also, but I expect it will turn up before the end of the voyage. The trouble is we are so cramped and there is hardly, if any, spare room.

I will now try and rewrite my letter which I started:

Saturday 10 a.m. Your letter posted. We hung around the rest of the morning except for 'Action Stations' (Lifeboat Drill) and had dinner about 12.30 p.m. It was very nice and consisted of meat, potatoes and beans with stewed apples for dessert. We strolled around the deck again in the afternoon (it was a fine day) and for tea at 5 p.m. there was bread and cheese and pickles. We shoved our hammocks up at 8.30 p.m. and as there is nothing to do, rolled into them. It is impossible to undress (no room) so we have to sleep with our clothes on.

It is very warm when we first get in but I usually wake up about 1 a.m. extremely cold.

Sunday: Up at 6.30 a.m. Breakfast – bacon & egg (!!) bread, etc.

'Action Stations' at 10 a.m. This lasts for about $\frac{3}{4}$ hour and afterwards I managed to get a wash and shave – impossible first thing in the morning owing to lack of accommodation. For dinner at 12.30 p.m. we had pork(!) potatoes and beans and a pudding similar to Xmas Pudding, for dessert. It was very nice and there was plenty of it. Food is the only thing which is satisfactory on this boat and I don't think the quality of that will last. By the way, during the morning I had my roulette game confiscated by an officer who said no gambling was allowed. "Crown & Anchor" and "Housey, Housey" however, seem to be still going strong. I expect I shall be hearing about that again shortly. A pity, because we were doing quite well. Still, 'Never mind, eh!'

For tea we had haddock, bread and butter, jam and, of course, a mug of tea. Johnny and I managed to fight our way in the canteen at about 7.30 p.m., and, after waiting about half-an-hour in the queue I managed to get a pint of beer (5d). We rolled into 'bed' again about 9 p.m. and I was unfortunate enough to have to sling my hammock next to the lavatory door. Still I slept a bit better so it could not have done me any harm.

Monday: Up at the usual time (6.30 a.m.) I then went on sick parade because of a sore throat I seem to have contracted. (No surprise to me!). By doing so, I unintentionally missed fatigues for which I was detailed.

John and I went for a walk around the deck as usual till 10 a.m. when we paraded at the usual 'Action Stations' which lasts about an hour. For dinner there was meat, potato and greens with ………. Dessert. We all noticed that …………… seemed to be diminishing. After …………………… lined up for the canteen (this takes about an hour) and I bought 6 bars of chocolate and a tin of Nestles Condensed Milk (!) which I later enjoyed. In the afternoon, John and I played cards together on the deck despite the fact that it was a miserable day. We got pulled up by the OC for not springing to attention when he passed. He added that we weren't on a pleasure cruise – as if we didn't know! We nearly told him so.

For tea there was sausage, potato, bread and jam and by 8.30 p.m. I was, once again, in 'bed'.

Tuesday: Up at 6.30 a.m. John and I went up on deck before breakfast to have a look round. I dreamed about you last night darling. I dreamed I was back at Watford with you and I was telling you I wasn't going abroad after all. What an anti-climax to wake up and find oneself on a ship. I wish I were back with you, my sweet. I am very homesick and heartily fed up with this boat. But to continue ..

Breakfast was porridge, liver, bread and butter with, of course, the inevitable cup of 'cha'. After breakfast I went to the MO for the thrice daily gargle which he prescribed. I then met John on deck and although the sea was quite rough …………..

For dinner we had a good portion of meat, one potato (they are always cooked in their skins) and some very nice peas.

There was plum duff for dessert. In the afternoon we lined up outside the canteen and I bought 60 cigarettes (1/9d) and another tin of Nestles. The weather was very bitter and it was raining so we did not stop on deck. We lazed about during the afternoon –

the sea air makes one very sleepy. For tea there was bread and jam, fish and an apple. John is on guard tonight and at the moment I am sitting writing this letter on our mess table.

Wednesday: Up at usual time. I dreamed about you again last night, darling. Instead of being in a boat, I was in a train and, as each station went by I knew I was getting further away from you. Apparently I had been able to get home and see you at the first few stations, so when we stopped at another station, presumably a goodish distance away, I hopped off the train and jumped into the driving seat of a lorry. I got it started but it broke down and there my dream ended while any minute I expected a policeman to come along and ask what was up. I wonder if it has any significance? For dinner we had rabbit, potatoes and beans and not very good tapioca for dessert. Our rations are certainly getting smaller – I thought they were feeding us too well the first few days. By the way, it seems as if we have been at sea for years and hard to believe darling, that I am away from you for only a few weeks. I hope we are not parted long. During the afternoon we got paid. Everybody got the same amount – 10/-. I have not broken into the money you gave me yet, darling. I learned, much to my disgust that I am on guard tonight. By the way ....

.... clean record by being sick. I do not think it was all due to the sea – which was pretty rough and claimed plenty of victims aboard – but rather to the tin of condensed milk which I insisted on having saying, of course, that I was tough and could take it. I was on guard from 8 – 10 p.m. and 2 – 4.30 a.m.

Thursday: Up at 6.30 a.m. after a nice 2 hours sleep. Washed and shaved. For breakfast there was haddock, bread and butter and tea. At 8 o'clock I was on guard again and, owing to the usual parade at 10 a.m. (Action Stations) was not relieved until 11.30 a.m. Dinner at 12 noon was meat, potatoes and beans and a very nice pudding for dessert. They certainly cook the stuff well here.

As I did 'overtime' on my last guard, I was told to parade at 2.45 p.m. instead of 2 p.m., for the next one. This was quite a short duty as I was relieved at 4 p.m. These guard duties are not tiring but very monotonous. There is nothing at all to do. We are just posted at different points throughout the ship just to spot any fires that start. For tea at 4 p.m., there was bread, butter and jam; pickles and corned beef. John bought some tinned pears in the canteen so I also had some of them. After tea I made my way to the canteen and bought 6 bars of chocolate and a tin of pears to return the compliment. After tea we made our way up on deck and I am sitting there now writing this letter. It is quite a nice day today and I think we shall soon be in warmer weather. By my watch it is now 6.30 p.m. so it is 8.30 p.m. at home. I wonder what you are doing darling? Are you reading a book in front of the fire or doing some washing or visiting friends? Or are you in bed? I shall be glad when I get a letter from you – although I don't suppose you will get this until 2 months' time at least. I would think we should reach our first port of call in about 3 weeks. What a life! Well, darling, will close now for the time being. Maybe I shall have a little game of cards with John before we turn in. It is certainly very monotonous on board – I shall be glad when the trip is over. Goodnight my love. I love you.

Friday: Up at the usual time. Did not sleep very well last night for some unknown reason. I dreamed about you again but the only part I can remember is sitting in a café with you. We had a slight tiff, but we soon made it up! I seem to do nothing else but dream at nights.

6.40 a.m. Washed and had porridge, liver and bread and butter for breakfast. It is a very fine day today – we are getting into the warmer parts but the wind is still rather chilly – and John and I sat on the deck during the morning. At 10 a.m. we had our usual parade which lasted about an hour and a quarter. For dinner at 12 there was meat, potatoes and beans (by the way I forgot to mention before that we always have soup in our mugs first) and stewed apples afterwards. During the afternoon we went up on the top deck as the sun was quite strong and played cards with the two other fellows who were on guard with me the first day you came to Watford.

At tea time I opened my pears and cream so did not want the fish that was offered. But I had some bread and jam and a cup of tea:

an officer told us that we should probably be able to post some mail in two or three days as we were calling in at a port. So, with a bit of luck, you may get this letter within a fortnight or so.

I'm sorry there's not much news to tell you, darling, but as you see our days are very much the same old routine – sleeping, lying on the deck and eating. I can't describe, for obvious reasons, the convoy and I can't tell you the name of this ship. I also can't tell you what it looks like because I haven't seen it from the outside, but altogether there are eight decks, and I should imagine it looks something like this.

(Simple sketch of ship)

John and I are on 'G' deck. I don't think actually it looks very much like the ship, but it's the best I can do. At the moment I am sitting at the rear end of "D" deck under cover. I should imagine the ship's tonnage is about --------------.

Saturday: At the time of writing this I am sitting on an open deck in the forward part of the ship and the time is 7.10 p.m. (9 p.m. at home). A few yards away there is a crowd of soldiers community singing, led by an officer with Joe (whom you met at Watford) playing the accordion. It is all very peaceful. The sea is as calm as a mill pond, there is a cool breeze blowing and twilight is descending. It is hard to believe that there is such a thing as a war on. I still can't believe that I am far away from you, darling. I am always thinking of you. I love you more than ever. I wish you were here with me. Here's what I have been doing today.

6.40 a.m. Got up. Breakfast at 7.30 a.m. was porridge, liver, bread, etc. I don't think I told you before that the bread is baked on the ship and is very nice.

It was rather chilly in the morning, but Johnny and I went up on deck until 'Action Stations' at 10 a.m., and when we had finished with that, I lined up at the canteen for 6 bars of chocolate. I was told that there was only enough for a couple more days! So it doesn't look too good.

For dinner at noon there was soup, pork, potatoes and beans and rice pudding. But I noticed that the rations are still getting smaller.

In the afternoon we went up on the top deck and played cards. It was very warm and the weather was lovely. We have been re-issued with our "topes" which were taken away when we boarded ship. Tea was at 4.30 p.m., for which there was pickles, jam, bread and butter. After tea I went for an audition for the ship's concert or concerts which are to be held sometime. We went up to the officers' lounge which looks very cosy and made me wish I had a commission. I expect I will hear more in a few days time. The trouble, I believe, is finding a big enough space to hold the concert. And that brings me to the opening of today's script. The time is now 7.30 p.m. and it is getting quite dark. (Twilight gets shorter in these parts).

There is a rumour that we may dock tomorrow sometime, in which case I will post this letter. I will also try and write a short one to Dad. Well, darling, I must soon close for today. The fellows are singing 'Just a song at Twilight' and have now started 'The Lost Chord'. It makes me feel very homesick and a longing to see you darling. My pen is now running dry, darling, so goodnight and may God bless you. I love you, my sweet.

Sunday: 12.45 p.m. I am sitting on the top deck (the Sun Deck) writing this. I am waiting for John who is having a shave. It is a marvellous day – clear blue sky, dark blue sea – just like it used to be on the Riviera. I wonder what the weather is like in England at the moment?

I shall soon have to finish this letter, darling, as people are handing them in for censoring. Very soon now I think we will be calling in at a port and I must not risk missing the post. I asked the officer when letters had to be in and he said he couldn't say exactly, but would like them as soon as possible. So I think it would be best if I handed this in sometime today. If I finish the letter abruptly you will know we have had orders to hand them in. I hope this letter reaches you. It will be a nice surprise for you to hear from me so early. With a bit of luck we may be able to post another batch in about a fortnight's time, which, I should imagine you will receive about ------ weeks after receiving this. Then, I think there will probably be an interval of -------- before you hear from me again. I think we should reach our final destination about

--------- from now, at the rate we are travelling. I shall write a short note to Dad and probably Do too. So you needn't trouble to inform him of my whereabouts.

Here's what I have been doing today up to the present.

6.40 a.m. Got up. 7.30 a.m. Breakfast – porridge, 2 kippers and coffee. Then I went up on deck with John and tried bathing in the sunshine – only there was no sun as yet. It was very close last night, by the way, and I undressed. Consequently I had a very good sleep.

There was the usual parade at 10 a.m., and then John and I went on Church parade. The sermon, naturally, was something about sailing on the sea of life where nobody gambles, swears or drinks excessively, blah, blah, blah. I felt a lot better after that!!!!
Dinner at 12 was meat, potatoes and greens and a very good plum duff which was very enjoyable. After dinner I went up on deck and here I am.

As there is nothing happening at the moment, I will write that short note to Dad. Don't go away. I shall be back.

Monday 9.10 a.m. I am afraid the short note to Dad and the children took longer than I expected. After I finished that I played cards with John till tea. For tea we had rissoles and bread and jam. After tea we went up on the deck and watched the sun set. It is really a remarkable sight. You remember how we used to watch it sink as we stood on Chiswick Station. Well, in these parts it sets about twice as quickly. It looks very eerie.

Here's what I have been doing today up to now.

6.40 a.m. Got up. 7.30 a.m. Breakfast. Porridge and liver. Had wash and then came up on deck to write this letter. I think, darling I had better hand this letter in today as time is getting rather short. By the way, I have just learned that the censorship is pretty strict, and that, instead of using a blue pencil, they cut the offending passages out which is rather unfortunate owing to my patriotic gesture of writing on both sides of the paper.

However, darling, it is too late to do anything now, and I haven't time to re-write the whole letter. The censoring officer has my sympathies when he starts wading through this lot. By the way, John asks me to tell you that his mother would be only too pleased to see you if you cared to call at Blandford Road, (Mrs. Collins) when you are around that way. They have even offered to put you up permanently if you get too lonely at Pitshanger Lane. So I leave it to you. John wishes to be remembered to you. Please give my regards to all your family. I shall still be writing you every day darling and am looking forward to hearing from you. My address is still R.A.RFFFZ, c/o Army P.O., No. 990. Keep care of yourself, darling and keep beautiful. All my love for ever. Your loving husband.

P.S. I have just 'subbed' this letter and re-written two pages as I think I gave some information away. I have just seen John's letter – there's nothing left of it. I hope I am luckier.

Date censored   At Sea
Postmark on letter
Manchester 6th May 1941

My darling wife,
    As you will see, I have handed in my previous letter to you and will now continue where I left off.
    Actually, at the moment, the letter has not yet been despatched. I am not allowed to say when we reach port or mention any dates at all. The censorship is far more strict than I thought and I expect my previous letter will be cut about quite a bit – especially as I wrote on both sides of the paper. There is a chance that you will receive this letter at the same time as the one previously. By the way, I hear they are also cutting out all 'kiss' crosses, which is, again, rather unfortunate. However, we live and learn and I will try and see whether you can receive this letter without any cuts. Nothing very much interesting happened after I handed your letter in yesterday, and I can't for the life of me,

remember what I had for tea. So I will continue this letter as from this morning.

Tuesday: Up at 6.45 a.m. Breakfast was porridge without sugar (which I left) sausages and bread. We had to parade this morning at 10 a.m. with Topes which we are supposed to wear now we are in the tropical zone. Curiously enough, though, it is still quite cool, due mainly, I think, to the gusty winds which we are experiencing.

After Parade I lined up at the canteen and at just about 12 noon managed to get served. I bought 60 cigarettes, 3 cakes and a tin of 'Ideal' Milk. They had run out of the usual cigarettes and were selling a South African brand – 20 for 6d! They are simply terrible and I consider I might just as well have thrown 1/6d overboard.

Dinner was the usual meat, potatoes and beans, and some unexciting rice pudding for dessert. After dinner John and I went up on deck. Having occasion to look at my watch I found it had stopped at 12.20 p.m. I re-wound and shook it, but it refuses to go. I think it may be caused by dirt clogging the works as quite a lot of grit is to be seen between the glass and the dial.

It is a lovely day today, but there is a terrific wind blowing. I fell asleep but woke up about 3.15 p.m. feeling rather cold. John was playing chess so I popped 'down below' and started this letter. It is now almost 4 p.m. and I will have to close soon as tea will be 'up'. I forgot to add that yesterday I had a salt water shower which was very refreshing.

I wonder what you are doing at the moment, darling? I expect you are sitting at your usual place puzzling out what has happened to that £5!! I don't suppose you finish till 5.30 p.m. now do you? I'd give anything to be sitting in that District Line train bound for Ealing Broadway at the moment darling. What a pleasure it would be to look out of the window and see houses, streets and parks instead of nothing else but water – which looks exactly the same today as it did a week back. Will now close sweet as tea is definitely 'up'. I shall be thinking of you.

Wednesday: Up at 6.40 a.m. Breakfast was porridge, haddock and tea. Yesterday evening, after tea, we went up on deck and played cards. About 7 p.m. Joe brought his accordion on deck and we sat and listened to his numerous 'discords' in the gathering twilight. (He wouldn't like that!)

Last night it was very hot indeed and a long time before I went to sleep. I shall be glad when we sleep on deck – if ever.

This morning, after breakfast, John and I went up to our usual place on deck and, as usual, played cards. It was a lovely day, blue sky, etc., and I knew it was going to be terrifically hot in the afternoon. Today, by the way, it was on Orders that from today onwards 'Topes' must be worn between the hours of 9 a.m. and 4 p.m. The usual parade took place at 10 a.m. which finished just after 11 a.m. We then continued cards until dinner time. Dinner wasn't so good today. Rabbit (not too fresh) potatoes (rather gritty) and parsnips (quite good). Dessert consisted of plain suet pudding – no jam or anything. Definitely a disappointing meal. I hope they are not all going to be like that in future.

After dinner we came up on deck again. The heat was really terrific and there was very little shade. I started playing cards but soon fell asleep. I don't know exactly where we are, but I hope it doesn't get much warmer. I woke up just before 4 p.m. and went to the canteen and bought six penny cakes which I thought would add variety to the army tea. By the way we are getting no pay this week. Apparently pay aboard ship is 5/- per week and as we got 10/- last week, they decided that the amount covered this week too. Rather unfair really as they didn't tell us at the time. Still that's the army all over. Tea was corned beef rissoles (which I didn't like) bread and jam. After tea I had a quick wash and here I am, back on deck again in my usual place. It is much cooler now and a pleasure to be on deck.

I am not looking forward to tonight down in our 'Black Hole'. However, they are allowing 5 out of every 18 men to sleep on deck every night. So perhaps there will be a slightly larger share of fresh air for everyone in future.

It is now about 6 p.m. (My watch won't go but I'm afraid nothing can be done till I reach India. I shouldn't be surprised if it is just clogged with dirt). There is nothing much more I can write, darling. It's surprising to me how much I do write considering how very little happens. You should be grateful for my journalistic training!! Till tomorrow (when, by the way, we have to parade in our tropical kit). I love you.

Thursday. It was very hot last night and I did not sleep too well. But as I had a sleep yesterday afternoon, I felt no ill-effects. First thing I remembered when I woke up was that it was the anniversary of our engagement.* It does not seem too long ago in some respects and yet, in others darling, it seems ages. So much has happened in that short space of time. I really think we have had the experience of three or four years crammed into one. I wish we could have spent this anniversary together. I think I would have liked to have spent the evening at 72 had I been home. I love you more than ever darling and, who knows, perhaps I may be home again by our next anniversary. We must look on the bright side, and, if we wish hard enough, the seemingly impossible may happen. I have been with you in spirit all day, darling, and am imagining myself at the moment sitting with you on the settee at 28. Time (at home) 7.40 p.m.

* *A day in April*

Well, my sweet, here's my record of today's events:

6 a.m. Got up early this morning as it was far too warm to stay in bed. Thought I might get a wash early, but found that hundreds of other fellows had the same idea. I did, however, manage to get one before breakfast which consisted of egg and bacon (a very small rasher) porridge and coffee.

During the morning John and I sat up on deck until parade at 10 a.m. The Indian crew (there are a couple of dozen Indians in the crew) were putting up canopies all over the decks, so that now practically all the ship is shaded. A good idea, really, but it is surprising how cool it makes everything. At times I feel quite cold being dressed only in shorts and shirt.

After parade I went below and packed my battle dress away in my kitbag (I expect it will be a long time before I wear that again). I also put on my white shorts in order to keep the khaki ones clean.

Dinner at 12 noon was chop, potato and beans with stewed fruit. Very nice, but not quite enough. After dinner on deck again. Played cards for a little while, but managed to find a spot where the sun was gleaming through and had a little sleep. The sun was not half as strong as yesterday. Tea at 5 p.m. was the usual pickles, ham (a very small portion) and jam. And that brings me up-to-date again, sitting here on the deck writing to you. We have very short evenings in these parts. It is quite dark by 7 o'clock so will close now and continue tomorrow. Au revoir, my sweet.

Friday: Up at 6.30 a.m. It was terrifically hot last night and I was bathed in sweat. It should be my turn to sleep on deck tonight, and I am looking forward to a rather cooler time. Breakfast was porridge and liver (which I did not fancy). I had a cold shower and then went up on deck. Parade as usual was at 10 a.m. and during this period the day's excitement commenced. A plane was seen approaching and, after circling once or twice, disappeared; but returned again at intervals. After we had presumed it was one of ours (as no bombs were dropped!) we guessed we must be near land. A few minutes later we saw a bird which heightened the excitement. Everybody was, of course, looking for land, but John and I got rather tired of straining our eyes and played cards. When we looked again just before dinner we could see mountains (which looked like dark clouds) in the distance. We went down to dinner which consisted of meat, carrots and potatoes, with a very good pudding for dessert. After dinner we went on deck and there was land, complete with mountains, trees (palm), houses, etc. all round us. Native boys were paddling around the boat in canoes and everything looked very nice after days at sea. I only wished you could have been with me darling. Don't imagine I am at all delighted at being all these miles from home – I still much prefer Ealing – but it was nice to see land again. Although I don't suppose we will stop here long, and it is very unlikely that we shall ever set foot ashore. During the afternoon we just lazed about and it being extremely hot, I occasionally watched the natives diving for pennies.

138

Tea at 5 p.m. was bread and jam and fish. And here I am again sitting on deck writing this letter. There is community singing going on at the moment, accompanied by an accordionist and an officer playing the guitar. The time is now 6 p.m. here and it won't be long now before it is dark.

I am afraid, darling, I can't describe what this place is like or where it is. But it is rather barren and I shouldn't like to come here for a holiday much. But as I said before, any land is welcome after endless seas.

Well, my darling, I think, once again, that's all for now. My previous letter should be mailed to you from here and I hope it is not torpedoed on its way. It should not take too long to reach you. I don't suppose I shall have the luck of hearing from you for a long while yet. I am eagerly looking forward to your first letter, darling. I wonder if you are writing to me every day? I expect you are. Well, goodnight, my sweet. I will write again tomorrow.

Saturday: Up at 6 a.m. after having spent the night on deck. It was much cooler, although still very warm. I did not sleep too well as the deck felt very hard after being used to a hammock. But as we do nothing much during the day, loss of sleep at night has little effect. Breakfast was porridge and fish with coffee. I had another shower this morning although there was a wild scramble for them. I have to line up for almost everything on this ship. For a wash, to get to the canteen, for all meals, for a drink – in fact, unless one is just sitting on the deck doing nothing, there is always a queue in which one has to take one's place.

Parade was at 10 a.m. as usual and after that I played cards till 12. We are still in port and are occasionally amused by the natives who crowd round the ship trying to sell fruit, etc. It is rather hard lines for them as we are not allowed to buy anything for fear of spreading diseases. A wise ruling really, but, of course, one or two break it.

Dinner was meat (which I think was pork) beans and potato, with stewed apples for dessert. Quite nice but again not enough. We had a pleasant surprise in the form of a bottle of mineral water which we are getting every day while in port. After dinner, I borrowed 3d from John and bought 3 cakes. (Yes, I am broke now until pay day, which I hope will be Monday).

We do not have to carry our lifebelts whilst we are in port, but I find them very convenient as a cushion. We also use them as pillows at night. They are not the round cork lifebelts, but two pads filled with cotton wool which go over our shoulders. When we are on the move we always carry them around even more so than we used to carry gas-masks ashore. During the afternoon we alternate between playing cards and resting. The heat is too great to walk around much (although it is now evening and, therefore, slightly cooler. I don't have to use a blotting paper when writing. The ink dries at once).

Tea at 5 p.m. was corned beef, pickles and bread and jam. By the way they have now opened the portholes so we get a little more fresh air below.

It is now 5.40 p.m. (7.40 at home) and I am finishing today's notes sitting on a raft on deck. John is looking over the side trying to read some signalling by lamp which is going on between the ships. I think I will now go and join him.

I wish I knew what you were doing at this moment, darling. Last night the Great Bear or the Plough was very distinct from where I lay on deck. I thought of you then and how often I had gazed at the Plough at Ealing when out with you of an evening. Well, my sweet, will close for today. All my love.

Sunday: I am going to close this letter now, darling as there seems to be quite a good chance that it will be accepted for posting. Will not write any more as I wish to hand it in as soon as possible.

All my love, darling and please keep cheerful. Your loving husband.

Author's note: *The port was Freetown, Sierra Leone (West Africa)*

Date censored   At sea
My darling wife,

I handed in my previous letter to you at dinner-time and I think
I fortunately got it in in time to go ashore with the mail. You
should, therefore, darling, receive two letters from me numbered
2 and 3 on the envelopes. I hope you get them safely. I will
continue this letter by relating today's events.

Sunday: Up at 6 a.m. Had a very bad night - nightmares, etc. -
and was pouring with sweat. I think it was due mainly to a pint of
beer which John treated me to last night. It is supposed to be
lager, but it is horrible stuff and it turned my stomach upside
down.

I slept 'down below' last night as most of the fellows went up on
deck Consequently, there were only about 3 in the room. John and
I are thinking of sleeping on deck tonight, however. I had a
shower first thing this morning. Breakfast was porridge and
kippers. After breakfast I shaved and then we went up on deck.
Parade was at 10 a.m. and during parade I noticed a few letters
being handed to the officer, so directly parade was finished I
rushed down below, concluded your letter with a short note, and
gave it in. Dinner was meat, Swedes and potato and rice pudding
for dessert. A very uninteresting and unappetizing meal; the only
delight being a bottle of mineral water. After dinner on deck again
and mainly slept, but had a short game of cards before tea. Tea
was rissoles and bread and jam. Up on deck again and writing this
letter to you. I will shortly be going down to collect my hammock
to bag a place on deck. Till tomorrow, my love.

Monday. Slept on deck again last night, but during the early
hours it started to rain and so we made a dive for the canteen
where we spent the remainder of the night. We were up at 6 a.m.
I had a shower and then breakfast which was liver, porridge and
coffee. After breakfast up on deck and played cards till parade
time. After parade continued playing cards till noon. Dinner was

141

meat, beans and potato with plums and custard. Not bad, but again not half enough, and had to buy 3 cakes to satisfy my appetite. During the afternoon we lazed about – it being very hot – and at 3.30 p.m. we received our 'pay' of 5/-. The Pay Parade was in our room below deck and it was terrifically hot. Sweat simply steamed off us.

We have had orders that, in future, we have to wear only shorts – no slippers or singlets – so we will look like a nudist colony by the time they finish with us! Tea at 4.30 p.m. was the usual corned beef and pickles, with bread and jam. It is now about 6 p.m. and there is quite a cool breeze blowing. It is delightful on deck in the evenings. A pity they are so short.

By the way, we are at sea again and we have been told that we shall get shore leave at our next port of call. Whether that means just a route march, I don't know. But anyway it is <u>something</u> to look forward to when there is nothing of interest to do all day. I can even do crosswords now to keep mentally alert and as there is no piano available for the troops, the only things left to do is to read or play cards. However, it won't last for ever, so I must grin and bear it until we reach our destination.

Will close now for today, darling. I'm afraid there is nothing much to tell you nowadays. I am hoping that perhaps you will receive my letters by Easter so that you will know I am O.K. All my love, darling.

Tuesday: Spent the night on deck again – or rather in the canteen – which is a far sight better than being below. Believe it or not but there is scarcely a square foot of spare space on the open decks when people start putting down their beds.

I was up soon after 6 a.m. Had a shower and shave and breakfast was porridge, sausages and bread. We went up on deck as soon as possible as the heat down below gets worse every day. The usual parade was at 10 a.m. and during this hour we had to do a bit of saluting drill. Apparently they thought we might not know how to salute with topes on! Even the process of lifting one's hand to the forehead is exerting in this climate. From 11 – 12 noon we rested in the shade.

Dinner was meat, greens and potatoes with currant pudding for dessert. It is agony having meals nowadays. Sweat pours off us like water when coming out of a swimming bath. It was bad enough when we were in the cooler regions – even then we had not enough ventilation below, but now conditions are really wicked. You remember I showed you a little book we were issued with – 'Health Memorandum for British -------'. Well practically all the advice contained in the ---- (*half page of letter cut out*) -------.

Although it is only 6 o'clock it is already so dark that I can hardly see to write, so will continue tomorrow.

Wednesday. I'm afraid I've started writing this rather too late to be able to write much before it gets dark, darling. John and I had to attend Guard Mounting Parade as 'Reserve Men'. Luckily we were not wanted. The time is now 5.50 p.m. (we put our watches on another -------- last night) and the sun has already set, so I shall have to hurry.

Yesterday for tea there was baked beans (but nothing like you serve them up) and bread and jam.

We slept on the deck again last night and I had the best night's sleep for a long time. There was a cool breeze blowing all night and it was very delightful. It started raining about 5.20 a.m. but I was quite ready to get up, so went below and had a shower. Breakfast was porridge and fish with coffee. During the morning there was the usual parade and a laze about until 12 noon. Dinner was chop, potato and peas with stewed fruit. Quite nice, but I still needed a few cakes after to satisfy my appetite. We are still getting that bottle of mineral water daily – but I don't suppose it will last much longer.

During the afternoon we had a short game of cards and then slept. It is much cooler today due to a strong wind that is blowing. But if one is not under cover, the sun is very hot. Must close now in haste, darling, as I can hardly see to write. It certainly gets dark quickly in these parts. Goodnight my love.

Thursday 4.40 p.m. Have started my letter before tea today, darling, so that I do not have to cut it short. Tea last night consisted of bread and jam, the usual bully beef and pickles.

As I mentioned yesterday it got dark very quickly so, soon after 6 p.m. we started looking around deck for bedding sites. After being turned away from a couple of places – as they were not under cover – we finally found a pile of rafts which John and Joe slept on and I slept on the deck between the rafts and the deck railing. It was rather cramped, but I had a good sleep. We don't suffer from lack of sleep as there is nothing to do after black-out except go to bed. There is the wet canteen where terrible lager, mineral waters and tea is sold, but the place is stifling at nights and crammed tight.

This morning we were up at 6 a.m. I had the usual shower and shave and then had breakfast which consisted of porridge, bacon and tomatoes, bread and tea. By the way, we have real butter for breakfast and tea – haif a pound between 18 men for each meal. After breakfast we lazed on deck till 10 a.m. when we had to go on parade. Feet were examined, but for what I am not sure. We have heard that we shall most likely get shore leave at our next port of call, so perhaps that's why. I think our feet must have got pretty tender marching about in slippers all day, with no socks. We went up on the sun deck at 11 a.m. and had a short snooze till dinner time. Dinner was pretty awful today. One slice of bully beef and a few beans with unsweetened rice pudding for dessert. I think that, if they are not going to feed us properly they should give us more than 5/- a week. I have spent nearly all mine already, mainly on food. And there is always razor blades, toothpaste, etc. to buy. However, perhaps they will make up for it by giving us a good tea today. Although I doubt it!

By the way, my watch is going again. This morning I decided, after much thought, to take the dial covering off, which I did successfully. I only had to blow on the face and it started going. So it was only dirt, as I suspected.

This afternoon we have been playing cards and, as the time is now 5 p.m. I think I will go below for tea. We put our watches -----

144

------- again today, so you are now only -------------- at home, and I expect you have just got home from the office. I wonder if I'm right?

We have passed ------------------. Today they ------------------------ but I did not go and see it as Army humour (or rather their idea of humour) does not appeal to me.

Friday: Slept on deck again last night after having a lot of trouble with our hammocks. We rigged them up early, but when we went to look for them later they had been taken down and another two put in their place. As we then could not find our own we took down these particular two and slept in them in a different part of the ship. You certainly have to keep you eye open on this ship. If you so much at blink at the tea-table someone would pinch the sugar out of your tea. Tea yesterday was the usual pickles and corned beef. There doesn't seem to be much variety nowadays at meals. I had quite a good sleep last night and was up at 6 a.m. We put our watches ------------------ which makes our time ----------------- yours now. My watch is still going O.K.

Had a shower before breakfast which consisted of porridge, coffee and kippers which did not taste too fresh.

It has been rather cool on deck today, mainly due to the wind. The weather is now getting more 'Englishified' although the sun is still very strong. My legs look like a couple of beetroots. I have rigidly refused to do any sunbathing – the idea seems pretty ridiculous to me. After all we shall probably have quite a long time in which to get brown.

At 10 a.m. we had ------------------ lesson till 11 a.m. Quite interesting, but I think I'll teach the ------------------ to speak English, rather than learn their lingo.

Dinner was again very meagre. <u>One</u> potato and <u>one</u> slice of meat; with about 4 stewed prunes for dessert. I think Stores must be getting short. I'll be glad when we reach port and they can load up again. During the afternoon we, as usual, rested and played cards. There was a special parade at 1.30 p.m. and we were told that we were to be inoculated. However, it has been put off till tomorrow when we shall have two inoculations and one vaccination – all at one go! I think I shall refuse to be vaccinated, however. Tea was again pickles and corned beef and I am now sitting on deck writing. The time is ------- at home and it is nearly dark, so once again I will terminate my penning for the day.

Saturday: Up at 6 a.m. Had quite a good night's sleep in the canteen, which, although under cover, is on deck and much more airy and roomy than being below. Actually it was rather cold last night and today the weather has been very cool. The sky has been overcast and the sea quite choppy. In fact the weather is similar to that off the coast of England – but we are not deceived!!

We managed to find a fairly warm part on deck after breakfast (sausages, porridge, etc.) and on the 10 o'clock Parade we attended an M.T. (Motor Transport) lecture as we weren't very thrilled with the Hindustani one yesterday.

From 11 a.m. to noon we had a short game of cards. Dinner consisted of <u>half</u> a potato, one very small slice of meat and about half-a-dozen peas. The currant pudding which followed was quite nice but I could have eaten two more similar meals.

At 1.30 p.m. (as I mentioned yesterday) we had to parade for our inoculations, but it was nearly 4 p.m. before Johnny and I were 'done'. I think the Medical Officers must have been a bit weary when the lot was finished.

I had quite made up my mind not to be vaccinated and won the first round with an officer (a captain) and when he said I would most probably get small-pox, be disfigured for life and finally die, I did not flinch and still refused! So he wrote 'Refused vaccination' on a slip of paper and sent me to the first M.O. for inoculation. After this jab I accidentally went to the 'vaccination' M.O. and when I realised my error said I did not wish to be vaccinated. He asked me if I knew the consequences and I said 'Yes'. And then he said did I realise it might not be fair to other people if I were disfigured or 'pegged out' and I started weakening. He then, of course, brought his full powers of persuasion into play and I finally succumbed. I feel all right at the moment, but if I don't write tomorrow, darling, I expect you will know why!

We have to hand in letters for posting again Monday – you know what that means, don't you? If you receive all my letters it really isn't so bad. You should hear from me far more often than you thought you would.

Well, darling, it is now 4.30 p.m. so will go down to tea – I was nearly too late yesterday. I may continue this afterwards. It is now 5.45 p.m. and I am sitting on the floor in the Canteen (where I hope to sleep tonight) continuing this letter. We put our watches -- ---------------- on another ----------. So tomorrow morning we will be ------------ Greenwich time.

Tea wasn't very interesting again. There was bread and jam and baked beans with some meat, which was supposed to be pork, but tasted like rabbit. We drew our hammocks out of stores immediately after tea and are now waiting for the canteen to shut (6.30 p.m.) when we can roll them out on the floor. I think I sleep better on the floor than in the hammock – there is more room.

My arm is beginning to hurt a little now, but nothing to speak of. John is curled up on the floor and almost asleep. I think he is going to have a restless night somehow. I don't think the inoculation will affect me much, although I wouldn't like to say that about the vaccination. I don't believe one feels anything at all until about 10 days after the 'operation'.

Well, darling, it is now ---------- at home and, if the weather is anything like it is here tonight, I expect you will have a nice cheerful fire going. I still can't believe I am very far away from you darling. Every day when I write to you I imagine that you have received the previous day's letter. I expect you have noticed that. I would give anything, darling, just to see you for a few minutes now. When I left you that Thursday morning I did not dream that I would not see you again before I left. But perhaps it was all for the best. We would only have had a miserable parting had we known, whereas we said au revoir as if we expected to see each other again in a few hours. All I do now is to look forward to the day when I see you again. I often lay in bed and think of what it will be like when I return. Back in the old train to Ealing Broadway. The bus ride to the top of the hill and the walk down the road to

28. I often wonder what your expression will be when you open the door and see me. I expect you will know when I am coming home, but I doubt if you will know what day I reach home. Of course I may phone you first and meet you at the office. I expect you romance in the same way, don't you darling? We are so much alike in that respect – both dreamers!!

Well darling I am beginning to feel a little tired and think I will 'tuck in'. I shall be dreaming of you, my love.

Sunday: Up at 6 a.m. Had a very restless night and my arm, apart from aching, felt like a barrage balloon. Didn't feel too good when I got up and as I couldn't get my shirt off (owing to not being able to bend my arm) I did not have a shower.

Breakfast was coffee, porridge and haddock (not very nice). After the meal John and I managed to drag ourselves up on deck (taking our coats with us as it was not too warm) and snoozed away peacefully until parade time. Attended the lecture on M.T. but did not feel in the mood to digest knowledge.

From 11 to noon we snoozed again and I almost felt like not arousing myself for dinner. However, I thought I had better although it was hardly worth having - a slice of cold meat and a small mixture of potato and beans with an overdose of pepper. Dessert was stewed apples – no custard or juice.

After dinner up on deck again to continue our snooze. We weren't lazy but definitely feeling the effects of the inoculations. It was a funny day; warm and clear blue sky but with a very cold wind. I had my overcoat over me to keep warm, yet when I got up my ankles were sunburnt.

Tea consisted of bread and jam and rissoles. The latter I did not fancy.

The time is now 5.20 p.m. (------- at home) and I am sitting on deck telling you of a very uneventful day. I still feel a bit groggy but better than I have done all day.

How have the raids been in London? We have the news on the wireless and a bulletin pinned up on the Notice Board every day. According to them, London has been having a quieter time lately, but of course, we don't know exactly what that means. Are you still thinking of going to Watford, darling? Or have you gone? I would still feel very much easier if I knew you were no longer in London. But you do what you think best. Will close now, my sweet, but will add a little extra tomorrow morning before I hand this letter in.

Monday: Up at 6 a.m. Had a much better night and arm was not half as painful. Managed to get my shirt off this morning and have a shower. My arm is still a little tender and stiff, but I am hoping it will be almost normal by tonight as I am on guard - worse luck. Breakfast was liver (no likee) porridge and coffee. To think I used to enjoy liver in civilian life! The army certainly changes one's taste for things.

I am not sitting on deck and the time here is 8.15 a.m. Apparently I have been making a slight mistake lately over our respective times for I find today that we are -----------------------

------- you now. That means that, if you are going to the office today (which I doubt) you will just be leaving home.

The weather today is quite warm – there is no cold breeze. We are wearing our boots today to get used to them once again as we shall wear them if and when we get shore leave.

Well, darling, I will close this letter now so I can hand it in at Parade time. I hope it doesn't take too long to reach you. I wonder if you have received my previous letter yet?

Au revoir, my darling. I love you with all my heart and will always be thinking of you. I wish I could hear from you but I don't suppose there is any chance until I reach my destination. All my love for ever.

Date censored   At Sea

My darling wife,

I am now starting my fifth letter to you since I left London. I do hope you safely received the previous ones. I handed in No. 4 yesterday lunch time and I expect now it is in the process of having large chunks cut out of it. I shall be very interested to see my letters when I get back and find just how strict the censorship is.

I will not write much this evening darling (Tuesday) as I was on guard last night and today and am feeling a bit tired. However, I will continue my non-dated diary as previously.

Yesterday, after handing in your letter during parade time, we went straight 'down below' and just hung about waiting for dinner. It was hardly worth waiting for however – one potato, one slice of meat and swedes (which I detest) followed by a very minute portion of unsweetened rice pudding. I hope they don't forget to load the ship with stores again when we dock. After dinner I felt very tired for some unknown reason and without waiting for John made my way up to the sun deck and fell asleep. I woke about 3 p.m. and suddenly remembered that Pay Parade was at 1.30 p.m. I rushed down and just managed to get my 5/- before the Pay Officer went. I then had a shave, etc., rushed through tea (the usual corned beef, pickles, etc.) and was on Guard Mounting Parade at 5.30 p.m. We hung about till about 6.30 p.m. when we were inspected. (How the Army loves to waste time!) and then, being first relief, I went straight on guard until 8 p.m. John and I considered ourselves lucky at being first reliefs as, besides missing half-an-hour (owing to a prolonged parade) on our first guard, during our second watch, the ship's clock went forward the usual 20 minutes (between 12 midnight and 2 a.m.) and so we did 20 minutes less on that guard.

I was on again at 6 a.m. and it was rather cold standing about in our tropical kit. About 7 a.m. I was rather cheered by sighting what I thought was land on the horizon – and so were other fellows standing on the deck – but it turned out to be a line of low clouds. However, the sunrise was well worth watching. Had breakfast directly I came off guard (porridge and sausages) and then went up on deck for the usual game of cards and a rest. Will close for now, my love, as I am feeling very tired. Will continue my 'memoirs' in the morning.

Over four days have elapsed, my darling, since I last wrote to you. I am very sorry but I am sure you will forgive me when I explain and describe the events of the last few days.

It is now Sunday (5.25 p.m. here - probably 4.25 p.m. at home) and as I am writing this I can just see land disappearing on the horizon. I wish I could tell you where we have been, but that of course is impossible.* But we have had a very good three days ashore - made all the more enjoyable by being able to stretch our legs after being cramped together for weeks. However, I will continue this letter from where I ended last Tuesday, although I expect, I shall not be able to write very much this evening. I am not going to bother you with such uninteresting details as to what we had for breakfast, but will try my best to give you a good picture of the place we have just left. It was about Wednesday, mid-day, when we first sighted land on the horizon and it was just as I had pictured it from descriptions I had read at home. As the buildings and landmarks became more distinct everyone began to get restless and crowded the railings.

*Cape Town, South Africa

I suppose it is hard for you to imagine how we feel when we see land and the thought of getting ashore again made us want to shout and cheer at the least provocation.

However, it seemed that we were approaching land very slowly, so we went and had tea as usual. When we came up on deck again we found ourselves quite close to the shore and everything was very distinct.

John and I stood looking over the railing watching one of the other ships put in to dock, and then suddenly we started moving ourselves.

The harbour came nearer and nearer and when we were able to read advertisements on buildings and see trains and cars on the dockside we nearly went mad.

We manoeuvred up to the side of one dock and for some time were amused by the antics of native dockers who would scramble

151

like a lot of children for a penny or cigarette. I suddenly noticed that a boy was selling papers on the lower deck, so I dashed down but was too late – there were none left.

I went down below and got John's and my hammock and, as I was taking them upstairs, a fellow stopped me and said that if I wanted a pass for tomorrow I had better go below again as they were being issued. So I dashed up and told John and together we went down below. When we entered our mess room we found everyone 'dressing up' and, on making enquiries, found that we were being allowed on shore that very evening.

So, amidst great excitement, John and I got ready, collected our passes, met Joe, and, after lining up for what seemed hours (actually about 5 minutes) were making our way down the gangway.

The first thing we noticed was, of course, the lights. Although we were still in the dockyard and it was only dimly lit, it seemed very cheerful and reminded us all of home before the war. The walk through dockland took about 15 minutes and all the time we were dodging freight trains that were shunting backwards and forwards. However, we finally made our way into the town proper and it was a sight for sore eyes.

Tall buildings brightly lit, electric signs flashing as in Piccadilly in peace time; hundreds of cars sped along the streets and the noise was terrific. The scene was more reminiscent of New York than London, especially as the town was built in 'blocks' - streets running straight in both directions and crossing each other squarely. The first thing we did was to go in a pub (as they shut at 8 p.m.) and have a lager, which rather shocked us by costing 10d a pint. For the rest of the evening we wandered around the streets looking at the shops, etc. We found that there were free canteens and dances for soldiers, but all were crammed full. In fact, the whole town was crammed full and, towards the end of the evening, we were getting rather tired of pushing our way through and resolved that, when we got ashore tomorrow, we would get as far away from the town as possible. We discovered that troops could get free rides on trolley-buses and other buses which seemed to hold possibilities for the next day.

We tried to get some supper before we made our way back to the boat, but everywhere was crammed full, so we just bought a few bananas and got back about 11 p.m. (our passes were available till 11.59 p.m.). We slept well that night and were looking forward to the following day.

(Will continue this in the morning, darling, as it is now getting dark. All my love)

We got up sharp at 6 a.m. on Thursday after a good night's sleep on deck. Parade, while we were in dock, was at 9.30 a.m., so we all rushed and got ready and for the first time, I think, we looked forward to a route march. Parade stretched out for over an hour until we were finally marched off the boat in section. We made our way through the dockyard and were soon marching through the main streets of the town. People lined the streets and typists, etc., were leaning from office windows and cheering – from appearances one would have imagined that the war was over and we were the victorious army returning home. Still it was quite pleasant but somewhat marred by continuous stopping and waiting caused by traffic lights which were as numerous as those in Oxford Street.

We returned to the ship just before 12 noon, had our dinner then waited for our shore pay and passes. Although these were due at 1 p.m. it was well on 2 o'clock before we got two native 10/- notes and a pass.

We made our way down town again and thought we would try the local beauty spot half way up a mountain from which the whole town could be seen. By the way, I forgot to mention that the citizens would go to no end of trouble to entertain us. Most of the people with cars picked up soldiers and took them around the districts – usually inviting them to their homes for a meal afterwards.

However, we three felt we would be independent and explore for ourselves. After all, we had £1 each!

We waited for a trolley-bus to take us to our destination, but apparently nearly everyone else had the same idea, and every trolley that came along was full up. Not to be outdone, however, we took another, emptier, bus which was not going to this particular place but which seemed to be going in the same direction, and went as far as the terminus. From there, using my unfailing sense of direction (!) we made our way half way up the mountain. It was a beautiful day and one could imagine oneself to be on holiday on the continent. I often imagined that you were with me.

We looked at the city from this height, and for some time we debated as to whether we should take the cable railway to the very top - but finally owing to the cost (3/- return) and the thought of risking our lives on that thin stretch of cable, we decided to postpone it. Three roads forked off from where we stood, and as we were wondering which one to take, a 'speed cop' came up and told us where they all led.

We tossed up between two of them and finally made our way down a road which wound down the side of the mountain. We came across a nice tea-room called 'The Round House' about half-way down which used to be a shooting box in the old days when lions roamed the countryside. Although we reckoned the tea would cost about 10/- between us for 2 poached eggs on toast, tea, cakes, etc., it came to only 5/3d. I must explain that the cost of living here is very high and things are much dearer than in England. Bars of chocolate, for instance, are 3d each; in fact it is hard to find anything costing less than 3d. Even in the fun fairs the machines have to have 3d bits put in the slot - so we didn't go in any of these places.

After having tea we left the Round House, the proprietor accompanying us part of the way. As we descended we could see a bay on our left which looked very inviting. We decided to visit it the next day.

Finally we came out into a suburb of the city and we leisurely strolled towards town. The suburbs looked very much like London suburbs and reminded me greatly of parts of the Uxbridge Road. The road began to get rather uninteresting, so we jumped on a bus to town. There we decided to take another bus to another suburb which was mentioned in a pamphlet we had obtained.

There was a dance with free refreshments at this place, but, as with all the other places of entertainment, it was crowded full.

So we had a little walk round, had a small supper and returned to town. We got back to the boat about 11 p.m.

The next day (Friday) we were up sharp at 6 a.m. again. By the way this day was the first anniversary of my being 'called-up'.* I have now been in the Army a year – but it seems more like a century. Instead of parading on deck this morning at 9.30 a.m. we lined up on the dockside, and so there was not so much hanging about.

Darling,

I couldn't get all this letter in one envelope. You will find it continues in letter No. 6 and possibly No. 7. Love.

* *April 18th*

Letter No. 6

The route march was quite enjoyable, but, of course, they are now rather dull after a free afternoon and evening, and we eagerly looked forward to 1 p.m.

We had dinner sharp at 12 noon and got our passes rather late again – just before 2 p.m. We made our way down town and took the same trolley-bus as yesterday to the terminus and then walked half-way up the mountain as before. This time however, we took the left hand road which led to the bay we had seen yesterday. It was rather a long walk, however, owing to the curve of the mountain road.

Eventually we tired of following the road when we could see the bay below us, so scrambled down the side of the cliff. This place looked rather like a quiet English sea-side resort. We found a nice little café – and, as it was too early for tea – just had a cup of tea and a bar of chocolate. The shops here, by the way, are crammed with chocolates and sweets. It is very difficult not to walk in and spend shillings on buying the stuff.

We then lay down on a grass patch near the sands (which are almost as white as snow) and listened to the waves washing up on the shore. At about 4.30 p.m. we took a bus going towards town again. It was a very pleasant ride. The sea on our left below us and mountains on our right above us. The road continually curved in and out, and together with the continental style buildings which lined the road, the scene was very reminiscent of the Riviera road between Monaco and Eze-sur-Mer. I don't think it was quite as pretty actually, the mountains weren't half as high and the road was not so picturesque. But it made me continually think of our holiday together on the Riviera, and I must admit I felt very sorry for myself at times.

We did not travel right into town but got off at the point where the other road led us to yesterday. We found a nice little café and I had an egg, onions and chips with coffee, which was very tasty and quite reasonable. We then went right back to town and as all the cinemas were full, made our way out towards the suburb to which we went yesterday evening.

On my recommendation we went to a cinema called the "Astoria" which was showing William Powell and Myrna Loy in "I Love you Again" which I remember had a good press review. It wasn't until the film started that I realised I had seen the film before with you. We left the cinema about 10 p.m., found a nice little café next door and had coffee and cakes.

We had a fright when trying to get 'home'. Every bus that came along was crammed full – people even sitting on the stairs. We tried to stop a car, but even they were full up with soldiers going back to the ships. Just as we were beginning to get panicky, about 11.30 p.m., a break-down lorry came along which John, Joe and I, together with other fellows scrambled on. After numerous adventures with other vehicles we reached the docks and got back to the boat with 5 minutes to spare. A few minutes later and we should have had tomorrow's shore leave stopped – definitely a narrow escape! We slept well again, and the next morning we were up at 6 a.m. as usual and washed and shaved, etc.

The route march this morning was more enjoyable. There was some military display in town and people lined the roads and cheered and clapped us heartily. I almost began to feel like a soldier!!!

We got our passes quite early today (Saturday) and, on my suggestion, we took a train ride this time to a place on the other side of the mountains. It is a seaside resort and not far away from town and is, I suppose, to this town what Richmond is to London. The trains were electric and were similar to the District Line trains, although not so comfortable and got their power from overhead cables.

The journey took about 40 minutes and, when we got to our destination, we were not unduly impressed. It was quite a nice place but reminded one of an English sea-side resort out of season; which, of course, is partly right, as it is nearly winter here now although the weather is like summer at home.

However, we found that there was a free tea in the pavilion for visiting troops in which we partook. It was not at all bad. We had our choice or cakes and sandwiches, etc., and two cups of tea. It certainly saved us a shilling or so.

We then walked along the coastal road which was very pleasing. The scenery was not exceptional – at least to me – but it was a very enjoyable walk with a nice fresh breeze blowing. We leisurely strolled for about 4 miles and then had a cup of tea and some biscuits in a small café. We were not so lucky this time as we were charged 2/-; but we can't always be lucky!

It was now about 7 p.m. so we took the next train back to town. We were going to do a little shopping but apparently shops shut in this country on Saturday afternoons.

Well, we got back to town and for some time we were stuck; we didn't know what to do for the rest of the evening. We tried to get in the main cinema which was showing 'Gasbags', but as the lowest price was 2/6d and John and Joe had seen it before, we decided against it. We hoped somebody would notice our plight and invite us home to supper, but no such luck. Finally we decided

157

to go out to the suburb where the café next to the Astoria was situated and have some supper.

Once again, however, we had the same transport difficulty – all the buses full.   Finally I managed to stop a car and, after a nightmare ride at about 60 m.p.h. along the main road, we reached the suburb.   We noticed a fair so, greatly bucked, we went to investigate.   It was a very disappointing show, just a swing and a couple of tame side-shows, so we did not stay more than a couple of minutes.   We started walking along the road for about 15 minutes and when we asked someone where the 'Astoria' was, found we had been walking in the wrong direction.

We made our way back, therefore, and finally found our café.   I had an egg on steak (a popular dish in this country) and chips.   It was very nice indeed and very reasonable.

We left earlier today in order not to have any trouble getting home and reached the docks about 11 p.m.   This, although we did not know it at the time, was our last time ashore.

We were up at 6 a.m. as before next day (Sunday) and were already planning our excursion for the day when we happened to look at Orders and found that all shore leave was stopped.   It was a great disappointment, but we had three really good days so we didn't grumble.

When we reach our destination I shall be able to tell you the name of this town if you haven't already guessed.   It is a grand place, and if we decide to leave England after the war, this country has distinct possibilities.

It is decidedly a wealthy country.   Everyone seems to have a car – and not a small one – but high-powered American streamlined automobiles.   As I mentioned before, the place is more like a miniature New York than anything else.

The women look amazingly fresh and youthful compared to their counterparts in England.   And don't think I am deliberately flattering you, darling, when I say that they are your type.   Blonde hair, very little make-up …….. curiously enough, you remember when I first met you I said you spoke with a slight accent and I said I thought your people might have come from Holland.   Well, they all speak the same way here. It is most remarkable. I think it must be your spiritual homeland!

I could write pages more describing the place to you darling, but today is now Tuesday and I shall get behind in my 'dateless diary' if I spend much more time on it. However, I expect I shall refer to it again and mention things I may have forgotten. At the first opportunity I shall send you, with my letters, a couple of pamphlets about the place.

Land finally disappeared from sight Sunday evening and now, once more, life goes on in its old monotonous, uninteresting way. On Sunday evening we were told to change back into Battle Dress – this puzzled us as the weather had been quite chilly whilst wearing tropical kit, and now the weather appeared to be getting warmer, this Order was issued.

I am not going to describe the meals since Sunday. They are the same as usual and as unappetizing as ever. On Monday afternoon we were paid 10/- to last us a fortnight. Directly afterwards I went to the canteen and bought a pipe, tobacco, toothpaste and two bars of chocolate, and bang went 4/2d! Not a very good start. Today, by the way, is Tuesday and an Order came out at 2.30 p.m. that we were to wear tropical kit again. What an Army! The time is now 5.45 p.m. (4.45 p.m. at home) and it is beginning to get dark, so I shall have to close.

I read in the newspaper that you had a bad air-raid last Wednesday night and also, apparently, one again on Saturday. I do hope you are all right, darling. I try not to think about it, but I can't help worrying. It's so hard to understand what actually has happened from news bulletins. Between the lines, however, I seem to sense that Fleet Street had rather caught it again. I wonder if you have moved to Watford yet, darling? I should feel much easier if you had.

Must close now, sweet, as it is getting quite dark and I have to draw my hammock. I shall be thinking of you tonight.

Wednesday: Up at 6 a.m. after spending night on deck. Had quite a good sleep. Had a shower and breakfast was porridge, some awful looking fish (which I did not fancy) and coffee.

After breakfast we were sent up on deck until 9 a.m. When we came down below again there was a kit inspection at 10 a.m. and we had to lay out our stuff. I was short of my forage cap and puttees and considered myself lucky not to have had many other things missing. Some of the biggest rogues in the world are on this ship and things are always disappearing.

From 11 to 12 noon we went on deck again. It was a warm day but extremely breezy. We tried to have a game of cards but nearly lost them overboard when we attempted to play.

Dinner was one slice of pork with one potato, followed by quite a good plum duff.

At 2.30 p.m. I had to report at the M.O.'s for vaccination. I explained, of course, that I was treated last week, but while I was there I had my arm bandaged. I am not troubled much with it, but my old dressing had fallen off.

By the way I was lucky I finally consented to be vaccinated last week. Those who refused were refused shore leave when we arrived at the port. Mind you, inoculations and vaccinations are strictly voluntary........!!

When I left the MO's I went to the library and as I couldn't find Johnny I curled up in a corner, filled up the old pipe, and started reading. The book is W.W. Jacob's 'Many Cargoes' which I think I have read before.

Tea at 5 p.m. was corned beef, pickles, jam and bread. Quite nice, but definitely getting very monotonous. After tea I went and listened to the 6 o'clock news. John's just gone to the M.O.'s to get his arm dressed, and I am sitting at our mess table writing this letter.

I expect all this is very monotonous for you to read after the many things I recounted during our stay ashore. But there you are, darling, I can't write anything interesting if nothing interesting happens. It should not be long now before we reach our destination; and then I shall have more to tell you. I must apologize, by the way, for this terrible writing paper, but it is the only kind they sell on the boat. Like the cigarettes, it is of the lowest quality. Anything is good enough for the ranks.

I am on guard again tomorrow – second relief this time. Not so good. Will close another day now, darling. I hope you are keeping well and are in the best of spirits. I know you will not worry too much. May God take care of you for me.

Thursday: Up at 6 a.m. Breakfast was bacon and egg – only a small portion, but nevertheless welcome. It was very breezy on deck during the morning, so we did not play our usual game of cards. Dinner at 12 noon was the usual uninteresting one potato, meat and carrots with plum duff for dessert.

At 2.30 p.m. I had to parade for the guard mounting which lasted about half-an-hour. My hours of duty were 4.30 – 6.30 p.m., 10.30 – 12.30 a.m., 4.30 – 6.30 a.m. (Friday) and 10.30 a.m. – 12.30 p.m. (Friday).

Once again I was lucky and dodged 20 minutes of my guard in the second two hours. The clocks went on 20 minutes at midnight. They also went on 20 minutes the night before so we are now 2 hours 40 minutes in front of Greenwich Mean Time. Taking into consideration the extra hour's summertime you have at home, makes us 1 hour 40 minutes in front of you.

The 4.30 – 6.30 a.m. guard was the worst and it was with only the greatest difficulty that I prevented myself falling to sleep.

Breakfast this morning (which we had to have a bit later) was porridge, some evil smelling fish (refused with thanks) and coffee. Dinner was the same as yesterday except that for dessert we had some unsweetened rice pudding for a change!

Since dinner I have been snoozing most of the time, making up for last night. John's been doing the same thing as he was also on guard last night.

Tea this evening was bread and jam, pickles and corned beef. It is now 5 minutes to 6 and it is getting quite dark, so will not be able to write much more tonight.

I am getting more homesick and missing you more every day now darling. I do wish this damn war would end. However, it's no good looking on the dark side – perhaps I may get on a draft going to Britain when we arrive at our destination! You never know.

Saturday: Got up a bit later this morning, just after 6.30 a.m. The reason being that we were on an open deck last night and also slung our hammocks instead of putting them on the floor. I had a very good night – woke up very comfortable.

Had my usual shower then partook of breakfast which consisted of porridge, sausages and tomatoes and tea. Up on deck afterwards and lay in the shade as the sun was very strong despite being only 9 a.m.

Paraded at 10 a.m. and had a very interesting talk on India by a Sergeant, mainly about the various common diseases there. I don't think I will take any risks like buying fruit from natives, etc.

From 11 – 12 noon sat in shade on deck again and made a few notes with the help of John on our Scarborough days for that book which I was always talking about. I think I will try and make a start on it when we arrive at our destination.

Letter No. 7

Dinner was meat, beans and potatoes followed by plum duff. The dinners really are the worst meals we get on board. Uninteresting and unappetizing.

It was terrifically hot during the afternoon and except for a little reading I am afraid I did nothing but sleep. I think we must be near the equator.

Tea was bread, butter, jam and baked beans. Quite nice, I suppose, but it's impossible to enjoy meals down below. It's like trying to eat in a Turkish bath!

The time is now 5.45 p.m. and although the sun is setting it is still very warm. I think today is really the hottest day we have known. If it were possible, I would sit in a cold bath all day.

Well, darling, I think I will have a pipe-full of tobacco and try to get cool. I might write a little more this evening.

Sunday: As you will see, darling, I did not write any more yesterday evening - mainly because it got dark so quickly.

We slept at the forward part of the ship last night (on deck) but I did not sleep very well owing to the intense heat. I listened to the six o'clock news at 9 o'clock, and then had a little chat with John and Joe before going to sleep.

Up at 6.30 a.m. this morning. Had the usual shower and breakfast was porridge, bacon and eggs and coffee. Quite enjoyable. Played a short game of cards until Parade time at 10 o'clock when, much to my disgust, I was detailed for Church Parade. We had a very short talk on India and found out that you could probably get out there for £17. However, as we don't know what is happening yet, it is no good thinking of such things.

I made my way up to where the Church Service was being held, but as nobody seemed to want me I buzzed off and played cards for the rest of the morning. By the way, we saw quite a lot of flying fishes this morning – hundreds of them. They look like large dragon flies, but they actually only skim the water.

Dinner was quite good, despite the heat 'down below'. The usual meat, potatoes and beans seemed to be a bit better cooked and we had some very tasty sliced pineapple (tinned) for dessert.

Played cards all the afternoon and had amazing luck as I seemed to win most of the time. John treated me to a bar of Cadbury's and a bottle of lemonade "seeing as 'ow I was broke" – and will probably continue to be until next pay day (next Friday).

Tea was quite good. Bread and butter, jam, a beautiful orange and haddock. They seem to be dishing up better food now that our journey must be nearing its end.

The time is now 5.45 p.m. and it is rapidly getting dark. I saw, on the news bulletin, that you have put your clocks forward another hour. So, although we are 3 hours in front of Greenwich Mean Time, we are only one hour in front of you now.

Must close for now, my darling. The bugler is playing some awful air which means a quarter of an hour to blackout and I must go downstairs and get my hammock.

All my love.

Monday: Had a troublesome evening yesterday trying to find a place to put our hammocks. It started raining about 6 p.m. which limited likely places considerably as the rain easily found its way through the canvas covering on the open decks. Finally, as we couldn't stand, at any price, sleeping down below in the heat, we took a chance and slept in the canteen, despite the fact that Orders had come out that day forbidding it. Consequently we had our names taken by an officer in the morning. However, we are not worrying, and nothing has happened yet.

Breakfast was porridge and liver, but I contented myself with a cup of tea and a plate of porridge. I am getting a bit browned off with grub aboard this boat. Played cards till Parade and continued from 11 – 12 noon. Dinner was awful, the usual stuff with terrible tapioca for dessert.

Continued our cards all the afternoon. There was a crossing-the-line ceremony at 4 p.m., but, as I mentioned before, I am not struck on Army humour. Tea was bread, butter, jam and boiled haddock. After tea I had a shave and then brought my hammock up on deck. Once again we got shifted and it started to rain, but the weather cleared up and we slept on top of some rafts, and I had a very good night.

Tuesday: Was up soon after 6 a.m. and had my usual shower. Breakfast was bread and butter, porridge and fish. But owing to the late arrival of the porridge and the horrible smell of the fish, I contented myself with bread and butter and coffee.

Came up on deck and I am now sitting on a raft writing this letter. The time is only 8.30 a.m. so there's not much more to write about yet. I will continue later.

(Later) Played cards till 10 a.m. During the Parade Hour we had a very interesting signalling talk by a Sergeant concerning the heliograph – an instrument that sends signals by the reflection of the sun's rays. Its range is 96 miles!

From 11 – 12 noon played cards. When we went down below, we found, much to our astonishment, that the portholes were open – the first time during the voyage. I don't know why they never opened them before, perhaps they thought they were too near the waterline. However, rather late in the day it seems, someone had a brilliant idea.

Dinner was the usual meat, potato, but with greens this time. Stewed fruit followed and when I complained about my portion I received a bit more. My second surprise today!

All the afternoon we played cards again sitting in the shade. The only way - although a pleasant way - of spending a hot afternoon.

Tea was bread, jam and hash. After tea I tried my hand at chess, but was rather easily beaten. However, I intend to improve during my stay abroad. John went down below and brought up our hammocks. We laid them out on the rafts as yesterday and after a lot of 'gassing' went to sleep.

Wednesday: Up at about 6.30 a.m.   Had usual shower and breakfast was quite good - sausage and egg. During the morning except for the Parade we alternated between chess and cards.

The sea is wonderfully calm now - hardly a ripple. Also most of the day there is a nice cool breeze and the last few days have been the most enjoyable (if that word can be used) of the trip. I must tell you, by the way, that I am endeavouring to grow a moustache. Nothing permanent, mark you, but we get up to all sorts of tricks to break the monotony. It's getting on quite nicely, and if this war lasts a few months I shall have a real 'walrus' and look a 'pukka sahib'.

Dinner was as usual with some nice plum duff for dessert. By the way we have minerals with our meals again now.

We played cards all the afternoon till tea which was not very exciting as it consisted of fish. It soon got dark after, so John brought the hammocks up and we settled ourselves in our usual rafts. We chatted away about home, etc., till quite late and then fell asleep.

Thursday: Up just after 6 a.m. and had a shower before breakfast. I had a good helping of porridge as I didn't fancy the fish they were serving. During breakfast John and I got a shock. The section Sergeant called out our names and told us we were on fatigues today and tomorrow for sleeping in the canteen against Orders. We had to report at 8.30 a.m. down one of the hatches to the bowels of the ship - a good distance, even below our mess decks (which are low enough). We wormed our way through a small hole and gingerly climbed down a long ladder. It was just like descending into hell; the heat was terrible. And the sweat pouring off our bodies made us all look like a lot of demons.

However, owing to the interruption of Parade hour, we were not down there too long. But even then it was bad enough – we had to shift large sacks of flour from one end of the hold to the other. We finished the morning at 11.30 a.m. and immediately had a shower as we certainly needed it – caked in flour and sweat.

Before dinner I managed to wash a shirt and handkerchiefs and so saved myself money. Dinner was meat, Indian turnips (!) (which I refused) and potato followed by stewed fruit.

We played a short game of cards till 2 p.m. and then went down the hold again. We had to work harder than we did in the morning. It is really an awful job. It was amazing how the sweat poured off me. I was only wearing shorts, but they were completely soaked. I was certainly glad when 4 o'clock came. I can't say I am looking forward to a similar day tomorrow.

We had another shower and, once again, felt clean and tidy. Tea was bread, jam, pickles and an orange. Quite good.

The time is now 6 p.m. (we put our watches on another 30 minutes last night – 1 hour 50 minutes in front of you) and the sun has just fallen like a big ball of fire into the sea; so it will soon be dark. (There is hardly a twilight in this part of the world). I must try and write during the day tomorrow as I have a lot to tell you, but will have to close now.

Friday: Up at 6.30 a.m. and had my shower as soon as I got 'down below'. Breakfast was tea, porridge and fish again! After breakfast I went up on deck till 8.30 a.m. when I reported for fatigues again. John was lucky and managed to dodge his, but I was finished at 10.30 a.m. and the work wasn't so hard as yesterday. So it wasn't too bad.

However, I was caked with flour and when I finished looked more like a loaf of bread than a human being. From 11 to 12 noon I read an American magazine which I found, and dinner consisted of meat, greens and potato (for a change!) with rice pudding. But the mineral water was quite nice.

This afternoon we were paid 5/- and another 10/- which we will receive in Indian money.

I shall have to end this letter definitely now, darling, as we shall arrive at our destination in a few days. I could post this ashore and maybe it wouldn't be censored, but I think it best not to for the following reasons:-

(a) I have written this letter with the answer in mind and have not given any information away.

(b) You will probably get it earlier if I post it on the boat. It will probably catch the next boat home.

(c) I don't know when I would be able to post this ashore, as we may be bundled straight on a train and have a few more days journeying.

I will, however, darling, continue writing and directly we get to our station send you another letter. If possible I will send you a cablegram.

I think my letters will be more interesting in future, darling, as, besides the censoring being less strict, I shall be able to name the places which we visited on our voyage. I shall also send you one or two pamphlets which will describe the places and give you a better picture of our time ashore.

Probably I shall have to send this letter in 2 or even 3 envelopes, as it is really a terrific bundle when put together. But I will number them on the envelopes so that you will know which is first. I wonder what the censor officer thinks when he sees my letters – I bet he doesn't trouble to read them all through!

I hope this doesn't take too long to reach you, but if there is an air mail for the forces – as I think there is – it should be only a matter of weeks and not months before you receive this.

I hope you are still keeping fit my love. I notice that air-raids on London have eased off lately; I pray it will continue to be pretty quiet.

I am quite fit, darling, although perhaps a bit lazy after a few weeks of comparative idleness – but I shall soon get that knocked out of me I expect. I also keep quite cheerful, although I periodically get fits of depression and curse everyone and everything connected with the war. I always think of you every day, especially as I lie awake in 'bed' at

nights. I love you very much darling. Don't forget to write to me often and send me any new photographs of yourself; and don't forget to keep as cheerful as possible. The sun is just setting and very soon now it will be dark, so I must close. I will hand this letter in in the morning to our section officer.

All my love for ever; Your loving husband.

PART FOUR

IN INDIA AND MALAYA

Gnr/Sig. Berry HW
974063
5th Field Regiment R.A.
Nowshera
India

8th May 1941

My darling wife,

   This is my first letter to you from India. My last letter, if you received it, was written on the boat two days before we docked. I have quite a lot to tell you in this letter, but before I start I must tell you that I love you with all my heart and am always thinking of you. I hope you are still well and are keeping as cheerful as possible, darling.

We arrived in this country last Monday (three days ago) about 10 a.m., but we did not disembark until 2 p.m. We hung about on the dock under cover from the sun until about 5 p.m. when we boarded a train. They were very primitive coaches – wooden seats, etc. – and, as there were no bunks, we guessed that we could not be going too far. Whilst we were waiting to start we were issued with one blanket, a mug and plate, and a piece of string (which nobody even yet knows what it is really for). We got rather impatient hanging about in the train, but finally at about 7 p.m. it started moving. We didn't get much chance to see the countryside as it soon got dark, but several of the stations reminded me of Ealing Broadway as there were electric trains as well as steam trains running, and when the 'electrics' flashed by they looked just like the District Line trains. The journey was made rather entertaining by the presence of numerous insects which rushed across the floor of the compartment. However, we are getting a bit more used to 'creepy crawly' things by now.

   We arrived at our destination – which was a place called DEOLALI (from which I am writing this letter) about 2 a.m. Much to our surprise they wanted an 'Advance Party' consisting of several officers, sergeants and four gunners to go on ahead. As they happened to come to our compartment for the four, the four of us who were at Scarborough together volunteered. We were lucky – we got a free ride to the camp and when we got there nobody seemed to want us, so we had a meal and picked some beds in a barrack room before the others arrived. However, it was 4 a.m. before we got to bed.

We didn't get up until about 9 a.m. (Tuesday) and then we had a look around. It is hard to describe this place as everything is so different from England. However, it is a huge camp covering, I would say, over a square mile. It includes a large internment camp in which are some Italians and Germans. They are, however, guarded by Indian soldiers.

This place is a kind of Depot and drafts are only here a few days before being split up and sent to different units. We were divided into 4 drafts and the whole five of us Scarboroughites: John, Joe, Jack (whom you met when you first came to Watford) Steve (who came to Mrs. Tucker's one night) and myself all managed to get on the same draft. We are all going to the 5th Field Regiment at Nowshera*. If you get a map of India you will find this place on the North-West Frontier about 20 miles from the Khyber Pass – so we should get some excitement.

*Now in Pakistan

It is a Regular Army Unit, so whether we stay there or move to some theatre of war remains to be seen. We shall be going off from here any day, and, as Nowshera is about 1,000 miles away, it will take us 2 or 3 days' train journey!

We don't do much all day at the moment as l) It is too hot between the hours of 11 a.m. and 4 p.m. and 2) We are just waiting to be moved. We have a very nice barrack room although it is nothing like we have ever seen before. About 60 people sleep in here, but, of course, it is very open, so that doesn't matter. The room is about 60 ft long and about 18 ft wide. Except for the tiles and beams the whole hut is made of straw matting; the windows, of course, have no glass. It is lovely and cool compared with the heat outside and, of course, that is all the structure is for. We live a very lazy life as we all have a 'boy'. He cleans our kit, does errands, etc., all for 8 annas a week (about 8d)!

Yesterday evening we went to the town travelling in a kind of landau and had a look round the native bazaars. There are plenty of bargains to be had and if I am out here long I should like to buy some silks like table covers for our future home. I thought of buying one and sending it to you right away, but the chances are it would be lost. I did, however, buy a lovely leather wallet for 12 annas and a shaving mirror and three handkerchiefs for 8 annas. It's all very interesting and different in a way, but give me England any day.

I shall not write such long letters now, darling, as I have to pay for postage and weight counts and, if the letter gets lost, you lose a long letter. The best thing I can do is to write regularly once a week and then, if only fifty per cent get through, you will get quite a number.

Another idea – before I start each future letter I will put a short note at the start explaining what was in my two previous letters so that if some are lost you will know roughly what was in them by the next letter. I am afraid letters take about two months to get home, so we will have a hard job answering each others' letters. However, we mustn't grumble.

The next letter I send you, darling, will probably be from the unit at Nowshera. Meanwhile this afternoon I am going to the Post Office (which I located last night, but too late) and send you a telegram telling you I am safe and, if possible, giving you my address.

I will therefore close now, my darling. I will tell you more about life in this country in my next letter. I haven't heard from you yet, darling. I hope I do so soon. I haven't heard anything about this one free cablegram a month which you mentioned before I left. Well, my darling, au revoir for now. I love you very much and every day I look at your photographs which I always carry. I am almost eager now to get into action and help finish the war so that I can get back. Do you still love me? All my love for ever.

173

P.S. You should get my telegram in about 4 days – I can't afford a cablegram. I am enclosing a pamphlet which we got at our last port of call which, as you probably guess, was Cape Town.

5th Field Regt. RA

Nowshera

15th May 1941

My darling wife and sweetheart,

Although I have headed this letter as being posted from Nowshera, we have not moved yet and are still at Deolali, near Bombay.

Every day we have been expecting to go, but as in England, we are still waiting about until something happens.

How are you, my darling? Last Thursday I sent you a telegram in which I said 'O.K. Write 5th Field, Nowshera, Love Harry'. I expect you have got it by now – I wonder if you had any trouble interpreting it? I shouldn't be at all surprised if you haven't sent me one back and it is waiting for me at Nowshera. I shall be glad when we move.

Nothing much has happened since I last wrote to you. Every morning we parade at 9 a.m. and then are dismissed for the rest of the day. These last few days, however, they have started gym at 6.30 in the mornings and now we are going to have lectures for an hour or so in the mornings.

This place, actually, is a Rest Camp – a place where troops have a holiday for a few weeks during the summer after, perhaps, being stationed at an uncomfortable spot. All I can think is that, if this is a rest camp and is supposed to be a cool place, what must the other places be like?

Between 9 a.m. and 4.30 p.m. the heat is almost unbearable, and it is impossible to do anything except stay in one's bungalow and either read, write, sleep or play cards. Sometimes it is too hot to do anything but sleep.

There is absolutely nothing to do of an evening. There is a very small cinema just outside the camp which has ordinary chairs for seats (I went there a few days a go and saw 'Sergeant Maddon') but otherwise we have to make our own amusements – mainly cards! To add to our discomfort we haven't been paid since last Wednesday week, but are hoping to be paid tomorrow when I will post this letter.

The only advantages here are that it is possible, for a small sum, to get everything done for you (if that is an advantage) and a fairly good canteen. Actually, the canteen is quite the best one I have seen in the Army, or expected to see. It is housed in a long bungalow similar to the bungalows we sleep in (in my last letter I said they were only 60 ft long; I meant 160 ft long) and contains pukka French polished tables and chairs at which we are served by smart Indians! It is almost like being in the Corner House!

Most things are ridiculously cheap. Mineral waters, which we drink all day, are 1 anna (1d) a bottle (if we have the money) and Players are ten for 3 annas, Woodbines 10 for 2 annas and other lesser known English makes (quite good actually) 50 for 5 annas! Tins of fruit are only 5 annas and the more expensive things are chocolate (3 annas) and, I believe, beer, although I haven't had any since I have been in India. By the way, one of the cheapest things we can get in the canteen is chicken and chips, roll and butter, for 6 annas!

Well, my darling, I regret there is nothing much more I can describe to you. The country is very barren round here, so it is not possible to give you a picture of it. I can tell you, quite definitely, that my views which I had on this country before I left England have not changed. I think India's a lousy country and shall be glad when we leave.

I love you very much, darling and every day I look at your photographs and imagine I am with you. I shall never forget, for a moment, the happy times we had together and am looking forward to the time when we continue our life together.

I will write to you directly we get to Nowshera or any other destination to which we might go. I shall be glad when I get a letter from you – I shall be annoyed if the Army lose them. Will close for now, my darling, and please believe me when I say I am always thinking of you and love you with all my heart.

Remember me to all at home. My love for ever.

Nowshera,
India
31st May 1941

My darling wife,

I love you.

Before I start telling you the news, I shall have to explain why there is no summary of my two previous letters at the top, as promised. Unfortunately someone 'swiped' my former writing pad on which I had, in shorthand, the contents of my previous letters from India. So I can only tell you briefly what was in my letters dated about May 8th (No. 8) and May 16th (No.9). I described our safe arrival in India and how we arrived at Deolali, a kind of Depot and/or Rest Camp. I described how we Scarborough-ites had all managed to get into the same draft going to Nowshera and gave a picture of the uninteresting scenery round here.

I will now commence this letter.

As you will probably notice, it is a fortnight ago since I wrote my last letter and although I don't suppose it will make much difference to the time you actually receive it, I don't want you to think I didn't trouble to write out of pure laziness.

Since my last letter we have been expecting (and fervently hoping) that we would be moving to Nowshera, but despite several 'alerts' we are still in this God-forsaken hole. I very badly want to get to Nowshera as that was the address I put on my telegram and perhaps there may be a telegram from you there. If so, I hope you are not worried because I have not replied – if I had known we were going to be at this dump so long I would have sent it from here. But, as I said before, we thought we were here for two or three days only.

We hang about here just as we did at home. They still don't seem to be able to make up their minds. There is practically nothing fresh to tell you. Each day the programme is the same, namely Reveille 6 a.m., P.T. 6.15 a.m., Breakfast 7.30 a.m., Parade 9 a.m.; followed by marching drill or something similar till 10 a.m., 'Siesta' 10 a.m. – 1.30 p.m., Dinner 1.30 pm., Parade 2.30 p.m. followed by a lecture to 3.30 p.m. Tea 4.30 p.m., Supper 6 p.m., Lights Out 10.15 p.m.

Most of the day when not on duty we either play cards, sleep or read. We very seldom go out of an evening as there is nothing to go out for. About once a week we go to the 'Garrison Talkies'. I went yesterday and saw 'Seven Sinners' with Marlene Dietrich. But it is impossible to really enjoy the film as there is a break every time they start a new reel.

The funniest thing is that they have the interval slap in the middle of the film – usually just as things are getting exciting!

How are you keeping, my sweet? I do wish I could see you or speak to you for a few minutes – I miss you terribly. I'm glad to see that London's been pretty free of air-raids during the last three weeks. I hope the good work continues.

<u>Sunday, June 1st</u> Nothing much to tell you today. Slept most of the day and in the evening from about 8 to 9.30 p.m. we played cards. I'm sorry there's nothing more I can tell you, my love, but things are really very dull and uninteresting.

<u>Monday, June 2nd</u> Our draft was on duty today and I found myself a Camp policeman. I was on patrol from 9 a.m. to 1 p.m. and then I was finished for the day. I had a short walk around the camp for about an hour and a half with another fellow and we went through a nearby village which is out-of-bounds in the normal way. It was quite interesting as it was a genuine native village and there were no white people about. The natives live more like animals than human beings and the smell in parts was terrible. We walked down to the local river and there saw the whole population washing themselves, their clothes and bullocks in the water. At first glance it looked like an open-air Lido. Have I mentioned before

that most of the carts are pulled by bullocks? They are much more common than horses.

We returned by about 10.30 a.m. so I 'hid' until 1 o'clock when my spell of duty was over.

There was a rumour going round today that we were moving on Tuesday, but, once again, it proved a false alarm. I am getting impatient and the thought that there might be a telegram at Nowshera makes me seethe. I do wish they could get a move on. You see, darling, you might get rather fuddled if I sent you another telegram giving my address here. Besides taking a lot of explaining, we might move directly I sent it and then things would be more chaotic than ever. I think I will post this letter Friday so will continue daily till then. Meanwhile I must try and drop lines to all the people to whom I promised to write.

All my love for the present (By the way, I have just realised it's Whit Monday today – what a life!)

<u>Tuesday June 3rd</u> Our draft was split into two on the 9 o'clock parade this morning – half on digging trenches (to keep the water away from the bungalows when the monsoons break any day now) and the other half, which I accompanied, sent on a route march. There was a cool breeze blowing so the walk wasn't too uncomfortable. I think however, we are all getting used to the heat.

During the afternoon, for about two hours we had a miniature cyclone and sand storm. The wind whistled and howled and great clouds of sand tore across the camp. When the storm finally subsided everything, including our blankets, etc. inside the bungalows was covered with sand. The sky has also been clouded a lot today and I distinctly smelt rain. It is surprising how easy it is to smell rain in a place like this when everything has been bone dry for months. During the afternoon I got a book from the library and read for the rest of the evening.

<u>Wednesday June 4th</u> Woke up at 6 a.m. to find it had been raining during the night. The sky was very overcast and there was a lovely smell of freshness in the air – more like an English summer. The monsoons haven't definitely broken yet – the rain comes down

in torrents when they do – but it has dribbled nearly all day today. We had some good news today. On Friday we are moving to Nowshera and so I will be able to see whether there are any telegrams for me from you.

The journey, however, is going to take 4 or 5 days by train! They certainly have a good railway system in this country. Will close for the moment as it is 5.30 p.m. and I want a shower before supper at 6 p.m. I love you, my darling.

Thursday June 5th There was no early morning parade today as we had to pack our things and wear our packs for a 'dress rehearsal' for tomorrow. Consequently we had a little longer in bed.

At 9.30 a.m. we went on the usual route march which lasted until 11.15 a.m. We had plenty of rests however, so it wasn't too bad. We didn't parade again until 3.15 p.m. when we were paid. We were all solemnly warned not to spend all our money tonight as we would require it for the train journey. It is surprising how the money does go. By the time we have paid the dhobi (laundryman) and boot boys and other similar debts we are usually left with about 5 out of our original ten rupees. I am stopping in this evening purposely to save money. If I go out I shall only go to the pictures and have some supper afterwards.

So, darling, this brings me up to date and my last letter from Deolali. It's been a luxurious and easy life really, but I have been getting rather bored. I shall be glad to get to Nowshera where we may do some work and where there may be a telegram from you. I hope you are still in the best of health, my love. You must believe me when I tell you that I am always thinking of you and am always dreaming of the time when we are together again. Please remember me to everyone. All my love for ever.

P.S. Friday: Just a last note to tell you we are moving tonight definitely at 6.15 p.m. I will write again directly I arrive at Nowshera.

15th June 1941

Sig. Berry H.W.
974063, 73rd
Bty.,
5th Field Reg. R.A.
Shinkiara Camp
Abbottabad
Nr.India

My darling wife,

As you will see from the above address, I have now moved from Deolali and am now with my Regiment.

I have had two very pleasant surprises today – a telegram and a letter from you. The telegram which read 'OKAY CABLEGRAM RECEIVED LOVE GWEN BERRY' was received here on May 28th, and it has been waiting for me. Your letter was dated 7th April, so the service isn't too bad. The only trouble is that it is numbered No. 4 so your previous letters have gone astray. It is maddening in a way, but perhaps they will eventually turn up.

Darling it is wonderful to hear from you again. I hope I don't have to wait too long before I get another letter.

Before I start answering your letter, I expect you would like to know what the place is like and what I am doing. As you will see from the address, we are not at Nowshera as the Regiment is under canvas for three months. We are miles from any town and on the North-West Frontier at the foot of the Himalayan mountains. We are not near the Khyber Pass, but on the border between the N.W. Frontier Province and Kashmir. Kashmir, as you may know, is the beauty spot of India and so we have a bit of it (the beauty) here. The scenery isn't exactly thrilling, but it is certainly better than if we were on the Khyber Pass.

We left Deolali on the 6th June when I posted my last letter to you and, contrary to all expectations, the journey took only 3 days. Life on the train wasn't too bad.

The food, of course, was not very good, nor was the sleeping accommodation. But as we had only four in a compartment we weren't overcrowded.

Our main discomfort was the 'creepy crawly' thing, cockroaches nearly as big as elephants which crawled about compartment. We arrived at our final station (I forget the name) on Monday June 9th. (I've just looked in my diary and found I had written the name of the station down. It is Havelian – I may have spelt it wrong, but you might find it on a railway map of India.) Outside the station were dozens of Army vehicles to cart us off to our regiment. But as the road was tricky they decided to postpone the journey until the following morning. We managed to scrounge a cup of 'cha' in the station refreshment room and then had to sleep as best we could where we could. I was lucky enough to scramble into a lorry, but the majority of fellows had to sleep on the platform.

We got up at 5 a.m. and had breakfast – three boiled eggs, bread and butter and a cup of tea and then commenced our journey to the camp – about 36 miles away. The ride was quite exciting. You remember those tours through the French Maritime Alps – well it was similar to that. The road wound up and up a mountain with a sheer drop on one side. But I'm afraid I didn't enjoy it as I did in France when I was with you.

Two hours later we arrived at the Camp. It is situated at the top of a number of hills on which have been built temporary roads. They twist around so much that to reach a place about a hundred yards away, one has to walk over a mile.

I share a tent with 5 other fellows and although it is a bit crowded and primitive, it is not at all bad considering. The food is very good (!!)

We have such things as porridge with milk, 2 fried eggs, bacon and chips for breakfast, and meat, fried onions and well-cooked vegetables for dinner and supper.

'Afters' at supper time is also 'tres bon' – bread pudding, apricots and custard, etc. They use plenty of sugar here and I enjoy eating. I usually have a second helping of dessert.

We had a very big and pleasant surprise on our second day here. We went to visit the MO and when we arrived who should we meet but a fellow from Scarborough who was in our Squad. To our amazement we found that, with the exception of about 2 fellows, all 24 Squad is here. They left England about 3 months before we did. What a coincidence! They are not in our regiment (there are two regiments here), their unit is a new one which is being trained to take our place on the frontier so we can move elsewhere. Last Wednesday we had an interview with a Captain and I managed to get a job in the Battery Office again. I am glad because signallers don't seem to have a very good time here. The Sergeant-Major said I was finished with signalling. They seem to be impressed with the fact that I can write shorthand and type fast. The daily programme is as follows:

5.30 a.m. Reveille: 6 – 7 a.m. Parade and classes: 8.30 a.m. Breakfast.

9.30 – 12.30 p.m. Parades, etc. 6 p.m. Supper.

As you will see, usually all work finishes at 12.30 p.m. as it is then too hot and everyone goes to sleep. I get into the office soon after 6 a.m. and I can finish by about 12.30 p.m. But I usually stop on a little longer.

Well, darling, I think that's all I can tell you about this place. We have to make our own amusements, of course, although a lorry takes fellows to the pictures twice a week – 30 miles away. It is a dreary dump and I shall be glad when we move. We still have natives to do all the dirty work, so we almost live the life of gentlemen.

In answer to your letter, I am glad you are still well, but I wish your first three letters hadn't gone astray. I hope I don't receive only one out of every four letters from you in future. I see you got my letter I posted whilst we were in port – I wonder if you got the one I smuggled off the train? And the ones posted from Freetown and Capetown?

I expect by now you know everything about life on the ship, so I won't repeat it. It seems funny to read you are sitting in front of a big fire when, at the moment, I would like to sit on a block of ice! I am glad NAPSOPA* have remembered me – I wonder if I shall receive the cigs? Don't bother to try and tell me any news as we have a radio here and papers with stale news. (There is, of course,

182

no piano here. I'm afraid I shall forget how to play!) I wonder if you got my letter in which I mentioned the anniversary of our engagement? I'm glad you are still keeping in touch with Eileen and Aubrey. I wonder if you have visited them yet? I <u>must</u> write to them soon.

My Trade Union at the time

    Well, darling, I think that's all for now. I hope you are still fit and still in love with me. Working in an office here reminds me of Watford. Despite the fact that I was in the Army, they were the happiest days of my life. How I used to look forward to the evenings, when I would be seeing you. I do wish I could see you occasionally now, darling. I am more in love with you than ever. I think of you continuously. I hope this damn war will soon be over.

    Supper is now being 'served' (actually served too). I love you with all my heart. I have been faithful to you darling, and will always be faithful. My love for ever.

Shinkiari Camp
Nr. Abbottabad
NWFP
India
28th June 1941

My darling, beautiful wife,
    I love you.
    I hope you are still keeping well, my sweet, and still love me. I think of you more and more every day and every afternoon during the 'siesta' I just lie back on my mattress and think of you. I miss you so much darling and shall be glad when the war is over. Now that Russia is in too, perhaps I shall be home sooner than I expected. I hope Russia helps us to win the war for if I had to go years without seeing you darling I think I would go mad.

I had another surprise last Saturday. Just as I posted my letter to you another letter arrived for me from you (Letter No. 3). I have been eagerly awaiting the first two letters, but they haven't turned up yet. I hope they haven't gone astray.

There is not much news to tell you darling since my last letter. I had a letter from Dad which arrived at the same time as yours last Saturday. He seems to have been keeping in touch with you and says you may go to Huntingdon for a week-end. I wonder if you have gone yet?

Life here for me is pretty much the same each day. I get in the office about 6.15 a.m., break off at 7.30 a.m. for breakfast, back to the office until about 12.30 p.m. when I have dinner. Then I go and sleep for the afternoon in my tent.

I usually return to the office just before 6 p.m. while the Guard is mounting in case anyone I have detailed hasn't turned up. Then I have supper and am finished unless I am on duty that day. The weather here has been terrifically hot lately – well over 100 degrees F. in the shade. It very seldom rains and when it does is accompanied by a storm. For a short time everything smells fresh, but in a few minutes the sun has vaporised the moisture and everything is dry and sandy again. I live in a perpetual bath of sweat (which is a good thing I suppose). The trouble is that we have no showers or any decent form of sanitation here. Water is fetched up to the camp every day by pack mules and kept in a kind of small swimming pool. To have a wash or a bath one gets a bucket-full of water and carries on as best as possible. After feeling a little more fresh and clean one dons one's clothes and 10 minutes later is as dirty and sticky as ever. What a life!

The food is still pretty good and that's the only thing that keeps my spirits up. A case of the stomach helping the mind. A couple of days ago I felt rather washed out and thought I was going to have malaria. However, in the evening I bought a pint of beer (the second since I have been in this country – getting quite a boozer!) and went straight to bed. I didn't sleep much as I wrapped myself up and simply poured sweat out. But I felt much better in the morning and have felt all right since.

Since I have answered your letter No. 4 I don't think there is much I can reply to in your previous letter.

It seems cruel to think of your writing to me thinking I was in England when, all the time, I was somewhere in the Atlantic. I see you mentioned holidays and that you were having one week in June. I wonder if you are on it now and if so whether you went anywhere? I wish you could pop over here and see me for a week – but I wouldn't wish you to stay here. It's not the kind of place for a woman to live in. I'm afraid I see nothing romantic or beautiful about India as you suggest; rather my description of it – filth and dirt – is more appropriate.

I hope you don't make a habit of getting on the wrong train of an evening – you see what happens when I'm not with you! And I expect you fall all over the place as you walk along. You make me feel very homesick when you say it is 'teeming with rain'. What wouldn't I give to be waiting for a bus to Ealing Broadway with the rain oozing down my neck. Lovely thoughts.

Well, darling, I think that covers everything. I am hoping that perhaps I shall receive a telegram from you soon – it's nice to receive something that you have written only 3 days previously. I could send you one if I could afford it, but 5 rupees minus 2 rupees and a bit doesn't leave much. I will now finish this letter, put it in an envelope, kiss the envelope and then give it to the Indian Orderly with $3\frac{1}{2}$ annas and say 'Post this letter immediately' and he will take a leisurely stroll to the post office (about a mile away) whenever he feels like it. Don't forget to write to your husband a lot and post your letters on ships that don't sink. Remember me to everyone and tell them I am coming back to you soon.

All my love for ever.

My darling wife,

I love you.

I hope you are still keeping well and that you still love me. Just after I posted my last letter I received two more letters from you – Nos. 1 and 2. It seems that directly I post you a letter I get one back from you.

There's still nothing much I can tell you. We are still stuck in this dump and nothing particularly interesting has happened during the last week.

There is now an open-air cinema in the camp, but I have not been yet. The sound apparatus is so loud that it can be heard all over the camp. Last night they were showing 'South of Pago Pago' and the sound of tom-toms assailed us all the evening. We could almost imagine we were in an oriental country!! Certainly I have seen or heard nothing yet in India which is supposed to portray the glamour of the East – it is just dry, hot and damned uninteresting. No snake-charmers, no native music, no nothing. There is one thing, however, that makes this country different from any other I have been in, and that is INSECTS. Thousands of 'em! Ranging from the ordinary common or garden house fly, of which there are about 10 times as many as there are in England, to whacking big scorpion spiders and centipedes which can put one in agony for a day if they take a dislike to you.

The other evening I went to my tent and lit the hurricane lamp. I could see there were quite a number of moth-like insects about, but did not take much notice of them. However, I went to speak to John in the next tent and, when I got back there were literally thousands of them swarming round the lamp and in my mosquito net. I managed to clear them away from one side of the net, crawled into bed and then yelled for John to come and put the light out. If I had attempted to do so they would have got into my mosquito netting. John and another much amused chap came across to my tent, but when they got there they were dumbfounded. There were even more moths and they were lying about an inch thick all round the lamp. They did not fancy entering and turning out the lamp, so they got a long pole and pulled it out followed by millions of the insects. They left it alight outside the tent which helped as the attraction kept the moths away from the tents. I learned afterwards that they were Monsoon flies – they were anything up to an inch long. The other day we caught a centipede about 5" long in the office. I haven't yet seen a big scorpion spider, but they are quite as big as this sheet of paper and move like lightning. I can honestly say I would rather be in a London blitz than have these things crawling about at night. However, I am usually careful about tucking in my net properly and searching my bed before I turn in.

You say in your first letter that if there is anything I need to let you know. Well, darling, I would like a prepaid telegram from you occasionally (if you could afford it).

I know there's not much to say, but it is nice to be only three days away from you and not three months. You understand what I mean, don't you darling?

By the time you have received this I expect you will have finished both your holidays – you have had one already. I wonder what kind of a time you had and where you went. I do hope you had as good a time as possible. I also expect that by the time you get this we won't be in this part of India. However, your letters will always find me if you address them to Nowshera. By the way don't waste money sending them by air-mail as they get here no quicker.

I hear that another mail-boat has come in so I shouldn't be surprised if I get some more letters from you directly I post this. I hope so.

Well, darling, the time is just 2 o'clock so I think I will go and have my afternoon's siesta. I will add a little more to this letter this evening and then post it. I shall be thinking of you all afternoon. I love you.

Tuesday: I'm sorry darling, I didn't finish this letter yesterday as promised, but there was such a lot of work to do in the office that I did not finish until 9.30 p.m. when I went straight to bed. I don't mind really as there is nothing else to do. Will close now, sweet, and give this to one of the native orderlies to post. All my love for ever.

xxxxxxxxxxx (I'll risk these being censored).

20th July 1941   Shinkiara
Camp

                                                                    NWFP
                                                                    India

Summary of previous letters posted included No.14 posted on July 14th which did not reach home. i.e.

Received your letters No. 6 & 7 which I answered. Hoped you would be careful on your bike. Description of Camp Cinema which I visited and saw 'Foreign Correspondent', very good. Hoped that Russia would hurry up and beat Germany so I could get back to you. No news to tell you from here.

My darling wife,

I am writing this letter in bed – the time is 8.30 p.m. and as the only light is from a Hurricane Lamp and I am under a Mosquito net which dims the light, I hope you will not mind if my writing is a little erratic. It is very hard to see.

I had a big surprise yesterday darling. I received your Air Mail letter No. 11. In my last few letters I have been telling you not to send by Air Mail as it was no quicker – but this one certainly seems to have arrived much earlier although not quite so quickly as you thought. It has actually gained on your previous letters – I have not yet received Nos. 5, 8, 9 and 10. But I am sure they will turn up.

Darling, it is certainly nice to have a letter from you so up-to-date. It makes you seem much closer to me. John also received an Air Mail card from his mother on the same day. I think you were lucky in this particular instance and just caught a plane – or they have improved the service.

Thank you for giving a resumé of your previous letters. I had read most of it except about the Blitz and the office being bombed. It seems to have been a very bad night – you are a funny girl the way you sleep through them. I expect I shall know more about it when your previous letters arrive. I'm glad you were not sleeping at the office, darling. I wonder if anyone was hurt? I'm glad you are still writing to me every day. I've explained in my previous letters why I do not – there is absolutely <u>nothing</u> to write about. If I didn't have your letters to answer I don't know what I should do.

Every day exactly the same things happen. I get up at 6 a.m., go to the office. Have the afternoon off if I can. Back at 5 p.m. and finish about 7 p.m. Then usually a wash and then bed. As you will see they are long working hours, but it doesn't matter as there is nothing else to do. Once a week I go to the Camp Cinema.

No, darling, as much as I should like it, I certainly advise you not to come out here. For one thing, it is very unlikely that we shall stay in this country and the other reason is the country itself. I cannot describe what a desolate place India is. The few towns like Bombay and Delhi, etc., aren't too bad (although I didn't think much of them from the train window) but apart, I believe, from Kashmir, the rest of India is very much the same; hot, dirty, barren and hardly any type of entertainment at all. I have not been to Nowshera yet, but I know it's terrifically hot. I can honestly say that villages like Godmanchester are paradise compared with the average town in India. They simply stink both literally and metaphorically. Even apart from all these disadvantages and even if you could get out here, I don't think you would enjoy the company.

There are only two types of people out here. The wealthy and officers on one hand and the ordinary soldier on the other. To be

189

a soldier's wife out here is terrible. You would be treated almost as a soldier yourself. Your companions would be the wives of other solders who, although they may be all right at heart, are not exactly the type of person I think you would like. They are probably all of the lower class in England. They get out here and find they can afford servants and, of course, it goes to their heads.

I don't know this from first-hand knowledge, but only by what I have been told – but I have no doubt it is true. No, darling, please keep away from this country. It's impossible to say how long I shall be out here, but I shan't be here for over a year after the war ends. I am not a regular soldier so have no special time to serve out here. If that gentleman you met starts praising Nowshera you take it with a pinch of salt. I expect he was an officer. Officers and rankers look at India through different eyes.

Thank you for sending me "The Star" newspapers. It will be nice to see one again.

On Friday I went to the Camp Cinema and saw the Marx Bros. in 'Go West'. It wasn't bad. The night previously they had Chaplin in "The Dictator". I did not go and see it but I heard the sound! I believe that was the last film we saw together wasn't it darling? I have been working quite hard in the office, and I shall be working harder still.

One of the fellows is on leave and today the other fellow went sick. So I am left holding the fort by myself. In the middle of this letter I had to get up and dress and detail a fellow for guard tonight.

The time is now 9.55 p.m. darling and I am very tired. Remember me to everyone and say I will be writing.

All my love my darling. I am always thinking of you and am longing to see you again.

I love you.

My darling wife,

I have just received your No. 13 letter by Air Mail (which still leaves Nos. 5, 8, 9, 10 and 12).

I am very relieved darling to have had this letter from you as I started writing to you on Monday, but could think of nothing to say. My letter started 'I am really in a fix this week, darling. I have not received any more letters from you and I simply don't know what to write about'. I then wrote another couple of lines and dried up.

It is difficult darling to know what to tell you. I know it is hard describing the daily routine at home, but when one is stuck in a place where nothing at all happens and there is nothing to do, it is twice as difficult.

Your letter arrived even more quickly than the last one. The postmark is 5th June and today is the 30th July. Not at all bad. I will try and send this to you by Air Mail – if I can scrape enough money together – 8 annas! (I believe). There is another way we can send letters home from here by air mail, via America. However, that costs 14 annas and only rich people like sergeants can afford that. I was hoping to draw 15 rupees this week (I have been saving(!) one a week) – but the Battery ran short of money and I got only my usual 7.

But to answer your letter:-

Your description of the book you are reading on the North-West Frontier, darling, made me grin.

Either Peshawar Cantonment is the exception that proves the rule or the author has a very fertile imagination. I think I have described, or tried to describe, this place in previous letters, and I can state most emphatically that there is no glamour, beauty, magical nights, eastern romance, 'West End' shops, barbed wire entanglements, spacious bungalows, Bournemouth Park-like gardens, or whatever in this dump. 'Dump' gives me an inspiration. Imagine a big rubbish dump with quite a number of trees, white tents dotted here and there and thousands of insects – that is a pretty good pen picture of Shinkiari Camp. Nowshera, I believe, is a little better. There is a bazaar there, but on the other hand the heat is terrific. When I get back I'll write a true book on India!

You ask me darling, if I still love you. What a question! If I didn't have you to think of, my sweet, I would go off my nut. I stay in bed a few minutes later in the morning to finish dreaming of you. If I go to bed in the afternoon I think of you all the time. Wondering what you are doing, how you are looking, and keep picturing to myself our reunion when I return. Every book I read I imagine the heroine (if there is one) is you, and I often get very angry with myself when I think of all the silly little quarrels I started when we were together. I won't quarrel any more when I get back, darling. Honestly, darling, I love you with all my heart and I shall always be faithful to you. Do you still love me, my sweet? I know you do.

I am glad to see you are keeping fit and well and doing plenty of cycling.

I sometimes feel a bit worried, darling. Don't forget to CONCENTRATE will you. I shall have to hurry back home and look after you.

The time is now 7.15 p.m. and as I am going to the 'Cinema' tonight I will close for now and continue in the morning. We got paid today. I went last Friday and saw 'The Ghost Breakers'. It was quite funny. See you in the morning, darling. Don't go away. I love you.

Thursday 8.15 a.m.: Good morning, darling. I went to the pictures last night and saw 'I want a Divorce' with Joan Blondell and Dick Powell. It wasn't as good as the previous ones I have seen. But it passed the time away.

Nearly every night now we have storms and downpours of rain. The monsoons are just about breaking in this region. Sometimes the lightning is so constant that it is as easy to walk about at night as in the day. By the way, a couple of weeks ago I received a 3/-

Postal-Order from NAPSOPA. Would you mind acknowledging this for me, and say it was a good idea to send cash instead of tobacco as it is possible to get 160 Woodbines for that amount here. I can't decipher the signature but it looks as if it might be something Branch (A lady I believe).

If we go abroad from this country I shall try and let you know. If we do and there is no air mail direct to where we then are, it is best to address your letters as follows:

73rd Field Battery, R.A., 5th Field Reg. R.A. c/o Base Air Post Depot, Karachi, India.

Meanwhile, until you hear to the contrary, keep addressing your letters to Nowshera as I expect we will return there first.

Well, my darling, I think that's all for now. I shall definitely send this letter by Air Mail although I have just heard it costs 14 annas! It will be interesting to hear how soon you receive it. I am eagerly awaiting your previous letters I have not received – especially the one acknowledging my letters from Freetown and Cape Town. All my love for ever, darling.

P.S. I did not forget June 7th. I am now working out when I must write to you to receive a letter on our anniversary. The news of the war seems quite good today. Perhaps it won't be long before we meet again. I love you.

Author's note: June 7th – six months married.

Shinkiari Camp
NWFP
9th August 1941

My darling wife,

I love you.

I have two letters from you to answer today, darling, so this should be a little longer letter than usual. I received your No. 14 about 5 days ago and No. 12 arrived shamelessly yesterday. I think I will reply to No. 12 first – you seem to have done a lot of interesting things in that letter. I wish I had received it before.

Things certainly seem to be much more difficult at home now than when I was there. It seems hard to believe that tomatoes could ever be worth 6/- a pound. As you say, darling, there is plenty of fruit to be had for the asking out here, but it is not advisable to eat much.   They are one of the main causes of dysentery – probably one of those 'horrid' diseases you have read about. I have had a few pears and peaches – but that is all. (Beg your pardon, I have also had one or two mangoes). But I keep off fruit as much as possible. I also very seldom eat meat now – it is not very tasty and extremely tough. I expect I shall be a pukka vegetarian when I return.

You certainly seem to be developing into a rough weather cyclist, but be careful of skids, darling. I am glad Joe is better and that Dad is keeping fit. You mention that you sent me a cable – I wonder if that was the one in reply to mine. I have only received one from you, darling – "O.K. Cablegram received. Love Gwen". If you have sent another one, I am afraid it has gone astray.

I'm afraid, darling, I cannot afford to send cablegrams – they cost half my meagre pay.   But they have started paying us on a weekly basis now (as in England) instead of monthly, so in future I may be able to save a bit more as I shall be getting 9 rupees a week (12/-). But it would help me a lot, darling, if you sent pre-paid telegrams (if you want me to reply), otherwise, although I am always broke for five days of the week, I would rather manage on what I get than break in on your allowance. The trouble is that we get so many 'stoppages' out here.   Boot boy, washing, barber, battery funds, sports funds and various other funds are deducted from our pay. It doesn't leave a married man very wealthy. But, as I said before, I can manage – but cannot lay out for telegrams, etc., unless they are urgent – as letting you know I had arrived safely.

What a pity it rained nearly all the time at Huntingdon, but I hope it made a change for you. Mrs Towgood seems to have taken a fancy to you. I hope you remembered me to her. Yes, darling, I received "The Stars"* two days ago (before this Air Mail letter). Thank you very much darling, they were very interesting, although the poor old 'Star' seems to be shrivelling up.

The London Evening paper I used to work for

Glad you got my No. 4 letter darling. I wonder if you are still receiving my letters regularly – I hope so. None of your letters have been censored yet. Please don't get depressed, darling, the war won't last for ever, although it seems ages since I last saw you. I find it hard to believe that I have been away from England for nearly 5 months. If the time keeps going as quickly as this it won't be long before we are together again!

Darling, it's no use your thinking of coming out here – you wouldn't be very happy as I have explained in previous letters. Besides, I may not stop in this country if the Far East flares up. So you wouldn't be any nearer to me. Some time in the future, sweet, when I have money, perhaps I'll bring you out here and we'll visit the few places that might be worth visiting – away from all the military. India at the moment reminds me of one big soldier's camp. Please put any idea you may have of coming out here out of your head, darling.

No, darling, I do not find your letters uninteresting – I think they are very well written. I'm sure mine must seem very dry – I can never think of anything to say. Some of my friends haven't written for weeks – they are simply stumped and can't write a line. I am always very much relieved if I have a letter of yours to answer. I think the book you are reading now by Sir William Barton is more true to life than the previous one. I am afraid I am in one of those lonely outposts you speak of. I still don't like Army life and you are right – the atmosphere is very military.

You say, darling, you are going to send me a cable every month, but I am afraid, as I have mentioned before, I have only received the one in answer to mine. I hope you have not been sending them and they have gone astray. I'd love to have another telegram from you. Offer my congrats to Herbert on his stripes. He certainly is a lucky devil, although I expect he has worked hard and deserved it. I don't think I shall ever do it. I was going on a clerk's course which might have meant promotion, but that has been cancelled now owing to certain uncertain affairs.

It's nice to know you have written to me each day – I wish I could do it for you. I'll have a go at it maybe next week – but it's not as if we have anywhere decent to write. I'm writing this in the office as I have finished work. It is really the best place when it is fairly quiet. No, darling, I shall not stay with the Army after the war – I still loathe every minute of it.

I am honestly, darling, thinking of you every minute of the day and am always putting the clock back $3\frac{1}{2}$ hours and wondering what you are doing. The time here at the moment is 12.35 p.m. (Saturday). It is only 9 o'clock at home and you are at the office. You have only just arrived and finished putting your hair straight, etc. At this very minute you are just settling down in your chair ready for the morning's work. Am I right? (I have just kissed you on the cheek whilst you were opening one of your account books).

I have not written to Mr. Sinclair yet, but will do so. I have not written to anyone except you and Dad and Do. It's not only laziness but also that 4 letters would cost a rupee – which is a lot of money. (Always on about money aren't I, sweet? But don't take any notice. I intend to manage on what I get).

(I am just going to dinner. I shall continue afterwards. It is pouring with rain).

1.30 p.m. Just finished dinner and typed Battery Orders.

As usual darling, there's not much I can tell you. Last Monday (August Bank Holiday) the Regiment had a holiday although I had to work during the morning.

During the morning a sergeant came up and asked me if I would play with the band at the Dog Show. I agreed although I was not very enthusiastic. When I got there I found, as I thought I would, a piano with two accordions and a drum. The piano was terribly old and out of tune and, as people crowded around, I can't say I enjoyed the experience. I promised to play during the evening, but when the time came I had not finished my work and got somebody else to play for me. I was not sorry because, after playing one or two numbers, the crowd got beery and started singing 'Nelly Dean', etc., and the band wasn't much good in such circumstances. I played for about 15 minutes later on, but then packed up and went to my tent. They were issuing free beer, but I only had one mug full. It is nothing like English beer.

Considering what could have been arranged with a little organisation, the day was very disappointing. But that's just like the Army – they can't even arrange a holiday properly.

That was the first time I had touched the piano since I left home, but it was impossible to settle down to playing with a crowd around – and I do like a decent piano.

Yesterday evening I went to the cinema and saw 'Arise my Love'. A very good and funny film – the best I have seen since I left home.

Well, darling I think that's all for now.

During the week I'll send you an Air Mail postcard telling you I have had no telegrams from you and what letters I have received. It costs only 4 annas compared with 14 annas by Air Mail letter.

Darling, I love you very much.

Do you know, sweet, that, since I have left England I have spoken to no woman (except a café waitress in Cape Town) all the time I have been away from you. I am going to try and keep this record until I see you again.

Remember me to everyone darling and please be careful on your bike. All my love for ever.

P.S. I've just thought. It will nearly be Xmas I expect when you receive this. I shall have to think of Xmas Cards soon – if I can get them. John sends his regards.

Note: This letter was received by my wife on 22nd December 1941

16th August 1941

In view of what I believed to be the uncertainty of the mail at home, I continued to number my letters and to enclose shortened versions of my two previous letters. This letter was numbered 18, and enclosed précis of letters nos. 16 & 17.

My darling wife,

I have received two of your letters this week. No. 9 on Monday and No. 8 yesterday. It seems strange reading 'back numbers' after having received later letters by Air Mail, and I have to re-digest the letters I have in order to get the run of things. I enjoyed reading No. 9 very much darling as you acknowledged my first two letters and telegram. It makes me feel less far away from you when you answer letters I have written since leaving home. I am expecting to receive an Air Mail letter from you within the next few days – I hope it acknowledges more of my letters to you. I have certainly been very lucky in getting yours. All I am waiting for now, I think, is No. 5 and No. 10. I expect they will turn up soon. They seem to get to this country on time but spend weeks being circulated round India trying to find me. The postal service isn't what you could call good here.

There doesn't seem much to reply to in No. 8 darling. You seem even then to be dashing around on your bike. I am almost dreading what might happen when I get home. I can imagine you waking me up in the early hours of the morning saying "Come on darling, get your bike ready. We are going to cycle to Brighton."

I hope you have learned how to mend a puncture, I was never much good at that job! You make me laugh when you say which rows are carrots, turnips and spring onions in your garden. Fancy serving spring onions for dinner and assuring people they are turnips. Or dipping carrots in salt and eating them raw.

No darling, I have written no articles since I have been out here, but I am making notes for a proposed book to be written when the war is over. It won't be an autobiography, but rather a satire on Army life. I shall probably name it something like 'I am not wearing Rose Coloured glasses, my eyes are naturally bloodshot'. (Vic. Oliver, I believe).

You make me very envious when you say you strolled along the river bank. I can imagine nothing better than strolling with you along the Thames near Maidenhead or Staines on a cool summer's evening. It must be heavenly.

I have read your No. 9 letter over and over again darling, despite the fact that I have read quite a lot of it in your later Air Mail letters and have replied to most of it. Fancy your receiving my first two letters and telegram within a few days of each other, and just after your saying that you thought of enquiring of my whereabouts. And also, of course, our Wedding Anniversary.

I am so glad you are getting on all right at the office. Have you had your 'rise' yet? When I get home it looks as if I shall have a wife rolling in money! Will you take me out, darling? We had no adventures at all on the way out here. As I mentioned in previous letters, the voyage was very uneventful – no scares or any excitement. We all felt as safe as houses.

I purposely mentioned our engagement anniversary so that you could work out the date from that. We were not allowed to mention dates. Thank you for letting Dad know I was O.K. – I was hoping you would do that.

Yes, darling, your conclusion about us being somewhere around Africa when I wrote was quite correct, and, as you know by now, we stopped at Capetown. I'm afraid I didn't think it such a wonderful experience, darling. It was taking me further away from you all the time. And that's not wonderful. My letters were censored on board ship by the officers. I don't suppose many, if any, of the letters from here have been touched.

I am quite amused at the thought of your pouring over Atlases to find Nowshera. I am glad you automatically presumed it was in India, otherwise you would have had a much longer job. The Battery is moving down there for a few days next week, but it's doubtful whether I shall go. I expect I will remain with the rear party here. I would like to go really just to see what the place is like. Darling, I'm sorry you had to have a cry, but I expect it will do you good as long as it doesn't make you feel too miserable. Sometimes I almost wish I could cry myself. I do miss you very much, darling.

How is "The Star" getting on? Are they rebuilding the premises or are they still continuing at "The Sketch".

I also can't believe I am all these miles away from you, darling. I would have liked you in a way to come out here, but as I have explained it is quite impossible. But never mind, darling, I don't think it will be long before I am coming back to you.

John has got a camera and I shall try and get him to take a snapshot of me one day. I will send it to you right away when it is printed.

I have been trying to keep a diary for you this week, and here it is enclosed all nicely typed. I am afraid, as I have warned you, it is very, very uninteresting. I am going to send you an Air Mail postcard with this letter just to let you know which letters I have received and to enquire about these telegrams you have mentioned in previous letters.

I hope you are still keeping well, I am as fit as can be expected in this country. I am always thinking of you, my sweet. I wish I could telephone you or see you on a television screen. I hope you haven't changed – that's silly because I know you haven't. The time is now 2.15 p.m. and I think I'll get some sleep. I have just been to the canteen to get a postcard, but they don't sell 'em. I expect I shall scrounge one from somewhere. All my love darling. Keep good.

Diary for an August Week in Shinkiari

Sunday August 10th

Got up at 7.30 a.m. (extra lie-in today, being day of rest). Breakfast was porridge, egg, sausage and chips with, of course, the usual cup of cha. Had a shave at the barber's and rolled into the office just before 9 o'clock.

Quite busy on usual office routine during morning making out Battery Orders, etc. Dinner at 12.30 p.m. consisted of sauté potatoes, peas, meat (none for me) and the inevitable cup of cha.

Went back to the office and cleared work by 1.30 p.m. Went back to my tent, undressed and went to bed. Slept right round till 5 p.m. It wasn't so warm this afternoon. A rather chilly wind was blowing. Rolled into office again about 5.30 p.m. but there was nothing much to do so went and had supper: Chips, peas and meat (not for me) with rice for 'afters'. Back to the office and decided to type out this diary for my next letter to you. The weather is typically English at the moment. It is cold, a chilly wind is blowing and it is raining. It is something like March at home. Well darling, that's all I've done today. I've made quite a splash over doing nothing at all – I'm sure it won't be at all interesting for you to read.

The time is now 7 p.m. and I am going back to my tent now and will probably be in bed before long. (There is absolutely nothing else to do on an evening such as this).

All my love, sweet.

Monday August 11th

Up at 6.15 a.m. this morning. Feel very fit. Got to office about 6.30 a.m. Did my usual work and then went to breakfast (2 eggs and mash, with the usual porridge and 'cha').

Shave and brush up and then back to office again. During the morning we shifted the furniture around in the office (which, by the way, is a tent), and then had a very pleasant surprise in the shape of a letter from you (no. 9 – by ordinary mail) which I thought was very interesting and one of the best letters you have written. Probably because you received my two letters and cable. I am replying to this letter now. Did not go to bed this afternoon as I was clerk on duty. It is much cooler today, more like an English summer and is probably the reason why I am feeling much more fit and cheerful. (Your letter, of course, darling, had a lot to do with it.)

Managed to get away about 3.30 p.m. for a bath (one foot at a time in a bucket) and drew two Bush Suits from Stores. (A suit specially for the hot evenings). It's made of thin khaki material and consists of slacks and jacket. The jacket is something after the style of a sports jacket and is very cool and comfortable to wear. Supper at 6 p.m. was stew (which I missed) so contented myself with a currant pancake and a cup of 'chaa'. (Dinner, by the way, was chips and peas – once again I gave the meat a miss).

It is now 7.20 p.m. and getting quite dark. The evenings are very short here. It is 4 p.m. at home and I expect you are having a cup of tea and cake in the office. I wish I were with you.

Tuesday August 12th

Got up at 6.30 a.m. Breakfast was egg and chips. Usual office routine during the morning. It is very hot again today and consequently I don't feel so lively. Dinner at 12.30 p.m. – scallopes and peas – as usual I had no meat. Supper was stew which I did not fancy and satisfied myself with the kind of currant pancake they dish up. Had an attempt on Joe's accordion for a few minutes during evening. Talked a little and then went back to bed to dream of you.

Wednesday August 13th

Up at 6.30 a.m. (getting later). Rolled into office, but soon rolled out again for breakfast and had porridge, chips, fried onions and some liver which was very nice and very tender. Nothing unusual happened during the morning, but I did not have much work to do. Dinner was sauté potatoes and greens (no meat). Had another good rest during afternoon, but it was very hot, although there was a funny chilly breeze at the same time. It is these cool breezes which are dangerous. When you are lying almost naked on a bed with sweat pouring off, and a cool breeze blows at irregular intervals, one has to be careful not to catch pneumonia. I wrapped a towel round my shoulders. Got up at 4.30 p.m. had a wash in the usual bucket and donned my bush suit, which fits where it touches. To the office, did a bit more work and then to supper which was mashed potatoes, tomatoes, onions and cucumber salad. It was very nice too. Does it make you envious? There was rice pudding for sweet.

Back to the tent and a chat with John and the boys, and went to bed about 9 p.m. Read a book for a little while and then to sleep (or rather tried to). It was so hot it was a long while before I finally dozed off.

Thursday August 14th

Up at 6.45 a.m. (later still). It is surprising, considering the amount of sleep we get how tired we wake up in the morning. I think it is definitely due to the heat and also to the fact that we sleep under a mosquito net. It tends, I think, to make it stuffier. Breakfast was porridge (which I missed) eggs and chips. Had a wash (not a very good one as there was not much water) and rolled into office. Nothing much doing – usual routine. It is now 12.20 p.m., darling, and I shall soon be having dinner and then have another forty winks. I expect I shall write you your letter today. I also intend to send you an Air Mail postcard at 5.15 p.m. I didn't have much of a sleep after all, I forgot pay was 'up' this afternoon. I did not have any supper except one of the usual pancakes. In the evening I thought I would go to the pictures. Got there and found they were showing 'Women without Names'. Unfortunately the projector broke down after about an hour and everybody had their money back, except for silly people like me who lost their ticket. I dunno! Came back and went straight to bed.

Friday August 15th

Up at 6.15 a.m. Breakfast was very poor. A couple of hard boiled eggs. So I just made do with a plate of porridge. Usual routine during morning. For dinner I had sauté potatoes and peas. Had a good sleep in the afternoon and got back to office at 5 p.m. Was quite busy during the evening and not finished till 7 p.m. Went back to my tent. Had a short game of cards with John (the first I have played since leaving Deolali) and lost 8 annas. Then went to bed. (Received letter No. 8 from you, darling).

Saturday August 16th

Up at 6.15 a.m. Breakfast was porridge, potatoes and peas. Usual work during morning. Dinner at 12.30 p.m. was a kind of salad again – onions, tomatoes, cucumber, potatoes. Stayed in office till 2.30 p.m. writing letter to you, then went for a lie down. Time is now 5.45 p.m. and I am just finishing this Diary so I can slip it into your letter. I might go to the pictures again tonight and will hold on to my ticket!

Note: This letter was received by my wife on 24th November 1941.

73rd Field Battery RA
5th Field Regt. RA
Nowshera
NWFP, India.
22nd August 1941

My darling wife,

As you will see from the above address I am writing this letter from Nowshera.

It is 7.30 p.m. and I am sitting in the Battery Office (being clerk on duty) and above my head is a big propeller whirling round and round creating a much-welcomed breeze.

I think things will be a little more interesting this week now we are here in decent barracks and with more to do, so I shall write this letter in the form of a diary, starting from this morning at Shinkiari Camp.

Friday August 22nd:

Was woken up by my boy at 4.30 a.m. who brought a cup of cha. Was very surprised to find the difference an hour earlier made – it was as dark as if it were midnight. Had plenty to do as we were moving off to Nowshera at 6 a.m. We are only going to be down there a week for firing practice on the ranges. Packed up all my kit and bedding and dumped it in the back of the Battery Office lorry. I sat in front with the driver and about half-a-dozen 'wogs' (natives) sat in the back. They are some of the Battery 'followers' (Barbers, cookhouse wallahs, etc.)

6 a.m. Moved off. We have 110 miles to go and hope to get to Nowshera by 1.30 p.m. The scenery is not much to look at – for about 30 miles we travelled back on the road we came along when we first arrived and, except for one pass through a range of mountains (nothing as spectacular as those we experienced in France) it was all very uninteresting.

The only interesting part was near the end of the journey when we arrived at a place called Attock on the River Indus. The Indus separates the North-West Frontier Province from the rest of India and there, on top of a hill, was a huge fortress built by the British years ago to stop hostile tribesmen coming further south. Since then, of course, the tribesmen have been pushed further north. Nowshera is about 20 miles north of Attock. We crossed the Indus by a long suspension bridge – a really wonderful piece of engineering carrying a railway and road (the former running above the latter). The bridge is the only way of getting from this part of the N.W.F. to the rest of India and it is closely guarded. At 7 p.m. each night it is closed. The Indus was really quite an impressive sight – with the mountains rising behind it to the north. It looked like the Hollywood version of the North-West Frontier. We arrived at Nowshera on time and I was pleasantly surprised with the place. (The Cantonment, of course. Not the native parts). It is set out something like a garden village, with lawns and trees, etc. in front of the bungalows. It is certainly more like England than Shinkiari – but then we are here when the weather is getting cooler. I believe it is terrifically hot in mid-summer. The bungalows are built of bricks and are very spacious and quite clean - and we have pukka beds to sleep on, so I shan't have insects crawling all over me tonight. The other clerks and I sleep in a room next to the office, but tonight, as I am on duty, I am sleeping in the office. I think I shall have a sound sleep tonight – I will enjoy that artificial breeze (you know how I hate stuffiness).

It is rather unfortunate in a way that we are confined to the area around the Cantonment owing to an outbreak of cholera in the district. But after Shinkiari, I personally, won't mind that. There is a cinema, billiard rooms, canteen, YMCA, etc., all in the Cantonment, so we will have more to occupy our minds during the evening. Of course it is nothing like any place in England and, after a few days, I expect I shall get 'browned off' of it. But after that dump Shinkiari, it is certainly a change.

Well, darling, it is now 8.10 p.m. and, as we have had a long day, I am feeling rather tired, so I shall pack up for now. (I have no difficulty in writing a letter here as there is an electric light in the office. Almost civilized again!)

I love you very much, darling. I wish you were with me tonight.

Saturday August 23rd

I was mistaken when I thought I would get a good sleep last night. Despite the fan whirling above, the heat was terrific and, on top of that, my mosquito net came down on top of me during the night and wrapped itself round me. I kept waking up thinking I was being strangled, but was too tired to get up and put it right.

Had a shower as soon as I got up (that's one of the advantages of being in barracks – having showers. You certainly need plenty of them in this heat) and then went to breakfast.

The dining hall here is also a great improvement on the tent to which we have been used. It is large, clean and cool (four big fans suspended from the ceiling) and there is wire netting all round the windows and doors so that the flies cannot get in. Definitely first-class.

There was nothing much doing today, the Sergeant-Major and Officers all being out on the ranges (as they will be every day whilst we are here) so I went to bed. I'm afraid I slept nearly all day to 5 o'clock. The heat certainly does get me. You know how tired I used to get sitting in front of a fire – you can imagine how sleepy I feel in this heat (although the weather is supposed to be getting cooler). Was occupied in the office till about 7 p.m. and then went to the camp cinema (The Lansdowne) and saw the Crazy Gang in 'O.K. for Sound'. Price of admission 9 annas. Came out about 9 p.m. and went to the canteen and had a lemonade and played billiards from 9.30 to 10 p.m. Then to bed.

Sunday 24th August

Got up about 6 a.m. Slept a little better last night, but it was still very hot. We had a violent storm during the night – rather in the nature of a hurricane. Did a little more work during the morning today, but broke off for an hour to have a game of billiards. Learned today that we are all going to be inoculated for cholera directly they can get the vaccine through. (Don't get alarmed. None of the white people have caught it yet and the native parts of the city are now out of bounds). Also learned we are going to return to Nowshera again after staying at Shinkiari for a few weeks. We return to Shinkiari on September 1st. Slept during the afternoon till 4 p.m. (still very hot). Then had a shower (not the first today!) and typed Battery Orders, etc. Finished work about 6.30 p.m. Went out in the evening to the local YMCA and found a PIANO. Or rather an apology for one. It looked more like a dressing table. However, I mucked about on it for most of the evening. My fingers are terribly stiff and it will take some practice to get them in trim again. I shall probably go there again tonight (Monday). I might take my music as not many people go to the YMCA. Met a couple of fellows I knew down there and we came back when they closed at 10 p.m.

Monday August 25th

Got up at 7 a.m. Had a very good night's sleep – it being much cooler. It is a lovely morning today; cool and made more pleasant by the breeze from the fans. I feel much fitter and cheerful despite the fact that I couldn't find my clean shirt this morning. Someone seems to have pinched it. But never mind eh! By the way, darling, I sent you an Air Mail postcard just briefly stating which letters I had had from you and which letters I have sent you. I hope you get it. It is numbered No. 20. I still have not received a letter from you – I wonder what has happened to the Air Mail? If I don't get one soon I shall have to send you a telegram.

Darling, the time is now 10.40 a.m. I think I will close this letter now and post it. I will continue this diary in my next letter. I hope you are still keeping well, darling – I am missing you very much, but I have a feeling it won't be long before we are together again. I will now take a walk to the post-office and post this letter. I shall kiss it before I put it in the letter-box. My love for ever.

24th August 1941

AIR MAIL POSTCARD

Darling,

At last I have been able to get hold of a postcard as promised in my last two letters. Have received all your letters up to No. 14 with the exception of No. 5 and No. 10. The first two I got were No. 9 on August 11th and No. 8 on August 15th. I have not had an Air Mail letter from you since 8th August. I hope they have not gone astray as I should have had one by now, shouldn't I? You mention sending me telegrams in your letters – I have not received any except the one acknowledging mine saying I was O.K. Have you sent any? I should like to have one from you. I am just writing you No. 19 letter. I hope you are receiving mine regularly. No. 16 sent by Air Mail – I can't afford to send them by Air every week. But I will send you postcards by Air. I am writing this in Nowshera. It is very hot here, but better than Shinkiari. Hope you are still keeping well darling – are you still getting about on your bike? By the way, John has been getting Air Mail postcards regularly from his mother, but also has not now had one for some time. The guns are firing over on the ranges and the noise makes me feel quite homesick. But it's been fairly quiet lately. I cannot squeeze any more in so will close. Remember me to all. Love.

I am afraid I have to admit that I haven't written to you now for over a fortnight! But don't think I don't love you any more, darling. I haven't felt much like writing because I have been in Nowshera Hospital since yesterday (Wednesday) fortnight. It is nothing very serious really. I went sick on the Tuesday evening and was admitted to hospital on the following day with a fever. It was not malaria, but Sandfly fever – a minor edition of the former caused by the bite of a small fly that can even get through the mosquito net. The disease is not half as troublesome as malaria because it doesn't keep recurring. After I had been in hospital about four days my temperature began to drop and I felt better. But then a sister noticed I was beginning to go yellow. I did go yellow too. I went more yellow and more yellow until I looked like a cowardly Chinaman. As I write this I am still yellow, although I think it is slightly fading.

Once again yellow jaundice is not a serious complaint. It is tiresome, depressing and inconvenient, but happily not serious. Some of the fellows say I'm lucky to have this as it is impossible to catch malaria afterwards; but how true that is I don't know. I hope it's true.

I'm feeling much better today, darling. That is why I am writing this letter. (I think it's because I had 3 letters from you last night darling – but will refer to them later).

There's nothing much I can tell you since my last letter. Life in hospital is very monotonous.

It is quite a clean place, consisting of 4 wards. Much better than the one at Shinkiari which was a marquee full of insects. But, of course, it is a Military Hospital, and, like everything connected with the Army, very badly organised. If we patients didn't keep reminding the orderlies what treatment we were supposed to have, we wouldn't get any. Every morning about 10 o'clock the M.O. comes round, asks one how one feels. One says "Fine", "Not so good", "Very Bad", or whatever one considers to be the best reply.

The M.O. nods his head in a wise way; prods one's tummy, knocks one about the chest, says "You look a bit better this morning" and strolls away. A few minutes later the Matron comes round and most of the previous conversation takes place again. Then a Sister comes round until one feels like a horse in a horse show. However, it breaks the monotony and, believe me, it is monotonous being in bed 24 hours a day. Every day I get the same food. Toast for breakfast (lately I have had liver too). Chicken and potatoes for lunch, with jelly for sweet. A pear or something similar in the afternoon. Toast and biscuits for tea. Fish, followed by jelly for supper. I am on a fat free diet, and that's why I have to have the above. I know it all looks very nice, but food out here is nothing like it is in England. A chicken, for instance, is only about half the size of an English one and is very tough with little flavour. Fruit is the same. Grapes are only the size of peas, and oranges and limes are juiceless and full of skin. The fish is not bad but we are a long way from the sea and it has not much flavour.

I shall certainly be glad to get out of this place and have some nice fried potatoes and other things cooked in fat.

This last few days, owing to my persistent requests, they have now started mincing my chicken as I am suffering from sore gums. I was also suffering from a barber's rash which spread all over my face and round my neck. But that has disappeared now.

Well, my darling, I think that almost completes everything I have to say about myself. I only get 5 rupees a week whilst in hospital, but that is plenty as there is nothing to spend it on. I buy a paper every day and yesterday bought two packets of Woodbines. (The first for a fortnight). What did make a hole in the money was when I sent the boy out for this writing pad, envelopes and pen and ink. It came to 3 rupees 12 annas (4/-). The cost of living is really very high out here except for cigarettes and food. The reason, of course, is that it all has to be imported.

It is now 12 noon and as 'tiffin' will be up in a few minutes I will continue later. I can see that this letter is going to be terrifically long. I have four of your letters to answer yet!

5 p.m.   I had a nice little sleep this afternoon, so will now continue this epistle until supper comes 'up'. As I have said before, darling, I have four letters of yours, Nos. 15, 16, 17 and 18. No. 15 I got after I had been in hospital a couple of days, and the others all came together last night.

I will now answer No. 15.

This letter arrived very much overdue, darling. It is dated 16th June and I did not receive it until the end of August.

It was only a few days earlier than the ordinary mail as I have letters from Dad and Do, both dated the beginning of June. Actually I think it is the postal service in this country that is to blame. It is very slack and inefficient as are most things in this country.   Sometimes we are lucky and they are delivered right away, and at other times they hang about in the Post Offices. For instance, I have not received that telegram you sent me (I shall take the matter up with the Post Office when I leave here), neither have I received those two Air Mail postcards you mention. I did receive, however, with No. 15 letter my second batch of 'Stars' – this one for week-ending 30th May. Thank you, darling.

But to answer your letter.

You seem to be quite an ardent cyclist now. I am glad you are keeping fit that way. I expect it helps to occupy your mind too. It has not been as hot as 120 degrees here in the shade because the hottest time of the year is passing. Also Shinkiari was considered to be a cooler spot – that's why the regiment was there. Certainly it was possible to sleep at nights.

I have seen pictures in "The Star" of the Temple. It certainly looks a mess. But perhaps when they rebuild it will be just as pleasant. As you know, I am not a great lover of old buildings and, if they have a good Architect on the job, it could be just as charming when we stroll through there again.

Darling, I wonder if you have received my first letter yet in which I advise you not to come out here. In every letter you have mentioned it, and in every letter I have told you to put all thoughts of it aside.

I must emphasize this because, I have an idea, that by the time you get this letter I will no longer be in this country. And you don't want to be alone in this country, darling. It would be hell. We shall have to continue to be with each other in spirit for the time being. But the war news is very encouraging and I shouldn't be at all surprised if it isn't over much sooner than most people expect. I've a feeling that we won't be long apart, darling.

Yes, we can get ice-cream here at a few places – but it is not very nice. Did I not used to like salad? I often fancy a cool salad out here. We sometimes get served with something resembling one for 'tiffin' and I enjoy it.

I don't think I will want to travel much when I return, darling. It's a very disappointing world – there's no place like London. I'm glad you went to Watford again. What a lucky girl you were to be taken over the brewery! It makes my mouth water. Do you know that since I left England I have not drunk as much beer as I did in a normal week at home? I simply can't afford it and, in any case, the beer is no good.

Darling, please don't envy my experiences. I have had no adventures and everything is very dull. I should like to get back to my old job when I return; where I can use my initiative and not be handicapped by a lot of red tape and ignorant men. I hate Army life. I'm sure now I shall never get on in the Army – I'm far too independent and cannot conceal my contempt for some of my superiors.

Your No. 16 letter with postmark dated 30th June is a particularly interesting letter. All your letters are, of course, interesting, but I particularly like those in which you acknowledge my letters. It seems as if we are 'getting somewhere'.

So you are still reading books on India. I think by now you must know more about this country than I do. In fact, I am sure of it. I hope that your brother Frank is exempt from National Service. I wouldn't like to think of your being all alone in that house but I expect you would move to Watford. I'm glad you soon got over your tummy trouble.

I'm glad you have received all my letters to the time of your writing. I think the postal service is really quite good, even if rather slow.

As I have not got my diary with me I cannot clearly remember what was in No. 8. You say it was my first letter from India, so it must have been from Deolali, although you do not mention it. I must say you seem to get my letters much quicker than I get yours. Ordinary mail takes almost 3 months to reach us and Air Mail takes anything from 6 to 8 weeks. Your No. 15 took 10 weeks!

Cape Town is certainly the best place we have come across so far. There is nowhere in India like it. But we began to tire of Cape Town after the third day. As I have said before, there is no place where there is so much to do as in London.

(Darling, this letter seems to be going on and on so I will have to continue on the back of the pages now. Otherwise I won't be able to afford to post it!)

No, darling, you are quite wrong. I am not enjoying my travels; I would much rather be at home with you. Also I have now lost my pipe and shaved off my moustache. The latter I could never succeed in keeping tidy.

As I have previously mentioned, you definitely know more about India than I do. And those tribes you describe – I've never 'eard of 'em. You see, although I am in the North-West Frontier Province I haven't been up to the actual frontier and haven't seen the Khyber Pass. This regiment used to be on the frontier but it has been released for more important work – which will probably take effect in the near future. I don't think it's much good making plans for after the war. Cape Town is O.K. but I want to come home first. Believe me, darling, these distant countries aren't very thrilling. I've come across no scenery as exciting as that which I have seen in Europe on my holidays. Also there is not the same local atmosphere. You embarrass me by trying to fix me up as a press correspondent. It is impossible for me to do anything like that in the Army. Besides, what news can I get in an out-of-the-way place like Shinkiari and Nowshera? The only news I get is from the local rag, and that's usually two days old. No, darling, you mustn't make such ridiculous suggestions again, otherwise I shall be forced to make a funny face at you. And I know you wouldn't like that!

We were absolutely forbidden to send any postcards or mail direct from Cape Town. So the fellow you mentioned was being very naughty and probably endangering the lives of other men.

I shall tell John of your visit to his mother. I have not seen him for a long time – he had to go back to Shinkiari when I went into hospital.

I'm afraid we are not such good friends as we were – but it's nothing much and there's no need to mention it to Mrs. Collins. I am glad you went to Yiewsley and saw Dad and Grandad, etc. I will really have to write to a lot of people now I am feeling better. I feel very guilty.

Darling, you are a funny girl mentioning a son whilst I'm thousands of miles away. I think you are very artful – I bet you wouldn't dare mention it if I were at home! But I don't think it's a thing we can discuss by letter. I have really given no thought to the subject and I have not and I hope I don't have, any adventures to describe. You funny girl – I love you.

Like you, darling, I have plenty of space to think, and I am always thinking of you. This last fortnight I have thought of nothing else but you and, when I was a bit low, I often hid my head under a towel and shed a few tears. I couldn't help it, especially when they played the gramophone here and put on 'Indian Summer'. Strangely enough that tune always reminds me of you and home – the melody is so unlike India and always reminds me of green grass, trees, and usually the Thames. It seems such an English tune.

It is now past 7 p.m. (it is quite dark at this time) and I must put my mosquito net up and get ready for bed.

I will continue in the morning and try and get it posted by Air Mail. Goodnight, my darling, I shall be dreaming of you.

Friday (12th): 8 a.m. Good morning, darling. I have just finished my breakfast (toast and liver) and will now write a few lines before the M.O. comes round.

I will continue by answering your letter No. 17 postmarked 8th July. Your first words are that you have sent me a cable which, as I remarked previously, I have not received. I shall certainly create a 'stink' about it when I get out. It's damn annoying.

You certainly seem to be making a success of your garden now – you seem to have sorted out the rows successfully. You ought to open a shop. Yes, my watch is still O.K.

All your spare time now seems to be spent on your bike. I hope you don't overdo it. I still feel nervous when I think of your riding along the Uxbridge Road and probably day-dreaming!

I know a few words of Hindustani. Just enough so the 'boys' know what I want. Many of the fellows who have been out here some time use a lot of native words even when speaking English, but I am trying to keep out of that habit. I think it sounds ridiculous. The heliograph I haven't touched since I first arrived in this country, but I think I could still work it.

I can read your letters quite easily which, I expect, is more than you can mine. I don't get much opportunity to play the piano now, but I expect it will all come back to me when I get home again. So Watford is still crowded with soldiers. I do wish I were back there with you, darling. I was very happy but I expect it was too much to hope I should stay there for the duration. But I often think of how unlucky I was at not getting a permanent job there. I don't think fate has been very kind to me. However, I might be considered lucky at being out here if Britain ever invades the continent.

Also, of course, there is no shortage of beer out here as you noticed in Watford. Unfortunately I can't take advantage of it.

I don't find your letters dull, darling. I love getting them and I really have felt a lot better since I received those last three. I hope I get another one. I should do if the Postal authorities here don't lose them. I have your postcards to look forward to. I must temporarily close now, sweet, and get ready for the M.O. I shall continue later. All my love.

11.30 a.m. Everything's quiet again, darling. The M.O. has been round and I can get up the day after tomorrow. So that proves I am getting better. I am gradually returning to my usual colour and am regaining my appetite. I will now answer your letter No. 18 postmarked 14th July.

I am glad you are still very well. I'm not surprised you get 'moods'. I get terrible ones myself, but I've felt a little more cheerful lately. The news is extremely good and I think that perhaps we may be together again sooner than we expected. If the war ends I should imagine our Army of Occupation would be taken from the regiments who have spent the duration in England and let the Middle and Far East Armies home first. That's my hope, anyway.

You make me very envious when you describe your visit to town. If only I were with you. I often picture Oxford Street and Piccadilly Circus – but, of course, the lights are all on and it is slightly raining. There's a fresh smell of moisture in the air mixed with the petrol fumes of passing vehicles; crowds of people thronging the pavements, dense traffic on the road all rushing and hurrying.

There is also a continuous roar in the ears and occasionally we did get a little tired of it all. But, darling, it's civilized. Everything is clean. People are polite. There's entertainment, parks, music. There are hospitals, decent doctors at every street corner. Shops where you can buy almost anything you want (Yes, even in war time, darling, although you are short of luxuries). Darling, I wonder if you realize how lucky you are to live in a 'civilized' country. I don't mind roughing it. I could 'rough it' anywhere in England, but things are so primitive out East. As I said before, in the main, India is heat, dirt, diseases, unintelligent white people and ignorant natives. The worst part of London is paradise compared with this.

I can't send you an Airgraph letter, darling. I've never 'eard of 'em. I don't think they make 'em here. However, I'll make enquiries. I'm glad my young brother Ray got his scholarship – I will write to Do. I hope you appreciate the fact that you've married into a very clever family. (It looks as if I am the 'dunce' of the family. Doesn't it?).

I've read of the shortage of cigarettes in England and I was wondering whether I could send Frank some from here. But I don't think for one moment it would be allowed. However I'll make enquiries.

I'm glad you are still managing to live fairly comfortably and don't let the war get you down. If things are too bad after the war we'll think of going to Cape Town as you suggest. But I would like to come home first.

It was nice of you to ask me what I would like for Christmas. As you say, darling, money seems to be the only thing. It certainly would be nice to have a little extra at Christmas for a few luxuries. I've often thought of what I can send you. When I'm better I'll have a walk round the bazaar and see if I can find anything useful. There's not much out here really and usually they are cheap Japanese things. But I'll have a good look.

I don't think there's much more to add. I was reading a 'London Opinion' the other day and think I will write a short article and send it to them or 'Lilliput' and see what happens.

I've an idea I will be returning to signalling when I get back to duty. I don't mind really, but I hate things like that happening behind my back. I shall probably have a row with the Sergeant Major.

It is now 12.45 p.m. and I can smell 'tiffin' so my usual chicken will be up in a minute. I will write to you every day now while I am in here, darling. Be a good girl and don't forget I love you.

All my love for ever.

13ᵗʰ September 1941   Nowshera
                                                                NWFP

My darling wife,
The day is Saturday and the time is 5 p.m. This morning I gave my letter No. 22 to a fellow to post by Air Mail. I hope you get it soon.

There's nothing much to tell you. I have had my usual meals, read a book and had a short sleep in the afternoon. The M.O. was very pleased with me today and I certainly do feel a lot brighter. I shall be glad when I get out of this place. The sister has just passed and asked me to send you her love – although she hasn't the slightest idea who you are. Still, I expect she feels she is doing her duty by cheering up the patients. I am just waiting for dinner to be served. I hope to have a change from jelly as a sweet. I mentioned to the M.O. this morning that I had had jelly twice a day since I have been here and he said he would see what he could do. At 'tiffin' today I had blancmange!

Will close for now then, my darling. If anything 'exciting' happens after supper I will let you know. Goodnight, my sweet.

Sunday September 14th – 4.30 p.m. As you see darling, I am still in the land of the living and still getting better. Nothing happened last night except my hopes were dashed and I had boiled fish and jelly again for supper. The latter I refused and sent it back with a thousand curses. Later I ordered some buttered toast (I'm not really allowed butter) and did I enjoy it.

The usual routine again today. The M.O. still thinks I'm improving but hasn't mentioned anything about getting up. My morning was rather spoilt by the non-appearance of the newspaper wallah.

I enjoy reading the 'Civil and Military Gazette' of a morning as it is our only link with the outside world. It's surprising how miserable I feel and at a 'loose end' when it doesn't turn up. By the way I have one of your photographs (the one I like best) perched up on my mirror on my locker by the side of my bed. The mirror is on a metal stand. On one side is the looking-glass and on the other an awful picture of some Indian film star. I tried to extract the young lady's face in order to insert your photograph, but I think the whole contraption will fall to bits if I try. That's why I have your picture balanced on the celluloid lip of the mirror. It looks quite good. I can lie on my bed and gaze at you.

For 'Tiffin' I had my usual chicken and the boy was going to bring me jelly again for the sweet, but I created such an uproar that the sister had to calm me with a jam roll and custard. I really won't be able to look a jelly in the face again for months.

Monday 6 p.m. Hello darling. I love you. Nothing extraordinary happened today; usual meals, etc. The newspaper wallah didn't turn up again and mucked up my morning's routine. For all I know the war might be over now.

This afternoon I had a surprise. Two surprises in one really – pleasant and otherwise. A parcel was brought in for me from the Watford W.V.S. (How they got my name and address I do not know). It contained two nice pairs of hand-knitted woollen socks and 20 'Weights'. All that was the pleasant surprise. On the outside of the parcel was written by the Indian Postal Authorities 'This cannot be treated as a War Comforts Fund Parcel as it contains cigarettes, and I had to pay 1 rupee 2 annas (1/8d) extra on the postage. Because of the 20 'Weights' I had to pay all that money. It's the principle of the thing that annoys me really. To think of those people sending hundreds of parcels to soldiers abroad and all having to pay 1/8d. I do wish I were out of hospital, but I shall take the matter up with the Postal Authorities as soon as I possibly can. They're the most inefficient lot of blighters I've ever come across in my life. And there's that matter of your telegram too … I foam at the mouth when I think of it.

7.15 p.m. Have just finished supper – usual fish and jelly – and am now feeling very tired, so will 'tuck in'. Goodnight my darling. I shall be dreaming of you.

Tuesday 4.30 p.m. Well, darling, another day is drawing to a close. One more day nearer the end of the war. Things have been a little brighter this morning. The news still looks remarkably bright and I feel very optimistic (the newspaper wallah turned up this morning). The M.O. said I could get up for a couple of hours each day now and also added that I could have butter on my bread in future. (I have just finished tea and had butter on my toast. Boy, did it taste good!). And to complete the morning I received another batch of 'Stars', Jun 14th to 20th. On the last one was a picture of the damaged 'Star' building which you mentioned in your previous letter. It doesn't say whether anyone was hurt.

I had a row with one of the sisters today. She is new and very officious. I was lying on the bed and she told me to get underneath the sheet. I said it was too hot. She said it was a hospital regulation that one must keep under the sheet until the afternoon. I counter-attacked by saying nobody else bothered about the ridiculous rules and why should I be uncomfortable for the sake of Red Tape. All she could reply was "Don't be awkward." Result, a Draw. To be replayed tomorrow. She's a nasty bit of work and everyone hates the sight of her. I'll wring her neck one day. You will notice, by the way, that I'm writing much smaller. I've decided I've been wasting too much space, especially as I reckon each one of these sheets cost roughly a farthing. Isn't it too, too, wicked!

Incidentally, I nearly got my discharge from the Army today. The bloke in the next bed to me was told he'll probably get his discharge for damaged kidneys. Only one bed out! Perhaps I'll have better luck next time. He was told he'll probably only be able to get as far as Cape Town, but he has relations there and is as happy as a sand-boy. He said he will try and get his wife out from England and settle down there. Some people have all the luck!

In order to pass the time away I am endeavouring to write a couple of articles and intend sending them to 'Lilliput'. Whether I will finish them or not I don't know. The trouble is I can't walk up and down the floor thinking, and I find it very difficult to write without this pleasant exercise.

I do an enormous amount of reading – on average 2 books a day at the moment. For some unknown reason I can't bear novels and read mainly books on politics and economics, autobiographies, etc. I am really getting terribly highbrow, my deah. I shall almost be one of the intelligentsia when I return. Seriously though, I have had time to study and have even been improving my maths. So perhaps the war will do me a little good after all. Anyway I shall be better fitted to play my part in building a better, brighter, more beautiful, bountiful, brilliant, beery Britain. Am I being ridiculous darling? I'm sorry. But when three unexpected things happen during a day I think my mind must become a little unhinged.

I can't stand the strain of a newspaper, butter and 'Star's all at once. They should have been spread out over a week.

I can think of no more nonsense, darling, so will now close for the day. Supper will be up soon - I expect it will be the same as usual. But I managed to scrounge some bread pudding at 'tiffin' today. It was jolly good. All my love. When am I going to get another letter from you?

Wednesday 7.30 p.m. Another day nearly gone. I wonder what you are doing at this moment.

Had some good news today. The M.O. said this morning that I could get up and that I would probably be discharged on Saturday! I got up this morning directly I was told I could do so and went for a walk just around the bungalow.

I did not go very far but it took it out of me and I slept like a log during the afternoon. It's surprising how exhausting it is to walk after being in bed a long time.

I got up again about 4 p.m., washed, had tea and went to the R.A.M.C. where I played billiards with a fellow for half-an-hour. I felt much stronger than I did this morning and was not a bit tired. I bought 6 whiffs at 1 anna each and smoked one. Not bad, but, on the other hand, not good.

Incidentally, I was looking at my diet sheet today and I noticed it included one bottle of beer a day. I queried this with the sister and the matter was looked into. It appeared that I should have had beer for the first five days I was in here. It was ordered but, apparently, someone else had it. Did I fume! Fancy missing free beer!

Tomorrow, I think, I shall ask to be inoculated for cholera as I missed it through going to hospital. I believe in taking all precautions in this country.

When I get out I'll try and get a photograph taken to send you. I'll also take a walk round the bazaar to see if I can find anything for you. I intended writing to the Post Office tonight about that parcel, but I feel too tired. I should sleep well tonight. Goodnight, my sweet. All my love.

Thursday 7 p.m. Here I am darling, sitting in a chair in front of my locker on which is perched your photograph. I am smoking one of the cigars I bought yesterday.

There have been no earthquakes or air-raids again today – I hope this letter is not too dull.

The M.O. confirmed that I should be discharged on Saturday but told me to be careful and keep off fats for another 3 weeks. That was a blow because I had been promising myself a nice plate of fish and chips.

For half-an-hour this morning I had a game of billiards and also (Ssssshh!) a glass of beer. Tiffin was the same as usual and then I undressed and went to bed where I had a good sleep. I have felt very tired today, but I suppose it's only natural after being in bed all this time.

Pay was brought round today – 5 rupees (the other 5 going to my credit). It's surprising how money goes in this country. Except for the last two days I have bought nothing except necessities like soap, hair-oil, toothpaste, writing paper, etc. and 5 rupees have gone on these alone. I bought some chocolate though yesterday - 4 bars of Cadbury's – 1 rupee (4d) each. I bet you're not paying as much as that in England even now. This evening I was sitting outside on a deck chair and a Methodist Padre came along. He was a very decent fellow and we had a long talk about world affairs and the rebuilding of sanity after the war. He asked me what I did in civilian life, and advised me to keep my writing up here. I told him how I hated army life and he was very sympathetic, but urged me not to give in. He left me his address at Peshawar and asked me to go and see him one Sunday if I could get leave. He promised to give me a day entirely free from Army influence.

It was nice to have a chat with someone intelligent and I should like to go, but doubt whether I could manage it. However, it made a break and an enjoyable half-hour.

This brings today's news to an end. A further bulletin will be issued at the same time tomorrow evening. (The heat's getting me again!) Goodnight, my sweet. Don't stay up too late tonight.

Friday: A Red Letter day today (or rather an Air Mail letter day). Two letters Nos. 19 and 20, and my first two postcards Nos. 2 and 4. The postcards, by the way, don't seem to be as reliable as the letters – I don't really think it is worth while your sending them. I will now reply to your No. 19 letter.

Yes, darling, I still remember 'Bitter Sweet' and the Chiswick Empire. I taught Joe to play it on his accordion at Shinkiari and I always had to chuckle when he played it. I shall never forget the look on the girl pianist's face when her partner kept insisting on repeating the tune until the curtain went up. All these little incidents are still as plain to me as if they happened yesterday. It doesn't seem possible that it happened nearly two years ago. Darling, you gave me a great fright when I read 'My darling, I'll let you into a secret. There is a possibility of you becoming an Uncle'. My temperature went up and up until I reached the word 'uncle' when I gave a great sigh of relief. It would have been better if you had started 'An uncle there is a possibility of your becoming'. Then I would have had no reason for becoming feverish. But after your asking in one of your previous letters whether I wanted a son, it certainly made me jump when I commenced reading that sentence.

Anyway, if it's true, give my heartiest congratulations to Joe and Mary and say I will be proud to accept the position as Uncle Harry. I'll try and get hold of a few adventures now I am assured of a good listener.

You can take it from me, darling I won't change. I am still as miserable as ever and I still wish I could re-organise the British Army, the British Hospitals, the Indian Post Office, and most other things in this country. I still keep rather to myself and I've met no men yet who were such good friends as Vern and Jimmy or Walt. Or anybody as big-hearted as Mr. & Mrs. Cox and Eileen and Aubrey. Or any superior as decent as Mr. Sinclair and some of the others at "The Star".

Also, or course, I have not met a woman yet who can compare in the slightest way with you, darling. I shall always be faithful to you.

I'm like you darling. You say you think you are becoming 'hard', now I am just the same. I prefer to be alone and think of you, than be sociable.

I couldn't tell you whether we get beef or not darling. I think we do, but the meat is so tough that I've never bothered to find out what it is.

I am now going to reply to letter No. 20 but will start on a clean sheet.

Darling, you are very optimistic regarding receiving letters from me. A month is not long between receiving batches of letters.

I am certainly receiving yours rather more regularly now by Air Mail, although sometimes I still have to wait three or four weeks. When you posted them by sea mail I never expected to hear from you again under a month. Actually I think Mail Boats leave roughly every 4 weeks.

You seem to be in a terrific muddle with regard to time at home and out here. Your mathematics are in a shocking state. Out here, I think, we are $5\frac{1}{2}$ hours in front of G.M.T. You are now 1 hour in front of G.M.T. – that makes us $4\frac{1}{2}$ hours in front of you. I may be a bit out but your half-hour is a long way from the mark. Why not have a look at the Time Map of the World in Piccadilly Station Arcade? That will put you right.

You are a lucky girl being able to go to Windsor and have a walk. There's nothing I would like better than a nice walk on a cool English summer's day. There are no 'walks' out here in the sense as a walk in England. Everything's so dull and barren. There is simply no place to walk to. I certainly wish I had been with you darling.

I wonder where you went for your holiday in September? To think I was in hospital while you were probably out in the fresh air. Still I expect I could have had a worse holiday. You mention August Bank Holiday – I wonder if you have my letter yet describing our Bank Holiday at Shinkiari? I expect you have received my letter by now describing our camp cinema at Shinkiari. We have two here at Nowshera – one camp and one private. They are both pukka cinemas compared with Shinkiari, but I like the latter best because the screen is clearer and the films more modern. Mind you, the cinemas here are nothing compared with even the worst in London. Even that one in Ealing which used to be a skating rink where one cannot stretch one's legs is 'de luxe' compared with these.

Nevertheless, I am grateful for small mercies, but won't it be lovely to sit in an Odeon again!

Yes darling, I am still very much in love with you – even more so I think (if that is possible). When I have a meal I put your photograph on the other side of my table and imagine you are having lunch with me. I have to be careful though. I mustn't speak to you or my neighbours might get too interested.

I will not answer your postcards darling because, as you mention, everything is in your letters.

I've nothing much to tell you today, darling. I am definitely discharged tomorrow, but I will probably be excused all duties for a week to pick up my strength. It will be nice to get out and get some decent food, but I have to keep off of fats for 3 weeks!

This afternoon I went to the canteen and bought a pipe and tobacco. It cost 2 rupees 14 annas altogether, but it will save me money if the pipe is O.K. Also I think it's healthier.

The time is now 6 p.m. and supper will soon be up. It should be 1.30 p.m. at home and you have just come back from lunch. I wish I could exchange what you have had for my boiled fish followed by jelly.

I will close this letter now and post it by Air Mail tomorrow. I expect I shall send my next letter by Sea Mail, but I will try and send Air Mail periodically. You see I have been able to save a few rupees in hospital. That's why I have been sending by Air Mail. All my love for ever, darling. Be a good girl and keep beautiful.

STOP PRESS.

Sunday, 21st September 1941 10 a.m.: Am just going out to post this letter. I have just been going through my diary and checking up the contents of my previous letters. I think the numbering is O.K.

Came out of hospital at 2 p.m. yesterday and am feeling O.K. Am excused duties for 5 days. Went to pictures last night and saw

'Flight Command' and then had fried tomatoes and eggs in the Canteen. It was like coming out of prison.

Didn't sleep too well last night. Had no mattress and noticed it after the very springy hospital bed. Up at 7.15 a.m. this morning. Shower and breakfast. A lot of my kit has been 'lost' whilst I have been in hospital. Shall have to do something about that.

That's all for now darling. Nothing has been said yet of my going back to signalling and I am sleeping in the office. Will continue Diary in next letter, but won't promise to send it by Air Mail. All my love.

Note: Air Mail letter received by my wife on 7th November 1941

22nd September 1941   Nowshera
                                                        NWFP
                                                        India

My darling wife,

Today is Monday and I have just returned from posting your letter. Last night I went to the YMCA with John where I had some supper and played the ancient piano. I'm afraid I don't enjoy playing these out-of-date instruments which are out of tune and half the notes not playing. We left about 8.30 p.m. and John and I and another bloke played cards (first time I have played for ages) until 10 p.m. I <u>won</u> 11 annas.

Whilst I was at the Post Office today I made enquiries about that telegram of yours I did not receive, but could get no satisfaction. He said it must have been lost at Shinkiari which, I expect, is true, but not much use to me. If I were you, darling, I would make enquiries at your end and see if you can get a rebate. Although I am still excused all duties I helped a little in the office today. The Sergeant Major seems to think I am 'swinging the lead' and keeps suggesting that the only reason I was ill was that I was not getting enough exercise. He has not told me definitely yet that I'm going back to signalling, but keeps slyly suggesting it. He is one of the most ignorant persons I have ever met and directly I get the chance I am going to ask why I have been dismissed from the office. If I don't get any satisfaction I shall ask to see the Major. I'm getting just a little tired of the way things are carried on in the army.

I felt rather queer in the evening and went to bed about 7 p.m. I had stomach-ache and a bad headache (the first I've ever had). I felt better about 9.15 p.m. and had a cup of tea and a cake, but it was a long time before I went to sleep.

Tuesday 23rd September: Hello, darling. I don't feel too good today – no headache but am suffering from indigestion. I did a bit of typing in the morning but finished about 11 a.m. Didn't have much dinner and have been in bed all the afternoon. It is now 5.10 p.m. and I am just going to wash. I had a pleasant surprise today. I went to the Pay Office to find out how much I was in credit owing to my being in hospital and found it was only 5 rupees. However, they discovered that the 3d per day extra for over a year's service which I applied for weeks ago, had never been credited to me. Consequently I had 30 rupees in credit. Quite a nice surprise. So I shall draw 30 rupees out this week and 25 rupees next week. I'm drawing it all out because I don't trust the army with my money. I never received that 30/- Proficiency Pay which was due to me and which I tried to get at Watford and Woolwich.

Wednesday 24th September: Another red letter day today, darling. Your No. 21 letter arrived and postcards 4 and 5. They have really arrived very quickly. Your letter is dated August 4th and No. 5 postcard August 11th - the latter having taken just over 5 weeks only. I think that must be the quickest one I have received.

I will continue my diary and then answer your letter. By the way, I received your second telegram this afternoon which you sent on June 30th! Apparently it's been all over the North-West Frontier looking for me – all due to the fact that the dithering Post Office officials spelt my name wrong.

I will enclose the telegram cover in this letter.

Last night (or rather evening) I went for a walk to the local park. I had heard a lot about it and how English it looked. I was told that there was a river and park seats to sit on. When I got there the first thing I saw was a wide muddy river with half of it dried up and a few lawns on the bank. I saw one seat which was facing away from the river. It was really a horrible sight. I'm afraid the fellows that have been out here for a number of years get a rather distorted view of things – they have forgotten what England and English things look like. We then walked (I was with one of the clerks) to the YMCA where I had a lemonade. Back to the barracks and in bed by 10 p.m.

(My eyes ache rather at the moment, darling – it is one of the effects of the jaundice. Also I am still suffering from indigestion, so will continue later or in the morning. I love you my darling).

Thursday 25th September: Hello darling. How are you? I am still suffering with my stomach despite taking doses of Andrews Salts. However I have to go sick again this evening (end of my 5 days excused duty) so perhaps they will condescend to do something about it.

I received your No. 1 postcard today. It took such a long time because of the Draft Address you put on, I expect. You silly girl – fancy taking more notice of the War Office than of me. However, I noticed you ceased doing it with No. 3 so I will forgive you. Now to answer your letter.

I'm sorry you lost your fountain pen darling. The office seems to be trying to imitate the Army. Still you mustn't grumble. If you knew the number of things I had 'lost' you would have a fit. You certainly seem to be getting my letters all right as I am getting yours. Things out here are not so cheap now as your friend's father believes. The war affects this country too and, as most things are imported, I think the cost of living (except for cigarettes, food, fruit and other home-produced stuff) is probably as high if not higher than in England. Toothpaste, writing pads, etc., are all very dear.

I think I have answered your queries re smoking and moustache in previous letters. I am, once again, smoking a pipe and I have

228

shaved off my dirty bit. (I'd rather look like Napoleon than Hitler!)

So John said he was having a wonderful time, did he? Most of the fellows who hadn't been abroad before were thrilled by the new experience, but I think everyone is a bit 'browned off' now. After Cape Town everything was rather flat for them. I am always thinking of you and will never be my normal self till I get home again. I'm absolutely fed up to the teeth.

When we were on the boat we were advised by a sergeant to forget everything about home and seldom write – otherwise we would keep thinking of it and comparing it with India. If we didn't, he said, we would live a 'miserable existence'. He was right, but I would rather live a 'miserable existence' than forget about you, darling.

(Will have to close for a few minutes as PAY is UP).

2.30 p.m. Back from pay parade – 30 Rupees!! I think I'll send you a telegram today. But to continue:-

I'm sorry about my being a year out in the dating of my letters – I hope you didn't complain to the Post Office about the time they were taking to reach you. My first letter cost 8 annas because of its weight. I'm afraid I don't bother about weight now. I do hope you don't have to pay anything extra on my letters. Especially the Air Mail ones. I'm glad you got my No. 10 letter because that's when I started my system of keeping shorthand notes of what I wrote – so I can tell roughly what I wrote all that time ago!

I don't think there was much to choose between Deolali, Shinkiari and Nowshera – I think maybe Deolali was the best. It was much cooler and not so many insects.

I can't tell you much about the North West Frontier as there is nothing to tell. In any case I have not seen much of it. But I must admit that the man who planned Nowshera Cantonment was pretty good. It is like an oasis in the desert. There is a system of irrigation – water runs round the lawns, etc., by a kind of gutter system. And certainly they have tried to make the place as pleasant as possible for the troops.

At first glance it looks like a Garden City, but all this is, of course, spoilt by the heat and mosquitoes. It is not such a healthy place as Shinkiari or Deolali and it's hard to keep fit in a place like this.

What a remarkable co-incidence that you dreamed I was ill just about 3 weeks before I entered hospital. It is certainly a case of telepathy or something like that.

Let me know when you dream I am home again.

So Watford is still full of soldiers. I suppose it hasn't changed much. Do you ever call on Mrs. Tucker?

I see you have started practising pram-pushing again. You are making me nervous, darling. In nearly every letter now you refer to babies. Would you like me to pinch a black one for you out here? (I said pinch). It would be quite a novelty for you. You would have no need to wash it; just use Cherry Blossom or something similar. And now, after that nonsense, darling, I will continue my diary.

Last night I was persuaded to go to the pictures, although my eyes ached I thought it might help me to forget my tummy-ache, so I went and saw 'The Arsenal Stadium Mystery'. I felt very tired when I came out and was in bed before 10 p.m. and had quite a good night's sleep. In the afternoon, by the way, we had to hand in our battle dresses, woollen pants, woollen vests, etc. (!!). Probably in the near future our letters might take even longer to reach each other – but, of course, I don't know.

This morning when I woke up I didn't feel too good, but managed to eat some breakfast. I did a little typing in the morning and bought a cup of milk and some fruit for dinner. I also bought a picture frame for 4 annas for your photographs. It is standing on the mantelpiece by my bed. I often wish you had signed your photographs before I left.

It is now 3 p.m. darling. I will post this letter by Air Mail today and also send you a telegram.

By the way I have just noticed that you have sent two No. 4 postcards. One dated 23rd July and one 10th August. Tut, tut, very careless.

No. 5 card made a good journey, beating your No. 22 letter. The first time a postcard has done that. You must have just caught a 'plane by posting it a little earlier. You say you have put the clocks back an hour - is that the second time? Your timing is still in a hopeless muddle, darling. We are $5\frac{1}{2}$ hours in front of G.M.T. You should be able to work it out from that.

Friday 8 a.m.: Good morning, my love. I couldn't post your letter last night because the Post Office was shut when I came back from Sick Parade. I saw the M.O. and have to go to hospital this morning between 8 and 9 a.m. to be examined. The whole trouble is, of course, that I am supposed to keep off fats. But nearly everything is fried here. I feel much better this morning (I have been taking some Andrews) but that's always the way when I go to see the M.O.

Last night I went to the pictures again and saw 'Andy Hardy's Private Secretary'. It was very good. Afterwards I went to the Y.M.C.A. and had some fatless food. Force, mash potatoes, beans, etc. I had nothing all day except fruit. It is now 8.20 a.m. and I think I had better walk to hospital. I will let you know the verdict.

9.45 a.m. Just returned from hospital. Nothing much happened. The M.O. just said I was looking much better as, of course, I am. He repeated the warning about 'fats' but when I told him the cookhouse fried almost everything, offered no suggestion. I have got to go sick again tonight. I am still excused duties (much to the Sergeant Major's disgust).

Darling, that brings this letter right up to date. I am now going to the Post Office to post this and send you a telegram. I will not give extracts from my two previous letters as you should definitely receive the Air Mail ones.

My darling I know you will always be faithful. I can definitely also say the same, darling. Except for the Sisters in the hospital I have not even spoken to a woman since I have been in India. None of those awful things you imagine has materialised. I don't drink, gamble or go with women. So you see, darling, I was right.

I love you very much, darling and shall never stop loving you. Physically I am in India, but my spirit is always with you. I won't change darling and please don't you change. I still love my darling Scatterbrain. My love for ever. Your loving husband and sweetheart.

P.S. Please excuse the bad writing, but I have no table and have to balance the pad on my knee whilst sitting on the bed.

Note: This Air Mail letter reached my wife on December 3rd 1941

27th September 1941

Nowshera
NWFP
India

My darling wife,

Saturday: It is 2.15 p.m. at the moment and I am sitting on my bed writing this letter. It is much cooler today – a nice breeze blowing. I have been in bed all morning – my tummy has been troubling me again. However, I feel much better now and will continue my diary.

I walked to the Post Office after leaving the M.O. in the morning and posted your No. 23 letter (which I forgot to number) and also sent you a telegram which read "O.K. RECEIVED 21 LETTERS. KEEP SMILING. HARRY". I thought you would be interested to know which letters I had of yours. I have received all of them except No. 10. Both sea and air-mail have improved lately, but I noticed the other day that the air-mail was suspended for a period round about June. That's why, I expect, I had such a long wait before receiving your letters 15, 16 and 17. They must have come by sea.

I had to go sick yesterday evening and was excused duty for another 3 days. I certainly can't do much with a perpetual stomach-ache; I think I must be going to have a baby!

I met John about 5.30 p.m. and we went to the Y.M.C.A where I returned the supper he bought me a few days ago. I had grapenuts, then tomatoes with coffee. I have to be careful what I eat! We came away about 8.30 p.m. and played cards in John's barrack room until 10.30 p.m. I lost 8 annas.

Saturday 27th September: Didn't feel too good this morning. The old tummy was misbehaving again. During the morning I received your No. 22 letter.

Yes, darling, Garston was the name of the place at which I did a long guard duty when I first arrived at Watford. I wonder if you found the Manor which we guarded and the farm where we slept in a barn. It was not on the main road. Funny you should go and see Mrs. Tucker after my enquiring about her in my previous letter – but I find that often happens. I do really think there must be some form of telepathy between us. Then again you mention if I still get things 'pinched' – that is answered in my previous letters. By the way, sweet, I can't understand what these rouges are you keep mentioning with regard to your lost fountain-pen. Is it something to do with lipstick, or do you mean ROGUES? You must have been writing too quickly and made the 'u' come before its turn!

I remember our wedding date every month, darling. In a few days time we shall have been married 10 months and then it will be only 2 months to our first anniversary. I shall really have to have a glass of beer on that night – perhaps John will buy me one! I don't remember your asking whether I could change a Postal-Order out here – I shall have to look through your letters again. But I can change them. I expect you have got my Air Mail letter No. 16 by now in which I remarked I had received a P.O. from the NAPSOPA.

So Joe is really going to be a father is he? Fancy my kid brother being a father. Well! Well! Well! You say that you and Mary are busy knitting. I presume you are knitting things for Mary's baby. Only you don't say!

I think that's about all for now, darling. The time is now 3.10 p.m. and it is getting hotter. Will continue later. Love.

Sunday 6 p.m.: Continuing my diary. During yesterday afternoon I had my promised 'crib' with the Sergeant Major who simply retreated all along the line – so I didn't get a chance to use all the words I had saved up for him. He said I can go back to my old job

233

.tter but will have to return to signalling when we go on ervice. That's O.K. by me.

ne evening I walked with one of the clerks round the bazaar in the native quarter which is called the 'loose wallah' bazaar. 'Loose wallah' meaning thief. We did not hang about too long as it was dark and not exactly a healthy place to be in at night. We then strolled round the R.A. Bazaar – which is more dignified – and after lengthy bargaining with a native 'salesman' came away with a table cover which, in my opinion, is a lovely piece of work. I am going to send it to you – I do hope it arrives safely. I also bought a lady's work-bag. I might send that to Do.

I have now only 6 of my original 30 rupees left! It's surprising how the money goes when one starts buying other things than cigarettes. Also I have been buying my own food and Andrews Liver Salts – so I shall have to go careful now until Thursday. I shall probably post your parcel then. Before coming home we went in the Y.M.C.A. and I had my usual grapenuts and tomatoes. I was in bed by about 10 p.m.

Today, Sunday, I have felt much better. No tummy trouble at all, but a headache in the afternoon. During the morning I had to attend a Court of Enquiry about some kit I lost whilst in hospital and the verdict was that it was due to the negligence of the Battery. I slept most of the afternoon.

The time is now 6.30 p.m. and I have just come back from supper. (I had dinner and supper in the cookhouse today – it wasn't too fatty). It is gradually getting dark now. They are having a black-out up here soon, by the way.

Will now say Goodnight to you darling and let you know what I do tonight tomorrow. All my love. I shall be thinking of you all the evening.

Monday 6.30 p.m.: Hello darling. Nothing much to tell you today. Last night I went to the pictures and saw 'Arizona'. This morning I felt quite fit and did some work – typing, etc., but felt very tired and depressed during the afternoon. I went 'sick' again this evening and asked to be put back on duty. The M.O. agreed but told me to go sick again in 3 or 4 days time if I did not feel

234

O.K. I don't know what I shall do this evening. I do miss you, darling. I believe I am going to have a lot of trouble posting that parcel off to you. I think I have to fill in numerous forms, etc., but will find out definitely tomorrow.

I hope you are still fit and well and keeping beautiful for me. I love you very much. Goodnight darling.

Tuesday: Back at work but, nevertheless, found very little to do. Did some typing in the morning. Had a short sleep in the afternoon and some more work for about an hour at 4 p.m. In the evening I had a game of billiards and then went to the Y.M.C.A. where I had some beans and tomatoes, followed by 'Force'. I also played the piano for about an hour. 'Home' and in bed by 10 p.m. On the whole I have felt quite fit today.

Wednesday 10.45 a.m.: Got up at 7 a.m. Nothing much has happened today so far. I was having a clear up of my kit this morning and, in my old wallet, found an old letter of yours written last October. In one of your paragraphs you said you had a horrible dream. You dreamed you hadn't heard from me for months and then you received a letter with a foreign stamp on. Your dreams certainly seem to come true sooner or later. You also dreamed I was ill a few weeks before I was, but what is very encouraging is the fact that you mentioned that you dreamed I had come home. I wonder how premature that dream is?

Yesterday, by the way, we had to make our Wills. I left all my Estates, worldly goods (including the Roulette game) to you. Seriously speaking though, we never discussed what you would do if anything did happen to me. If......! But I want you to promise, darling, to keep as cheerful as possible and to carry on in just the same way. I wouldn't mind what you did so long as it made you happy. I shall always be near you darling and doing my best (if it is at all possible!) to make you happy. But I don't think anything unpleasant will happen to me. I <u>know</u> I am coming home again to you darling.

I am expecting another letter from you any day now. Tomorrow (when we get paid) I shall post off your parcel. I am afraid, darling, it will have to be our wedding anniversary, Christmas and your birthday present. I don't know whether I shall get much chance to buy anything else.

I received two more batches of 'Star's a few days ago. They don't seem to arrive very frequently. You must have sent off over 20 by now and I have received 6 only.

5.15 p.m.: I felt very sleepy this afternoon and slept from 2 to 3.30 p.m. I have just had a shower and changed from shorts and shirt to a Bush Suit and am now going to supper. I don't know what I am doing tonight so will now say 'goodnight' darling in case I go out. I love you with all my heart.

Thursday 6.30 p.m.: I am sitting in the office writing this letter as I am clerk on duty. I am sitting at the Sergeant Major's table as there is a table-lamp which comes in very handy. I have felt fit all day today, darling. This morning I got my old job back of running the Guard Roll and typing Battery Orders, etc. The fellow who had been doing it in my place had made a dreadful muddle of everything so I have been busy 'organising'. I think that's why I feel better – you know how I like organising and getting some kind of order out of chaos. I do wish I had some important job of administration in the Army. I <u>know</u> I could do it better than anyone else. But to return to the daily events:-

Last night I felt very weary but went to the 'Royal' Cinema – a cinema outside the Camp – and saw 'Bottoms Up'. The sound and clearness of the film was, I think, better than the Camp Cinema. The only trouble is that they show such old films sometimes that I forget I have seen them before until I recognise some incident or other. 'Bottoms Up' I must have seen about 7 years ago. They do, of course, show more modern films – 'Philadelphia Story' is on at the Camp Cinema tonight. I should have liked to have seen it.

I spent my remaining 4 annas on a lemonade and egg sandwich, and was in bed by 9.30 p.m.

Today there is nothing much to tell you as I have been in the office all day. This evening I intend to try and write an article. If I finish it I shall send it to 'Lilliput' and ask them to return same or cheque to you at home. If it comes back I should be obliged if you would try 'London Opinion' or 'Men Only'. But don't try and sell it to

'The Star' or 'News-Chronicle' because it is not the type of thing they buy – even if they had room. So please don't do anything to 'embarrass' me again.

I have not been able to get out today to post your table cover, but will have a good try tomorrow.

I have just been reading some Orders which appeared whilst I was in hospital and discovered that I can send an Air Mail letter for 8 annas if weighing less than $\frac{1}{2}$ oz. Also I can get 4 x $3\frac{1}{2}$ anna stamps a month for $2\frac{1}{2}$ annas. I shall have to investigate further. Will close now darling. I will conclude and post this letter tomorrow. I hope you are keeping fit and have received my telegram. Goodnight, my sweet. I love you.

Friday October 3rd 2.15 p.m.: I am going to conclude this letter this afternoon darling and post it. Again I feel very fit. Even fitter than yesterday. I think I must have been in need of mental exercise rather than physical exercise. I finished my article last night and will send it to 'Lilliput' so I expect you will be seeing it soon with a rejection slip! I don't know what to think of it. I have not the slightest idea whether it is good or bad. But the 'exercise' has certainly done me good. I wish I had tried writing before in my spare time.

I got up at 6.45 a.m. sharp and felt fresher than I have for ages. I haven't done much work up to now. I am waiting for the O.C. to give me the details for tomorrow's Battery Orders. I have not gone to bed this afternoon because I don't feel tired!

I shall probably go to the Camp Cinema tonight. 'Philadelphia Story' wasn't on last night after all, but is tonight. Have you seen it darling? I believe it is very good.

I am going to see if I can get some brown paper this afternoon to wrap up your table-cover. You would be surprised if you knew how difficult it is to get simple things like brown paper in this country.

I should get another letter from you tomorrow. All my love for ever.

P.S. I love you. Je t'aime. Ich lieberdiech (I don't know it in Hindustani!)

Stop Press:

Sunday 5.30 p.m.: I'm sorry I have not posted this before, darling, but I have been busy in the morning and felt rather queer in the afternoons. I have not felt so bright these last two days – my tummy again. I think it was caused by having some forbidden bacon on Friday night. I can't post your letter in the evening as the Post Office shuts at 4 p.m. I have wrapped up your parcel and will send it off tomorrow. I have just received a letter from Dad. The stamps on this letter cost me only 10 annas. A special concession. We are allowed four a month – so that's my quota for the next four weeks. Will close now, darling, and have a small trot to the Post Office. All my love for ever.

6th October 1941   Nowshera
                                                          India

My darling wife,

I posted your letter last night and this morning I sent your parcel off. I hope you get it. I registered it, but I don't suppose that will guarantee its arrival. I have not received this week's letter from you yet – it should have arrived Saturday - I have also been expecting a telegram!

I have felt a bit better this afternoon – less pains in the tummy. It is still, of course, the effects of the jaundice. I am still slightly yellow. It takes a long time for the effects to entirely disappear.

Last night I had a game of billiards from 7 to 8 p.m. and then went to bed. Today I have been very busy in the office (no afternoon sleep) and tonight I am clerk on duty.

At the moment (7.10 p.m.) there is a blackout practice until 9.30 p.m. It is just like old times. I have a black pair of gym shorts shading the electric light and blackout material over the windows. Some officers, including the O.C. are acting as wardens and I have already been warned about a chink of light showing! It reminds me of the times the warden used to knock at home. Do you still get him calling?

(The Sergeant Major's just been in to say my light's showing - but I proved it wasn't. He then walked into the other office without any blackouts up and switched on the lights. He was caught by the O.C.!!)

Yesterday I received another week's supply of 'Star's (for the middle of July I think) and I have read every word in them.

I have sent my article off to 'Lilliput' and might try to write another article tonight. Will close now and send my goodnight kisses by telepathy.

Thursday 9th October: I am sorry I haven't written during the last two days, darling, but we have been very busy all the day (including the afternoon) and when we have finished about 6 p.m. it is getting dark. There is a proper blackout here now for a week or so and, as we have no blackout material, we have to stay in the dark (if we stay in). So you see, darling, I have not been able to write to you in the evening. The time is now 5.15 p.m. (we were finished earlier today) and so I am able to continue this letter, but I shall not be able to write for long as it is getting dark.

I did not do much Tuesday or Wednesday. As I mentioned before I am very busy in the office. On Tuesday evening I played billiards for an hour in the Regimental Canteen and then went to the Y.M.C.A. Yesterday I did the same.

It is getting very much like home here now – in one respect. The sirens go, planes come over and there are explosions. All very realistic but, of course, no one takes as much notice of the whole affair as they would if it were real.

Today we got paid. Only 5 rupees this week (after 50 in the last fortnight). I haven't got much to show for it – money goes even faster here than at home. I reckon, although 1 rupee is supposed to be worth 1/6d it has no more spending power than 6d in England in peace-time. Even here, during peace-time, the rupee had only the spending power of 1/-.

I have been expecting a letter or/and telegram from you darling - but no. I should have had an Air Mail letter from you last Saturday, but I expect I will get two together.

239

I will probably send this letter by sea mail because of the financial position. Or perhaps it would be better if I left this to next week and then send it by Air Mail. I could send you an Air Mail postcard this week.

I am feeling much fitter again now – the tummy is almost normal. I shall certainly keep off all fats though. Goodnight sweetheart. I love you.

Friday 10th October: Hello darling. I love you. I received your telegram today. There was no date of despatch on it, so do not know how long it took.

Last night I played billiards in the canteen again – I am still pretty duff. On the table on which I was playing the cloth was torn and the native Babu (fellow who looks after the tables) tried to blame me for it. Anyway he made a complaint to the N.C.O. in charge, so I expect I shall hear more about it.

We have just heard that we are being paid again on Monday instead of next Thursday, so I will be able to post this letter in a couple of days' time.

6 p.m. This afternoon, as I expected, I had to go and see the Regimental Sergeant Major about the billiard table. I told him that it was torn before I went to the table. Finally he went over to the canteen to inspect the cloth himself.

The cloth had been taken off the table and it was in a terrible state – all patches underneath, etc., and it didn't need much effort to tear it.

The Sergeant Major gave the Babu a good talking to and told him to pay more attention to his job, etc. Definitely a victory for me. Will now close, darling, as I am going to the pictures. Goodnight sweetheart.

Sunday 12th October 5.15 p.m.: Hello darling. Will continue my diary from Friday. In the evening I went to the pictures and saw 'Come Live with Me' which was quite good.

On Saturday morning we weren't quite so busy as usual. I learned, to my disgust, that now we aren't getting paid until next Friday. A nasty blow – especially as I am broke already. During the afternoon we all had a sleep – the first for a long time – at the suggestion of the Sergeant Major. The Battery Office was closed up and we all had a good snore.

I was rather at a 'dead end' in the evening, but I had a game of snooker and spent the rest of my time with the canteen wireless. At 9.15 p.m. I heard a programme from England which I forgot the title of, but it had the tune 'All Pals Together' as the signature tune. At 9.30 p.m. I heard the news. By the way Big Ben struck 4 o'clock just before the news commenced, so it seems quite definite that we are $5\frac{1}{2}$ hours in front of you now. Nothing much to tell you about today. Had another sleep this afternoon and am now eagerly awaiting supper as I feel quite hungry.

I'm afraid I can't even afford to send you a postcard this week now, darling so will send you a fortnight's news on Friday. I hope you won't mind. I still have received no letter from you. I wonder what's holding them up.

By the way darling, you are a funny girl for answering telegrams. There's no need to waste two words saying 'cable received' – I know that by your telegram. Also 'received' was spelt 'recd'. I don't know whether you spelt it that way, or the Post Office, but if you did, darling, it doesn't save you any money by shortening words. 'Received' costs just as much as 'Recd', as 'Antidisestablishmentarianism' costs the same as 'I'.

Well, my sweet, it is 5.30 p.m. and I hear food calling me. I have certainly regained my appetite. I am feeling very fit again. I hope you are. I am going to try and get a game of table tennis this evening. All my love for now.

Monday 9 p.m.: I am clerk on duty tonight, so have not been out this evening. Something rather unfortunate has just happened. Earlier in the evening my watch-strap broke and the watch fell on the floor. It didn't seem to have any effect at the time, but I have just noticed that it has now stopped. I took the glass off and shook it. It went for a few minutes but has stopped again – I think for good. I shall have to save a few rupees now to get it repaired.

But it's a damn nuisance, especially as it has been going so well and keeping good time.

To continue my recording of daily events. Last night I was taken to another canteen by the two fellows you met on guard with me at Watford and we played table tennis all the evening – and it is not a very cool pastime in this country. However, I think the exercise did me good.

Nothing interesting has happened today except a storm which came suddenly upon us about 5.30 p.m. I've seen storms (which include sand storms at Deolali and Shinkiari) but never have I seen such a violent one as this. The sand was so thick that, looking out of the office window, it looked just like a bad London fog. Visibility was limited to about 2 yards. The wind was howling and almost uprooting the trees; the lightning was practically continuous, and combined with the thunder, the scene was reminiscent of a typhoon as portrayed in an American film. All the electric lights went out about 6 p.m. and did not come on again until after 8 p.m. It is still slightly raining and there is a nice cool smell of moisture in the air reminding me of home. I suppose it is beginning to get cold in England now – it doesn't seem possible that this is October out here. Of course, it is much cooler, but it is still hotter mid-day than the normal English summer. Darling, that's all the news for now. I've just taken another look at my watch, but it's not going. I am off to bed now. Goodnight sweetheart.

Tuesday 6.15 p.m.: I am sitting on the veranda outside the Battery Office writing this letter as it is lighter here. I think the blackout ends tonight, thank goodness. It has been just like being back at home this past week. Sirens going during the day and loud bangs at night. But it will be nice not to have to worry about blackout tonight.

Nothing exciting has happened today. My watch is still stopped. Tonight I have borrowed 5 rupees and think I will have a game of billiards. Life without money in a dump like this isn't too bright.

Nothing much more I can add darling. I hope I get a letter from you soon. I haven't had one for over a fortnight! Goodnight darling.

Friday 6.30 p.m.: I'm sorry I have not written for the past two days, darling, but I have been very busy and have been glad to get out and away from it all in the evening.

However, I will continue my diary from Wednesday. In the evening the powers that be decided to give us a little 'do'. They weren't being benevolent however, as it was paid for out of the men's Battery Funds (8 annas a month per man). Instead of 5.30 p.m. supper was served at 7 p.m. and we had the following:

Roast potatoes, roast chicken, sausage and tomatoes with 1 bottle of beer. 'Xmas' pudding and one packet of 'Players'. It made a change and the food was quite good. There was no speech making or regular 'do' afterwards. However, the beer made me tired and I went straight to bed.

On Thursday evening I played snooker and table tennis and then had some supper at the YMCA. Not very interesting, I'm afraid. Today has been rather an unfortunate one for me. I had to go on Parade this morning as we were being inspected by some big-wig. We had our backs towards the sun and just as the B.W. was talking to an officer in front of me I began to 'pass out'. The colonel noticed it and instructed the man next to me to fall out and take me in the shade. I soon felt better. Actually four other people had to leave the ranks too – it was certainly a silly idea to have the sun beating on our backs; although it is now mid-October, it is still very hot mid-day.

After the parade I received your letter No. 23. So it seems quite definite now that Joe is to be a father. Good luck to him. It's funny you should have seen a film called 'Rage in Heaven' when you wrote, as it is on at our 'local' tonight. I would like to see it but don't think I can afford it. I have only a couple of rupees left – I think I will try and post this letter by Air Mail for 8 annas. I believe it can be done for $\frac{1}{2}$ oz letters and, although this will weigh more, I will chance it. I may get away with it. I want to post this letter tomorrow as it may be some time before I can post a letter again!!

This evening I went and broke the glass of my watch and the hour hand and minute hand both came off. It is certainly in a sorry state now. I shall have to save hard to get it repaired.

10 p.m.: I suddenly stopped writing because people kept coming in the Battery Office and worrying me. I decided on the spur of the moment, as I wasn't feeling too cheerful, to go to the pictures and see 'Rage in Heaven', but when I got there the cheapest seat was half a rupee, so I did not go. I then went over to the canteen, met Joe, and played billiards and jawed for the rest of the evening.

I am now sitting on my mattress (we are sleeping on the floor, having handed our beds in) writing this letter.

Incidentally darling I dreamed of you last night. It was a very vivid dream. I was back home and we were walking along a road near Finsbury Park and, on turning the corner, met Joe and Mary. It was all very clear. I wish it had been true.

I shall post this letter tomorrow morning, darling, as it may be the last chance I shall get. I am definitely finished with office work now and am going back to signalling. It will make a change.

I hope you are getting my letters O.K. - I had to wait 3 weeks to get yours, despite the fact that you sent it by Air Mail. Sometimes it is very quick and other times not much quicker than sea mail.

I did not forget our 10 months' wedding anniversary on the 7th. I have been trying to get a suitable card to send you for December 7th, but cannot find one. There is one of a sorts, however, in the parcel I have sent you. I do hope you receive it.

I have not sent Do's present off yet. I have been trying to find something to buy the children and Dad, but have had no success. This is a dump. However, please tell them I have not forgotten them all and will send them all something sooner or later.

Well, darling 'Retreat' is now sounding so I think I will close now. Be good darling. I am always thinking of you and love you with all my heart. Goodnight and au revoir, darling. Love for ever.

18th October 1941
Saturday:

My darling,

It is exactly a week ago since I posted No. 25 letter by Air Mail. I am sorry I have not continued writing in diary form this week, but we have been moving and, as you can probably see by the 'address' above I am, once again, on board a ship.

---------- about six lines censored ----------

It is very difficult to know what to write. I am being very cautious as I do not want this letter to be cut about as you say one or two of my previous ones were.

I think the best idea is to give you a rough description of the boat which we are now on.

It is not the same vessel as the one we came out on (although she is with us in the harbour) but is of a very similar design. We are not half as crowded as before and consequently life is a little more comfortable. Also the canteen is a little bigger and includes a PIANO – a very good one too; the best I have come across since leaving home. I have been playing quite a lot. There is also a cinema on board (free I believe) and tonight there is a Show. I will, of course, have a 'basin full'.

Yesterday we were paid in English money! - (a great thrill to have tanners and bobs again after annas and rupees) and received a fortnight's pay - £1. Last night I bought a pint of beer and played the piano for an hour or two.

It was almost like old times and it was the best evening I have had since I was in England. And I did only have one pint of beer, darling. That's all we are allowed per day, so I can assure you I did not get blotto, or even slightly blotto!

Everyone is issued with a ticket entitling them to one pint of beer and is optimistically labelled 'NOT TRANSFERABLE'. However, a really determined man can get hold of two or three from people who don't drink – either by persuasion or payment. But I am not as determined as all that.

On boarding we all thought we were going to get cabins, but to our disappointment have the same kind of accommodation as before. But, as we are not overcrowded, it is not too uncomfortable. The only other important item – food – is middling, but, at the moment, far better than we received on the former boat.

Our daily life is very similar to the previous trip. A parade at 11 a.m. and the rest of the day practically to ourselves except for guard duties and fatigues. As I mentioned before I have left the office now and am one of the 'mob'.

There's a nice view from where I am sitting. Different types of ships in the bay and the port in the distance. India looks quite a nice country from outside – very much like a bad apple with a nice rosy skin. I hope we never return to this country again – although where we are going may be worse. If we continue in this way it looks as if I shall have been round the world two or three times before the war ends. I am beginning to feel dizzy already.

I hope you are keeping well, darling, and cheerful. I keep as cheerful as possible although I occasionally get great fits of depression and don't care a hang for anybody or anything connected with the army.

The time is now 9.50 a.m. and I have to hand this letter in for posting, so will now close. I don't know when you will receive this letter, but directly we arrive at our destination, I will, if at all possible, send you a telegram with my new address.

All my love, darling.

P.S. I will continue the letters day by day in future. I'm afraid they will be undated, but I expect you will be able to work it out. I don't suppose you will receive this till nearly Xmas.

Note: This unstamped 'On Active Service' letter franked 'Received from HM Ships' reached my wife on 21st January 1942

30th October 1941   On Board

My darling wife,

I did not post letter No. 26 at the port of embarkation as I was mis-informed about the time that letters had to be handed in. However, I will post it with this letter at our next port of call – I don't suppose it will take any longer to reach you.

I have not been writing every day as promised and I should have had to be very careful in not giving information away in the form of dates, etc.

We have now been at sea for a few days and, as I mentioned previously, will be calling at a port soon. We are hoping that we will get shore leave, but no one actually knows anything. Since my last letter nothing startling has happened. The sea has been very calm and the weather very hot. Today, however, there is quite a wind blowing and the sea looks more like --------------. I wish it were!

I have done another Guard on the ship and also have been on fatigues on two mornings.

This trip is still much more comfortable than the one out to India, although it still leaves a lot to be desired. However, there is no need for grumbling as this voyage should ------------------------ ------------------------------------.

Every day has seen the usual routine – 6 a.m. Reveille; 7 a.m. Breakfast; 11 a.m. Parade; 12 noon Dinner; 5.30 p.m. Supper; (or tea whichever one likes to call it) 8 p.m. a cup of tea; 9.30 p.m. bed time. The rest of the time we have to ourselves unless we are on guard duties or fatigues.

I have been playing the piano most evenings and, I must admit, have had my ration of one pint of beer.

It's been rather expensive and I am now broke a week before the next pay day. But I think it was worth it. It made a very pleasant change and has kept me in a more cheerful mood. Also, of course, there may not be the chance again of having a pint of beer, or playing the piano for, maybe, the duration. So I looked upon it as a kind of 'last fling' although a very poor kind of 'fling' compared with the ones we have had together at home.

The sea air, too, definitely agrees with me. I wish I had been able to get in the Navy when I was called up – I think I would have been a lot happier. At night I sling my hammock on deck and usually have it next to the side of the ship. It is quite pleasant to lay on a swinging hammock and watch the sea roll by below. It gets dark very quickly here. Blackout is about 6 p.m. I have dreamed about you nearly every night since I have been on board, darling. I think it's because I imagine we are going home again ----------------
-------------------------------.

I received two batches of 'Star's on board before we left port. The last week in July and the first in August. I have not had a letter from you since we left our former station, and I expect it will be quite a time before I hear from you again. However, as I promised in my previous letter, I will send you a telegram if it is at all possible when we reach our destination. And, I expect, I shall still be able to send letters by Air Mail.

Well, darling, I don't think there is much more I can tell you. I suppose it is beginning to get chilly in England now – I wish I could see a nice rainy, cold, typical London day for a change.

I hope you are still keeping fit. I still think the war won't last much longer. I am always looking forward to the day when we are together again. I will continue this letter, darling, for the remainder of the voyage and it will be posted, I expect, when we reach our destination. All my love for ever, darling.

Note: This letter 'On Active Service' and franked 'Received from H.M. Ships' was received on 21st January 1942

4th November 1941   *On Board*

My dearest Gwen,

As you will see, we are still at sea at the time of my writing this letter although we hope to reach our destination in a couple of days' time.

Since last writing to you we have had an evening ashore at a port* of call – which of course I can't mention at the moment. It was not very interesting, partly, of course, because I was 'broke' and also because, although it was a capital, it had none of the usual town attractions. For instance, there was only one cinema and, as far as I could see, no theatres. The trams were funny affairs. They had no sides – only a roof covering. They looked rather like the pier trams at English sea-side resorts. We landed at about 4 p.m. and wandered around until 9.30 p.m. No doubt, if we had landed earlier, we could have gone for some nice walks outside the town and along the sea front, but as it was getting dark there was nothing else to do except stay in town. There were canteens opened for soldiers and a kind of reception committee similar to that of Cape Town. But in no way could it be compared with our stay in Cape Town. Most of the evening I spent walking around the shops and in a canteen where one could have as many cups of Ceylon tea as one liked, quite free. They also sold cakes, etc., and in one corner of the room was a 'band' – piano, trumpet and drums (natives, by the way) – in front of which soldiers were dancing with the local white women who were running the canteen. Needless to say, I did not dance.

Note: *Colombo, Ceylon.

I often wish I were back home. It must be getting chilly and raining now. Lovely thoughts!!

I am really feeling very homesick, darling and am getting rather fed up with being pushed around the globe. The only thing that brightens me up is the thought that the war won't last much longer now. I hope I'm right.

This letter will have to be posted tomorrow, so I will add more later. I am sorry I have not been writing every day as promised, but I have felt really too depressed to do anything lately. I am feeling a little better today though.

Wednesday: I have just found out, darling, that I should have posted this letter last night. But I shall have to try my luck this morning.

I am extremely fed up this morning. Last night I 'lost' (or to put it more crudely they were stolen) a pair of shorts in which I had my wallet, money and various other things. Lots of other fellows also lost their kit and personal property. I don't mind losing a pair of shorts, but I had a lot of personal effects in my wallet, including the photographs of you. I can't do anything else except hope that, by some miracle, they will be returned.

Well, darling, will finally close now. The next letter I send you will, I hope, be by Air Mail. Keep smiling, darling. All my love for ever.

The following morning we left port again and are, once again, surrounded by acres and acres of water with nothing to look at except the other ships in the convoy, and nothing to do except guard duties, fatigues and parades.

Yesterday afternoon I went to the cinema. It is only a small place, but quite comfortable. And free. The screen, ten feet away, looks just about as big as the screen in an Odeon Cinema from the very back row in the top gallery. But the picture is very clear and distinct.

Yesterday I saw 'Irene' which I believe you mentioned you had seen. I have also seen, at previous shows, 'The Story of Irene and Vernon Castle', 'Knights of the Range' and 'French Without Tears'. Yesterday the show was rather spoilt by the continuous 'jumping' of the film. However, one cannot grumble.

Yesterday also I had my first lesson of a course in O.P.A's work. (Observation Post Assistant). The point being that the signaller might have to take over an officer's work in an emergency. It is not very interesting and I don't like the work much. By the way, my official job now is wireless operation at the O.P. (Observation Post).

I have not been playing the piano much these last few days – I have not been in the mood! I have been feeling very depressed these last few days for no apparent reason at all. Yesterday, on the morning's parade, I came over giddy again and had to fall out. I don't think this part of the world agrees with me at all.

Sign. Berry H.W
974063
73rd Field Battery RA
5th Field Regt. RA
Malaya
19th November 1941

My darling wife,

It is over a fortnight since I posted my last letter to you, but I have not had much opportunity of writing before owing to our moving, also not knowing, until a few days ago, our official address, or how we posted letters. Thank you for your telegram which I received two days ago – yes, I am quite well again darling. I have not sent you one yet, but I am hoping that Mrs. Collins will let you know where I am as I know John sent a telegram home with our new address.

As you will see I am no longer in India, but a little further east – Malaya. I'm afraid I cannot tell you in which location we are stationed, but we are near a fairly-sized town* and I find this country a far more pleasurable place than India. It looks more like England, and the climate is not so hot. But I will start from the beginning.

*Ipoh

The day following the day I posted my last letter, we arrived at our port of disembarkation.° I don't think I am allowed to mention this but you should be able to guess it. We docked about 11 a.m. About half the regiment disembarked soon after as they were travelling by road and taking the vehicles. I left with the second batch about 8 p.m. in the evening. We did not, therefore, see much of the port, but it looked a very nice place and all the trees looked very green. Quite a change from India. We marched to the station from the docks (about a mile) where a train awaited us.

°Singapore

251

It left at 10.30 p.m. and we were told we would arrive at our destination the following afternoon. We made ourselves as comfortable as we could sleeping on the wooden seats, the floor, etc. I slept on the luggage rack and was quite comfortable. The following morning when I woke up we had stopped at a place called 'Blue-pencil'. Later we learned that a train had been derailed in front of us and we should probably remain stationary all the morning. We were allowed to have a walk round the town whilst we were waiting and, although it was only a small place, it looked quite decent and the surrounding trees and grass looked very refreshing and green. I always thought Malaya would be very much like India, but I was wrong. The people (mostly Chinese) are cleaner and look healthier. There is none of the filth or smells one sees and breathes in India, and the heat is not so torrid. They have quite a lot of rain here – it rains at least once a day, and consequently, there is not that barrenness so typical of India.

About 2 p.m. the train started again and we rolled merrily onwards through green forests and rubber plantations. At 3.30 a.m. (although we didn't get off the train till 6.30 a.m.) we arrived at the station nearest our final destination. The town looked a grand place in the morning light. Big white buildings, spotlessly clean. (I forgot to mention that, coming up in the train, we noticed how modern and tidy the towns looked. The buildings would be outstanding in London and some of the stations were marvellous examples of architecture).

There were a number of lorries waiting to transport us waiting outside the station driven by Ghurkas, and, after a ride of 4 or 5 miles, we arrived at our camp situated plumb in the middle of a rubber plantation. The huts are similar to those we had at Deolali, although a little more strongly built I think.

I have not done much since I have been here. I have been to the town on three occasions. The regiment runs lorries to take us there and back; every evening starting at 6 p.m.

It is quite a large place – as Eastern towns go – and has various places of amusement. Western style cinemas (including a Gaumont-British 'Rex'), dance halls, canteens, etc. The dance halls are funny places. They are quite free to enter and have dance hostesses who charge 30 cents a dance. One buys a book of tickets at the pay desk and presents one to any slant-eyed Chinese maiden who takes his fancy. They also sell drinks, but they are very dear – about 50 cents a glass. I only go in these places occasionally for a few minutes to listen to the band. Paying the equivalent of 9d for a short dance and 1/2d for a glass of beer does not appeal to me. By the way you will have noticed that the money is cents and dollars out here. I now get 5 dollars a week (a dollar being worth roughly 2/4d) and it does not go very far. The cost of living is very high in this country and a dollar seems to go no further than an English shilling. There is a rumour that we are going to get Colonial pay (another 6d a day) soon, but I don't bank on it. Things are cheaper in the camp NAAFI. It is possible to get a packet of cigarettes for 5 cents and a bottle of beer for 25 cents.

There is also a good YMCA in town where they have billiards, table tennis, wireless and a PIANO, and one can get a good meal there quite cheaply. Nevertheless a dollar still seems to go very quickly. I feel much fitter here than in India, mainly I think, because the climate is cooler and damper. One of the curses is mosquitoes. They are not malaria carrying ones, but they certainly bite! Everyone gets bitten several times an evening and they are extremely irritating. Otherwise we are in a fairly healthy spot. Each town has a 'Health Area' of about 5 miles radius and that is why the mosquitoes here are not of the malarial type. It might be quite a different story if and when we move from here into the jungle. Most of the troops in this country are, by the way, Aussies, as you probably know.

Up to two days ago I was, once again, a signaller. I have been doing fatigues and guards but, because of the cooler weather, have almost enjoyed it. I made up my mind never to work in an Army office again. However, a couple of days ago I was told to report to the Battery Office, where I was told to report to the Regimental

Office as I was, in future, to be employed there. Whether this is permanent or not I do not know, but I shall be glad when I find out whether I am a clerk or a signaller.

I am writing this letter in the office. I am, once again, clerk on duty and it is now 9.30 p.m. and I am feeling very tired. I shall not be able to post this letter until Friday (Pay Day) so will close now and continue tomorrow. Goodnight, my darling.

Thursday 20th November: I am sitting on my bed writing this letter. The time is about 7.30 p.m. and it is pouring with rain. (I am sorry this writing is so faint, but I think someone must have watered my ink).

I have felt quite fit today and the office wasn't too dull. The grub here is not too good. Besides breakfast (always shrivelled bacon and bread) we only get one hot meal a day. (Meat, potatoes and maybe stringy beans or carrots). The evening meal consists of simply a sandwich or bread and jam. All my 'spare' money goes on food.

I said in my last letter that I had lost your photographs when my wallet was pinched on board ship. I now find I did not, luckily I kept them in the picture frame I bought at Nowshera and packed it in my pack. I was much more cheerful on finding them safe, although it was annoying losing my money just as we had been paid. Still 'Never mind-eh!'.

I'm afraid I won't be able to send your telegram this week as promised owing to the financial situation. But I shall be sending you one in a week or so to reach you, I hope, on our Wedding Anniversary. I don't suppose you will receive this letter till nearly Christmas.

I notice that the local newspaper is published in the town here. I think one evening I might try my hand at writing an article again. It would be a novelty to see something in print again.

Well, darling, I don't think there is anything more to add for the present. I shall post this letter tomorrow by Air Mail (50 cents). Ordinary sea-mail is free from here as where we are now counts as Active Service. I am hoping to get a letter from you soon. My last one was No. 23 received on 17th October! I expect they will arrive in a batch from India.

If you receive this letter anywhere near Christmas I will take the opportunity of wishing you as merry a Xmas as possible (I shall be thinking of you every minute that day) and hope that the new year will see us together again sometime, darling. I don't think the war will last much longer now.

Please remember me to everyone and give them my Xmas regards – Herbert and Hazel, Frank, Muriel, Joe and Mary, Eileen, Mr. & Mrs. Cox (if you see them) and Uncle Tom Cobleigh and all. All my love, darling.

P.S. I hope my Xmas present is now well on its way to you. When I get that Postal Order you promised me I intend to get my watch repaired if it does not cost too much.

There were no more letters from Malaya. The Japanese invaded on the night of December 7th 1941 (My first wedding anniversary!)
However, my wife did receive one telegram and three cablegrams – all sent from Post Offices that were still 'open for business' during the war.

POST OFFICE TELEGRAM: RECEIVED EALING, MIDDX.. 2 DEC. 41.
'TELEGRAM P.O. RECEIVED. ADDRESS MALAYA. LOVE. HARRY BERRY'

CABLE & WIRELESS LTD. DATED 9 DEC. 41:
'CONGRATULATIONS ON ANNIVERSARY. BEST WISHES. LOVE. DARLING. BERRY'

CABLE & WIRELESS LTD. DATED 5 JAN. 42: (CENTRAL STATION LONDON)
'OK. DON'T WORRY. ALL LOVE XMAS. HARRY BERRY'

CABLE & WIRELESS LTD. DATED 17 FEB. 42 (CENTRAL STATION LONDON)
'OK. RECEIVED 31 LETTERS 8 POSTCARDS. BELATED BIRTHDAY GREETING. LOVE. HARRY BERRY'

This last Cablegram I managed to send from a small Post Office a few minutes before the staff evacuated.
Singapore fell to the Japanese on 15th February 1942.

The cablegrams from Malaya and Singapore were the last communications my wife received from me for a long time. It was over a year – late March 1943 – before she received a curt letter from the Royal Artillery Record & Pay Office, Foots Cray, Sidcup, Kent, which read:

'Madam,
Army Form B104-83A
I have to inform you that a report has been received from the War Office to the effect that (No.) 974963 (Rank) Gunner Dr i/c (Name) Henry William Berry (Regiment) Royal Artillery, is a Prisoner of War in Taiwan Camp.
Should any other information be received concerning him, such information will at once be communicated to you.
Instructions as to the method of communicating with Prisoners of War can be obtained at any Post Office.
                    I am,
                    Your obedient Servant,
                    Officer in charge of Records'

Some weeks later she received her first POW card from me which had been sent (when I was still in Singapore) from Changi. It read:
'Darling, Don't worry. I am in the best of health and really very fit. Keep smiling. Give my love to all. Love, Harry. No. 974063 L/Bdr. H. Berry.

PART FIVE

THE WAR AND CAPITULATION

It was, of course, impossible to write to my wife, or even keep a diary, during the short but hectic war in Malaya. My regiment, the 5th Field Regiment, Royal Artillery, was in action from the day the Japanese landed at Kota Bharu to the final capitulation of Singapore.

Soon after returning home after the war I wrote "I was a 'Guest' of the Japs in Tokyo" and "First to meet the Japanese in Malaya" both of which were published in "War Illustrated" in October 1946* and January 1947.**

The accounts which follow of "The Fall of Singapore," "Changi" and "Rude Awakening," I wrote about the same time but were not published.

*Vol. 10 No. 244 October 25, 1946
**Vol. 10 No. 250 January 17,1947

The following was first published in "War Illustrated" on January 17th 1947.

FIRST TO MEET THE JAPANESE IN MALAYA

We arrived at Kota Bharu on the night of December 5th 1941. After the opposite side of the Malay Peninsula where we had been stationed for the past month, our new camp did not impress us. We were about 30 miles outside the town, our 'barracks' being wooden huts in the middle of a rubber plantation. Everyone was heartily fed up with rubber plantations, and we were to get even more tired of them during the next few months. The most popular song among the isolated British troops was a parody, 'I hope that I shall never see another blinkin' rubber tree!'

In the middle of our first night there we were called on parade and informed that a Jap convoy had been sighted heading towards Malaya and it looked as if they meant business. We 'rookies' from England were confident that it was a false alarm. After weeks of standing-to on the British coast at the beginning of the same year prepared for the oft-threatened German attack, we were inclined to be sceptical. But this time we were wrong and, on the night of December 7-8th the blow fell. The Japs had commenced landing operations at Kota Bharu and we were officially at war.

Our unit was the 73rd Field Battery of the 5th Field Regiment, Royal Artillery, and we were the only British troops of the 9th Indian Division which had the job of defending the whole of the north-east corner of Malaya. The rest were Indians, mainly Hyderabad State Troops. We climbed into our vehicles and in convoy formation rolled off towards the battle-front.

Dawn was breaking when we arrived at our rendezvous. The vehicles were parked and camouflaged and we awaited further orders. Except for the occasional explosions in the distance and the faint hum of aircraft it seemed fairly quiet. Excitement rose when, early in the afternoon, a despatch rider who had accompanied some officers to the front returned with what we took to be authentic news.

259

"You'll be back in your camp by this time tomorrow, boys!" he told us. "The Air Force has sunk hundreds of landing barges and the Japs have been beaten off!" We congratulated each other, gave silent thanks to the Air Force and began to look forward to relaxing in our camp bunks. Our optimism was short-lived. A few hours later we were ordered to advance and go into action. The Japs had returned at a different part of the coast and had already been successful in establishing a beach-head.

A half-hour's journey brought us to the aerodrome on the other side of the town. We pushed our 4.5 Howitzers into position well hidden by the trees surrounding the airport, dug trenches, and waited for the order to fire. Nothing startling happened, so we commenced making ourselves 'at home'. We brewed tea and the cooks prepared a bully-beef stew. There was not much activity on the airport, but we knew that sooner or later the Japs were bound to come and bomb either us or the nearby hangars. With great fatalism we refused to let that worry us. The immediate consideration was rest and something to eat and drink. The future would look after itself. Suddenly a shout went up.

"Take cover! Here they come!" The faint hum of approaching aircraft grew louder, and presently we saw them. There were five, and they confirmed the impression we then held of the Jap Air Force. They were all ancient biplanes and, as they sailed slowly over our position we couldn't help chuckling. "Wait till the Spits and Hurricanes get on their track" we told each other. "It will be sheer slaughter!"

But as they passed right overhead we gave gasps of astonishment. They weren't Japs. They had the circular red, white and blue rondels on their wing-tips! Someone suggested they were our training planes getting away whilst the going was good, and it seemed the only reasonable explanation. It was a long time before we realized that we had very few aircraft in Malaya and those we had were nearly all out of date. Neither did we appreciate at the time the splendid fight our pilots put up in the 100 mph crates against the superior Jap craft.

Our confidence was again shattered when, a few minutes later, we saw a squadron of low-winged monoplanes approaching from the north. "At last," we said. "Here come the Spitfires!" We stood out in the open and cheered, but rushed for cover when they started dive-bombing and machine-gunning the drome. This time it was the Japs.

Before we went into action that night we saw most of the hangars on fire and all the aircraft on the ground destroyed. Our air arm had ceased to function.

As soon as night fell we received the order to fire. I was a signaller, and grew more miserable as the night wore on, trying to get messages through on a faulty line and to hear and make myself heard above the continuous noise of the howitzers only ten yards away. Then it started raining; and indeed it knows how to rain in Malaya. I had orders to try to repair the cable leading

260

to our other troop of guns. Having no torch I had to grope my way through the undergrowth, and when I reached 'Eddy' Troop I found they had ceased firing and were preparing to move. I dashed as fast as I could in the darkness back to my own lines and with more luck than judgement managed to find my vehicle.

The main route from Kota Bharu that night looked like the London-Brighton road on a Bank Holiday. Hundreds of vehicles were trailing each other with headlights full on. If the Jap Air Force had thought to come our way then all would have been lost. And so for the next fortnight the battle raged along the 50 miles to Kuala Krai. Days and nights had little meaning for us. We slept and ate when we could. It was impossible to stay in one position for longer than 24 hours as the Jap pilots would spot us. So we would go into action for as long as possible, beat a hasty retreat, and find a 'hide' a few miles further down the road then go into action again. So it went on. A queer nightmare without beginning or end.

None of us knew exactly what was happening. We didn't even realize that the war was going badly for us and that on the other side of the peninsula the Japs were making a far speedier advance.

Having a knowledge of shorthand, it became my job (when we weren't actually in action) to tune in to the BBC every night and take down the news. We felt quite proud when the announcer stated that British troops in the north-east of Malaya had made contact with the enemy. It often struck us as quaint that people in London 5,000 miles away knew more of what was going on than we did. Although we thought we were putting up quite a good show, we realized it couldn't last. Losses among the Indian infantry were enormous and we were always in danger of being cut off by the enemy thrust through Penang. Eventually we were finally driven back to Kuala Krai where the road ended and the railway remained the only way open to the south and safety. One by one, whilst still firing, the guns were withdrawn and hauled to the station. All night we worked loading guns, vehicles, ammunition and other war material onto the open railway trucks, and as dawn broke we pulled out en route for Kuala Lumpur, some 200 miles to the south, and to what we thought would be a rest, with time to overhaul our equipment and strengthen our defences. Strange how optimism refuses to die, even when one knows the odds are piled heavily in the enemy's favour.

But such was the speed of the Jap advance that within a few days we were once again in the front line. By January 11th Kuala Lumpur and its aerodrome had to be abandoned. And the sad story continued until February 15th 1942 when at Singapore we received the order to cease fire – and we commenced our weary three and a half years as prisoners of war.

FALL OF SINGAPORE

It was the 15th February 1942.

British and Australian artillery were lined up along the waterfront of Singapore where no further retreat was possible.

Perspiring gunners were firing off round after round – the shells just clearing the roofs of the Government Buildings on the other side of the road.

There was a continuous thunder of explosions as the Japanese planes bombed and machine-gunned the streets jammed with refugees and soldiers. The Jap artillery shells were landing all round us with a sound like a thousand clanking iron chains.

The buildings around us had been hurriedly converted into hospitals and were all displaying large Red Crosses.

I was seated by a telephone in a surface air-raid shelter a few yards in front of the main entrance of the famous Raffles Hotel. From the lounge came the sound of a pianist and singers. The gunners' way of passing the time when allowed a few minutes respite from manning the guns. It was impossible to sleep. I was reminded so much of a London blitz which I had so often experienced only a year previously.

Singapore had only a few more hours of life under the British flag. But were we downhearted? Definitely NO.

Hadn't we been told that, if we could only hold out until February 14th the sky would be black with Allied aeroplanes? Weren't the British and American troops even at this moment landing at Penang? Weren't British paratroops overcoming all opposition at Kuala Lumpur, and hadn't they captured over four hundred Japanese aeroplanes which were being handed over to the RAF? It was just a matter of holding out for just a few more hours.

Looking back it seems unbelievable that grown men should have believed such stories. But nearly everyone did. And, as if in confirmation, Japanese air attacks had definitely diminished in intensity during the past few hours.

Everybody had great faith in Churchill. He wouldn't allow this stronghold of the Far East to fall to these little yellow men. All we needed was an Air Force. We had enough men.

There was a terrific artillery barrage. Orders for two hundred rounds of gunfire were nothing to the British soldiers who were manning the guns in relays by day and night.

Being attached to the Regimental telephone exchange I was one of the first to suspect that there was 'something in the air'. The Command Post Officer was called to the telephone to take an important message. I did not hear the conversation or the 'Yess's' and 'Hmm's' of the officer on the receiving end.

But as he went out I heard him mutter "So this is the end." Even then I didn't realise it meant surrender. I thought the Japs were probably asking for an Armistice.

From four o'clock onwards the noise of battle gradually diminished until it was passed around verbally that an Armistice had been signed and the cease-fire was going to sound. But nobody knew for certain what was happening.

The nearest we got to the truth was when a Runner came in and reported that the Union Jacks were flying at half-mast and that the Governor had made a speech saying that we had offered to surrender, but the Japs had refused to accept this and insisted on an Armistice owing to the great defence we had put up. It was a long time before we heard that it was actually the opposite way round. The Governor had asked for an Armistice in order to bury the thousands of dead civilians, but the Japs insisted on unconditional surrender.

The Nippon Army did not enter Singapore that night, but agreed to enter in the light of morning in order to avoid any incidents. Feelings were mixed. It was a temporary relief to be able to walk peacefully along the street again without fear of a shell landing in front of you, or a plane machine-gunning your vehicle. But there were other reactions. Some men broke down and cried at the humiliation of defeat. Some men refused to give in and continued fighting.

That night the streets around the Government buildings were crowded with the sleeping forms of British, Australian and Indian troops.

Everyone shared their possessions with everyone else irrespective of race, creed or colour. Everyone mutually agreed to have one last go at the Japs if they tried any 'funny stuff'.

But the official entry of the Emperor's troops the following morning passed without incident. The first Japs entered on captured British motor-bikes. The rest followed in every kind of transport – Japanese, British and American lorries. Even now the British did not realise the terrible consequences of the defeat. Jap guards were sent to check up on arms and guard captured equipment. A typical British officer suggested to a bespectacled Japanese guard that he could sit down if he wished. The Jap politely refused but accepted a cigarette. Most of the invading army had a tin of English cigarettes attached to their belts. Many were wearing British tropical uniforms.

About 80,000 British troops were ordered to surrender, including an entirely new division which had landed only a few days previously.

"If we can keep alive for six months we shall be free," said the O.C. And everybody agreed. It could be only a few weeks before Britain and America sent out some more aircraft and other arms to the East, and once they did that the Japs would be forced to surrender.

So, what with one way and another we were not too pessimistic about the outcome. It was inconvenient. We couldn't write or receive mail from home. We wouldn't be able to walk exactly where we pleased or eat exactly what we wanted – but all this would be only temporary. We had the whole might of the British Empire and the U.S.A. behind us – to say nothing of China. And

Churchill – well, could you imagine him allowing Singapore to stay in the hands of these little yellow men for very long?

That night we slept on the lawns of the waterfront. A solitary Japanese sentry stood guard with his rifle over our regiment of over 500 strong. It was almost laughable.

The lights in the Government Buildings were on nearly all night. Behind the drawn curtains we knew that General Percival and his staff and the Governor of Singapore were offering terms to the Jap Generals. It was weeks later before we were finally convinced that Singapore had been surrendered unconditionally.

In the morning, after leaving all our small arms dumped on the sidewalk, we jumped on to our vehicles and on orders from nobody we knew who, drove to a golf-course on the outskirts of town. Here were dumped hundreds of abandoned vehicles of all shapes and sizes.

We quickly made ourselves at home and, as two of our trucks were packed with tinned food – tomatoes, cheese, bacon, etc. - our cooks soon had two fires going and we had a good meal. There was no thought given to the hungry days ahead.

Our first shock came later that morning when we found we had to walk about 20 miles to Changi Gaol in the north-east corner of the island. The Japs said we could take three vehicles with us; two for food and one water wagon. "Not enough," said the British officers. "We have bedding, camp stools and other personal effects. You don't expect us to carry them, do you?" "O.K." said the Japs (or words to that effect). "If that's the way you feel you can take just one vehicle – the water wagon." And one vehicle – the water wagon – it was. Even then many of the officers found room to pack their kits around and on top of the tank.

That afternoon we started our weary march. As artillery men having ridden in lorries at every possible occasion and walking only when absolutely necessary, it left us in no suitable condition for the long trek in a tropical climate.

"No food will be taken," was the order. "The Japs will search everyone for foodstuffs and if found will probably shoot first and ask questions afterwards."

So all the 'tinned stuff' was left behind. Very daringly I tucked two tins of bully beef away in my haversack – as did many others. I thought it might go nice with biscuits later. I didn't stop to think where the biscuits were to come from!

We couldn't understand why the Australians were driving lorry loads of foodstuffs up to Changi. Only later did we realise that if there were such an order not to take food with us, the Aussies had decided to take no notice of it.

I think that 'simple' walk to Changi was almost my worst experience of the war up to that time. Only the previous day I had accepted a new pair of boots as my old ones were worn out. Unfortunately they were one size too small. I started the march optimistically with a kit-bag and carrying a large office type-writer I had picked up during the retreat. After a mile or so both were deposited in a ditch and there were half-a-dozen painful blisters on my feet.

There were no Jap guards accompanying us. It might have been an ordinary peace-time route march except that, long before we were half-way to our destination, there was no further attempt to march either in step or in line. Many men took off their boots and walked in their bare feet and most of them, like me, threw away the extra kit they had optimistically started with. We were still marching when night fell. As we limped through the almost English-like country lanes with a clear moon above throwing our shadows out in front of us it was very difficult to credit that we were now prisoners of war of the Japanese.

Men were cursing and dropping out. They refused to march any further and decided to sleep by the road-side and find their way to our destination in the morning.

This was mainly the fault of the British officer in charge who, with every good intention, no doubt, kept shouting "Only about two more miles now boys!" This was encouraging at first but soon became monotonous and finally nobody took any notice of his remarks at all.

We finally reached our journey's end – Roberts Barracks – in the early hours of the morning. The cooks who had travelled on the water wagon had a very welcome cup of tea waiting for us, but no supper. We didn't yet appreciate what food shortage meant and when the cooks said they hadn't enough food in store to give us a meal we were rather bewildered. However, we were too tired to worry too much and on entering the barracks in which we found a number of cast-iron Army beds, threw a blanket across the bare springs and quickly fell to sleep.

Most of us were up at dawn and had a quick look around our new quarters. Changi was a pleasant spot on Singapore Island and Roberts Barracks stood on a hill. From the top storey one could overlook the sea or a wide expanse of the island. We congratulated each other. If this was to be our prison camp, then life wouldn't be too bad. Not a Jap guard in sight.

But we were shaken when we queued up for breakfast. A spoonful of oats, two army biscuits and a pat of butter. "That's all you'll get and that's all you're going to get in future," said the cooks, "until the Japs issue us with some more food." And they were right. Except for a slight variation of the two ounces of bully beef for the mid-day meal and a cup of cocoa for supper.

"I'd eat ANYTHING," a despondent gunner said to me, "even _raw_ oats." Little did he realise he could be eating raw snails in a few months time!

We spent five days at Roberts Barracks and except for the lack of food, life was not too bad. We were occasionally irritated by the British O.C. holding Parades and making us cut the grass around the building, but we started organising debating societies and other pastimes. I had a weakness for lying *on my bed but I decided I could best occupy my time by writing a book – if I could finish it before we were liberated!*

But all our ambitious plans suffered a set back when we suddenly received the order that we were to move. Roberts Barracks, being situated in such a healthy position, was to become a hospital. We groaned at having to move – especially when we found we were going to be 'billeted' in Changi Jail. But no-one really begrudged the sick having beds to sleep on in a fairly decent and undamaged building.

We packed what kit we had and walked the two miles or so to Changi Jail. Only the Royal Artillery Regiments of the British Army were to be imprisoned here, but even then the place was overcrowded. The Japs were finding 80,000 prisoners rather a lot to find accommodation for.

Our regiment was unlucky enough to be allocated the eastern quarters of the Jail. Two or three men shared a cell made for one. It was little larger than a pantry with a stone slab in the centre serving as a bed. There was also a WC in the corner but nobody used them as the fresh water system was not functioning.

Life was decidedly getting grimmer but still bearable. Once again we started to organise ourselves. A library was opened. Classes were started – shorthand, economics and Physical Training. A Camp Magazine was suggested and got under way. But once again the blow fell. We got the order to move. "Don't let it get you down," said the Brigadier. "The Japs are trying to undermine your morale."

We were quite sure that all the Japs in the Far East would not get us down, but we did object strongly to having to make three or four journeys carrying officers' kit to our new quarters. Most of the Other Ranks were travelling light, but the officers still held on to their camp beds and other items they had picked up. Some even had easy chairs!

This time the Artillery Regiments were split up. Our regiment was allocated some native shacks on the sea front and a couple of European-type houses. These were in a terrible state. The rooms stank. WC's and drains were clogged up and the dead bodies of Malay and Chinese civilians lay in the rooms, in the gardens and on the sea-shore.

It was not a pleasant job cleaning up and burying the dead, but soon the quarters began to look a little more respectable. We were feeling more energetic because we were now getting an issue of rice from the Japs. Even more encouraging was the fact that we were in the centre of several coconut groves and although only the most athletic of us could climb the trees one could usually find an odd coconut or two lying on the ground.

But once again our tranquil existence was short-lived. We again got the order to move.

But we were now getting used to these 'inconveniences' and although there were the inevitable groans, the men took it in their stride. We also appreciated that the Japs could not possibly organise so many prisoners in a few days and, as we hadn't been troubled by them personally, decided that the best thing to do was to keep calm and obey orders.

We met the rest of the Artillery Regiments in our new 'Area' and our first impression was that, except for Roberts Barracks, they were the best quarters we had had so far. The Camp area was about half-a-mile square. In the centre was a huge sports field with two football pitches, a rugby pitch and a cricket and hockey pitch. All marked out and ready to be used. The 'barracks' were primitive but built of wood with quite strong roofs. And as rain was the only disadvantage of Singapore's fairly reasonable climate, we had nothing much to grumble at.

The few months we spent at this camp were probably the easiest of our POW life and if we had only known this at the time we might possibly have been more contented than we were.

CHANGI

Because Changi was a peninsula on the north-east corner of Singapore Island and surrounded on three sides by water, the Japs thought it an excellent place in which to keep P.O.Ws. It was a good idea from their point of view as few guards would be needed to patrol the mile or so 'frontier' dividing Changi from the rest of the island.

It wasn't such a bad idea from our point of view. Changi had always been recognised as one of the healthiest spots on Singapore Island and had always been used by the British services. There were modern barracks with wide verandahs useful for giving extra shade from the tropical sun. There were cultivated meadows, coconut groves and sports grounds. So we considered ourselves fortunate in more ways than one, that the Japs had picked on this particular spot for our prison camp.

The Indian and Ghurka troops who had fought with us in Malaya were segregated from the British and Australians. They were taken to another part of the island and, from what we heard, were not treated too gently if they refused to take up arms against the British.

Changi was then divided into sub-camps. The Australians were together. The Royal Artillery regiments were together. The 18th Division which had arrived just before capitulation shared one area and was the unluckiest. There were hardly any stone or wooden buildings in their area so the majority had to live under canvas.

On the other hand, most of the Singapore Volunteer Force had well-constructed brick buildings to live in. Some were very pleasant villas by the sea. It was all a matter of luck.

Our area was probably the smallest in Changi, but we had few men to accommodate – about 1500. As regards living space we had little about which to complain. Our area was about half-a-mile square. The buildings were wooden with thatched roofs and large open windows (no glass). Apart from the rats (which we ignored) they were comfortable enough in the warm Singapore climate and we were well sheltered from the frequent tropical rain storms. We slept on a blanket on the floor – far more comfortable than the bare, rough ground to which we had become accustomed during action.

Food was somewhat of a problem. Rice took some getting used to as a staple diet and most men suffered with their stomachs. We had a small allowance of meat, flour and vegetables, but the army cooks excelled themselves and did their best with the limited rations. Meat would go further when mixed with ground rice as also did flour.

Favourite dishes were 'Changi Slabs' (a hulk of baked wheat and rice flour) and 'Changi Pies' (minced meat mixed with rice, covered in pastry and baked in an empty herring tin.)

The men adapted surprisingly quickly to their new mode of living and the camp was made more ship-shape.

Parties were out scrummaging – collecting wood and other useful items from the deserted settlements and villas. A cookhouse was built. Latrines were erected and, although basic, were quite sanitary. Damaged vehicles were salvaged, the engines removed, and used for local transportation. They were just larger editions of the 'soapbox' cart and there was fierce competition for the privilege of driving these man-powered vehicles.

Showers were installed and then entertainment was born when a set of drums and two pianos were found in reasonably good working order. This led to the building of a 'theatre' with stage, curtains and even footlights powered by car batteries. A church was built. Apart from writing sketches and songs and taking part in the camp concerts, I produced a 'newspaper'.

This was typed on the salvaged office typewriter with six carbon copies which were then distributed and read by everyone from the Brigadier downwards.

I named it "The Rumourist" because I could guarantee that everything in it was a genuine rumour. The headlines were sensational – 'Wavell sweeps across Burma', 'Yanks land up-country', 'Won't be long now, boys'. I found myself almost believing my own copy at times! But it certainly helped to keep morale up.

So now we had a church, a theatre and a newspaper.

At the time it reminded me of films I had seen of the birth of communities and towns in the American West. But although we had a theatre we had no dancing girls!

And although we had no Sheriff, we had Law and Order because we were still under British Army discipline.

Rude Awakening

Little did we know at the time that the first nine months of POW life under the Japanese were to be the best for many years to come. Life was fairly quiet and pleasant, and we were waiting only for the Allied Forces to come and rescue us, which, we were convinced would not take long.

Our blissful existence was suddenly shattered when the Japs started organising working parties. Several hundred men were sent to Singapore to work on the docks and building roads. Others were sent 'up country' – which turned out to be the notorious Burma Railway. (I volunteered for this, but, fortunately, was rejected). Finally they started sending us overseas.

In October 1942, eleven hundred of us, mainly Royal Artillery personnel, were told we were being posted and that we would be boarding a ship in the Singapore docks.

We presumed it would be Japan, and, although we did not fancy the idea of moving further East and further away from the Allied Forces coming to rescue us, we did believe that we would be better off. "We are bound to get more to eat, and it will probably be European food," we told ourselves. And from what we had heard of Japan we knew it should be a better, more temperate climate than that of Singapore.

But it was a very nasty shock when we saw the 'Liner' on which we were to be passengers. It couldn't have been more than a 4000 tonner and looked (and was) a dirty old tramp steamer made in Scotland in the early part of the century.

We didn't think it possible that the Japs could crowd the whole 1100 of us in that small vessel. But they did plus 1100 Japanese troops who were going home.

To add insult to injury the name of the ship was 'England Maru'. Conditions were vile. The ship had three holds with wooden partitions built around the side of each hold. The prisoners occupied the bottom of each hold whilst the Japanese troops had the upper 'berths'. We had been wise enough to bring some of the Red Cross food which had arrived in Singapore a few days previously, otherwise we would have been very hungry indeed. Our rations were a fistful of rice three times a day with some foul-tasting greasy stew. It was very hard to get any drinking water and that was dirty and tasted salty.

It was not long before men started to go down with dysentery. I caught it myself after only just a week at sea. For ten days I had nothing except Japanese tea (no sugar or milk). Four men died and were buried at sea.

The Japanese began to get worried in case their own troops became infected and radio'd for advice. They told us they were going to divert to Taiwan and were highly pleased about it. "You have no need to worry," they told the sick prisoners, "directly we dock you will be taken away in ambulances to a very nice hospital."

The ambulances turned out to be one army lorry and the hospital was a bamboo shack in a very primitive prisoner-of-war camp.

The camp was situated just outside Taihoku and consisted of a number of bamboo huts. Geography books had told us that Taiwan had a mild climate, *but none of us, dressed only in our Japanese issued green-dyed sackcloth had ever been so cold before in our lives as we were that first winter.*

I was in the 'hospital' for three months. Rations were extremely poor – reduced by one-third if you were not working – and there was little, if any, medicine. An emergency appendicitis operation had to be carried out on one of the prisoners by the Japanese doctors, but without anaesthetic. There wasn't any! They told the patient to remember he was a soldier and be brave. He was brave, very brave, and only screamed once as the knife went in. But it was quite unnerving for the other occupants of the ward. But worse was to come. There was an outbreak of diphtheria (which I never realised until then could be fatal). Men were dying every day. The illness started with a slight 'wet' cough at the back of the throat which developed rapidly. Within a day or so the victim choked to death. The final moments were horrifying. One man got out of his bed and attempted to run down the ward screaming "I don't want to die". He then collapsed and died. Another, opposite me, went more quietly. His last words were "A nice sausage roll." How I managed to escape the epidemic in my weakened condition I do not know.

But I did, and was finally discharged as 'fit' and sent out to work with a gang of walking skeletons. I weighed just over 7 stone.

But with the approach of summer and the warmer weather we began to feel a little more normal and after our day's work carrying earth and rocks around in baskets (we think we were making a park) we set about organising ourselves again. The concert party was re-formed and gave shows. Although the Japanese put many difficulties in our way we managed to get by and keep morale fairly high.

After a year of this existence, the Japs decided it was time to start splitting us up and interchanging us with prisoners on other camps on the island.

But three of us were told to report to the Japanese Camp Commandant.

"You have been selected," he told us, "for a very special purpose. You will leave tomorrow at 8 o'clock in the morning and you are going to the finest camp in the Japanese Empire. You have nothing further to worry about. You will be well treated and receive a Red Cross parcel every day."

It was obviously too good to be true and we knew there was a catch somewhere. But at that moment in time we couldn't work it out.

The following day we started our journey. Before we left the island we were divided into two groups, one of ten and one of eight. The larger group, we were informed, was to be known as the 'Technicians' and the remaining eight of us the 'Cultural Group.'

Before we set sail the Captain made a speech saying he would do all he could to get us safely to Japan.

We were happily unaware then of the large number of ships that had been sunk by American submarines.

270

```
                                 Tel:   Foots Cray 2291
                          Royal Artillery Record Office
                                         (Field Branch)
                                             Foots Cray
                                         Sidcup,  Kent.
                                     Date:   11.3.42
```

Dear Madam,

According to the records in this office your HUSBAND
974063 GNR. H.W. BERRY, Royal Artillery was serving
in Malaya when the garrison of Singapore capitulated
on 15th February 1942. Every endeavour is being made
through diplomatic and other channels to obtain
information concerning him and it is hoped that he
is safe, although he may be a Prisoner of War.
Immediately any information is obtained it will be
sent to you, but in the meantime it is regretted
that it will be necessary to post him as 'Missing.'

Yours faithfully,

Officer in charge.

271

PART SIX

THE DIARY OF A P.O.W.

NOVEMBER 4TH 1943 TO FEBRUARY 7TH 1944

NOVEMBER 4TH 1943 TO FEBRUARY 7TH 1944

Name & rank:- BERRY. H. GNR.
Nationality:- BRITISH
P. O. W. Camp of Taiwan.
Date:- 17TH SEPTEMBER 1943

SERVICE DES
PRISONNIERS DE GUERRE

TO:

Mrs. H.W. BERRY
28 PITSHANGER LANE
EALING. LONDON. W.5.
ENGLAND.

PASSED
P.W. 2719

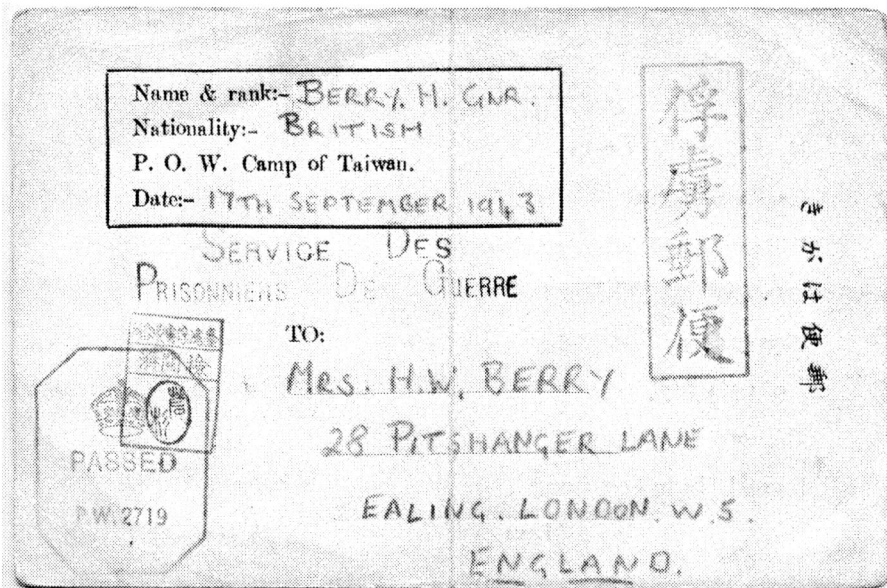

**Front and back of allowed standard card from
Taiwan P.O.W. Camp September 1943.**

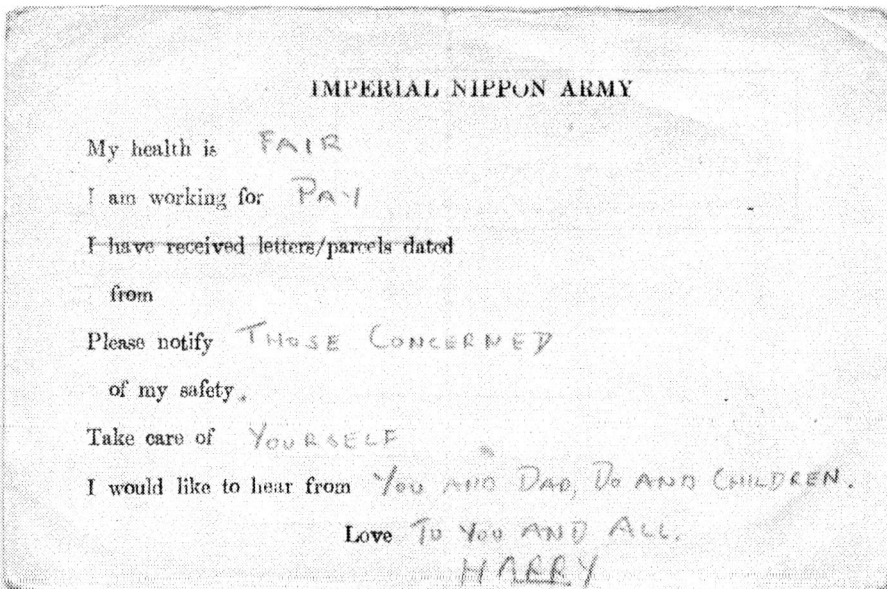

IMPERIAL NIPPON ARMY

My health is FAIR

I am working for PAY

I have received letters/parcels dated

from

Please notify THOSE CONCERNED

of my safety.

Take care of YOURSELF

I would like to hear from You AND DAD, Do AND CHILDREN.

Love TO YOU AND ALL.

HARRY

November 4th:

Left Taihoku (Taiwan) POW Camp at 08.00 hours with two others for unknown destination. Told only that we are going to an excellent camp with plenty of food and no worries! Driven to station and then left by train at 9.30 a.m., arriving at Takao port at 4.30 p.m. where we were told we were going on a ship. Some hitch and the 18 of us (others picked up from various POW Camps down the line) go to a nearby POW Camp (Haiti) arriving there about 10 p.m.

November 5th & 6th:

Waiting at Haiti POW Camp. No work. Food not bad.

November 7th:

Left Haiti Camp at 1 p.m. Driven to local station and then on to Takao. Board vessel 'Matsu Maru'. (Similar type of accommodation to that of "England Maru" on which we sailed from Singapore to Taiwan about a year ago). No smoking and not allowed on deck except for occasional P.T. for 15 minutes. But conditions generally much better and cleaner than the "England Maru." Touch of diarrhoea. Food good. Pap (soggy barley) for breakfast; rice stew for Tiffin and supper. Times of meals 9.30 a.m., 2 p.m., and 5.30 p.m. Vessels holds occupied mainly by Dutch POWs.

November 14th & 15th:

Arrive at Moji, Japan. Disembark and the 18 POWs from Taiwan are split into two parties – 10 'Technicians' and 8 'Culturals' – I being in the latter group! Hang around in a large hall being sorted out all afternoon and evening. Finally leave for local railway station at about 10 p.m. with rest of draft. Train very crowded. Now know we are going to Tokyo. Spend night and all following day travelling in train.

November17th

Arrive Yokohama at 10.30 a.m. Journey was quite comfortable considering. Received food three times a day packed in wooden mess boxes. One containing fish and pickled seaweed, another with odds and ends (kind of hors-d'oevre!) and one of rice. Got on quite well with Japanese guards who are all quite friendly; some of them speaking fairly good English. A better type to those we had in Taiwan. At Yokohama Station the draft is split up and we eight 'Culturals' take an electric train to another station about 20 minutes journey. Walk from station to Omori POW Camp (apparently an HQ Camp) arriving there about 11 a.m. Have to sign a paper saying I won't escape(!) and have kit searched. My notebooks and 'Rumourist's (paper I 'published' in Singapore are kept for censoring. Finally shown into a barrack room where there are other 'special' prisoners, including some of the band of the 'Loyals' Regiment, journalists and artists, etc. Arrive too late for 'tiffin' which was being served, but we were each issued with a loaf of bread. Later received winter clothing (British Army kit) and 4 blankets.

December 1st (Wednesday):

Birthday today; 27 years old. Reveille 6 a.m. Breakfast: Stew, bread and 'cocoa-mixture'. A party of 14 left for the Special Camp in the morning. We were told we are following later. Made two trips across the bridge linking our small island (reclaimed land) with the mainland to collect vegetables for cook-house. Tiffin: rice and fried vegetables. Decent ration. Washed two shirts, vest and socks in afternoon. Nice sunny day but rather cold. Dinner: stew, (made very thick with rice, barley and beans). Good. Listen to band rehearse for concert tomorrow evening.

'Presento' from Japanese of toothbrushes, tooth-powder, soap, soap-boxes, toilet paper, hygiene masks, notebook and paper. Unfortunately not enough for one for each man. 'Tenko' at 8 p.m. instead of 8.30 p.m. To bed at 8.45 p.m.

December 2nd (Thursday):

Reveille 6.30 a.m. Tenko parade. Breakfast: stew and sweet potatoes (good helping of both). Do not feel too good. Cold is very bad in head and am having giddy spells. To bed after breakfast. In 'draw' for 'presento' and win soap box and tooth powder. Missed the three things I needed most – notebook, pipe and towel. Japanese newspaper 'Nippon Times' for December 1st arrives. Not much news. Given card to write home. First one I have seen which allows actual writing instead of printed cards reading 'I am well/I am not well' etc. Lie on bed for most of morning and played cribbage from 11 to 12 noon. Tiffin: fish rice (about 5 sprat- like fish). Excellent. Listen to talk on music by Bandmaster of the 'Loyals' and then went to bed again. Cold now very bad. Wore overcoat and hat when not in bed. Supper at 6 p.m. Thick stew and good helping of rice (excellent). Listen to rehearsal in evening for concert postponed until tomorrow. Not very impressed. Would like to have a go myself. Tenko at 8 p.m. Had cigarette and so to bed!

December 3rd (Friday):

Reveille 6.30 a.m. Tenko parade outside. Told to bring mugs filled with water and had to gargle with it whilst hanging around in the cold! Breakfast: stew and beans (good). Weather still very cool, so went back to bed to keep warm. Another party of 38 consisting of Americans, Norwegians and Italians arrive in camp and are to be billeted in our barrack-room. I move down from 'upstairs' (higher bunks) in company with four others. Place is now crowded but should be a little warmer. Tiffin: thin slice of meat, stew and rice (fair for here but good for Taihoku). Made bed down in new position after meal and read 'Red House. My Story by A.A. Milne'. Smoked pipe which Capt. Marsdon gave me yesterday evening. Have now only one cigarette left and no

277

dog-ends. First time I have run short since leaving Taiwan. Brought Diary up to date about 3 p.m. Continued reading and general 'yasume-ing' in afternoon. Supper at 5.30 p.m. Meat flavoured with stew and noodles (excellent). Noodles are easily the most satisfying meal I have had since being POW. Concert has been cancelled again due to Italians being billeted in the Bath House where concert is held. We hear semi-officially that the Special Party will still be in this camp for Xmas, but one can never tell what is actually going to happen. Listen to band practice and chatted to one or two of the new Yankee arrivals – submariners and airmen. Tenko at 8.30 p.m. And so to bed.

December 4ᵗʰ (Saturday):

Up at usual time and had so-called gargle as yesterday on parade. My cold is, I think, a little better. Breakfast: sweet potatoes and soya bean extract stew (good). Had 'cat's lick' and then back to bed. Quite a sunny day but very cold wind blowing.

Continued reading Milne (not very good) and had a glance at the 'Nippon Times' for December 1ˢᵗ. Tiffin: Rice and fish (excellent). Occupied afternoon by reading and started darning my socks which contain more holes than wool. Pulled old sock to bits to obtain wool. Pair of white Japanese socks issued in afternoon. Supper: Rice and stew (very good). Weather turns very cold. Band plays in evening. Glad when 'Tenko' and bed-time comes. Very cold.

December 5ᵗʰ (Sunday):

Felt very cold all night, particularly my feet. Will have to try and make my bed warmer tonight. Notice that there is a thin coating of ice in gutters whilst on Tenko parade. Breakfast: sweet potatoes and stew (fair). Back to bed immediately afterwards as it is still very cold. Gets warmer about 10 a.m. so start darning socks again. Tiffin: rice and stew (very good). Finished Milne's mystery story in the afternoon. Not very good. Finished darning socks. Now I have 3 pairs without holes for the first time since Singapore – NOT including new Japanese issue. Had shave and wash. Not a very thorough wash as my cold is very bad and I do not want it to get worse. Suggest to 'B.J.'(Bowen-Jones) who produces shows that I could help with Xmas concert. Don't know whether anything will come of it. Not very impressed with B.J. as a producer. The trouble is, of course, we don't know how long we shall be in this camp. Personally I don't think we shall be here then. Borrowed 10 fags from Harry Hines as cigarettes did not turn up yesterday. I must cut down on my smoking. Supper: rice and stew. (Quite good. Plenty of fat in stew but rather thin).

However I am not hungry and that is something. How long, I wonder, is this easy life going to continue? Listened to band in the evening. It consists of 1 cornet, 2 trumpets, tenor sax and violin. Does not sound too bad considering. Glad when Tenko came as it started turning rather chilly.

December 6th (Monday):

Much warmer during the night, but looks as if day might be chilly as sky is becoming overcast. Breakfast: stew with mainly soya bean extract and sweet potatoes (good).   Back to bed immediately afterwards, but then have to volunteer for trip across bridge to mainland where we tie up empty straw vegetable sacks and stack them on lorry. Told to fall in at 11 a.m. again, but will try and dodge that one. Back to bed at 9.30 a.m. Have a cigarette. Bring Diary up-to-date. Go to sleep and miss 'fatigues' which was at about 11.45 a.m.   Not entirely laziness as chest is very bad. Got a new shirt from stores in exchange for ragged one I was originally issued with. Have now two good thick English Army shirts. Tiffin: fish and rice (fair). Rice was 'down' on yesterday.

Played cribbage with Harry Hines in afternoon and then lay in bed till 5.30 p.m. Dinner: beans and stew (fair). Once more smoked my last cigarette after dinner and managed to find enough dog-ends for pipe-full later. Very cold in evening. Played cribbage to while away time. Glad when bedtime came. We have to start 'Vigilant Guard' tonight. One hour each man. We have been excused Guards up to now, but, as with the newcomers we have 48 people in the barrack room, we have to do them. Should work out about once every 5 nights. Not too bad. Tomorrow is December 7th, my Wedding Anniversary. Something important should happen tomorrow – perhaps we will move or the war will be over! Be glad when things start moving. Do not feel too happy here as all my friends are in Taiwan. Even the two fellows who left Taihoku with me went to a different camp and there seems to be no one in this party who fits in with my temperament. However, it should not be long now.

December 7th (Tuesday):

Wedding Anniversary today. Three years married and only three months of married life. What a world to live in! I wonder what Gwen is doing today. Breakfast: English potatoes and stew (fair). Managed to find some tobacco from the linings of my pockets and had half a pipe full. Played crib, read and slept for an hour in morning. Tiffin: rice and stew (V.G.). Finished reading book by early afternoon. Am longing for a smoke, but cannot find any more grains of tobacco in my pockets. Had a 'bombshell' about 2.30 p.m. We have been told officially that we are no longer a 'Special Party' but will be going out to work tomorrow with the other working parties and that we are drawing working clothes and mess boxes right away. Whether this is temporary or permanent we cannot discover. One interpreter says we shall not be moving and seeing the other twelve, and the other says it is only temporary. I knew something would happen out of the usual today. One can never tell what is *going to happen next in this country. I am not looking forward to working tomorrow, but we must grin and bear it. I have had, at least, a month's 'yasume' and perhaps it may be better in the end than staying in Taiwan. The latest news is that we are definitely no longer a 'Special Party' and we are NOT leaving the camp.*

Washed pants and vest and drew working kit and mess boxes from Stores. Supper: stew and rice (V.G.). No music this evening as everyone is talking about the 'catastrophe' and debating the reasons. Many still think the work is only temporary until we are wanted for the 'special work'. At 'Tenko' the Americans and Norwegians are told they will have to go to work tomorrow too – causing further 'panic'. Go to bed wondering what work will be like tomorrow.

December 8th (Wednesday):

Up about 15 minutes before reveille as there is not much time to get ready and have breakfast. 'Tiffin' is drawn at 5.15 a.m. by 'Toban' and packed into our wooden boxes. Breakfast: sweet potatoes and stew (V.G.). Ration seems to be slightly better than when we were 'yasume-ing'. Rush breakfast but find I am ready in plenty of time for Parade at 7.30 a.m. Feel quite happy and enjoy walk to beach. Morning is cold and misty. Very interesting to walk along a road again with traffic and see civilians and shops, although I notice that the shops do not have much in them and there is practically no food on display. Start working (digging) at about 8.30 a.m. Surprised by 'yasume' at 9 a.m. which is officially ten minutes but lasts half-an-hour. Work with Norwegian sailor aged about 62. He can certainly handle a shovel better than I. Stopped at 11.20 a.m. for Tiffin which was rice and fried vegetables packed in our boxes. Wish I had a mess <u>tin</u> as it could be heated up. Luckily there was plenty of hot tea going. Started work again about 12.30 p.m. Talked with fellow who was in the Middlesex Regiment in Hong Kong and time went very quickly to another 'yasume' at 2 p.m. Continued work till about 3 p.m. and then finished.

Arrived back in barracks about 4.20 p.m. Legs felt a bit tired but otherwise I felt happy. The work is certainly much easier than in Taiwan and there is no one shouting all the time. Also although I believe the weather is actually colder, feel much warmer due to winter clothing and, no doubt, better grub.

Didn't feel so happy in the evening as there were no cigarettes up. Supper: beans and stew (fair), but did not enjoy it as stew was cold due to my having to have it in borrowed mess tin. Broke my stew bowl together with mug this morning. Am now in a fix as regards utensils. This is the second one I have broken. Evening very cold so went to bed after supper, but did not go to sleep before Tenko

.

December 9th (Thursday):

Up ten minutes before Reveille. Was on guard last night from 11 p.m. to midnight. Breakfast: loaf of bread (not English size!), cocoa mixture and stew (excellent), but was rather spoilt by having to rush for work parade. Do not feel very fit today. Tired and limbs ache. Might be due to exercise yesterday or maybe beri-beri. Work much the same as yesterday – shovelling dirt and stones through a sieve. Working with Nobby Clarke. Tiffin: Mess box full of rice with 3 fish (V.G.). Was going to borrow someone's mess-tin when finished and warm it up, but decided I could not wait for that. Sat by fire and had hot cup of tea. At about 2 p.m. six of us were detailed to unload a barge of timber. Heavy work, but have long final 'yasume' whilst awaiting other gangs to finish. Felt very tired marching back to barracks. Notice that most of the vehicles are running on charcoal gas. Arrive back at 4.30 p.m. Washed, etc. Felt happier when finished supper of rice and stew (V.G.). Stew was hotter as I had it divided into 2 china bowls with rice in a mess tin.

Felt a lot more happy also when cigarettes turned up at 7 p.m. Concert tonight but decided not to go. Scoured some mess tins, so will definitely have a hot mid-day meal tomorrow – as long as there is not too much rust!

December 10th (Friday):

Up ten minutes before reveille. Breakfast: Beans and Stew (V.G.) but spoilt by usual rushing about. Easiest day's work I have had for many a month. Did not start until 9.30 a.m. and finished morning at 10.20 a.m. Had meal of vegetables and rice (ate most of my veg. for breakfast as I could not pack it in box) heated in mess tin. Very successful. Really enjoyed it. By the time we started afternoon's work it was 1.15 p.m. Had 15 minutes' 'yasume' and cup of tea at 2 p.m. and finished 'work' at about 2.45 p.m. 'Yasume' until other parties had finished at 3.45 p.m. Ended day feeling quite happy although legs have been aching terribly and am very glad we were not on any heavy work. Supper: noodles and stew (V.G.). Not so many noodles as usual. Am 'Toban' this evening. Wash down tables, etc.

December 11th (Saturday):

Up just before Reveille. Breakfast: sweet potatoes and stew (V.G.). Fine day but bitterly cold wind. Was on same site as yesterday (across ferry) but different job – pulling huge logs out of the water. Told we were finished when ten had been pulled ashore. All done with the aid of winch. Tiffin: fish and rice heated in mess tin (V.G.). Finished job in afternoon at 2.20 p.m. Wind dropped and day was far more pleasant. Back in barracks at 4.20 p.m. Supper: rice and stew (V.G.). Tried to borrow a stew bowl but found R.S.M. wanted a 'price' for it. So decided to let it slip. To bed until 'Tenko'.

December 12th (Sunday):

Up at 6.20 a.m. Breakfast: sweet potatoes and stew (fair). Most of potatoes were bad. Nice morning with no wind. Easy job again – just digging. What a difference to Taiwan; this is more like working in the British Army! The only thing I miss now is the Sunday off. One does not get much chance for washing clothes, etc. However, POWs can't have it all ways. Had hour and a half for tiffin – rice and vegetables heated (V.G.). Unloaded logs from barge in afternoon and was finished before 2 p.m. Afternoon somewhat spoilt by cold wind that blew up and also because somebody stole my spoon. I still have a fork, but I must get hold of a spoon in case we get a Red Cross parcel for Christmas. 'Yasume' until 3.30 p.m. when we were marched back to barracks. Dinner: rice and stew (good), but rice slightly down. Very cold this evening and was glad when Tenko was announced at 7.30 p.m.

December 13th (Monday):

Breakfast: sweet potatoes and stew. Nice day again but wind still bitterly cold. Had very easy job today with shovel as 'Hanchow' did not even stay with us. I kept my coat on all day and did very little work. Tiffin: fried vegetables and rice heated. Very nice but rather disappointing as rice ration was considerably down. Food seems to be going down considerably lately. Decided to finish work at 2 p.m. as 'Hanchow' was not about. The afternoon turned warmer so lay in sun until just after 3 p.m. 'Fell in' about 3.45 p.m. and marched back to barracks. Washed, etc., and also washed shirt, vest and Jap. pants. Supper: stew and beans (poor). Beans were very low indeed and stew was thin. Compared with European standards it was just about as much as one would have in a snack bar of an evening after eating well all day – minus the bread. Had smoke and went straight to bed, getting up for Tenko at 8.30 p.m.

December 14th (Tuesday):

Up before Reveille. Breakfast: sweet potatoes and stew (good). Still feeling hungry from yesterday. On truck job today. Harder work than usual but still 100% better than Taiwan. I also feel much stronger when shovelling and loading. Had good break for tiffin: heated rice and fish (V.G.). Did one load after 2 p.m., 'yasume', and finished about 2.30 p.m. Hung around until 3.50 p.m. Back in barracks at usual time. Much warmer today as there was no cold wind. Hope it keeps up as I am on 2nd relief Guard tonight. Supper: rice and stew (fair). Low portion of rice.

December 15th (Wednesday):

Warmer this morning. Breakfast very poor: Pumpkin stew only. Bread was expected in but did not turn up. Nice day today and have easy job with shovel in morning. Glad when Tiffin came as was feeling hungry. Nicely cooked rice with added curry which I bought yesterday. (Two boxes for 60

282

sen from canteen). Rice was not too good for quantity however. Had a rotten afternoon loading trucks with stones and filling a barge – just six of us. Had to do 11 loads, not finishing until after 3.30 p.m. Worst working day I have had since Formosa. Supper: Stew and beans (G), but beans lower than usual. This is definitely as bad as the grim days in Taiwan. Lower rations and harder work always seem to come together. Think I will try and get on the boat job tomorrow and get extra food. The work cannot be any harder than this afternoon. The order has just come through that we have to strip to the waist on Tenko tomorrow and rub ourselves down with a towel. Crazy! The end of a perfectly bloody day.

December 16th (Thursday):

Up at 6.20 a.m. Sentry stood in barrack presumably to see if we towelled ourselves down before Tenko parade as per orders yesterday. However he did not trouble us and I did no towelling. Breakfast: Sweet potatoes and stew (V.G.). Plenty of veg. in stew. Rushed it down in order to get on 'Boat' party, but was turned off it by Hanchow along with other fellows from same barrack. Job did not look too promising – mixing cement on barge, but luckily it came on to rain so job was cancelled about 10 a.m. Hung around fire in hut and had tiffin about 11 a.m. Rice and vegetables which we heated up and added curry (Excellent). Rice was up on yesterday. Arrived back in barracks at 1 p.m. very thankful for Yasume. Went to bed during afternoon. Today looks like making up for yesterday if the supper is decent tonight. Supper: Rice and stew (V.G). As I remarked yesterday; less work and better food seem to go together. To bed until Tenko and then bed again.

December 17th (Friday):

Up at 6.15 a.m. Breakfast: Stew and beans (V.G.). Saved some of my beans which I mixed with haversack ration of rice and veg. for Tiffin. Was unlucky enough to get caught for station working party on morning parade. Enjoyed 45 minute ride to station through town. It reminded me very much of parts of London – the trams, traffic, etc. But that is because I have seen very little town life since leaving home, I suppose.

Thought day was going to be easy but turned out to be bloody. I found it a physical impossibility to lift the planks of wood off the railway trucks and was on the verge of passing out once or twice. No break until tiffin: rice, vegetables, beans and curry, heated (Exc.). Meal was steamed which was a great improvement on the Beach Job heating – it was hot but not burnt! Owing to the difficult work, however, I was not so satisfied after the meal as I would have been with light work on the beach. One of the fellows got knocked out by the 'Hanchow' during afternoon as he, too, was getting too weak to carry planks. A small portion of sweet potatoes was served at 3.30 p.m. with a 10 minute 'yasume'. "Crumbs from the rich man's table!" Have easier job after this unloading truck of charcoal, but was very thankful when 4.30 p.m.

283

and end of work came. I shall definitely do all I can to dodge this job in future on physical grounds. How the fellows carry on this kind of work every day I do not know. Arrived back at 5 p.m. just in time to hear "Come and get it." Had hurried wash and then supper: stew and noodles (V.G.). No flavouring or fat with stew however. Made bed after supper, shaved and had another go at getting my hands clean. Went and saw an American Officer who is going to complain about treatment of the fellow hit today. Enjoyed smoke with pipe full of dog-ends which I scrounged during day. Tenko 8.30 p.m.

December 18th (Saturday):

Did not sleep too well – stomach troubles. Breakfast: sweet potatoes and stew (V.G.). Back to Beach Job again this morning, thank goodness. Very easy morning. Tiffin: heated rice and fish (ex.). Finished just after 2 p.m. except for small job. Glad day was easy as I was feeling very tired after yesterday.

Back in barracks 4.10 p.m. Made bed, etc. and had bath. Supper: rice and pork and curry stew (V.G.). Stew very thin but tasty. Rumour that there is only pumpkin for breakfast for next 3 days. Food is certainly getting grimmer here. Went sick after supper and got some powder for diarrhoea, and ointment for sores. Buy bottle of canteen pepper for 30 sen. Shall have to find some cash from somewhere now for cigarettes as I have 35 sen only in pocket. Pepper, like curry, very poor quality, not worth buying. Tenko 8.30 p.m. To bed.

December 19th (Sunday):

Breakfast: Rice and stew (G.). Small issue of rice but better than pumpkin-only breakfast promised. Save half rice and mix with tiffin ration. Nice day, quite warm. Get lousy job on beach; stone carrying. Very tiring. Tiffin and rice, veg. heated (Ex.). Finished about 1.30 p.m. – none too soon for me. Do not leave for barracks until 4.30 p.m. as some men are caught cooking white rice in mess tins. Arrive at Bridge to see bread being taken into camp from lorry. Have to carry bundles of wood. Great surprise this evening – issue of Red Cross M & V – one between two to go with supper of rice and stew (V.G.). Great rumours of more Red Cross up for Xmas now! Supper not till 6.30 p.m. To bed afterwards till Tenko – am on guard again tonight 4-5 a.m. – Brrr! Go to bed for hour before Tenko. I wish we had Sunday 'yasumes' as at Taiwan. I certainly miss the break and the Church service.

December 20th (Monday):

Up at 6.15 a.m. Did not sleep too good. Breakfast: Stew only. Good and thick supposed to contain 50 tins of M & V, but nothing else. Enjoyed morning loading wheelbarrows with gravel to make cement. Tiffin: Rice and fish (fair) – rice low and small fish. Felt very weak on continuing job – these low rations are certainly beginning to tell. I feel as weak now as I did in Taiwan. I wish now I had never left and things there were definitely improving. Finished work about 2.45 p.m. Back to barracks at 4.20 p.m. Supper: Stew and beans (poor). Very thin stew and small ration of beans. Very bad day today for food – perhaps they are saving it for Xmas. Should be better tomorrow as it is supposed to be bread for breakfast and fried veg. for tiffin. I hope so. Enjoyed pipe full of dog-ends after supper. To bed till Tenko. Hear Order has just come out that no-one is to get up before Reveille tomorrow and that rub down with towel must be carried out in 2 minutes and other similar orders. Discipline is certainly tightening up in camp.

December 21st (Tuesday):

December 21st (Tuesday):

Very rushed this morning owing to new order about reveille. Men were caught on Tenko parade for not bringing cups for gargling – I was lucky. Breakfast: Bread and stew (Ex.). Save crust for Tiffin. Nice warm pleasant day again. Had job on concrete-making contraption – more like Heath Robinson than anything I have seen before in my life. Had a very hard day shovelling without a break, loading a truck through a chute. Cannot keep this heavy work up on the rations. However, have good break for Tiffin. Hot rice with fried veg. and bread some of which I semi-toasted (Ex.). Two men lost their bread – Japanese Toban blamed. Had decent break at 2 p.m. but did not finish till about 3.30 p.m.

Felt very tired and weak walking 'home' – just as I used to at Taiwan. Perhaps things will get easier again when boat party finishes. Things have definitely changed for the worse since we arrived. Nothing extra seems to have arrived for Xmas and there appears to be no cigarettes tonight. What an outlook! Have just learned that I am 'toban' this evening. Am now waiting for "Come and get it!" Supper: Rice & stew. Jap 'presento' of pipe and two razor blades this evening, but still no fags. Interpreter supposed to have said definitely Red Cross parcels for Xmas. Hope it is true. Swept floor. Tenko 8.30 p.m. Bed.

December 22nd (Wednesday):

Up at reveille. Breakfast: Pumpkin stew (poor). No rice or anything extra. On cement mixing today. Nice and warm again. Felt much strain in lifting cement bags. Tiffin: Rice and fish – heated. Very tasty but could eat twice as much. Collapsed in afternoon trying to heave cement bags on chap's back. So had 'yasume' till job finished about 3 p.m. Back in barracks at 4.25 p.m. Still no fags. But some more veg. turned up. Found 4 Irish spuds which I ate raw and enjoyed. The food situation and work is certainly very grim. Only 3 more days to Xmas – I hope I never have to spend another one in captivity. Supper: Beans and stew; tasty but not very filling. Roll on Steak & Kidney pies. Tenko 8.30 p.m.

December 23rd (Thursday):

Up at 6.15 a.m. Washed, etc. before Tenko. Breakfast: 4 Irish potatoes and stew. Quantity good, but neither spuds nor vegetable stew properly cooked. Feel very depressed and miserable this morning. Wish the damn war would end. Had a good day on beach – was lucky enough to be picked as Toban. Hardest job was fetching buckets of water, but rest of day was easy – collecting wood, lighting fire and heating rice. Was congratulated by three of the party on my 'cooking'. Tiffin: heated rice and green vegetables (Ex.). Collected wood for about 10 minutes after, and party finished work at 1 p.m., so I finished too. Yasume until 3 p.m. Back in barracks. Carried coal over bridge and found American Red Cross parcels had arrived – hurrah! Bit disappointed they are not British, but still very thankful. Rumour of sugar and cocoa issue tomorrow. Supper: Rice and stew (Ex.). Things are looking brighter now. Found enough 'dog-ends' to have a good pipe after supper. Looks as if cigarettes are 'up'. Bought 30. Tenko 8.30 p.m. To bed.

December 24th (Friday):

Very restless night and feel very depressed. Breakfast: Irish potatoes and stew (Ex.). Had very cushy job on beach today – cleaning up some kind of barracks. Rained during morning so had mid-day meal about 10.30 a.m. Also heated rice, fried fish and some mashed potato which I had saved from breakfast. Was excellent. Took things very easy just sweeping up and digging holes, etc. Finished at 3 p.m. Back in barracks and saw lorries with Red Cross parcels outside. Learn as soon as we get in that they are to be issued this evening. Have very great disappointment as they are 80 parcels short, so we are being issued one between two to start with. I share one with Harry Hines. Parcel contains: 1 tin powdered milk; 1 tin of Bovril 'Bully' (12 oz); Kraft cheese (½ lb.); Tin of Salmon (7¼ oz); Tin of grape jam (6 oz.); Tin of Rose Mill Pate (6 oz.); 1 tin of meat roll (12 oz.); 3 tins of butter (3¼oz.); 3 tins of corned pork (3¼ oz); 2 tins chopped ham & eggs (3½ oz.); 2 tins Kup Kafay (Coffee) (4 oz.); 2 bars of soap; 8 packets of soap powder; 12 vitamin C tablets; ¼ lb cube sugar; 2 bars of chocolate (¼ lb each). At the same time the Japanese issued 20 cigarettes,3 tangerines and 1 apple.

Directly we opened the parcel I set to on the concentrated chocolate. Directions said take ½ hour to eat but I got rid of it in almost half a minute. At the same time I scoffed my portion of cube sugar. For supper I had: ½ tin of corned pork, the stew (very poor), good helping of noodles coated with ½ tin of butter and the rest of my cube sugar. I then finished up on the tangerines and apple. Still feeling hungry, I opened my tin of corned pork and finished that off just before Tenko. Rather disappointed in the Chesterfields – they don't taste much different to the Japanese cigarettes. Still feel hungry in bed. I haven't really appreciated the taste of the things I have eaten. So excited and hungry. Didn't go to sleep for a long time. Rumour says there may be another parcel between 2 tomorrow. I sincerely hope so. Felt nice *and warm in bed. Tenko was not till 9 p.m. So ended Xmas eve. If I continue eating at the same rate I shall have nothing left by tomorrow lunch time!*

December 25th (Saturday):

Christmas Day. Think a lot of Gwen and home. Last night, by the way, I handed in my postcard to Gwen as follows:

"Darling. This is the best Xmas card I can manage this year. I hope you had a pleasant Xmas. I am thinking of you every minute. Received one letter dated 2.8.42 on November 18 this year. I am hoping to receive lots more some time. You will notice change of address. My love to you and all at home. Harry."

I hope it reaches Gwen safely. Reveille at 6.30 a.m. and Tenko. Do not make bed up. Biscuits and sugar issued (less than small tea-bowl of sugar) and about a dozen different biscuits. Ate all biscuits right away except 2. Breakfast was delayed by Catholic Church Parade which did not start till 8.50 a.m. Had loaf of bread and cocoa from cookhouse. Added butter with bread and sugar with solidified cocoa. Followed this with the stew which we kept until Church Parade was over. Had to parade at 9.25 a.m. for Japanese 'presento', (for good workers) of gloves, socks, etc. None of us newcomers received anything. After parade ate the tin of chopped ham and eggs and then Harry and I shared the meat pate. At 11 a.m. all we had left of parcel was a tin of milk, salmon, cheese and jam between us, and I had one tin of meat roll left. I could still eat more! Had cup of coffee also.

Washed shirt, vest and socks to save myself eating more. Tiffin: Pork flavoured stew. Mixed rice with half portion of jam. Felt really full at last. 15 more parcels (American) and 4 British, with odd tins of M & V and bully were allotted to room of 47 men. Went to bed and tried to sleep off grub while 4 section leaders split up parcels into groups of 47 different items which were drawn for.

I drew: 1 tin of tomatoes; 2 tins Bully; tin margarine; tin coffee and a portion of chocolate, sugar, raisins and 2 packets of cigarettes. Supper: Fried fish and loaf to which I added ½ tin of bully, cheese and 3 biscuits. Saved bully and biscuits for supper later. Had ½ bowl of rice given to me by Norwegian. Went to concert. Still feel very full, especially after cup of chocolate issued from cookhouse to which I added sugar and milk. Decided I would be able to finish bully, biscuits and rice when on guard. On picket 3 - 4 a.m. Had not been to sleep – stomach rolling all the time. Could not touch bully, etc.

December 26th (Sunday):

Boxing Day today, but we go back to work. I think this Xmas was the most miserable one I have spent – even worse than last year when I was at least a prisoner with fellows I knew well. However, feel much happier today – despite the fact that I slept very little last night. Up at 6.25 a.m. Had Bully and biscuits and some of my buckshee rice with morning stew for breakfast. Excellent but stomach still troublesome and not improved by usual rushing of breakfast. However, walk to work seems to settle stomach a bit. Doctor took my number for light work. Late at getting on job as there were extra parties for railway jobs and 'Yasume' men had to complete beach party. Lovely day and quite warm, had nice easy time on trucks. Tiffin: heated rice and veg. and small bits of pork with gravy powder added. Also had spuds which were issued for breakfast. Excellent; the most delicious outside Tiffin I have had. Finished work at 2 p.m. but left for barracks at usual time.

Supper: Stew, small portion of rice mixed with half-tin of salmon. Followed by rest of rice mixed with milk and sugar. A very satisfying and economical meal. My mind and stomach now seem to be balanced again as regards food. Perhaps I can make my little bit of my parcel last a few days now. Swapped tin of coffee and 20 Chesterfields for bottle of frying oil and old pair of socks for extra ration of beans tomorrow and half 'going-out' rice.

December 27th (Monday):

On 'trucks' at job today. Had good tiffin of heated rice and vegetables with gravy powder. Finished job just after 2 p.m. supper good: stew, 2 rations of beans and half tin of pork hash. (Other half I had for breakfast).

December 28th (Tuesday):

Up before Reveille. Just missed getting sent on station job in morning. Breakfast: Thick stew and rice (Ex.), but bit of a rush to finish. On easy job this morning – shovelling. Had tiffin at 11.30 a.m. 1½ rations of rice with fried fish. Added frying oil and soup powder. Excellent, both in quantity and quality, but stomach is a bit troublesome. Can't wonder at it really! Half holiday for 'beach' party today – arrived back in barracks about 1 p.m Stomach very troublesome, so lay on bed for couple of hours before washing, etc. Supper: rice and stew and about 1/3rd tin of Bully. Made sweet with rice and sweet milk. Tried to swap tomorrow's bread issue for bully or something, but finally swapped half-loaf for ration of beans tomorrow night. Bought apple from canteen which I am saving for tomorrow (11 sen). Tenko 8.30 p.m.

December 29th (Wednesday):

Up at 6.20 a.m. after very troublesome night with stomach. Breakfast: stew, bread and cocoa mixture. Save bread for tonight. On beach again (trucks). Managed to dodge the Station again. Stomach pretty painful first

288

thing but eased up by tiffin. (Rice and bully mixed with gravy powder, followed by apple). Finished job about 2.30 p.m. On arrival at barracks had to carry sacks of POW mail across the bridge. Only just made it, but very pleased to help – about 200 sacks with 5000 letters in each. I should get some from home, I hope. I expect they will take some time to sort out. Also rumours of further Red X parcels arriving for the New Year. Harry Hines just informed he has to prepare to leave for another camp tomorrow. Another friend gone! I shall have to find another unfortunate now! Supper: stew, beans with bully, followed by bread, butter and cheese (Ex.). Heavy meal, but stomach seems to be taking it. Hope I have a better night tonight. Emptied 'Milko' tin in order to use as mess tin tomorrow as I have to hand Harry his tin back. All I have left of Red X parcel now is tin of spiced meat, tin of margarine and a little cheese. Also have little sugar and milko left, and frying oil. I certainly have enjoyed it – I hope we get another one before long. I should be able to make it last longer now I have got over that hungry feeling and excitement of seeing European food again.

December 30th (Thursday):
No beach party today and had to go to the station job. Had bad night and a thoroughly miserable day on the job. These station jobs are definitely too heavy for me. Didn't take much interest in food. Glad when day finished.

December 31st (Friday):
On station job again. Stomach very, very bad. Had to go sick on job before starting work and was allowed to 'yasume' all day. Managed to eat a little tiffin. Back in barracks about 5 p.m. Could not manage supper of stew and noodles so gave half noodles away for someone to do my picket from 12 to 1 p.m. So ends another year. I hope in the New Year things look up for me. I have never been so miserable and unhappy in all my life as I have these last few days. Went sick this evening and managed to get excused work tomorrow

.

January 1st 1944 (Saturday):
Up at usual time after slightly better night. Had to get up at midnight so saw New Year in. Managed to eat breakfast of stew and rice; also ate fish from midday ration. To bed after breakfast. Had 'tiffin' of cold rice at 11.30 a.m. Am feeling hungry again – a good sign. In bed all afternoon. Ate big supper of stew and 'buckshee' stew, rice and half meat roll – last of Red X parcel, bar margarine. Went sick in evening but missed sick parade much to my regret as practically all sick were excused today. However, doctor promised to see what he could do for me tomorrow morning. I don't suppose he will do much. Tenko 8.30 p.m. Bed.

January 2nd (Sunday):

Up just before reveille. Breakfast: stew and Irish potatoes. Report sick on work parade and much to my, and about 20 others, delight, we are all excused work, by Japanese orderly officer. Back into barrack room and in bed most of morning. Tiffin: rice and boiled vegetables heated in mess tin (Milko tin). Open tin of margarine and melt some with rice over charcoal fire smuggled into barrack room. Ate last of corned pork which I intended to save for tonight.

Have definitely got my appetite back now. The Japanese, by the way, issued nothing special to eat on New Year's Day; but neither did they for Xmas. It would have been a poor do without the Red Cross parcel. I'm sure they had a much better feast (apart from the Red Cross) in Taiwan. Still, if it is due to our blockade, I don't mind so much. I hear the Japanese themselves did not do too well. Supper: rice and stew.

Offered to do watch for extra stew. Against my usual policy, but must make up for food I have missed during last few days. Went on sick parade in evening and the same orderly officer was on duty. All were excused work again. Tomorrow a doctor has promised me a light work tally for the beach party when it starts again on Wednesday.

January 3rd (Monday):

Did not get up in such a hurry as I have day off. Breakfast: Stew and Irish potatoes. Mix margarine with potatoes. To bed and sleep until 10.15 a.m. when I go on sick parade. Am told to report to doctor for light work tally before noon. Am feeling much happier again now – seem to have got over fit of depression. Probably due to the 3-day 'yasume'. I wish the Japanese would issue the remaining Red X parcels. Tiffin: Heated rice and fish to which I added oil and re-heated over the charcoal burner. To bed in afternoon again. Extra blanket issued this morning now collected back! Supper: stew and rice and beans (poor). I am certainly missing the Red X food now. Get light work tally from M.O. which he tells me has to be returned tomorrow night! Extremely cold this evening and am very glad when Tenko is announced at 7.30 p.m.

January 4th (Tuesday):

Up at 6.25 a.m. Work today. Breakfast: stew and 2 Irish potatoes (poor). On beach again and on trucks. Very cold out to start with, but warmed up slightly. Tiffin: heated rice and fried vegetables, to which I added oil (V.G.). Finished job just after 2 p.m. and 'yasume'd' until 3.45 p.m. when we marched back to barracks. Supper: rice and stew. Added margarine to rice (Ex.). Also 'niggled' a quantity of margarine. Have not much left now and there is no bread tomorrow! As there are not too many pages left in this notebook will only enter unusual happenings in future. I think the average day in this camp has been amply described. Smoked some dog-ends in pipe.

290

Intend to save last packet of 'Camels' to sell when market price goes up further. It is now, I believe, 3 yen. Have to do guard tonight from 12 – 1 a.m. in exchange for the buckshee stew I had the other night. It is bitterly cold too – the last time I shall do that. Tenko 8.30 p.m. Bed.

January 5th (Wednesday):

Breakfast: rice and stew (Ex.). No beach party today so get on to boat party and hope for the best. M.O. said I could hang on to light work Tally, but that won't be of much use when there's no Beach working party. Left Camp by launch. Ate going-out ration of rice, beans and vegetables on launch, on supposition that we get a Tiffin on the boat – which is usual. Start unloading coal dust from freighter in the hold, but at about 10 a.m. 30 of us are transferred to another boat from which we unload pig-iron. Horrible stuff to handle. Very glad when Tiffin time came. Packed in a wooden box, it consisted of white polished rice, 2 decent sized grilled fish and some carrots. About the tastiest mid-day meal I have had for some time. Afternoon seemed very long and had to work very hard.

Was presented with a pair of white gloves by Hanchow, but I practically wore them out handling the iron. We were the last of the three holds to finish at about 3 p.m. Back to barracks, after a lot of hanging around, by lorry. It's been a very hard day, but I prefer it to the Station jobs – and there is the extra ration which helps one along. Supper: rice and stew (good), but still feel hungry despite the extra food. I wonder if there is a Beach party tomorrow. Write card to Gwen after supper and send it in for the censoring. Doubt if it will ever reach her. Tenko 8.30 p.m. Bed.

January 6th (Thursday):

Snow on ground this morning. First I have seen since leaving home. On beach (trucks) again today. Snow thaws about mid-day. Saw flight of about 500 Jap planes in afternoon – some sort of display I suppose. Tenko 8.30 p.m.

January 7th (Friday):

Gwen's birthday today. On beach again (trucks). Very chilly wind but no snow. Address envelope and send Xmas card to Gwen which reads:

"My darling wife. Due to the kindness of a Japanese Roman Catholic priest I am able to send you this rather belated Xmas Card. I hope you are still keeping cheerful. We had a pleasant surprise on Xmas Eve - an American Red Cross parcel - one between 2 men. It was grand to see European food again – I was excited as a child. I thought of you a lot at Xmas, also of Dad, Do and the children. I hope we are together again soon. Today is your birthday – Many Happy Returns of the Day, darling. I am keeping fairly fit and cheerful. I am longing to see you again. All my love for ever. Harry."

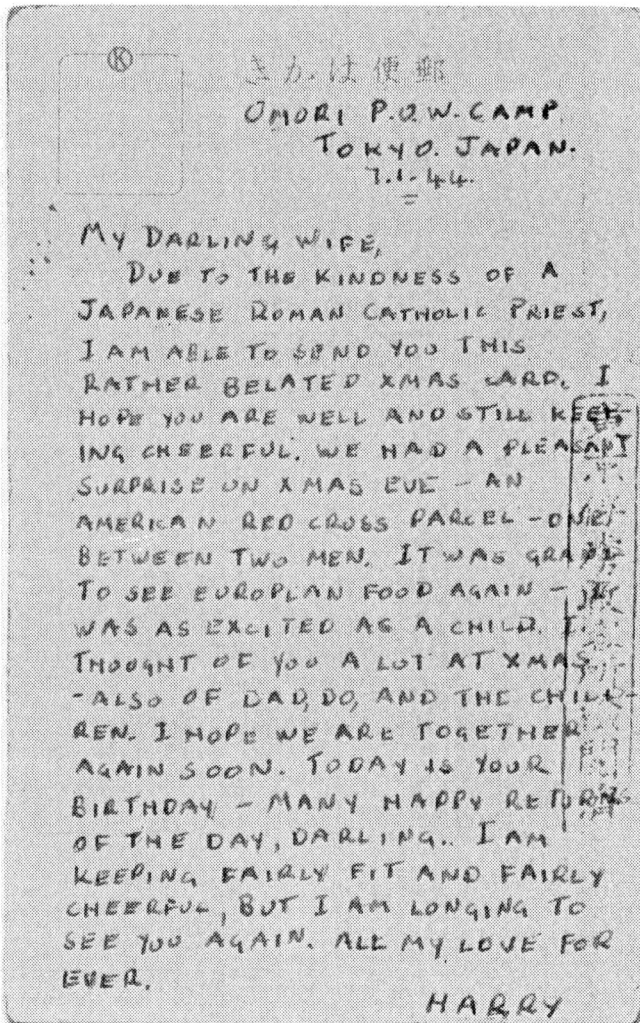

郵便はがき

OMORI P.O.W. CAMP,
TOKYO. JAPAN.
7.1.44.

MY DARLING WIFE,
    DUE TO THE KINDNESS OF A
JAPANESE ROMAN CATHOLIC PRIEST,
I AM ABLE TO SEND YOU THIS
RATHER BELATED XMAS CARD. I
HOPE YOU ARE WELL AND STILL KEEP-
ING CHEERFUL. WE HAD A PLEASANT
SURPRISE ON XMAS EVE — AN
AMERICAN RED CROSS PARCEL - ONE
BETWEEN TWO MEN. IT WAS GRAND
TO SEE EUROPEAN FOOD AGAIN — I
WAS AS EXCITED AS A CHILD. I
THOUGHT OF YOU A LOT AT XMAS
- ALSO OF DAD, DO, AND THE CHILD-
REN. I HOPE WE ARE TOGETHER
AGAIN SOON. TODAY IS YOUR
BIRTHDAY — MANY HAPPY RETURNS
OF THE DAY, DARLING.. I AM
KEEPING FAIRLY FIT AND FAIRLY
CHEERFUL, BUT I AM LONGING TO
SEE YOU AGAIN. ALL MY LOVE FOR
EVER.
                        HARRY

Japanese birthday card for Gwen from Omori prison camp. 7th Jan 1944

January 7th (Cont):

Cigarettes up in the evening, but only two packets. They are now 23 sen for 10. What a difference to Taiwan at 4 sen. It doesn't leave much margin at 10 sen a day to buy anything that may be available. Borrow money to pay for them – hope to get an advance from Capt. Marsden as he promised yesterday. Two more of 'special party' left today. I wonder if I will go, and if so, whether conditions will be better or worse. Very, very cold tonight. Glad when Tenko came.

293

January 8th (Saturday):

Very miserable night – couldn't get warm. Easy job on the beach but very chilly. Warmed up about mid-day. Saw another flight of about 300 Nip aeroplanes. Back to barracks to hear I have 'Yasume' tomorrow – hurrah! Shall be able to do some washing, etc., if it is not too cold. Tenko 8 p.m.

January 9th (Sunday):

Yasume today. Bitterly cold again. Spent most of morning in bed. Tiffin: not so good as on going-out ration. Did some washing in afternoon and got warmed up a bit. Managed to find Capt. Marsden who gave me 50 sen to pay for cigarettes I had the other day. Paid back Bud. Used last of Red X (the margarine) on supper of stew and rice and beans. Felt very depressed and miserable again today – shall be glad when something happens. Capt. Marsden tells me he found a letter for me in the Post Office. Hope I get it soon. Tenko 8.30 p.m.

January 10th (Monday):

Good breakfast and good 'going-out' ration today: rice and stew and grilled fish. For the past week we have had rice for all meals, there has been no noodles or bread since Xmas. On beach again – trucks. Chilly in morning but turned quite warm during day. Strong wind blew up about 4 p.m. but still a lot warmer than yesterday. Good supper of rice and beans and meat stew. Rumour of further Red X being issued sometime in future. Had fingerprints taken. Felt a lot happier when weather is warmer, but will be glad when war is over. Am thoroughly fed-up with POW life and am feeling very homesick and also longing for European food. Finished last Camel cigarette from Red X. Am now on dog-ends in pipe again. Tenko 8.30 p.m.

January 11th (Tuesday):

Bitterly cold wind in morning, but otherwise fine sunny day. On trucks again, but not so easy as usual owing to wheels of trucks being clogged with sand from last night's storm. Only did 13 instead of 14 loads in usual time. Arrive back in camp to hear 600 odd more Red X parcels have arrived – but whether we will get any or not remains to be seen. It is doubtful and no one is optimistic. No bread arrived for tomorrow – looks as if that is finished. Tenko 8.30 p.m.

January 12th (Wednesday):

Bread arrived in camp late last night. Had good breakfast of loaf, ersatz chocolate and good stew. Nice day today but cold wind kept blowing up. Got job on beach pulling logs out of water. Not bad but legs ached by end of job at 2.30 p.m. Two tangerines up from canteen at 2½ sen each in evening. Good meals all day today. Good 'taking-out' ration of rice and veg. and supper of rice, beans and good meat stew. Got nasty cold and don't feel too good. Tenko 8.30 p.m.

January 13th (Thursday):

On guard last night – 2nd relief. Did not sleep too well. Felt very cold. Had rotten day on trucks owing to people rushing job. Legs ache terrifically – and could only just walk home. Feel too tired to go sick. Think I will sleep well tonight however. Perhaps I will feel better in the morning. Meals quite good today but rice ration rather lower. Had a good tiffin cooked in two mess tins; Veg. issue and half breakfast rice in 'Milko' tin and rice and beans plain in mess tin. Felt no more satisfaction as regards hunger at mid-day however. Shall have to rake up 2 dollars from somewhere to buy Bud's mess tin which I have been borrowing. Am out of cigarettes again and none in canteen. Might just as well give up smoking. To bed till Tenko at 8.30 p.m.

January 14th (Friday):

Feel very weak this morning. Bad cold and legs very weak. Was lucky enough to get job of Toban, which gave me some rest, but felt very miserable and under the weather all day. Went sick in evening, but it is hopeless. Japanese doctor says, "You will have to be examined," and then dismisses me. Just a waste of time, I could have been in bed. Has been nice clear day and very warm considering time of year. Have trouble with Japanese NCO over opening of windows at Lights Out.

January 15th (Saturday):

Cloudy this morning but not too cold. On same job as yesterday except I was not 'Light Duty' but had easy job shovelling sand. Learned that I was excused duty last night for today after all – a misunderstanding on my part. Shall go sick and try my luck again tonight. Had good tiffin of breakfast half rice, tiffin ration and fried fish. Felt much fitter and happier today – cold seems to be improving. Go sick in evening. Am excused duty as there is no beach party, but it has to count as an official 'Yasume' as the Japanese doctor will be absent. Tenko 8.30 p.m.

January 16th (Sunday):

'Yasume' today. Made bed up first thing but went back between blankets about 10.15 a.m. Had good ration of rice for tiffin – more than I have seen for a long while. To bed again in afternoon and made up for sleep lost last night when legs were very painful. The M.O. has got it down as 'neuritis'! Sick again in evening and am excused duty tomorrow. Have been very cold today. Tenko 8 p.m.

January 17th (Monday):

No work today. Spent all morning in M.I. Room waiting for examination. Boring, but warmer than barrack room as there is a stove. Finally examined and notice complaint is put down as 'polyneuritis'. Have to report again in afternoon. Am given drink of yeast and injection in back-side – same as beri-beri patients. Am excused duty until further notice. Good supper of rice and stew. Am told by Capt. Marsden there are 4 or 5 letters from Ealing waiting for me. New Order is read out in evening that all sick in future have to report to leather room for work daily – just my luck! Tenko 8.30 p.m.

January 18th (Tuesday):

Potatoes again for breakfast. Hope they run out soon as it makes a very poor breakfast compared with rice. Go on wood collecting fatigue at 8.30 and then start in leather shop. Don't do anything all morning as no-one has shown 'new' sick what to do. Good rice ration with one fish for tiffin. Have injection and yeast drink in afternoon at 2 p.m. Don't think I will stand this 'sick' life for long – the injection is painful. I would rather be on the beach. Finish 'work' at 4 p.m. Toban tonight – good supper of rice and stew (food looking up again) but spoilt by getting cold due to lecture by Japanese NCO. Had another yeast drink after supper. Listen to band playing. Am on guard again tonight – 2nd relief (again). Tenko 8.30 p.m

January 19th (Wednesday):

Good breakfast of stew, bread and 'chocolate'. To work in leather shop at about 9.30 a.m. Did 2 hours guard last night – mine and Bud's (for his mess tin) which solves one of my difficulties. Very easy day, but cold sitting around doing nothing. Scheme is afoot to treat leather workers as work party at usual rates of pay, etc. Whether I shall stick it or go back to the beach I do not know. Had injection and yeast in afternoon. Cigarettes up in evening – borrowed money from Capt. Marsden who told me to see him whenever I wanted any money. Tenko 8.30 p.m.

January 20th (Thursday):

Very poor breakfast of spuds and stew. To work in leather shop again. Felt very cold all day – think I must have a chill. Had injection and 3 cupfuls of yeast in afternoon (doubling up). Also wangled dose of Vit. B powder. To bed immediately after supper – not feeling too good. Up at 8.30 p.m. then Tenko!

January 21st (Friday):

Good breakfast of rice and excellent stew. Out on wood collecting fatigue at 8.30 a.m. Report to Leather Shop about 9.45 a.m. Good ration of rice for tiffin. Feel better today. Had marvellous sleep last night – dreamed of Gwen and all at home – probably due to good dose of vitamin B. Finished before 4

296

p.m. Get weighed and find that I only weigh 51.6 kilos! Good supper of rice (barley and rice – no millet) and fried vegetables. Also two oranges from canteen at 10 sen each. Tenko 8.30 p.m.

January 22nd (Saturday):

Had a lemon given to me by Dawson after breakfast – very acceptable. Issue of 'fruit' to sick after tiffin – only bits of apple cut up but anything edible is always acceptable. Hardly did any leather work in afternoon owing to injection and yeast from M.I. Room. Had 3 cups of yeast. By the time this was over leather shop had closed. Very cold today but cold seems to be improving slowly. Still have a bad chesty cough. Tenko 8.30 p.m.

January 23rd (Sunday):

Another day in leather shop. Turned out 2 patterns. Finished at 4 p.m. Fine day today and warmer. 2 cups of yeast at 7 p.m. Tenko 8.30 p.m.

January 24th (Monday):

General yasume today. Kit inspection in morning. Good ration of rice for tiffin. 21 Americans arrive from another camp and are moving again tomorrow. They had 8 Red X parcels issued to each man! Received two letters. One from Gwen dated 2nd February 1943 and one from Do dated 28th April 1943. Made me feel very homesick. Good supper of stew and rice. Tenko 8.30 p.m.

January 25th (Tuesday):

Much colder today. In leather shop again. Received another letter from Gwen dated 1.7.43. Food good today. Tenko 8.30 p.m.

January 26th (Wednesday):

In leather shop again. Had injection in afternoon. 'Presento' from Nips of toothpaste, toothpowder, pencil, notebook and 2 razor blades and jock-strap. Bath at 5 p.m. Had double ration of rice and beans for supper for which I traded half of next issue of loaf. Felt no fuller but decidedly warmer. Tenko 8.30 p.m.

January 27th (Thursday):

Sunny day, but very cold wind. Injection in afternoon. Capt. Marsden tells me he cannot help me financially as promised owing to having to pay 40 yen for clothes. Very good supper of greasy noodles with meat, etc. and thick bean stew. Tasty but, of course, not enough. Receive pay of 80 sen for work from 8th to 15th December. Tenko 8.30 p.m.

January 28th (Friday):

Warmer today. Did washing in morning, then injection. Reported to M.I. Room in afternoon. Nearly all beri-beri cases sent out to work tomorrow but I dodged it owing to sick parade lasting too long. Expect I will be out on Sunday, however. Toban today. Tenko 8.30 p.m.

January 29th (Saturday):

Leather shop and injection in morning. Also cup of yeast. Told I am out to work again tomorrow when on afternoon sick parade. Not sorry. Report at 7 p.m. for yeast but told it is a mistake as I am not a beri-beri case! Enquire about a Light Work tally. Much warmer today. Bath in evening. Tenko 8.30 p.m.

January 30th (Sunday):

Out to work again. Very cold and miserable day. Work seems to have tightened up on beach rather more. Felt very tired in evening. Evensong at 7.30 p.m. but I was in bed. Tenko 8.30 p.m.

January 31st (Monday):

Much more pleasant today – warmer. Out on job again digging, but feel very weak. Decide to go sick again in evening and am excused duty. Turns much colder in evening. Tenko 8.30 p.m.

February 1st (Tuesday):

On sick parade again this morning, but am told to report for work again tomorrow. Rice ration increased by about 20 per cent today. Hope it keeps up. Swapped tomorrow's fried fish and 'chocolate' for half supper rice and beans tonight and medium bowl full of 'kori'. Feel very satisfied after supper – first time since Red X parcel. Find I am on yeast again at 7 p.m. and after Tenko each night. Tenko at 8.30 p.m.

February 2nd (Wednesday):

Out to work again. Fine day but very windy. Feel much stronger and happier -- probably due to extra rations. At work on concrete machine. Boil up kori for tiffin. Have another extra ration of rice for supper. Feel very satisfied again – lovely feeling. Half-apple from canteen – free. Another letter from Gwen dated 28th April 1943. Injection and yeast at 7 p.m. Tenko 8 p.m.

February 3rd (Thursday):

Very cold today. Snow fell but did not settle. Have decent job on beach – trucks. No pushing as they are pulled uphill by a winch. Ideal in warmer weather. Received another letter from Gwen dated 17th June 1943. Cigarettes up from canteen in evening. Swapped my next ration of bread for two rations of rice and stew. Injection and yeast. Tenko 8.30 p.m.

February 4th (Friday):
Warmer today but drizzly. Had day on trucks – feel very tired. Noodles for supper. 3 tangerines for 10 sen from canteen. Also pay up – draw 1 yen, 20 sen. Tenko 8.30 p.m.

February 5th (Saturday):
Warm again. On same job as yesterday but used Light Work tally. Had job shovelling. Still very tiring. Get some more 'kori'. Tenko 8.30 p.m.

February 6th (Sunday):
Warmer today. On trucks again. More pleasant than yesterday but feel very tired at end of day. Tenko 8.30 p.m.

February 7th (Monday):
Warm day. Tiring job sifting as Hanchow stood over all the time. Double ration of rice at night. Best day for food I have had in this camp. Another letter from Gwen dated 28th April 1943. Tenko 8.30 p.m.

WEIGHT CHART   Kept on inside front cover of diary

19.2.44	..	50.2 kilos
31.3.44	..	54.8 kilos
21.4.44	..	58.7 kilos
15.6.44	..	61.6 kilos
2.7.44	..	63.1 kilos
7.8.44	..	64.0 kilos
21.9.44	..	64.8 kilos
24.10.44	..	65.8 kilos
15.11.44	..	63.9 kilos
18.12.44	..	62.8 kilos
22.1.45	..	64.8 kilos
21.3.45	..	65.0 kilos
26.4.45	..	65.2 kilos
26.6.45	..	63.1 kilos
23.7.45	..	62.0 kilos

MY DARLING,
THIS IS MY FIRST LETTER. GLAD YOU RECEIVED CARDS. THE SECOND YOU RECEIVED WAS ACTUALLY MY FIRST – FROM SINGAPORE. I HAVE RECEIVED 23 LETTERS FROM YOU SINCE ARRIVING IN JAPAN – THE LATEST DATED JULY 15TH. ALSO LETTERS FROM JOE, HAZEL, MARGARET AND DO. CANNOT POSSIBLY REPLY TO ALL. CONGRATS. TO MAY & HAZEL. TELL DO LETTER MADE ME VERY HOMESICK FOR GOOD OLD TIMES. AM LONGING TO SEE DAD AND CHILDREN AGAIN. SHALL I RECOGNISE JOYCE, RAY AND BERYL? YOUR GUESS ABOUT DIET IS RIGHT. BUT I SHALL ENJOY RICE PUDDING – IN FACT I WILL ENJOY ANYTHING EATABLE. MY DAYS OF FUSSINESS ARE OVER. AM HOPING PERHAPS TO RECEIVE PARCEL FROM YOU SOMETIME – WITH SOME CHOCOLATE! I HAVE NO TIME FOR STUDYING BUT I AM NOW AN EXPERT NAVVY.
REMEMBER ME TO ALL.
MY LOVE FOR EVER. HARRY.

June 1944

Since my last diary notes there have been many changes in this Omori POW Camp. Summer is now here and food, because of slightly improved rations and warmer weather is not now the sole topic of conversation; although it is still possible to eat two or three rations without feeling unduly over-laden. (If one is lucky enough to get any 'gash'). The Beach job is no more. Everyone now works on railway stations. Up to now I have worked on three – Shinagowa, Onagi and now Shibaura. Of the three, I prefer Shinagowa owing to the shorter hours, lighter work and the copra which is always (or nearly always) possible to eat. I have put in an application to return to this job and am now awaiting the reply. Physically I am much fitter – due again to better rations, warmer weather and the large amount of copra I have consumed whenever possible. But I am still below the average as regards strength and still find it very difficult to carry anything heavy. I do not think, however, that I shall get much stronger under the circumstances.

June 15th (Thursday):

'Yasume' today owing to inoculation yesterday – the fourth in as many weeks. Up at 5.15 a.m. Washed and took blankets out for airing and de-flea-ing. Arm is a bit stiff but otherwise not too bad. Had good sleep last night after doing two hours picket – 1st and 2nd relief (for breakfast rice, stew and

30 cigarettes). Breakfast: rice and kori and split beans and stew. Washed pyjamas and cleaned up, and then had a 'kip'. Very annoyed at losing about 25 cigarettes and a fork during the morning. Do not expect either to turn up again. 'Fatigue' of fly-swatting in cookhouse from 11 to 12 noon. Lunch: rice and a pretty good stew. Inspection by a number of Japanese Officers directly after dinner.

Yasume'd on bed most of afternoon. Supper: rice and crushed beans and soup. Swapped my half packet of Red Cross tobacco for ration of rice, but afterwards wished I hadn't, as there were bags of 'gash'. Air raid siren went just before supper. Blackout shades on. Tenko at 7.20 p.m. Lights out immediately afterwards and then bed. Real or practice?

June 16ᵗʰ (Friday):

Up just after 5 a.m. Tenko 5.30 a.m. 'Toban' today. Saved half of my breakfast rice as I had some left over from last night. Washed rice buckets. Work parade 6.45 a.m. In lorries to Shibaura Station. Very easy morning unloading 'Kaisha' (railway truck) of long iron rods – about 8 of us. Break for tea at 10 a.m. Hour for lunch at 11.30 a.m. and then unloading Kaisha of Sheet metal. Again very easy. Earth tremor at about 2 p.m; the worst I have yet experienced. The whole place shook like a cake-walk for about 30 seconds. Finished about 4 p.m. Washed on job and back to barracks. Supper: Rice and crushed beans and fish. Lots of 'gash' again – including 'burners' (over-cooked rice). Had to keep most of it in mess box and tins as Tenko was at 7.30 p.m. on parade ground. I had to wash rice buckets. Tenko 7.50 p.m. Lights out 8 p.m. Refused to do picket for 20 cigarettes. Ate some of my 'gash' before going to sleep.

June 17ᵗʰ (Saturday):

Up at 5 a.m. after good night's sleep. Feel pretty fresh. Morning on cold side for June. Ate some of 'gash' from last night before Tenko at 5.30 a.m. Breakfast: Rice and stew. Had to stow half of breakfast rice away and also another ration offered which I accepted. Plenty of food nowadays on job.

Unloaded one 'kasha' of wood planks (very light). Usual gang of Micky Price, Nobby Clarke, 'Boo-Boo' and myself. Finished at 10.40 a.m. Had tea and then found we were finished for morning. Rice ball 'presento' for tiffin. In afternoon about a dozen of us moved some ships' spares and a winch about 100 yards. Quite easy once we got going but a slow job and very boring. Gloomy day and started to rain about 3 p.m. Finished just before 4 p.m. Back in barracks 4.45 p.m. Had hot wash (stripped) in bathhouse. Finished rest of 'gash' from this morning before supper. Very amused to read account of day in diary for December 17ᵗʰ last year. Supper: rice and stew. Had plenty of 'gash' afterwards; altogether amounting to about 5 rations! Tenko 8 p.m. Lights out 9 p.m. Did 2 pickets 12.30 – 2.30 a.m. for 30 cigarettes and 2 rations.

June 18th (Sunday):

Up at 5 a.m. Did not sleep very well during night as I did not feel tired. Breakfast: rice and stew. Easy working morning again unloading light timber from 'kasha'. Finished about 11.15 a.m. Had dinner and slept till 12.30 p.m. Had horrible afternoon loading charcoal from lorries (in bags) into a Kasha. Got relieved however about 3.15 p.m. so packed up and had 'bath' under tap. Had my wallet stolen from shirt pocket with 4 yen 20 sen in it when I left in on form for about 10 minutes. Have good idea who took it but no proof. Back in barracks 4.30 p.m. Weighed and went 61.6 kilos. Heaviest yet since being POW. Very good supper of fish, crushed bean stew and white rice. Also had some 'gash' stew. Tenko 7.30 p.m. Lights out 8 p.m. Air raid alarm apparently still on.

June 19th (Monday):   1944

Up at 5.15 a.m. Feel very tired this morning. Breakfast as usual. Had some 'gash' offered so kept 'working-ration' on shelf. Easy day loading poles and planks on lorries. Finished 3 lorries by 2.30 p.m. Very little traffic in at the station lately. Back in barracks 4.20 p.m. Supper: Rice and stew. Gave 20 cigarettes to someone to do my picket tonight as I was not feeling too well. Went to MI Room and asked MO to look at my eye which has been discharging all day. Tenko 7.30 p.m. Lights out 8pm.

June 20th (Tuesday):

Up at 5.10 a.m. Breakfast: Rice and stew as usual. Got to work rather later as we had to wait for lorry. Notice number of houses being pulled down during journey – ARP against fire-spreading I presume. Tried a new Hanchow on the job and had quite a good day. Finished 7 kashas; 1 of rice and beans, 4 of straw mattings and 2 of empty soya sauce barrels. Felt quite pleased with myself at lifting rice, etc. Am definitely getting much stronger. Had curry soup 'presento' at lunch. Back in barracks at 4.20 p.m. Shaved. Supper: fish and rice. No gash around tonight, but managed to get hold of a few more pieces of fish for which I had to wash fish basket. Went to MI Room and had a few small boils on my legs attended to and also cut on head which I got by knocking it on ceiling. Tenko 8 p.m. Raining in evening. Last few days have been rather cold considering time of year; especially in evening.

June 21st (Wednesday):

Breakfast: Rice and stew. Quite a good stew of soya cake and crushed beans. Had 'contract' of 3 kashas of wood to do on job again. Usual gang. First one was easy but remaining two were rather heavy. 'Presento' of beans for dinner: quite good. Finished contract about 3 p.m. Back in barracks 4.15 p.m. Had bath 4.30 – 5 p.m (Time allocated to our hut). Supper: good *curry soup and rice. No 'gash' tonight but did not feel particularly hungry. No blackout tonight. Tenko 9 p.m.*

June 22nd (Thursday):

Up just after 5 a.m. Breakfast: rice and crushed bean stew. Good and very filling. No boats today thank God. Not much doing on job today. Unloaded toilet paper, bricks and firewood. Loaded 4 lorries with empty boxes in morning. Some fellows got drunk whilst unloading alcohol. No stew for dinner today. In afternoon unloaded 'Kaisha' of tinned salmon onto lorries. Finished just after 3 p.m. Had good wash. Back in barracks about 4.30 p.m. Supper: rice and stew (with potatoes). Accepted ration of rice for picket. Also given 20 cigarettes. Went to MI Room and had boils on my legs seen to again. Tenko 8 p.m. Lights out 9 p.m.

January 24th (Saturday):

Up at 5 a.m. Slept like a top all night lately but always feel extremely tired most of day – Night Starvation! Easy time on job again today loading lorry with heavy timber in morning. Same in afternoon – one lorry of tin-pan. Good soup 'presento' at lunch time. Finished about 3.45 p.m. Back in barracks 4.30 p.m. Bath tonight. Supper: Rice, crushed beans, stew and fish.

Arranged to do picket for 30 cigarettes. Cigarettes up tonight – 50 per man. Signed for pay – 2 yen, 80 sen (rate is now 25 sen a day). Do not receive cash now, but pay is put to one's credit in canteen. Tenko 9 p.m.

June 25th (Sunday):

Up at 5.10 a.m. Breakfast: rice and stew. Had a little 'gash' rice offered which I took out with me. Not much 'gash' flying around these days. Easy day again unloading 'Kaishas' of metal pipes and then started 'Kaisha' of wood. Soup at mid-day, very tasty. In afternoon took turns with other gangs in loading lorries with coal. Very easy and plenty of 'yasumes'. Finished about 3.30 p.m. Had wash. Took long time getting back to barracks owing to 'bioki' (sick!) lorries. Went on sick parade with boils before supper and was told to try to work another day by Jap medical Orderly. Had two boils lanced. Very painful. Supper: white rice and stew. Very good. Had rest of boils 'dressed' after supper and changed library book. Tenko 8 p.m. To bed and asleep before lights out.

June 26th (Monday):

Up at 5 a.m. after a good night's sleep, but still feel tired. Think boils must be cause and am run down. Roll on Yasume Day. Breakfast: rice and stew. On job rather later this morning. One Kaisha of empty boxes in morning. Finished about 10.45 a.m. and stayed in shack for lunch. Soup again! Did Kaisha of wood in afternoon and helped another gang unload Kaisha of cattlecake. Finished 3.30 p.m. Washed. Back in barracks 4.30 p.m.

Supper good: stew with potatoes and noodles and good ration of rice. Rumour of 60 grams cut in rice on 1ˢᵗ of next month. Big surprise tonight – picture show on square. First film I have seen for 2½ years. Four films altogether. 'The Castle' (shots of an old Japanese castle): 'Mount Fuji' (with English commentary): 'Schooldays in Japan' (in English again) and one on Swimming which I missed owing to it getting rather chilly. Made a nice change. Hope we get some more. Tenko 10 p.m.

June 27ᵗʰ (Tuesday):

Up at 5 a.m. Very hot this morning – hottest I think this year. Felt much better on job today due, I think, to boils healing up. Easy day unloading cattle cake. Presento of rice ball with beans for lunch. Finished about 3.30 p.m. Had 'bath' under station water-tap. Back in barracks 5 p.m. Had remaining 2 boils dressed. Shaved. Supper: rice and fish. Very poor. Arranged to do picket for 2 supper rations. Tenko 5 p.m.

June 28ᵗʰ (Wednesday):

Washed, etc., and made bed after picket finished at 4.30 a.m. Very hot again today. Had hardest day yet on job, but fairly easy morning unloading wood and crushed beans. Soup presento lunch time. Unloaded Kaishas of boxes containing something and cement bags in afternoon. Finished early about 3 p.m. but very hot and tiring as I worked with regular gang at about twice the speed of my gang. Had to keep dipping head under tap to stop sweat going in eyes. Back in barracks 4.30 p.m. Had bath. Supper: rice and fish (squids). Quite nice, made a change. Had extra ration due to me. Also had another one offered later which I accepted. Always the same; either no gash at all or it all comes at once. Yeast also 'Up'. Very nice. Tenko 9pm. On picket.

June 29ᵗʰ (Thursday):

Yasume day today, thank the Lord! I certainly need it. Breakfast: rice and stew. Also had more rice and stew mixed offered which I accepted. Meant to do a lot but lay in bed all day. Stomach very upset and did not enjoy meals at all. Accepted extra ration at lunch time which I put into mess box and saved. Did a little washing at 3.45 p.m. Offered dinner rice I couldn't stomach to Yorkie. First time for a long while I have had to give food away. Supper: rice and stew. Ate lunch time ration. Changed book in library. Tenko 9 p.m.

June 30ᵗʰ (Friday):

On picket last night 3.30 - 4.30 a.m. Day started well on job. Unloaded Kaisha of brushwood and 2½ kaishas of boxes. Soup presento lunch time. Had 'damni' afternoon – 2 of us to empty an 18 ton 'kaisha' of coal. Managed to finish it about 3.45 p.m. after much 'buggero' from Hanchow. Had bath under tap which I needed! In barracks about 4.45 p.m. Very happy at receiving 2 letters – one from Gwen and one from Adami. Supper: rice and fish. Had extra ration due to me. Passed time away by writing a rhyme about 'Dodger Green' and got Nobby Clarke to illustrate it. Tenko 9 p.m. Very surprised to find American Orderly Officer taking it instead of Japanese. Everyone presumes there will be an Air Raid practice tonight.

July 1st (Saturday):

And yet another month. New scheme started on job today – every man is supposed to deal with 25 tons, but today it didn't work out. Couldn't start till about 9.45 a.m. owing to lack of lorries and our contract was to load 4 kaishas of asbestos rolls which, in any case, only made 64 tons. Managed to do just under 3 kaishas by 4 p.m. Absolutely impossible to do more.

Each kaisha had to have 750 rolls each weighing 22 kilos in it. Noticed ship at dock-side with huge hole in bows. Had bath under tap although it is bathnight tonight. Decide not to have warm bath on arrival in barracks owing to lack of soap. Have to economise! Apples up from canteen just before supper – one per man. Supper: good thick curry stew. The best, I think, I have had in Japan, and rice. Also had some gash. Felt very satisfied – almost too satisfied. Spent rest of evening writing rhyme. Tenko 9 p.m.

July 2nd (Sunday):

Bad day on job today. Started off trying to load 90 kilo sacks of Kori. Nearly broke my back! Then went on salmon. Loaded about 3 'kaishas'. Very hard and monotonous work and very few breaks. Came on to rain about 3.30 p.m. Finished at 4 p.m. Bathed under tap. In barracks about 5 p.m. Supper: rice and salad. Good, but rather cool this evening and would have preferred soup. Washed dishes and smoked last cigarette after supper. Feel very tired and limb weary. Tenko 8 p.m.

July 3rd (Monday):

Day started well on Shibaura Station. Unloaded 'kaisha' of straw bags and light metal pipes till 10 a.m. Spent rest of day loading cement bags from lorries. Not too bad a day. Finished 3.50 p.m. Bathed as usual. In barracks 5.10 p.m. Went to MI Room and had a couple of boils seen to on my legs. Supper: fried fish and rice. Tasty, but poor piece of fish. Still felt hungry after meal but managed to scrounge cigarette. Felt very tired and a bit feverish. Tenko 8.30 p.m.

July 4th (Tuesday):

Busy day on job. Air Raid warning went about 9 a.m. The real thing I think. Independence Day in America today. Loaded 4½ 'kaishas' of salmon. Soup 'presento' for lunch. Finished at 4 p.m. Bathed in barracks at 5 p.m. Blackout tonight at 7 p.m. Supper: rice and fairly good stew. Managed to find some dog-ends tucked away in Red X box – so I had a smoke. Tenko 7 p.m. Lights Out 8 p.m.

July 5th (Wednesday):

Had a good mind to go 'bioki' (sick) on job today, but finally decided not to. Hung around till about 9 a.m. as I seemed to be an odd man. Finally joined same gang as yesterday as one of their men went sick. Quite a steady day loading kori and big bags of beans. Am amazed at being able to carry heavy loads which, 2 months ago when first on this job, I found I could not manage. Miserable weather today – raining most of time. No soup 'presento' today. Just because it is colder and people feel more hungry! Managed to get some toilet paper. Finished about 4 p.m. Had to wait around for lorries. Back in barracks 4.45 p.m. Baths for our hut at 5 p.m. Went to MI Room for treatment but nobody there. Supper: fried herring, green vegetables and rice. No black-out tonight, thank goodness. Went to MI Room after supper and had 3 boils on leg lanced with old razor blades! Very painful, but much better after. Had smoke. Tenko 9 p.m.

July 6th (Thursday):

Breakfast: rice and stew. Vegetables in stew almost raw. Raining again this morning. Boils very painful. Asked 'Foo' (Jap i/c) if I could go 'bioki' (sick) but he suggested trying 'slow-motion'. Took it easy in morning, unloaded one 'kaisha' of some kind of roofing. No soup again today. Went 'bioki' again in afternoon and had yasume. Back in barracks at usual time. Shaved and had two more boils squeezed. Supper: fish again and rice. Very poor. Turned rather chilly. Handed 87 sen into canteen as nobody must now have any money. Soap issued at charge of 5 sen. Tenko 9pm.

July 7th (Friday):

Breakfast as usual. Cold this morning so wore a shirt underneath tunic – first time for weeks. Had 'Rich Man' as 'Hanchow' today – loading boxes of various things all day. Turns much warmer, in fact definitely hot. Had good dinner: rice and beans presento. Did not eat working ration until evening. Finished rather late at 4.25 p.m. Busy day, but light work. Bathed under tap. In barracks at 5.15 p.m. Supper: good thick curry stew and rice. Felt very satisfied. Towel, razor blade, issued from canteen. Total cost 35 sen. Did first two pickets.

July 8th (Saturday):

Late in starting out for work today – about 7.30 a.m. Had air raid practice by Shinagowa Station. Had to jump out of lorries into Air Raid Shelters. Did not start work until 8.45 a.m. On boxes. Broke off at 11 a.m. for a few Air Raid 'tips', i.e. how to get into Shelter, etc. More boxes and kori in afternoon. Finished at 3 p.m.

Bath night. Burnt rice 'up' before supper. Managed to get some in the rush. Supper: rice and fish. Had a very busy evening as I was Toban and also Sweeper-up being last relief on picket. Tenko 9 p.m.

July 9th (Sunday):

Yasume today. Thank goodness. Washed dishes and did 'benjo fatigue' and then slept till lunch time. Very good rice issue for lunch. Lazed till about 3 p.m. when I swept bed-space down. Washed a few things and brought blankets in which I had pegged out in the morning. Supper: rice and good noodle stew. Managed to get hold of kettle for a private brew. Gramophone and band play out on Square. Great surprise when order came that there was no Tenko and Lights Out when we pleased. Most people however, were in bed by 10 p.m. Felt very tired but did not 'drop off' till about 2 a.m. Had attack of diarrhoea.

July 10th (Monday):

Back to work again. Could not eat breakfast stew – gave it to Nobby Clarke. Did not feel very well in morning but had easy time as I and another fellow were 2 odd men. Unloaded kaisha of wire netting with 4 other men before 'cha' and helped unload kaisha of tin afterwards. Finished about 11 a.m. Good stew presento. Loading bean flour in afternoon – very easy. Back in barracks 5.20 p.m. Get bowls made up.

July 11th (Tuesday):

Easy day on job unloading one kaisha of coal (closed kaisha). Excitement on job owing to some men drunk on Saki. Curry stew for supper. Cigarettes up.

July 12th (Wednesday):

Unloaded empty drums first thing in morning and then went on cattle cake – about 4½ kaishas. Had to keep going most of time. Bath night. More instruments arrive in camp but no piano.

July 13th (Thursday):

Not such a good day today. All morning on Saki. Very short lunch hour. Good 'fry' with 'taking out' ration which, however, I ate before breakfast. Straw-covered boxes and rice in afternoon. Bathed on job. In barracks 5.20 p.m. Supper: rice and stew. Dried fish up from Canteen. Feel very tired and weary. Have done so for last few days. Lay on bed till Tenko.

July 14th (Friday):

Good night's sleep but still feel tired. Get on parade and find that 'Boats' are on – but in the end turns out for best. Did not start till late owing to launch being stuck in mud. Get to Shibaura about 9 a.m. Do 2 hours work unloading small boat of coal and finish. *Apparently Salt boat, which we were supposed to be on, never turned up. Had dinner (ship's ration) and then returned to barracks by launch. In barracks 1.30 p.m. Was going to do some washing but no water, so slept till 4 p.m. Shaved. Feel much better now after good sleep. General Yasume tomorrow too! Very poor supper – just a fish head with rice. Tenko 9 p.m.*

July 15th (Saturday):

Up late this morning – did not have time to make bed, but doesn't matter as today is a General Yasume. Practice fire alarm went just as breakfast was dished up so did not start eating till about 8.30 a.m. Very poor breakfast indeed – half a bowl of soup and small ration of rice. Grub definitely on downgrade again. Spent morning cleaning and washing bed space, etc. Dinner at noon. Poor again. Watery stew. Sports start in afternoon. Spend time alternating between lying on bed and watching sports. Had bath before supper. Listen to band on parade ground after Tenko at 7 p.m. Went to bed at 9 p.m. although Lights Out not till 10 p.m.

July 16th (Sunday):

On boats today – Salt boat. Hard going all day. Finished at 3.30 p.m. Felt very tired. Tenko 8 p.m.

July 17th (Monday):

Boats again – as yesterday. Did not finish until 4 p.m. Had rice ball at 3 p.m. in addition to mid-day ration. Stomach not too good today – probably due to drinking iced water whilst steaming with sweat. Plenty of 'gash' around today. Weather is very hot – too hot actually to work – especially in hold of a ship!

July 18th (Tuesday):

Another sweltering hot day and on boats again. Don't know how I stuck it – was almost literally swimming in sweat. Started at 7.45 a.m. and did not finish until 3.30 p.m. No break except ¾ hour for dinner. Thank God I have a yasume tomorrow. Had bath on shore and arrived in barracks 4.40 p.m. Nobby Clarke feels bad after today's experience – tell him to go on sick parade.

Pretty poor fish for supper, but plenty of gash rice flying around, so did not feel hungry. On 2nd relief tonight. Also did first for Nobby as he was not well and I am Yasume tomorrow.

July 19th (Wednesday):

Yasume today and I certainly need it. Spent nearly all day in bed as I did not feel too good. Headache, etc. Felt worse after supper so went to MI

Room and had temperature taken. Was 103°F! Was given 'Shoskin'(?) ticket for tonight, but was told I am not excused tomorrow, but to report after.

July 20th (Thursday):

Did not have bad night but still not OK. Go to MI Room after breakfast and as I still have temperature of 101°F put on sick list. In bed most of day. Supper: fish and rice. Ate a little extra offered by Nobby, but am not really hungry. Have to go on Tenko as Shoskin ticket was handed in.

July 21st (Friday):

Did not have too good a night's sleep – did not drop off until 3 a.m., mainly due to pain of boil on left wrist which seems to have infected arm. Am on 2/3 rations starting from breakfast this morning (rice only), but it does not worry me as I seem to have lost appetite a little. Went to MI Room after breakfast and had boil attended to. Also had temperature taken by MO. Am given one more day in barracks. To bed and slept till dinner time. Pretty good stew. Now weigh 63.1 kilos. Still going up. Plenty to eat at supper time.

July 22nd (Saturday):

Helped clean room in morning. Shaved. Reported to MI Room about 9 a.m. and am cleared for duty tomorrow. Had boil on wrist cut – still very painful. Slept for about one hour and a half to dinner-time. Feel much better today and occupied time in afternoon by washing clothes and writing some rhymes about the lads on the job. Good salad with cucumber and fried veg. for supper. Had to have boil cut again. Very painful operation. Tenko 9 p.m.

July 23rd (Sunday):

Out to work again today. Get put on big bags of Kori, for which we got a rice-ball. Finished about 4 p.m., having completed tonnage. Supper rice and good curry stew.

July 24th (Monday):

On boxes all day today on job. Fairly easy and plenty of yasumes between loading lorries, but got a bit tiring towards end of day. Back in barracks 5 p.m. 2 boils on backside very painful – have them dressed in MI Room with bit of paper. Band played on square. Tenko 9 p.m.

July 25th (Tuesday):

Did not sleep very well owing to boils – can only lie on back. Joined a 'bioki' gang on the job – all boil sufferers. Had 'damn' day – on coal and bricks. In barracks 5 p.m. Have boils treated. Later wished I had gone sick as other fellows were excused. Supper: noodle 'pork' stew and rice. Stay in bed till Tenko at 9.30 p.m. Tenko not over until 10.40 p.m. On picket to 11.30 p.m.

July 26th (Wednesday):

Still cannot sleep on my side. Join with gang who were on big bags of beans. Boils very painful but got through morning O.K. Kept raining at intervals but we were lucky enough to be under shelter most of time. Very easy afternoon unloading empty boxes. Had rice ball at 3 p.m. – a reward for being on 'Beans'. Back in barracks at 5p.m. No hot baths tonight but swimming parade. Did not go on it but had cold bath. Supper: Sweet stew (my first) and rice. Tenko 9.30 p.m. Lights out not until 10.30p.m. Suited me fine as I was on first relief.

July 27th (Thursday):

Seven officers (POWs) came to Shibaura today, including Capt. McGarth. Joined same gang as yesterday on big bags of beans. Fairly easy day. Rice ball at dinner time, but no soup. In afternoon unloaded 'Kaisha' of beans and I carried the bags on my back for the first time – 80 odd kilos in weight! Showers all day. Got wringing wet but dried quickly when sun came out. Also rained going back in lorry. Had to change bed position in barracks. Now sleep below instead of on top. Supper: Good 'cocoa' stew and rice. Had boils treated and now getting better. Cannot make beds now until after Tenko. Tenko 9 p.m.

July 28th (Friday):

Joined same gang on Shibaura Station as yesterday. Very hard morning loading rice, beans and cement. Shoulder is now red raw with carrying. Good dinner: 2 stew rations and official brew. Easy afternoon unloading rice – not many lorries. British and American Officers now acting as 'Checkers' -- very little work for them. Finished about 4 p.m. Had shave with Red Cross cream.

Forgot to mention previously I had also pipe and tobacco issued day before yesterday from American Red Cross. Supper: Rice and salad. Had boils treated and also graze on shoulder. Otherwise feel pretty fit this evening. Write some more rhymes. Tenko 8 p.m. Lights Out 8.30 p.m.

July 29th (Saturday):

'Yasume' today. Cleaned 'benjos' and then washed clothes first thing in morning Lazed around rest of day. Plenty of 'gash' today. Couldn't sleep much because of flies which are much worse on lower deck than up above. Good tomato stew for supper – best for many a month. Tenko 9 p.m.

310

July 30th (Sunday):

'Fry' for going-out vegetables today. Ate mine before Tenko as I usually do nowadays. Very nice. Miserable day today. Raining all the time. Not much work at Shibaura – probably due to rain. Had easy but monotonous day with wood and split cable drums. Finished about 3.20 p.m. Back in barracks 4.10 p.m. Had thorough wash down (bath house not available). Then to MI Room. Had boils and graze on shoulder dressed. Supper: Rice and stew. Tenko 8.30 p.m. Lights Out 10.30 p.m.

July 31st (Monday):

Very hard day at Shibaura. On embargo; sugar, salt and cigarettes. Did our tonnage (126½ tons) and finished about 3 p.m. Feel very tired, especially as I had to carry on left shoulder owing to graze on right. Back in barracks 4.45 p.m. Searched by Guards. Unusual thing, but nothing found. Supper: Rice and stew. Felt very weary and lay on bed space most of evening. Wrote one or two rhymes. Glad when Tenko came at 9 p.m.

August 1st (Tuesday):

Still feel rather stiff from yesterday. Join same gang on job. Tinpan. Promised rice ball but did not get it. Probably get it tomorrow however. Heavy going in morning but eased up in afternoon owing to lack of lorries. Back in barracks 4.45 p.m. Supper up early. Salad of potatoes and cucumber on rice. Feel very hungry. No gash around tonight. Tenko 9 p.m.

August 2nd (Wednesday):

Get on Working parade at 6.45 a.m. and are all pleasantly surprised when Orderly Officer tells us to yasume. (Shibaura party only). Apparently due to not enough 'Foos' being present. Had good sleep as we were not called out till 11.15 a.m. Ate working ration before leaving barracks. Very easy afternoon with gang on wood and big wooden tubs. Get back to barracks early. Good tomato stew for supper.

August 3rd (Thursday):

Fairly easy day on coal, empty gas containers, mats and bags of coal. Issue from Canteen. Buy red and white pepper and soap powder. No lights in barracks – out of order. Tenko 7 p.m. Bed.

August 4th (Friday):

Join another gang today. Josey, Bell and Cornwall. Did one lorry of wood before 10 a.m. and kaisha of glass afterwards. Finished morning about 11 a.m. No soup today. Kaisha of paint, coal and pig iron in afternoon. Back in barracks 4.50 p.m. Supper: fish, cucumber and rice. Definitely an improvement in quality of food lately. Plenty of gash rice also obtainable. No lights again. Tenko 7.30 p.m. Bed. (Had 2 letters from Gwen dated 18th January & 27th July 1943. Better late than never!)

August 5th (Saturday):

Good night's sleep. Disappointed at seeing there was a boat party on this morning. Thought I was going to miss it but was detailed at last minute. Coal boat. Very hard day but feeling pretty fit and so did not mind it so much. Rice ball at 2.45 p.m. besides usual extra dinner. Finished 3.30 p.m. Had hot bath on shore. Back in barracks 4.35 p.m. Had boils dressed and then ate 'going out' ration which I did not have time to eat on boat. Swimming parade tonight, but did not attend. Supper: Good thick curry stew with meat in, and rice. Plenty of gash. Band played on square. Tenko 9.30 p.m.

August 6th (Sunday):

No boats today thank goodness. But had very hard day on Shibaura. Morning not too bad. Found a few potatoes in bottom of 'straw mat' kaisha which I baked for dinner. Very nice. Horrible afternoon loading horse food of some description. Finished about 3.25 p.m. In barracks 5.10 p.m. owing to lorries being 'bioki'. Supper: fried 'herring' which consisted mainly of the head. Worst evening meal for a long time. Feel very tired and depressed after today's effort. Could not get boils dressed as MI Room was closed when I went about 7 p.m. Tenko 7.30 p.m. Lights Out 9 p.m.

August 7th (Monday):

Feel very tired today. Could sleep anywhere. Joined 'Kalin'(?) party on job today and had fairly easy time. Much cooler today and plenty of rain but managed not to get too wet. Back in barracks 4.45 p.m. Had wash only tonight owing to rain. Supper: rice and pretty good stew. No gash because I am feeling pretty hungry!

August 8th (Tuesday):

Had accident on job today. Only just started work when I dropped a box (which we were loading into a kaisha) on my foot (about 9.15 a.m.). Had to go 'bioki'* immediately. Very painful and quickly swelled up. Had to be carried from lorry over camp bridge and into barracks. Go on sick parade and get excused with compensation. Supper: rice and fish. Tenko 8 p.m. Lights Out 9 p.m.
  * Sick

August 9th (Wednesday):

Yasume today although I am excused work. 'Lucky' in a way as there were several fatigues to do bringing vegetables, etc. across bridge. Foot less painful today but still cannot stand on it. Very exhausting having to hop all

312

over place.   Managed to bathe in evening although procedure rather complicated.

August 10th (Thursday):
Bioki again today. Spend most of day on bed owing to difficulty of moving.

August 11th (Friday):
Same as yesterday except I can manage to walk on foot today although it is badly swollen and still painful. Get into trouble when going to MI Room in evening owing to misunderstanding order of Japanese NCO. Tenko 7 p.m. Lights Out 9 p.m.

August 12th (Saturday):
General yasume today. Foot still painful but can hobble about. Wash clothes, sleeping mat and general clear up in morning. Sports on in afternoon, but had good sleep on bed. Just managed to have bath before water ran out. Water situation very grim – it hasn't been on all day. Supper 5 p.m. 'Squids' and rice – very tasty. Concert in evening. Pretty poor but suppose could not expect much owing to lack of rehearsal. Wish I could get in and do a turn – but rather difficult. Lights Out 10 p.m.

August 13th (Sunday):
Had wash just after 5 a.m. Lucky I did so as there was no more water all day. Went to MI Room in morning - foot still swollen. Dinner was very tasty – sweetened egg fruit. On bed and read most of day. Supper: salad, rice and plenty of gash again tonight, but had to rush it owing to Tenko being at 7 p.m. No lights tonight and smoking only till 7.30 p.m.

August 14th (Monday):
Did not sleep much last night – sleeping too much during day! To MI Room in morning. Foot still swollen. Read again most of day. Nice to be able to do a bit of reading again. Have now read 8 books since I have been sick.

September 7th (Thursday):
Lt. Kato leaving Camp. New C.O.

September 8th (Friday):
New batch of about 120 Americans arrive from Philippines. Put in No. 5 Barracks.

September 14th (Thursday):
To MI Room in morning and agree to go to work in morning. Have now been sick with foot since August 9th. Not too bad now but still slightly

swollen. Have enjoyed 'holiday' and spent time mostly reading. Must have read over 50 books. A welcomed change and exercising of mind instead of the body for a change. Am awaiting with interest next weighing day to see how much I weigh now. Am told I look much fatter. Ambition is to weigh 70 kilos so I can afford to lose a few lbs when winter comes again. Weather is now much cooler than when I was previously working. Donned winter shirt for first time today – although, I hope, not permanently yet.

September 15th (Friday):
To work again.

September 20th (Wednesday):
Had to go sick again this evening with foot – too painful to work with. Am not on compensation however and have to work in leather shop.

October 3rd (Tuesday):
To work again. Foot seems better.

October 18th (Wednesday):
Send broadcast message to Gwen. (!)

November 1st (Wednesday):
See first American planes over Shibaura.

P.O.W. LETTER

DARLING. I HOPE YOU ARE WELL AND STILL
IN THE BEST OF SPIRITS. I AM VERY FIT AT THE
MOMENT AND FEELING QUITE CHEERFUL. I
AM RECEIVING SOME OF YOUR LETTERS TO
WHICH I AM ALWAYS LOOKING FORWARD. HOW
ARE ALL AT HOME? I HOPE THE PIANO IS
BEING TUNED UP READY FOR ME! I AM LOOKING
FORWARD TO SUNDAY AT HOME AGAIN.
MY LOVE FOR EVER.
Harry.

P.O.W. LETTER

Tokio
No.   CAMP
Date: 19th April 1945

MY DARLING WIFE. I HOPE YOU ARE WELL.
I AM STILL O.K. I HAVE NOT RECEIVED ANY
LETTERS FOR SOME TIME – THE LAST FEW
WERE OF THE 25 WORD VARIETY. I AM DYING
TO SEE YOU AGAIN – WHAT A DAY THAT WILL
BE! YOU WILL HAVE A LOT TO TELL ME. ALL
THE PLAYS, FILMS, ETC. I HAVE MISSED:
MEANWHILE DON'T WORRY. HAVE A GOOD
TIME AND KEEP SMILING. LOVE.
Harry.

This gap in my daily dairy (apart from June 16th and 17th) between November 2nd 1944 and August 15th 1945, deserves some explanation.

The short answer is that I no longer had the time or inclination, as I had now become an expert thief and was cheerfully robbing the Japanese Army of its rations by looting on the railway sidings and docksides, I was no longer hungry and pre-occupied with food. I was fitter, stronger and mentally alert.

So, despite the heavy American bombing of Tokyo during this period and seeing the whole city burnt down, I was far more occupied with writing songs and sketches and producing camp concerts than recording the destruction of Japan's capital city.

As far as I was concerned it was first things first and On With the Show.

And the Diary was temporarily forgotten.

May 10th 1945:
Concert: "Let's Go!", produced by Harry Berry

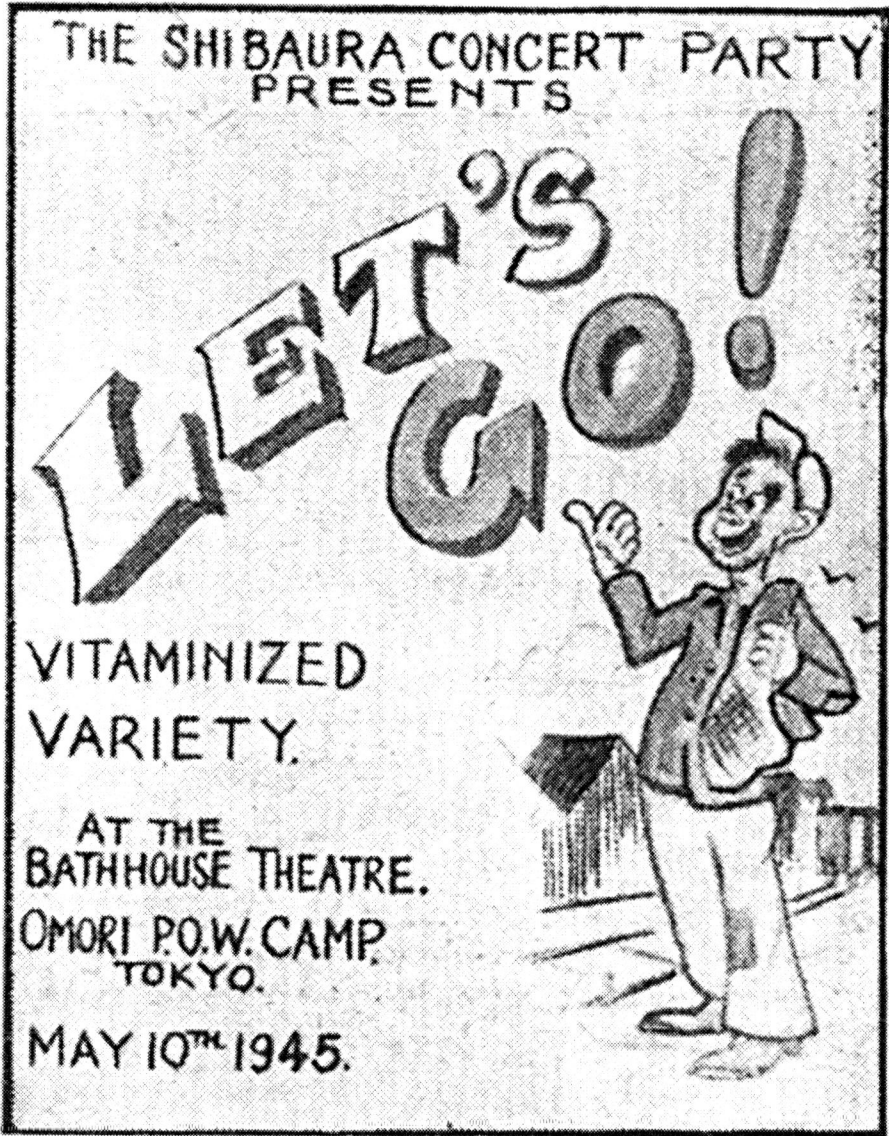

"Let's Go!"
This poster was drawn by Harry's best mate, artist Derek "Nobby" Clarke.

1. THE SHIBAURA TOBAN SHACK. — THE SHIBAURONS.
2. MASTER OF ALTO RAKKO.— C.STEWART, F.BAKER, P.STOCKER.
3. SHIBAURA SERENADERS.— R.CONSTABLE, F.PIDGEON,
   G.BLANCHARD.
4. LIGHTING SKETCHES. — D.A. CLARKE, I. COOK,
   (A) HEARD IN BLACKOUT.   C.CAUL, P.STOCKER.
   (B) LOVE IN A PARK.
5. THE WANCHAI BOYS.— M.GIBLIN, J. McCADDEN.
6. RECITATION. — J. BELL.
7. THREE OLD LADIES. — G.BLANCHARD, J. COOK,
   A. GREEN.

COMPERE— CAPT. H.S.BADGER.

INTERVAL.

8. BYE.BYE BLUES.(TAPDANCE.) — J. MONTEITH.
9. HOLLYWOOD IN O~DRI.— J. BELL, G.BLANCHARD,
   H.KERSHAW, E. BROWN.
10. CARTOONS & CHUCKLES. — D. A. CLARKE.
11. THREE IN A BAR.— C.CAUL, H.KERSHAW, E. BROWN
12. WHAT HO! WHAT HO! — HARRY BERRY.
13. FOUR KRAZY KOSSAX~M.GIBLIN, J. Mc.CADDEN,
    T. ALLEN, C.WANLESS.
14. THE TOBAN SHACK.— THE SHIBAURA CHORUS.
15. FINALE. — THE SHIBAURONS.

WITH
LEN AUSTIN'S ORCHESTRA.

PRODUCED BY
HARRY BERRY.

DIRECTOR, LT. G.M.BORDEN.
MUSICAL DIR; D.M. AUSTING. ARCH.
STAGE MANAGER, SJ.DE.L.BIRCHELL.
ASSTS, A.G.LEWIS, K.TMTL. I. STILL.
MAKE UP, I.T.R., LUCIA.
COSTUMES. J. GROAT.

Programme of "Let's Go!" showing Harry as the producer

318

Back cover of "Let's Go!"

319

June 16th:

Once again I commence my Diary. Things have changed a good deal since last October. I am probably as strong now as I shall ever be – able to carry 200 lbs on my back all day whilst walking up planks and stacking in the warehouses. Still working on Shibaura Station. Our station and Shiadome Station are the only two jobs continuing now. The rest have finished. New drafts have arrived at Omori and other drafts have left – due to the war situation. Not many people in camp at the moment. We are all hoping we shall be moving out of Tokyo shortly. Have done some entertaining lately. On May 10th I produced a Shibaura Concert which was a great success. I also visited local P.O.W. 'hospitals' and helped to cheer them up. I certainly feel a different person now to 18 months ago. Considering everything, I am living as well as can be expected. I am no longer perpetually hungry and am seldom short of a smoke!

June 17th:

Quiet day on the station. Loaded two 'kaishas' of odds and ends. Soup at dinner. Gave my 'going-out' ration to Nobby Clarke who is on a 'yasume'. Bathed on job. Back about 5.30 p.m. Dutch mess tins issued from Stores. Won't fit, but will get it seen to tomorrow.

July 19th:

Concert: "In Camp Tonight", produced by Harry Berry.

August 9th:

Concert: "Sing, Say and Play", produced by Harry Berry.

PART SEVEN

FREEDOM AT LAST

AND THE JOURNEY HOME

THE FIRST DAYS OF FREEDOM

August 15th 1945:

Today, I believe, is going to be the greatest day of my life. I am not quite sure yet – but almost. But to start at the beginning. For the past three days I have been working on the Camp air-raid shelters.

This morning we were up as usual at 5.30 a.m. for the usual breakfast of rice and soup when the air-raid sirens went. However, the 'all-clear' sounded a couple of minutes later so the camp working parties left at 7 a.m. I stayed in the barracks doing odd jobs and then went out onto the beach to saw some logs.

It was a very hot day but the clouds were low when we heard, but could not see, a squadron of planes passing overhead. We were ordered to get into the Shelter, but no bombs were dropped so we presumed they were Japs.

Up to now I had heard nothing unusual, but during lunch – a piece of cucumber, dried fish and beans – I heard someone mention 'Speech to Nation'. On asking what it was all about I was told that the Emperor was making a speech at 1 p.m.

As time went by excitement and speculation ran high, but despite various 'confirmations' I refused to believe the war was over and even told my neighbour I would wash his rice-bowls for him if it were true.

There was no official work parade in the afternoon, but we were found odd jobs to do. Many Jap Officers and soldiers and the office girls were seen to be crying and the Japanese Colonel gave a sickly smile as he told the air-raid shelter builders to 'ki-didi' (Hurry!). But still nothing definite had been heard.

The first outside working party to come in – from Shiadome Station – brought confirmation. They had been notified that the war was over by the German consular. There was further confirmation from other incoming working parties. Everyone was excited but kept cool. It was almost too good to be true. My doubts were slowly disappearing. Plenty of rice suppers were given away. The Canteen Officer issued five cigarettes unofficially on 'spec'. By 7 p.m., still nothing official had been heard from the Camp authorities and it seemed as if the camp routine was to carry on as normal.

Supper was very hard to digest (rice and green soup) as nobody felt particularly hungry.

I went out onto the Barrack Square with my neighbour, sat on a log and talked of home. The evening drew slowly on. The Band asked for permission to play but this was not granted. Tit-bits of news kept seeping through. We knew at 7.20 p.m. about Tojo and the War Minister. Just before Tenko at 8 p.m. Commander Maher (U.S. Navy) gave us the 'low-down' as far as he knew of the day's happenings. He warned us that we were still under the discipline of the Japs and not to cause any trouble.

There is no outside work parade tomorrow. I am on 3rd relief picket – 10.30 p.m. to 11.30 p.m. But nobody will be able to sleep tonight. Not only because of the fleas and bugs, but particularly because of nervous excitement.

Some people were literally sick with nerves. I went to sleep soon after getting into bed after my picket duty and had a good night's sleep.

August 16th:

No outside work party today. Paraded at 7.15 a.m. Cleaned up camp and then finished work. Everybody still talking of events and asking each other for news. Was shocked to hear the air-raid siren go at 10.15 a.m. Nobody seemed to know exactly what it was for. Received several cards from Gwen. Mail is now being issued very quickly as they are not being censored. It is a great effort to eat meals although the soups are now thick and pretty good. The remainder of the canteen cigarettes were issued today. We had been getting five every five days, but they have now issued the total available – 21 per man. So that's the end of those. Tenko 8 p.m. Lights Out 9p.m.

August 17th:

Slept pretty well although everyone else was pretty restless. Many chaps sleeping outside owing to the epidemic of fleas and bugs – particularly the latter which emigrate at night! Several people were sick and had stomach troubles during the night. All due, I think, to nervous reaction. Home-baked bread for breakfast this morning. Certainly enjoyed this much better than the usual meal. Paraded at 7.15 a.m. Did almost half-hour's work today tidying camp and then finished. All kinds of rumours floating around about Yank Fleet being at Yokohama, etc. One does not know what to believe. More cards from Gwen – the latest dated May 5th! Air raid alarm went again about 10.30 a.m. Also saw B29 as high as usual circling around in the usual way. Can't quite make it out. Washed hat this morning ready for tomorrow. After lunch put blanket and kit out in sun to air. Try to read, try to play piano, try several things. But no good. Outwardly I do not feel particularly excited, but the old nerves must be pretty taut.

Very hot today – we are now in the hottest time of year. Issue of soap, 'benjo' paper, vitamin pills. Day seems to drag terribly. Had to do small fatigue after supper and consequently escaped fly-killing at 7 p.m. Disquietening news this evening of hitch in peace talks and that Yanks cannot land at Yokohama owing to Jap Army not wanting to 'pack-in.' Hope it is not true. Tenko 8p.m. Lights Out 9 p.m. Was sleeping alright until 11.30 p.m. when noise of people stirring woke me. Saw other chaps all catching bugs and passing comments on their numbers. Could not see any around my bed space, but to make sure got up and looked through blankets. They were swarming! Immediately collected three blankets and rain cape and slept on air-raid shelter outside. Fleas (which breed in the sand) were pretty bad, but preferable to bugs. Rather comical that having escaped being bombed out, as were most Nips, we now have to evacuate because of bugs!

August 18th:

Did not wake up until Reveille Bugle at 5 a.m. Did not sleep too comfortably. Reveille was at 5 a.m. apparently because of Jap Colonel in camp. Bread for breakfast again and very nice. Paraded at 8 a.m. by our own (Allied) Officers, in groups. All nationalities together and services together, etc. They are now trying to resort to Army discipline. Helped clean room after Parade. Got a table without much trouble from former Leather Shop to use for bed in open tonight. Library is sharing out books. I have managed to collect quite a good few – 'Buried Alive' by Arnold Bennett, 'Plays of Tchekov', 'The Barretts of Wimpole Street' and several others.

Days seem to drag now. Lots of wild and depressing rumours floating around that Nip Army is refusing to pack in etc., despite the Emperor's Order. Air-raid siren went again during dinner time. Still don't feel particularly hungry. Have to force meals down – oh for some sugar. Read and lazed about in afternoon. After supper rested on bed-table. Am looking forward to sleeping on it tonight. Japs are making a row in their quarters. They are drinking a lot of Saki. During Tenko, Kato, who used to be Commandant of this Camp about 12 months ago, came into the room. He was slightly blotto. Made a very dramatic entry and with outstretched arms cried "The War is over. The Emperor's word is absolute." He then went right round the room shaking hands with everyone. He said "I will sing you a Chinese song." He started up in Chinese but ended up singing "Goodnight Sweetheart." He sat on the table and said "I want to do something big and clean. I want to wash an elephant," and several other such tipsy remarks.

Capt. Badger then made an announcement that nobody was to sleep outside tonight. Just my luck. Lights out at 9 p.m. For about an hour and a half there was a great uproar in the Nip quarters. Some of their NCOs armed with swords tried to break into the Special Prisoners hut, but luckily they were stopped by the guards. The Colonel finally arrived on the scene. He doubled the Guard and assured Commander Maher (U.S. Navy) that no harm would come to us. The bugs then got so bad that – orders or no orders – I went out to my table-bed and had a good night's sleep.

August 19th:

Tenko 5.30 a.m. Bread for breakfast. Immediately afterwards fix blankets over my 'table-bed' to keep sun off and sleep most of morning. Fish soup and rice for lunch. Back to bed again after lunch and read Tchekov's plays in between dozing. At 3.30 p.m. have salt water bath and then shave. Play piano for about half an hour. Sell pair of Japanese socks to departing Japs in No. 5 Barracks for 6 cigarettes. Some of the lads get flying jackets given to them by the Special Prisoners in appreciation of 'gash' given to them. Tenko 8 p.m. Lights out 9 p.m.

August 20th:

Tenko 5 a.m. Paraded at 7 a.m. at which we were told by our own Officers that we had to continue working in order to keep fit – and other usual 'bull'. Actually, of course, they are beginning to throw their weight around again after years of having no authority as POWs. We have had nearly four years of hard work with a 'yasume' every 10 days and now that the Japs are letting us take it easy, our own officers are objecting! Some of the lads told Capt. James exactly what they thought. No bread for breakfast today. Cleaned up No.5 Barracks in morning finishing at 10 a.m. Read the 'Barretts of Wimpole Street' till lunch. Slept all afternoon and read part of 'King John.' Typed more copies of songs from my shows for Commander Maher and others. Slept out in open again. Wonderful night.

August 21st:

Still no news of peace developments. We work in morning only and have afternoons off. But I did no work except composing a new song 'Dreaming that I'm Steaming on a Steamer Home to you' and a new script for the next concert. An Order today, reputed to be Japanese, that we cannot sleep outside any more, but personally I think it is our own Officers being awkward. Despite whole hut being cleaned and sprayed this morning there are still millions of bugs. God knows what we are to do tonight. Night time comes. We try to stay inside but impossible, so we all start moving. I grabbed a table and have it just outside the door. Capt. James comes along and asks what we are doing. We tell him and he goes to see Oban and we get permission to sleep outside. The Government suffers a defeat!

August 22nd:

Bread for breakfast. Water fatigue across bridge in morning. Japs don't look too cheerful. Starts raining mid-day and gradually gets worse. By the evening we realise a hurricane is blowing up. No question of sleeping outside tonight. Play piano in evening. *Tenko* 7 p.m. No lights owing to gale. I am on 2nd relief picket tonight. Some people chance sleeping on wash-stand, others in Bathhouse. But most return. Gale blew up terrifically during night. Horrible night's sleep owing to bugs. Glad when morning came.

August 23rd:

No bread this morning. Pleasant surprise – people from Propaganda Camp arrive. Fence pulled down around Special Prisoners' hut. Get rusty nail in side of foot but do not think it very bad. Got it treated right away. Talked with Don Bruce most of day (fellow I came with from Taiwan). Had plenty to talk about.

They did not have such a pleasant time in the Propaganda Camp and are certainly not as fit as we. Everything turned out for the best! (for me!). Nobby, with party of 40 to Shinagowa to repair camp after gale. Fence *around our camp blown down too. Surprise parade called about 5 p.m. Speech by Japanese Colonel. He thanked us for our obedience to the Japanese orders during our term of imprisonment. Said there was an armistice in progress which looked as if it might materialise, but that, if it didn't, Japan would fight on. Assured us that the Emperor's word was always obeyed. Told us to beware of Russian Communists against whom Japan was a shield. Said that the Army was disarming and becoming loyal citizens of the Emperor. Apologised for any ill treatment which may have occurred owing to some patriotic Japanese being temporarily mentally unbalanced with excitement. Told us he had done his best for us as regards rations and treatment. We had been much better off than the civilians. Hopes we would co-operate with Japanese and cause no incidents until we left. Commander Maher (USA) then replied. He thanked the Colonel for all the things he may have done as regards rations and assured him of our co-operation till we left. Earlier today we were informed that we were to have nothing to do with two of the chaps from the Propaganda Camp who were now under arrest.*

There is to be a concert on the 26th so I am now getting busy, having been excused fatigues. No lights again tonight. Played piano till 8 p.m. Tenko. Didn't sleep at all during night, probably due to Vitamin tablets and chocolate we were issued with today. Tried sleeping outside – it rained. Tried sleeping in bed space – bugs. Finally lay on a couple of forms. Did get some sleep.

August 24th:

Quite an exciting day today. On morning Tenko Mr. Parker collected 200 yen from our barracks (I got paid about 45 yen yesterday) as the canteen manager was going out to try and buy some cigarettes. Busy typing for forthcoming concert. Wrote Fire Station skit and my own act. Party went to Shinagower again today to help repair camp after hurricane. Swiss Consul visited there. Had 50 fags issued per man in morning – the result of manager's successful purchase. Fellow called Raye comes back from jail. Looks a complete wreck and has lost 4 toes. Swiss Consul arrives about 2 p.m. Chatted quite a lot but did not speak to me. 10 more cigarettes and 5 biscuits issued this afternoon. Felt very tired but busy on concert. Got Joe Edge to orchestrate music of my new song 'Dreaming on a Steamer'. Tenko 8 p.m. Looked as if it might rain but Nobby and I chanced it. Had a good night's sleep.

August 25th:

Tenko at 5 a.m. Informed this morning that Yankee planes are coming over and will drop food on camp any time after 6 a.m. Am now waiting for them. Several odd ones appeared and circled the camp giving recognition signals, but the first big 'raid' was at 10.30 a.m. when they dived right over the camp and dropped packages with and without parachutes. It was certainly a marvellous sight. We saw altogether 3 or 4 different types of planes. We could also see them circling over Shinagower. Several of the small planes dived and dropped packages of cigarettes, etc. – personal presents from pilots with attached notes. One said something like "Sorry this isn't much, but there is much more on the way. Keep your chin up. God bless you all." The pilot was off the 'Yorktown'.

They came over about twice again in the afternoon. The weather was not too good and similar to an English April. Showers one minute – the next sunshine. But we all stood out in the open, rain or no rain, stripped to the waist standing on roofs or anything else available and cheered and waved like mad. One pilot must have seen one of our Yanks who was standing on the roof signalling him to dive. He dived straight towards him and just skimmed the fence. Managed to do a bit of rehearsing in afternoon of 'Arnold Ramsbottom' sketch. Chocolate issue same as 3 days ago. Had bath. Band played in hut after supper. Had a talk with Perkyn about Propaganda Camp and POWs. Tenko 8 p.m. As lights were not out till 10 p.m. rehearsed in Cobblers Shop. Slept out in open at first but it started to rain, so I returned to barracks.

August 26th:

Raining nearly all day today. Typhoon reported hitting Osaka. No planes over. Very busy tonight with concert. On feet from 5 a.m. to 10 p.m. Had a shave with cream dropped by planes. Other drops include cigarettes, candy, soap, chewing-gum, tobacco and tinned meat. I drew a bar of Lifebouy Soap! Dashing around all day arranging programme, rehearsing my script and my own act and arranging other people's rehearsals. Stage and Lighting also had to be set up in the afternoon. I couldn't get the usual assistance from Bill Barber as he was busy in the office. Everything looked pretty hopeless – I couldn't get co-operation from anyone. At 6 p.m. hardly anything was ready and I could not find people for make-up, etc. We were supposed to start at 7.30 p.m. but actually started at 7.45 p.m.

Like most shows that look a shambles at rehearsal, it was a great success. We had five acts supplied by people from the Propaganda Camp. I had my 'Ramsbottom' sketch, my own act and accompanied the 'Wanchai Bros' on the piano. Everything went fine. The Ramsbottom sketch went over really big and I was afterwards told that my act was the best in the Show. Whether it was or was not, I was certainly feeling on form. The show finished at 10 p.m. and we all sang Auld Lang Syne. The Show was held in the Bathhouse. It was a great treat for the B29 fellows. Slept out in the open tonight. Had a marvellous sleep. Did not wake until Tenko Bell sounded.

August 27th:

Plenty of activity today. Tried to get some sleep in morning but planes were passing overhead and making too much noise! They glide in low with flaps down, drop the stuff – sometimes with parachute and sometimes without. Finally I went up on the Benjo roof and waved and cheered the pilots as they swooped by. They could be seen quite easily. Several parachutes broke and one package went right through the office window. Another package dropped contained ham sandwiches, etc. Today also the lads put the home-made British and American flags on the roof. Also in answer to a message as to what we required wrote 'Food, Candy, Home, Thanks' and several other things until Maher put a stop to it. Quite a load of stuff dropped today. Saw a big escorted transport plane land at airport. We've had white rice for breakfast and dinner today. A try to detail me for fatigues in afternoon, but I said I wouldn't do them as I had three days fatigues producing Concert(!) I didn't do them.

One of the planes this morning was photographing and cards were dropped which read 'Ernie Hoberecht, United Press War Correspondent. Pronounced 'Ho-bright'. Many more packages were dropped. Two planes dropped eight huge parcels with messages containing names of their crews. Some of the parcels fell into the sea, but most of them were fairly well aimed despite the parachutes sometimes breaking. It was grand standing on the roof trying to signal the planes to come in low. Had a short sleep in open in afternoon, then bath. Japanese issued bag of 'sweets'. Good supper of stew flavoured with bacon, and white rice, but had to give half my rice away. American cigarettes issued in evening (I drew Chesterfields) and one bar of Hershey's Candy, one packet of spearmint between two and one packet of Lifebouy between two. Everybody's feeling very happy this evening. This is better, I think, than any Christmas I have had. Played some swing records on gramophone. Roll Call by Commander Maher. Tenko 8 p.m. Lights Out 10 p.m.

August 28th:

Another exciting day today. Planes circling round nearly all day and making drops. They dropped a Newsletter today from the 'Yorktown'. Also 'Time' Magazine, newspapers and other books. Have been getting up-to-date with the news. Nobby drew 'Thanks Boys' on one of my sheets and we held it up on the Benjo roof. The planes dived right over the roofs to read it. Some were trying to signal by lamp but we could not read what they said. Did small fatigue in morning. Fifty more fellows arrived from a Factory camp today. Quite a number of B25, B26 and B29 crews about also. Learned from news-sheet that landing operations start today. A big target is made out of parachute and placed in Square – also a couple of wind sleeves.

Another issue of 20 cigarettes and sweets and later a 'supper' ration box – one between two. They contained a tin of meat, biscuits, chocolate, 3 cigs., spearmint and toilet paper. Went on 'Spotting duty' for an hour from 4 p.m. outside barracks. Target is now placed outside camp. Took the opportunity of going swimming in sea. The biggest thrill came just before supper when a

B29 came over and dropped a terrific load packed in a 50 gallon gasoline barrel. Unfortunately some landed in the sea and most of the foodstuff was destroyed. Lots of clothing also dropped. Notes also dropped saying they are stripping the ships to supply us – but they can't supply any women. Another says they have landed and we shall be released tomorrow or the day after.

Japs issue tin of oranges today. Also had an issue of jam and milk dropped by American planes. Had the bacon-flavoured noodle soup for supper and then went the whole hog and had jam, oranges and milk on my white rice. Played piano for a few minutes after supper. Certainly great to play a decent piano again. (It has now dried out). We learn from the Newsletter that British ships are in the vicinity – the "Duke of York" under Frazer. Won a tin of nuts in draw which I shared with 'Nobby' Clarke. Turned out to be peanuts. Went to bed 9 p.m. Slept well.

August 29th:

Had tin of meat with breakfast this morning. Food now raining down (from planes) like manna from heaven. This morning Japs issued 2 tins of salmon per man. Then we had issued (from planes) one ration box per man; a packet of cigarettes, spearmint and candy. My box included a tin of bacon and cheese, biscuits, candy, cigarettes, lemonade powder and sugar. Even now I might have missed out an issue of something. I have. Soup!

A great morning with planes. 'Tuxan' dropped. I managed to get hold of a newspaper dropped. One case of goodies went right through a back window of barracks and smashed place up. Luckily no one was in or they could have been severely injured, or even killed. We have been lucky not to have had any accidents as the Yanks are not using parachutes now and some of the boxes are very big and heavy. Had bowl of sweet cocoa this morning instead of stew. Marvellous. Grand standing on roof watching U.S. planes. The bigger bombers come over very slowly with their wing flaps down, sail just over the huts and then drop the loads. The 'Fighters' drop packets of cigarettes and written notes with the pilots waving and obviously enjoying themselves as they swoop down. I'd love to be able to pilot a plane. Can now see battleships out in the distance – three of them. The boys have painted a message on roof that Pappy Boyington is in Camp. Apparently he is a well-known American pilot with about 20 enemy planes to his credit and who is quite well-known in the U.S. I held up a sheet with 'Thank you boys' written on it. I shall have to wash that off soon. Have just been detailed to go across bridge to collect water.

330

POST OFFICE TELEGRAM 30th August 1945
SAFE ALLIED HANDS, HOPE TO BE HOME SOON,
WRITING ADDRESS LETTERS AND TELEGRAM TO:
LIBERATED P.O.W. c/o AUSTRALIAN ARMY BASE
POST OFFICE MELBOURNE, AUSTRALIA.
HENRY BERRY

August 30th:

I am writing this on board the American destroyer USS Runels. The events since I discontinued this Diary on August 29th seem like a dream.

On the afternoon of the 29th about 4 p.m. I went for a swim. Many planes were circling overhead and kept diving down low. In the distance we could see battleships and a white liner (presumably a hospital ship) which appeared on the horizon. Excitement was running high when somebody shouted "What's that?" Everybody stared out to sea and in the distance, heading towards the camp, were launches. Nobody doubted that they were anything else but a landing party and everybody was right. As they drew near we could see three launches, the last one flying the Stars and Stripes. Everybody went mad. From out of nowhere came the home-made Union Jacks, Stars and Stripes and the Dutch flag. Everyone dashed along the beach shouting and guiding the barges in. Some men swam out to meet them. The American commander then came ashore and said we were leaving immediately. The camp was in an uproar. There was a mad rush to collect what kit we had – one big melee. Scrambling for pants, jackets, vest and cigarettes. But nobody really cared that much. Soon there would be enough for everyone.

Embarkation started almost immediately with the sick. At the same time Shinagower was being evacuated by the barges. The Americans went first and then the odds and sods – the British remaining till last! Not many people slept that night. Everyone wandered around chatting to the U.S. Marines.

Today I started writing an hour by hour account. I found an American naval photographer who said there were a couple of English newspapermen aboard. I gave him my article with a note and told him to hand it to the English press. He said he would. Whether it will get home or not I do not know. We finally left Omori Camp at 4 a.m. the following morning. It was great to finally say 'Goodbye' to Japan. A 45 minute trip brought us to the Hospital Ship (on the 30th). Reveille blew soon after we boarded. We had a shower. We were examined by doctors and I was found to be 'A1' for transportation home. We were issued with American naval kit and a Red Cross bag holding toilet requisites, etc.

Then we had breakfast. Boy, what a meal. Real ham and eggs. Fruit, cereals, coffee, milk. Everything. I shall never forget it. Afterwards I read some English newspapers supplied and then dozed – first in one of the beds and then, when new arrivals came – on the deck. We had dinner on the hospital ship and then, in the afternoon, we who were passed fit, were transferred to the American destroyer. We were each given an American dollar – (about 150 of us). Had supper and another terrific meal and then a cinema show on deck in the evening. 'Silly Symphony' and 'Crazy House'. I then went to bed and slept like a top except for one bad dream when I woke up thinking I was still in Omori.

August 31st:

Up about 6 a.m. Had stroll on deck. Breakfast: toast, fruit, orange, chocolate drink. They certainly do things in style on American ships. Started raining, so slept and read during morning. Am troubled by stomach-ache, but decided to chance lunch. Still raining. Lie on bunk again in afternoon except when Destroyer moved further along Tokyo Bay. Supper is now up, but I am not having any owing to stomach. The American prisoners have left for a bigger transport and we are now waiting to be taken on a British ship. Meals were excellent. About 7 p.m. (just as cinema was about to start) the launches arrived to take us to HMS Speaker, a converted aircraft carrier. Most of the boys were sorry to leave the Yanks as they had been very decent to us. We gave them three cheers as we left. We arrive on the British vessel, are shown our bunks and given blankets, mattresses, mug and utensils, etc., and then have supper. Nobby and I have a walk around and examine 'Seafire' plane in hangar. It was damaged. All the rest (26 carried) have been taken off to make room for more prisoners. Had a good night's sleep.

September 1st:

Up at 6 a.m. Washed, etc. More prisoners board today. Shall be glad when we get moving away from this blasted country. Skipper gave a talk saying he was honoured at having us aboard. He added that he did not know where we were going. I heard on radio that Liberators were being prepared in England to bring us home. Rain cleared up a bit in afternoon. Had stroll round the landing deck – certainly an ideal ship to take us on. Plenty of room to move about. Saw film in evening – a Mickey Mouse, two other features and then 'Hanover Square.' Have not thought much of the modern films I have seen so far. Stroll round deck in darkness with Nobby after show. Slept well.

September 2nd:

Up soon after 6 a.m. Hope to get moving today. After wash, etc., heard gunfire. Strolled around deck. Breakfast: Ham and eggs, bread and butter. Slept and strolled round deck till lunch. Missed broadcast ceremony of Surrender on 'Missouri' owing to falling asleep. Marvellous 'Celebration Dinner' of Turkey, roast potatoes, greens and duff. Immediately after dinner wrote letter to Gwen. Only allowed one letter so could not write much. Had to post it on ship by 3 p.m. Had tea about 4.30 p.m., cake, butter and tea.

Cold ham and sauce for supper. Walk around deck for about an hour – then to bed.

September 3rd:

Up soon after Reveille. Stroll round deck. It seems pretty official that we leave at 2 p.m. About 11 a.m. Pay was up. Before paying out, the skipper told us where we were going – Manila. The reason being that the ship has to return to take on more POWs. Where we go from Manila, he didn't know. We were then paid the equivalent of £5 per man sterling. (Five Australian pounds and four American dollars). After dinner we all paraded (including Ship's crew) on Flight deck as we were leaving, as the crews of the other British vessels wanted to have a look at us. We sailed round and past about a dozen ships – including the King George V and the Duke of York. All the crews were on deck and cheered us, banged gongs, let off fireworks, etc., as we sailed past. It was rather embarrassing. What we have done to deserve this I do not know – the cheering should have been the other way round.

I stayed on deck until we left Tokyo Bay and then went below and slept till supper time. After supper went and saw film 'Practically Yours' but it was very hard to understand the conversation. Was going to stroll round the deck after the film but weather was blowing up and it was raining. Stomach didn't feel too good, so went to bed. Six years ago today war broke out!

September 4th:

Up soon after Reveille. Had salt water shower and then went up on deck. Marvellous day, but strong wind blowing. This ship certainly pitches – I hope we don't get into any really rough weather. Supposed to be a Concert tomorrow, but everyone I ask is feeling too sea-sick. Buy seven packets of fags at Canteen. Only 5d for 20! Read in Newsletter that cables have got home and BBC announced that HMS Speaker had left Tokyo with POWs. Had no supper, stomach wasn't feeling too good. Played piano in afternoon. Went to pictures in evening – 'Princess O'Rourke'. Best one yet but still, in my opinion, poor. To bed 10.30 p.m.

September 5th:

Got up when I thought Reveille had gone. Had bath, etc. and then found time was only 4 am.! Played piano in morning. Rum issue and 20 Ardath cigarettes. Didn't enjoy rum much. Slept most of afternoon on deck. Pictures again in evening. This time a Tarzan film. It was terrible. I am really surprised at the low quality of the films we have seen since we have been released. Strolled on deck after cinema. Took mattress up on Hangar deck as it is cooler. Heard that Tanker accompanying us had broken down.

September 6th:

Up at 6.15 a.m. On deck. Notice we are hardly moving – if at all. On deck again after breakfast. Can see Okinawa in distance. At about 9.30 a.m. we part from escorting destroyer and tanker which is going to be towed into Okinawa. Another rum issue and a packet of cigs. today. Play piano and then have dinner. Slept on bunk during the afternoon but woke up bathed in sweat. Took a salt water shower and had shave. Then up on deck after tea until supper. Spend odd moments reading newspapers, magazines, etc. Am now fairly well up on news. To pictures again in evening. This time 'Lady, let's Dance.' Still pretty poor. Stroll on deck afterwards. Take mattress up to hangar. Am now writing this in the Reading Room and intend to write something for tomorrow's concert.

September 7th:

Nothing much happening today. Nice day. Spend most of time on deck. Quite a lot of rushing about deciding what I am going to do in concert tonight. In the end decide to do my turn only as I don't feel like doing a lot of work. Rum issue at 11 a.m. Played piano till dinner. Concert started at 8.30 p.m. Was rather a washout owing to bad acoustics and noise of engines. There was a microphone but it wasn't much good. Really could not get going with my turn owing to this, but 'Song without Words' went over O.K. Had photographs taken on deck in afternoon.

September 8th:

Slept in hangar again last night. More land sighted today – the Philippines at last. Rum issue at 11 a.m. – then went to sleep till dinner. Tried to sleep again after dinner but finally went on deck. Did some washing and had a bath. Warships sighted on port side – look like a couple of aircraft carriers and destroyers. Rumour that we are to stay in Manila for 10 days. Hope it is not true. Received photograph taken yesterday, this evening. Still have not found shirt which I lost this morning.

September 9th:

Arrive in Manila at 8 a.m. Go ashore about 10 a.m. Straight to Camp. Find a lot of chaps from my regiment, but not John Collins.

HMS Speaker
(Tokyo Bay)

2nd September 1945

My darling wife,

Here I am again. Free, fit as a fiddle and longing to get home to you again. I hope you are still well.

334

The last letter I had from you was dated June 4th this year. The Japs released a lot of letters from home when peace was declared. I am sorry you had not heard from me for such a long time, but we have been writing pretty regularly once a month and even sent telegrams!

I am aboard a British vessel at the moment, but we have not yet set sail. I was in the first POW Camp to be liberated by the Yanks – what a sight that was! I still don't know exactly what I am allowed to say. I don't know whether the certificate on the back of the Air Mail letter still has to be conformed to. * However, I don't think I am giving away any secrets.

The Japs haven't treated us too well, but luckily since being in Japan I have been working on a railway station. So what the Japs didn't give us, we stole! I have learned (among other things) to walk up a plank carrying 200 lbs on my back. I think I can safely say that I am stronger and tougher than I have ever been. We used to work from 7 a.m. to about 4.30 p.m.

I've kept my brain alert by producing shows in camp about once a month. I've written several songs for you, darling; one at least I think should be publishable.

I hope all are well at home. I don't suppose I will recognise the children (my young brother and sisters). Give my love to them all. It won't be long now – who knows, I might beat this letter home!

Although I am well now, I have been very cold and very hungry. Hungry enough to enjoy eating ANYTHING. Just on two years ago I weighed 7 stone 12 lbs. I can honestly say, darling, that it was the thought of you that kept me going in those days. However, it is all over now – thank God.

We've had marvellous food since we've been released, especially today. We've just had roast turkey, roast spuds, etc. for the celebration dinner. Quite a change from rice and soup. Darling, I could keep writing for hours, but this is all I am allowed at the moment. Directly I get the opportunity I will write again – also to Dad and Do.

I am still very much in love with you, darling, and am always dreaming of our re-union. Believe me, if I get a chance to fly home, I will do so. I don't think I have changed much – if I have it is for the better! Thank you for all your letters, darling. They meant a very great deal to me. All my love for ever.

Your loving husband.

*The following had to be signed by the writer:-
"I certify on my honour that the contents of this envelope refer to nothing but private and family matters."

THE WAR OFFICE
Telephone: Mayfair 9400
Curzon Street House
W.O. Ref. SS/330/120/60
London W.1.
(Cas. P.W.)

9th September 1945

Madam,

I am directed to inform you with pleasure that official information has been received that your HUSBAND 974063 GNR H.W. BERRY, ROYAL ARTILLERY
Previously a prisoner of war in Japanese hands, has been recovered and is now with the Allied forces.
The repatriation of recovered prisoners of war is being given highest priority, but it will be appreciated that some time must elapse before they reach the United Kingdom.
Information of a general character regarding these recovered prisoners, including their movements before they reach home will be given from time to time on the wireless and will be published in the press.

I am, Madam,

Your obedient Servant,

Mrs. Berry
Ealing, London W.5.

336

THE DIARY:

1945

September 10th:
Busy all day queuing up for issue of kit, etc. Wrote letter home. Everything we want is for our asking here. Cigarettes, cigars, chocolate. Living like Lords. Went to pictures in evening. Rained, but am used to being in rain now. "Underman" – best film seen yet. Camp is in horrible muddy state due to rain.

September 11th:
Had medical today. Passed A1 in everything. M.O. says I am in pink of condition. Pictures again in evening. "The Long Shot" – pretty good.

September 13th:
New fellows came into camp today. Look for John Collins (best man at my wedding) but has not arrived yet. Spent evening with Danny Goldberg (of my regiment and with whom I used to do 'double-act' in Singapore and Taiwan POW concerts) and others singing with Jack Kirby playing guitar. Had couple of bottles of beer in evening.

September 14th:
Pictures in evening. Saw "A Song to Remember". Had 3½ tins of beer before going to bed.

September 15th:
Another draft leaves this morning. Have a good mind to see somebody about getting onto a draft. Drew pay this morning. 40 pesos, equal to £6.5s. Now have about £10 on me and can't spend it.

Manila
Philippine Isles

10th September 1945

My darling wife,

Just a short note to let you know where I am and what I am doing. Yesterday morning we arrived in Manila harbour at 8 a.m. At about 10 a.m. we disembarked on landing barges, then onto army lorries and straight to this camp.

337

There are about 2000 ex-POWs here from Japan, Formosa, etc. We are under canvas about 15 miles outside Manila and are being looked after by the Americans and the Red Cross.

They are really treating us like Lords. Everything is free at the canteen – chocolate, biscuits, cigarettes, cigars, films. So last night I had my first taste of beer for $3\frac{1}{2}$ years! Yesterday we sent off cablegrams via an Australian contingent which is here. You should have received it by now. It may mention Melbourne where we expect to fly to next week. All this is very nice, but I am still dying to get home to you, darling. It shouldn't be long now.

By the way, I've come across my regiment here – at least, perhaps I should say, the survivors. Some of them are in a horrible state. I can't find John. He and two other former 'Scarborough-ites' went to Japan about 9 months ago. I believe this Jap convoy was practically wiped out, but some people were saved and I am still hoping to see John. Perhaps his mother has news. If not, don't mention what I have written. Poor Joe Hamline (remember he met you at Watford when I was on guard duty) died about 2 weeks before the war ended – malnutrition.

God – I've been lucky. People from my regiment who have met me are astonished at my fitness. They say I have never looked so fit before – and they are right. I have been very busy since we have been here collecting kit, etc. I have now enough equipment to last me to the next war!

Well, darling, I must close now. Give my love to all. I hope your sisters are O.K. Remember me to Frank and my regards to Herbert, Hazel and the baby.

There are three things I want to buy when I get home. A car, a radiogram and a piano. We'll live in a tent! All my love, sweetheart.

POST OFFICE TELEGRAM:
14th September 1945

AM SAFE AUSTRALIAN HANDS HOPE TO BE HOME SOON
WRITING
ADDRESS LETTERS AND TELEGRAMS TO LIBERATED P/W CARE
AUSTRALIAN BASE P.O. MELBOURNE

HARRY BERRY

Manila

P.I.

12thSeptember 1945

My darling wife,

Just another short note to let you know I am still here. I am afraid my hopes of going home by plane are diminishing. Although a hundred left a couple of days ago by air I think most of us will be returning by sea.

Yesterday I had my medical. Passed A1 in everything. The doctor was amazed at my fitness. He didn't believe I had been a P.O.W. for $3\frac{1}{2}$ years. I was supposed to have two teeth out, but I said I'd rather not. I am terrified of dentists. I would rather meet a Jap any day!

The sun is shining here again today. The last two days have been almost constant rain. The camp is pitched on what used to be a paddy field, so you can guess the state it is in. Mud all over the place.

I hope we don't have to hang around here too long. I am tired of being a P.O.W. I am tired of being a soldier, and I am tired of being over here in this stinking East. Excuse the adjective, but I really mean it! I am looking forward to one of those good, cold, drizzly, foggy, London days.

Well, darling, there's not much to add at the moment. I am simply waiting for developments. I am longing to be with you again. The last time I kissed anyone was that morning I left you, and now I have four years of kisses saved up for when we meet again in a few weeks' time.

I checked up my measurements, weight, etc., with those in my original Pay Book. I am still roughly the same weight and size, but I have put on two inches around the chest. I don't think I have lost any more hair!

Au revoir for now darling. I am looking forward to receiving, maybe, a telegram from you. All my love for ever.

Manila P.I.
12th September 1945

My darling wife,

The time is now 10.30 p.m. and I am sitting in the Camp Canteen writing this letter. I have just returned from the open-air cinema where I have seen some crazy musical (the name I forget).

I have already written to you once today, but this is really just a 'Good-night' note. This is the time darling I miss you most of all. At home we should have probably just left the pictures and would be having a snack in Lyons or the Express. Then we should probably stroll slowly up Castlebar Hill to home (I suppose you would still have your glass of milk) and then bed. Now I have to go back to my tent alone and then perhaps I can dream of you.

Darling, I can't write any more. This place will be closing soon and I want to post this letter tonight.

But this is just to let you know I am still very much in love with you and longing to see you again.

Goodnight my darling. I hope the morning when I wake up and see you by my side won't be long in coming. My love for ever.

Manila, P.I.
13th September 1945

My darling wife,

I love you. As you see by the address I am still in the same place. We have, however, been told to stand by and <u>might</u> leave tomorrow – I hope by plane, but I think by boat. But as long as we are moving and going in the right direction, any transport will do.

I haven't been doing much today. This afternoon I was packing my kit in the hope that we would be moving soon. I also read all your letters I received in Japan. Darling, you have been very brave – I am proud of you. I did not receive any letters until I arrived in Tokyo from Taiwan – most of them during the past six months.

Thank Mr. Sinclair for his card. It was very nice to know I was not forgotten at the office.

I hope you are still keeping up your horse riding. It sounds attractive. By the way, I still have your two photographs which you gave me before I left home. I am afraid I lost my watch and cigarette lighter in action.

Well, darling, it's nearly 11 p.m. and time for bed, so I will say Goodnight. All my love, my sweet. It won't be long before we are together again. If we don't move soon I shall swim home!

Goodnight, my love.

Manila P.I.
14th September 1945

My darling wife,

I have just returned from the camp cinema where I saw 'A Song to Remember'. Gracie Fields is supposed to be coming here on the 17th – I hope I am not here to see her!

No news yet of moving. A small draft is leaving tomorrow, but where or how they are going nobody knows. The war has been over a month now and still I'm not on the right side of the world. If nothing happens tomorrow I think I'll do a little enquiring. I hope you have received by now a note from my friend Chris Gandy who left for home by plane about four days ago. He told me he would drop you a line saying I am O.K. I received news of John today. Apparently he is still in Japan and O.K. I may see him even now before I leave here.

Nothing much more to add, darling, except that the days seem terribly long now that I am so near to seeing you again.

All my love, sweet. I hope I have some definite news tomorrow.

15th September 1945
Manila P.I.

My darling wife,

A month ago today the war ended and I am still a long way from home. I certainly hope that by the time you receive this letter I shall be on my way.

There has been no news concerning my moving today. A draft of about a hundred left by plane. I suppose it will take time as there are about 2000 of us here, but I shall do what I can to get myself moved soon. I think it will be within the next four days.

We got paid today – 40 pesos (about £6.5s). With the money I received on the boat I have now about £10 and nothing to spend it on! As I have told you in previous letters, everything here is free. We are even allowed one and a half pints of beer a day. We have been given Australian paybooks and we can draw £2.5s a week – if and when required.

I have just returned from the pictures – I go practically every night. I saw 'Junior Miss' – rather an amusing comedy. I also happen to have read the play in book form in the prison camp at Omori. There's nothing else to add, darling. I'll be glad when I get out of here. I don't like camps of any description now!

All my love for ever.

Manila P.I.
16th September 1945

My darling,

No developments today.

This afternoon I wrote to Hazel and Mr. Sinclair. Whilst I am here I am going to try and write to everyone who sent me a letter in Japan. Tomorrow I shall write to your sister Margaret and my brother Joe. I see in one of your letters that he and Mary have two children now, but you don't say whether boy or girl. And Violet too! You know, darling, with all these babies flying around I shall have to bring back half-a-dozen or so black ones so that we can be in the running. I daresay I could get some in exchange for a few cigarettes. Or maybe we would get them cheaper in England – say for a couple of bars of soap. From what I can gather in the newspapers there is an extreme shortage of soap – amongst other things – in England. Today I have been buying soap and toothpaste (at last a use for my money!). If I see anything else that may be useful I will buy that too. Of course, there is not much variety in our canteen, but if we stop anywhere on the way home and I can get you any material I will do so.

A few cablegrams are arriving here now. I am hoping that maybe I will get one from you.

I am sorry to hear about your aunt. I hope Margaret isn't too upset. Are you living at Wimbledon now? I am still addressing your letters to Ealing.

I have just returned from the pictures where I saw 'To have and have not' – pretty stupid.

Well, darling, I think I will get some shut-eye now. I am very much in love with you, darling, and feel very miserable at being stuck here away from you. But I suppose I must be patient.

All my love, sweetheart.

P.S. Enclosed is the lyric of the song – "My Song Without Words" – I wrote for you. Don't show it around too much in case somebody copies the idea. It's the best thing I have ever done. I wrote it whilst in Formosa.

'My Song Without Words' was the camp's "Top of the Pops" both in Taiwan and later in Omori Camp, Tokyo.

Verse:

If I were some composer, like Mendelssohn of old,

I'd write a song and tell the world about you.

How far away you are today - How much you mean to me,
How lonely every second seems without you.
But I've no song except for one
In my deepest dream.
The melody is memory,
My thoughts a simple theme.
Chorus:

My Song without Words is no hit, that I know

You won't hear it played over your radio
My Song without Words is my memory of you.
The smile that you smile
And the way that you walk
That light in your eyes
And the talk that you talk
My Song without Words is my memory of you.

Now I'm confessing, that when expressing
My thoughts - Words seem in vain
At composition, I'm no musician
But you inspire a haunting refrain
So why should I try to write a song, when I know
Melody lingers wherever I go
My Song without Words is my Memory of you.

17th September 1945
Manila P.I.

My darling wife,

Tonight, for a change, I am writing to you on American Red Cross paper. If any other type of writing material turns up I'll send that to you too. Variety is the spice of life!

Another big draft was called out this morning and I was not on it. So I went up to the Orderly Room and said "What the Hell!!" or words to that effect and the officer told me there was another draft being made up this evening and I should probably be on that. So I shall now have to wait till morning to find out. If I'm not on it

344

I shall go stark raving mad, or at least, I shall be a little aggressive. They're not too good on organisation here but I expect things will work out. My friend Derek is on today's draft (he lives at Watford) and if he gets home before I do he will write to you.

I have just returned from the pictures where I saw 'Christmas in Connecticut' – a very good comedy. But I am awfully anxious to see Christmas in London.

There's nothing happened today to tell you about, so I'll get this letter posted. I was going to write to Joe and your sister, but it is a bit late now.

I really think I shall have news of moving tomorrow.

I get so impatient being here darling when I am longing to be with you again.

All my love.

18th September 1945

Manila, P.I.

My darling wife,

I am writing to you a little earlier today. It is about 5 p.m. I was not on any draft today despite the large numbers leaving, so I have just written to the Officer i/c Drafts asking him whether or not my name and particulars have been mislaid. So I ought to get away soon – or land up in clink!

This latest draft seems to be going via India and it is very overcrowded. It might all be for the best therefore. As I have told you before, I was in the first POW Camp to be released, but when we finally reached Manila by aircraft carrier, we found some ex-POWs already there, having arrived by plane. I have been pretty lucky as regards drafts whilst a POW so perhaps my luck will hold now and maybe I shall eventually fly home.

It has been a horrible day today – raining cats and dogs. There is mud all over the place. I am afraid it has washed out the pictures tonight. My friend Derek Clarke who left today has given me his ration ticket, so I shall probably get drunk tonight. Don't be afraid of my going 'astray' – it's impossible here. I shall probably go to bed feeling very homesick.

Well, darling, I think supper is up. I'm not particularly hungry, but I had better go.

All my love darling. I am thinking of you every minute. Some people have received letters and cables from home. I am hoping to get one from you soon. My love for ever.

19th September 1945

Manila P.I.

My darling,

I have just received your letter of August 22nd together with cable of September 1st. It was only by luck I got hold of them. A friend told me there was mail at the Post Office which you had to collect yourself. So I immediately splashed through the mud to the other side of the camp and searched through the B's. Besides your two there was a letter from Dad and a wire from "The Star". That's the way things are run in this Camp. There is no information given at all. You have to find everything out for yourself.

Darling, you cannot imagine how happy I was to get a real letter from you again. I was so excited I couldn't eat any supper. I am still feeling rather hot and bothered. I am very thankful that you and everybody at home are in the best of health. I am really very fit although I am getting very annoyed at still being in this hole when most of my friends have gone.

I did not get your radio message, but I am glad my letters home were speeding up. I think I must have received most of your cards this year.

Thanks for all the news. I am glad you have been looking after yourself and found a good friend to keep you company. Remember me to Muriel and Frank. I hope Muriel's very happy. I wasn't far wrong when I presumed Herbert was a Major. Give him my congratulations on his promotion. I hope he is fit and that he stays in England with Hazel. I have already written to you once today – this afternoon. The time is now about 7.30 p.m.

I have just found out that it is possible to send 'wires', so I will send one tomorrow.

Darling, I love you very much and am longing to be with you again. I think I shall be home easily by our wedding anniversary. I think I will go to bed now. I am not feeling too good- excitement I think. I will send a wire and write again in the morning.

My love for ever.

19th September 1945

Manila, P.I.

My darling wife,

Would you believe it? Another draft is leaving today and still I am not on it. Immediately I went to the office and complained. They took particulars and said they would look into the matter right away. They admitted that some of the names might have been mislaid. I guess the Army is still the same be it British, American or Australian. The only thing organized is chaos. If I'm not home within the next six years you might come and settle down out here! It's pretty deadly, but it would be nice to see you again. (It's a pity all these sarcastic remarks aren't going to the right quarter).

It's been a horrible day again today. Rain, rain and more rain. I never saw so much mud in all my life.

As I told you in my letter yesterday, I intended to get slightly 'blotto' last night. I had nine beers and it hardly affected me until I went (or tried) to go to bed.

Every time I tried to lie down somebody hit me on the head with a sledgehammer. Then I developed hiccoughs. This went on until I thought of trying the hara-kiri cure, but I suddenly remembered the showers. So at one o'clock in the morning I went and had a cold shower and it did the trick. But I've learned my lesson. I daren't look at beer today.

Well darling, there's no news. I'll write again tomorrow. All my love.

347

20th September 1945

Manila, P.I.

My darling,

Here I am still in the same dump. Another draft was made up for a plane-load today – 10 men – and I missed that! I went along to see the Major i/c and he assured me that I would probably leave tomorrow with the other 28 men left of the original draft to reach here. The liar!! However, I'm hoping for the best. You know I have been pretty lucky with drafts since being a POW, so perhaps it is all for the best. But to think I could be with you in a few days by plane! But there is one disadvantage of going by air – you are allowed only 50 lbs of baggage, and my cigarettes and cigars weigh nearly that much!

I sent you a 'wire' this morning – "Wire, letter received, also Dad's. Hope leave Manila soon Writing. Love. Harry." You should get it within four days.

Gracie Fields is appearing at the Main Theatre in Camp tonight, but I think I'll go to the pictures. It has stopped raining today – I hope it keeps fine now.

I get so depressed, darling, not being on the move. I'm longing to be with you again. However, by the time you get this I shall definitely be on a boat. I hope we don't have to spend another long period in India. All my love, darling.

21st September 1945

Manila P.I.

My darling,

Good news today. The authorities have suddenly realised that there are men still here from the 9th September. There are 27 of us and it has finally been admitted that our papers have been lost. Today we went through the whole process again;   medical

348

examination (my third since being released) and filling in various forms. They promise that we should be on the next draft and I have just heard that there is a draft leaving tomorrow. So goodbye Manila, and good riddance. It is about 10 p.m. now. I have just returned from the pictures. It started raining just after the programme started and, believe me, it is a regular monsoon. But the old British Bulldog spirit is still there – I refused to budge. Let it rain – who cares? I like getting wet now. It doesn't matter so much when one wears hardly any clothes.

Tonight, for the first time, I wore long trousers. Usually all I have on is a pair of underpants. The trousers are soaked, proving that the more clothes you wear the more inconvenient it is! I really don't know how I am going to get on when I have to wear civilized apparel. And as for evening dress – ugh!

There are now hundreds of POWs arriving every day and from information received I expect John to arrive any day. He was quite fit and in Japan nine months ago.

Well, darling, I pray I'll be on my way to you tomorrow. It will be the greatest day of my life when we meet again. I have always been very much in love with you and have always been faithful to you.

I have had no contact or interest with women at all since we parted. My dislike of the East includes the people who live here.

Give my love to all, darling, and carve a large chunk off for yourself.

THE DIARY: 1945

September 18th:
  Friend Derek (Nobby) Clarke leaves on draft.
September 21st:
  Authorities admit my papers lost! Am processed again. Hope to leave tomorrow.
September 22nd/23rd:
  Board U.S. Troopship with other British POWs for San Francisco.

Manila P.I.
23rd September 1945

My darling,

Just a short note to let you know I leave tomorrow at 12 noon – by boat.

I can't write any more now because the canteen is just closing.

All my love, my darling. I am on my way now!

5th October 1945

At sea aboard the U.S.S. Joseph T. Dickman

My darling wife,

At last I am really on my way home. I finally left Manila on the 25th of last month and am now bound for San Francisco. I was a bit disappointed at not getting on a British boat and going home the shorter way round, but I don't suppose there will be much difference in travelling time. We might have gone to India and spent another month there! I will be able to say I have been all round the world now.

It is expected that we will cross the American continent by train for New York, but, of course, we do not know definitely. We are due to dock at Pearl Harbour on the 9th, where I will be able to post this letter by air-mail.

Today is Friday, 5th October, and as we are crossing the International Date Line, tomorrow will also be Friday 5th October. Two pay days in one week. Not bad, eh!

There's not much to write about. The sea has been pretty calm and all I do all day is sleep, read and eat. The ship is pretty crowded with both British and American troops, but as I used to say in the bad old days, I'd go home by barge if I could get one. So I can't grumble. By the way, we are supposed to reach 'Frisco on the 15th.

I hope you are still keeping well darling. I am always dreaming of you. I expect you are getting my letters from Manila by now.

I won't write any more today, but I'll add a few lines later just before posting. I can't write too much because I am sending this by Air Mail and we are allowed only an ounce in weight. Goodnight, my darling.

6th October: Yesterday, darling, I received your telegram sent to HMS Speaker. It was delivered to this ship just before we left Manila and has taken all this time to reach me. I am glad you received my first letter. It's nice to be able to keep in contact with each other with intervals of days instead of years!

I have just heard we are supposed to be stopping for 42 hours at Pearl Harbour, so perhaps we shall get a few hours ashore. I should like to stretch my legs. There is no room for exercise of any description on this vessel. It is now 7.30 p.m. and I shall soon be going to bed as there is nothing else to do.

All my love, darling.

7th October: Will close this letter now, darling, as I will have to post this tomorrow. There's nothing interesting happened today to tell you.

All my love, darling. Keep good!

TELEGRAM DATED 'EALING 18 OCTOBER 1945'
Office of Origin: SAN FRANCISCO CALIF.
"ARRIVED YESTERDAY LEAVE ANY DAY SEE YOU SOON ALL MY
LOVE DARLING - HARRY"

**PICTURE POSTCARD OF ST. JOSEPH'S ORATORY, MONTREAL,
CANADA DATED MONTREAL OCTOBER 25**

Darling,

Train has stopped for few minutes. Hope to catch 'Queen Elizabeth' at Halifax in few days time. Won't be long now! All my love.

THE DIARY 1945

October 10th: Arrive at Pearl Harbour (no shore leave).

October 11th: Depart from Pearl Harbour.

October 16th: Arrive United States. Pass under 'Golden Gate' Bridge. Huge sign reading 'Welcome Home' on Alcatraz! Disembarked at Fort McDowell, Angel Island (in San Francisco Bay) for 'processing'. Not allowed on mainland (no visas!).

Americans ask if anyone wishes to join U.S. Army! One chap volunteers.

October 19th: Left Fort McDowell at 6.30 p.m. Arrive at a railway station at 8 p.m. Train leaves at 9.30 p.m. With much difficulty and perseverance manage to open windows for fresh air.

October 20th: 5.15 a.m. Bakersfield. Had breakfast. Lunch at Barstow. Nice place with Spanish-type girls. Bought Gwen some lipstick and scent. Very expensive.

October 21st: 8 a.m. Winslow. Had breakfast. Arizona very Mexican. Painted Desert. Gallup (New Mexico) 10.45 a.m. Indian type town.

Bought two pairs of stockings for Gwen. Albuquerque. Bought six pairs of stockings. Supper.

October 22nd: La Junta (Colorado) 6 a.m. Had breakfast. Town not yet awake. Very nippy. Saw Woolworth Stores. Lunch at Dodge City. Walk around town. Buy 3 lipsticks. Kansas City 7 p.m. Busy town with big station. Had quick walk around station area. Interviewed by press and had photograph taken. Talk to Yanks in next train just arrived from Europe. They say England's O.K. Leave 10 p.m.

October 24th: 9 a.m. Chicago. Train does not go to centre of city but waits around on branch line in industrial area. Have Red Cross biscuits, candy, etc. Leave about noon. Train picks up two Dining Cars. Arrive Detroit 5.30 p.m. Disembark onto station. Red Cross women with cigs. and chocolate. Have photo taken again. Change onto Canadian train. Dinner served as leaving Detroit.

October 25th: Pass Toronto at 5.30 a.m. Breakfast in 'Diner.' Montreal 2 p.m. Red Cross women on station with cigarettes, chocolates, fruit, etc. Send two cards home. Met Red Cross woman on station born in Finsbury Park.

October 26th:	*Arrive Moncton (New Brunswick) at 10 a.m. Quick walk around town. Raining. Cigarettes, matches and fruit from Red Cross. Arrive destination 4.30 p.m. In barracks miles from anywhere!*
October 27th:	*To nearest town – Truro (Nova Scotia) in evening. Bought presents, etc. Played piano in YMCA.*
October 28th:	*Play piano in Canadian Army's Mess Hall in evening.*

Airport Station
Debert
Nova Scotia
Canada

29th October 1945

My darling wife,

By the time you get this letter I shall be almost home. Tomorrow we embark on the Queen Elizabeth at Halifax and set sail on the 31st. We should cross the Atlantic in less than four days. It will be wonderful to be with you again darling.

We arrived here three days ago after a 6 day train journey from San Francisco – from where I sent you a telegram. I have only just found out it is possible to send Air Mail letters from here. It would have been no good sending you a letter by surface mail as that takes ten days.

My thoughts are always with you, darling. It's marvellous to think we shall be together again in a week's time. I shall never leave you again.

I hope you are in good health despite the food rationing. Believe me, darling, after what I've seen of the world, I'd rather be hard up in England than a millionaire in any other part of the globe – especially when I have a wonderful wife like you.

I don't suppose I shall get another chance to write, so the next time I say 'I love you', I will be able to do so with my own lips.

All my love, darling.

Airport Station

Debert, N.S.

29th October 1945
7.30 p.m.

My darling wife,

I sent you a letter this morning which I said would probably be my last before I get home. But this afternoon I was lucky enough to get two of your letters from the Post Office dated September 2nd and September 4th. Yes, darling, when I mentioned the piano in my letter from Omori POW Camp I knew the war could not last much longer. Japan was in a terrible state. We used to have to ride about 5 miles to work every day and we could see the conditions. Also we used to smuggle newspapers into camp and we could guess Germany was nearly finished. You were a silly girl, darling, getting so excited. But I don't blame you. I might have cried myself if anyone had encouraged me. By the way, I don't know whether you will be able to meet the "Elizabeth" when she docks at Southampton, but if you are, do you think it would be wise? I shall probably be very emotional when I meet you darling, and I don't suppose you will be any calmer. Mind you, I expect everyone else will be the same so I'll leave it to you to do as you think best. It will be a hard job to keep control when I see England again, and if I saw you too I should probably go completely haywire! However, darling, I'll leave it to you. I expect we shall have a few preliminaries to go over when we land and before we are allowed home. Perhaps the Red Cross will advise you. I am glad you kept so fit, darling. Don't believe what you read in the press about ex-POWs. I felt quite sorry for myself when I read some of the accounts.

Thank you for all the office news. I hope Mrs. Collins has heard from John by now.

Like you, darling, I have a tooth to come out, but, unlike you, I have not had it out yet. I didn't want to take the chance of meeting you with my face swollen. It's a good excuse isn't it darling? But it really doesn't ache all that much.

354

I am glad you didn't try to send me a parcel, darling. The Japs would only have pilfered it or lost it. I'll try and bring you some chocolate home.

Well, darling, this page is nearly full so I must close. Look after yourself, darling. I am terribly in love with you and can't imagine what I've done to deserve a girl like you for my wife. Goodnight, my love.

Airport Station
Debert, N.S.

30th October 1945

My darling wife,

Another last letter! Just a short note to let you know we are leaving here about 5 a.m. tomorrow for Halifax and the Queen Elizabeth. Reveille is at 3 a.m.! Believe me it's pretty cold around here at that hour. But who cares!

I haven't much news to tell you, darling. I went to bed early last night – about 8 p.m. – trying to get rid of a cold before I get home. But I have not yet succeeded.

By the way, in my letter I posted aboard the Dickman, I said I hoped to get shore leave. Well – we didn't. And at San Francisco we were put in any Army Camp on an island in the bay, so I didn't get a chance to stretch my legs before I arrived here. The nearest town is Truro – about ten miles away. I went down there one night, but there's nothing much to do except go to the pictures. However, I had a walk round Woolworth's and other shops.

Well darling, I have now got to go and have 'chow' (dinner to you) so will say au revoir for just a few days.

Shall we go for a walk next Tuesday afternoon, darling? All my love.

THE DIARY 1945

October 30th:
  Play piano in canteen in evening.
October 31st:
  Reveille 3 a.m. Breakfast. Parade at 5 a.m. Board train and leave at 7 a.m. Board "Queen Elizabeth" at Halifax. Set sail 2.30 p.m. Plenty of room aboard. Meet Mr. Powell, American correspondent of "The Star", going home. What a coincidence! Have a chat.
November 1st:
  Nice, but windy day. Walk around deck in morning. Sleep in afternoon. Red Cross kit issued.
November 3rd:
  Concert in evening. Wee Georgie Wood comperes. Did my act and sung 'Song without Words.' Wee Georgie says I have a 'hit' and will try and get it published when we arrive in England.

POST OFFICE TELEGRAM
November 5.45 (Monday)

ARRIVED SOUTHAMPTON TODAY THINK HOME TUESDAY EVENING ALL MY LOVE DARLING   HARRY.

That was the end of my diary and the last war-time correspondence with my wife.

We docked at Southampton on November 5th. I saw some rockets bursting in the evening sky and thought, 'Even after six years of war we still don't forget the Guy.'

Thinking back, however, the rockets might have been for us and the Queen Elizabeth, but that didn't occur to me at the time.

After I had telegraphed my wife we were 'sorted out', given some pay and told to take what medals we thought we were entitled to. The following morning we boarded the train.

We arrived at Charing Cross Station about mid-day and for the first time for over 5 years I felt FREE. No more orders, no more being organised – I could now do exactly as I pleased in my own sweet time.

I managed to dodge the Red Cross and other volunteer helpers (bless 'em, but I wanted to look after myself now) and decided to take a taxi all the way home.

But where were the taxis?

I approached a lady in some kind of – what I took to be – naval uniform. "Can you tell me where I can get a taxi, please?" I asked.

"Where are you going?" she enquired.

"Ealing."

356

"I'll give you a lift."

"Thanks very much," I said, "but I wouldn't dream of troubling you. I'll take a cab."

"Nonsense," she replied, "you won't find a cab. I'm in the W.V.S. (Women's Voluntary Service) and it's our job to look after you chaps. Come with me."

There was no way out of it.

But it was a nice ride to Ealing. A car to myself with an attractive chauffeur. I began to feel like a V.I.P.

Looking out of the window I found it hard to believe I had been away for nearly 5 years – London hadn't changed all that much. We reached Ealing and I guided her through the streets to the house. She stopped, I got out, thanked her and said goodbye.

"I'll wait till you go in," she said.

I grinned. I knew why she was waiting. I wouldn't be the first overseas serviceman she had taken home only to find the bird flown! But I knew better. I knocked at the door.

There was no reply. I looked round. The WVS was still there; an anxious look on her face. I knocked again and this time it opened and there was my wife in dressing gown, curlers and tears.

"You're early," she sobbed. "You said this evening and I wanted to look beautiful for you." We fell into each other's arms. "You have never looked more beautiful," I said.

Later I turned round to wave goodbye and thanks to the W.V.S girl. But the car had gone.

Ref D3/P.O.W./REPAT
R.A. Records (Field)
Foots Cray
Sidcup, Kent.

10.11.1945

Dear Madam,

I am pleased to inform you that information has been received to the effect that your HUSBAND GNR.DVR.i/c 984063 H.W. BERRY, Royal Artillery arrived in the United Kingdom on 5.11.1945.

It is appreciated that you are probably already aware of this information.

Yours faithfully,

Officer in Charge.

357

Gunner Harry Berry's

THE PLACES BELOW ARE MENTIONED IN THE LETTERS,

1 SCARBOROUGH, UK	6 FREETOWN, SIERRA LEONI	11 SINGAPORE
2 WATFORD, UK	7 CAPE TOWN, SOUTH AFRICA	12 IPOH, MALAYA
3 WOOLWICH, LONDON, UK	8 DEOLALI, BOMBAY, INDIA	13 KHOTA BHARU, MALAYA
4 GOUROCK, GLASGOW, UK	9 NOWSHERA, NWFP	14 SINGAPORE
5 SOUTHAMPTON, UK	10 COLOMBO, CEYLON	15 FORMOSA

wartime travels 1940-1945

BUT THE EXACT ROUTE IS UNSPECIFIED.

PART EIGHT

SONGS AND RHYMES WRITTEN FOR P.O.W. CONCERTS

AND PUBLISHED ARTICLES

SONGS FROM FEPOW SHOWS 1942 – 1945

1. "Song Without Words" Easily 'Top of the Pops' in Changi (Singapore), Taihoku (Taiwan), and Omori (Tokyo) POW Camps.

2. "Ijo Arimasen" Taiwan 1943. My translation may not be all that correct!

3. "The Bucket Swing" Taiwan 1943. We could always hear when the daily ration of rice and soup was being carried from the cookhouse to the various barracks. The rations were contained in wooden buckets and as they swung on the metal handles they squeaked! "Buckets are Swinging" was the call that used to go out when the rations were on their way.

4. "Somewhere across the Ocean" Taiwan 1943. Well received but never reached the popularity of "Song Without Words."

5. "We're in trouble again" Singapore 1942. Signature tune for double act 'Berry & Berg' (Harry Berry & Danny Goldberg).

6. "Dawberry Swing" Singapore 1942. First tune I wrote as POW. Dawson played drums and I played piano Hence Dawberry Band was formed.

7. "Dreaming that I'm Steaming" Tokyo 1945. Written in great hurry for final concert when war ended. Hence similarity to 'Tiptoe thru Tulips' which would have been changed if I had had more time.

8. "Goodbye" Tokyo 1944. Corny but cheerful chorus for concert finale.

9. Selection of 'Boisterous Ballads' (Harry Gribble and Fish).

   Words and music by Harry Berry (ex Gnr/Sig.R.A.)

   These songs were recorded on to tape by Harry Berry in 1987. Self accompanied on electric organ

   Copyright. Now Linda West ©

363

ORIGINAL SONGS BY HARRY BERRY   Singapore 1942

My first composition (!) for the Changi Concert Party. We found a piano, then a set of drums, and then a drummer. His name was Dawson, hence **"The Dawberry Swing."**

> The Dawberry Swing
> Will make you sing
> Make you dance like anything
> The Dawberry Swing will swing your blues away
> Now if you're sad
> Things aren't so bad
> With a little rhythm from the rhythm lads
> The Dawberry Swing will swing your blues away
> Now if you wish then we will demonstrate
> Just listen to the drummer make a break ....
> The Dawberry Swing
> Will make you shout
> Keep you going when the rice runs out
> The Dawberry Swing will swing your blues away.

Then I teamed up with a chap called Goldberg and we formed a double act, 'Berry & Berg.' We finished the act singing **'We're in Trouble Again.'**

> We're in trouble again
> In fact it's our middle name
> We never seem to do the right thing
> Tho' we try from the start, we always land in the cart
> And we're in trouble again.
> When we walk down the street
> We pass the people we meet
> It really is a crying shame
> They can see from afar the kind of fellows we are
> That we're in trouble again.
> It's hard to see why this should be
> It makes us sad,
> Compared, perhaps, with other chaps
> We're not so bad
> But when we grow old and die
> And take a trip way up high
> We guess the Guardian there will complain
> And just for a gag
> He'll send us back for the flag,*

And we're in trouble again.

* When working parties left the confines of the camp, they had to carry a Japanese issued flag to show they were 'official.'

Taiwan 1943

'My Song Without Words' was the camp's "Top of the Pops" both in Taiwan and later in Omori Camp, Tokyo.

Verse:
If I were some composer, like Mendelssohn of old,
I'd write a song and tell the world about you.
How far away you are today – How much you mean to me,
How lonely every second seems without you.
But I've no song except for one
In my deepest dream.
The melody is memory,
My thoughts a simple theme.
Chorus:
My Song without Words is no hit, that I know
You won't hear it played over your radio
My Song without Words is my memory of you.
The smile that you smile
And the way that you walk
That light in your eyes
And the talk that you talk.
My Song without Words is my memory of you.

Now I'm confessing, that when expressing
My thoughts – Words seem in vain
At composition, I'm no musician
But you inspire a haunting refrain
So why should I try to write a song, when I know
Melody lingers wherever I go
My Song without Words is my Memory of you.

"Somewhere Across the Ocean"

Verse:
Every second, every day, since the day I went away
I'm dreaming – of one I adore
Though the years have drifted by
Still I know that she and I
Will meet again tomorrow
No more tears of sorrow.
Chorus:
Somewhere across the Ocean
Somewhere across the sea
Some day I'll be returning
To someone who waits for me
Somewhere across the mountains
That's where I long to be
That's where my thoughts keep turning
To someone who waits for me
Remember how we used to watch the setting of the sun
Sinking in a sea of gold
All those little things that made life so much fun
A rainy afternoon - An English country lane
A stroll beneath the moon - A continental train

Verse
Someday when skies are clearer
Someday when life is free
Sometime I'll be returning
To somewhere across the sea.

Tokyo 1944

'Ijo Arimasen'

Verse:
Now tho' you haven't so much time for studying
Of many foreign languages it's true
Yet here's a phrase that's really worth remembering
Just listen whilst I translate for you
Chorus:
Ijo Arimasen, you must learn to say,
'Cause Ijo Arimasen means everything's OK.
When you're feeling lowdown

And things look far from bright
Say Ijo Arimasen, that means everything's all right
Don't let troubles trouble you
Do the same as me
Bango all your blues away
Ichi, ni, san, see
So when the day seems dreary,
But you're on that final ton,
Sing Ijo Arimasen, that mean's everything A.1.

(This was my translation of Ijo Arimasen. It may not be correct! 'Bango' meant 'number off' and " ichi, ni, san, see" is one, two, three, four)

"The Bucket Swing"

In Omori there's a new sensation
It's a POW creation.
It's the latest thing in swing,
Makes you want to dance and sing.
Just listen to me do
While I expound to you.
Chorus:
They've been truckin' down the line,
Now the boys are feeling fine,
'Cause they know it's time to dine,
When they hear the Bucket Swing.
Don't delay it's getting late,
See them stomping through the gate,
Even Harlem's out of date,
When they hear the Bucket Swing.
Now tho' they can't go slumming in some low speakeasy bar
Yet they can always go to town
With a hey-nonny-nonny and a hot cup of cha.
When they know it's time for grub
See them give themselves a hug,
Everyone's a jitterbug
When they hear the Bucket Swing.

(The evening rations of rice used to be carried from the cookhouse to the huts in wooden buckets which used to squeak as they swung on the metal handles. Hence "The Bucket Swing")

"Goodbye"

Goodbye, until we meet again,
    Goodbye, don't sigh.
    We'll be back with another great revue,
    Till that time, the best of luck
    To all of you.
    Goodbye, and though we can't remain
    Just cast away your blues.
    And it won't be all that long
    'Fore you join us in a song
    Goodbye, goodbye, goodbye.

Tokyo 1945

"I'm Dreaming That I'm Steaming (on a Steamer home to you)"

    <u>Verse:</u>
    The stormy seas of life have nearly ended
    A peaceful breeze is soothing angry foam
    Everything again will be plain sailing
    When that dreamboat wends its way back home.
    <u>Chorus:</u>
    I'm dreaming, that I'm steaming
    To a homeland where the skies are blue
    Yes I'm dreaming, that I'm steaming
    On a steamer home to you
    I'm dreaming, that I'm sailing
    Like a pilgrim to be born anew
    Yes I'm dreaming, that I'm steaming
    On a steamer home to you.
    No more stormy weather
    The reefs and rocks are gone
    Soon we'll be together
    Everything is fine now on.
    When the sun sets on the sun-deck
    And the shadows whisper day is through
    I'll be dreaming whilst I'm steaming
    On a steamer home to you.

(The final rather hurried composition for the last POW Concert in Omori, 26th August 1945, 3 days before being released)

ORIGINAL LYRIC – Tune not remembered   Tokyo 1945

"When we meet once again, Sweetheart."

Verse:
Now tho' you're far away dear, you're always in my mind
I'm thinking of you every night and day
I think of all the things we'll do
Of the happiness we'll find
When peace and gladness really come to stay.
Chorus:
I'll be wearing tailored clothes
We'll visit all the West End shows,
When we meet once again Sweetheart.
I'll never look at rice again
We'll live on oysters and champagne,
When we meet once again, Sweetheart.
Now I don't care if winter's in the air.
Skies are always blue whenever I'm with you.
We'll say goodbye to strife and gloom
And have a second honeymoon
When we meet once again Sweetheart

We'll have a great big celebration,
There'll be no more inoculation
When we meet once again Sweetheart
We'll have credits we can spend
I'll be 'shushin' for weeks on end
When we meet once again Sweetheart.
Now I don't care if winter's in the air,
Skies are always blue, whenever I'm with you.
I'll never push another truck
We'll push a pram if we're in luck
When we meet once again, Sweetheart.

'HARRY GRIBBLE'

Harry Gribble was a mythical character who haunted Omori POW Camp. If anything went wrong, or anything went missing – we blamed Harry Gribble. Even the Japanese heard about him, but whether they realised he was quite fictitious we never knew. He was so famous that I wrote a 'Boisterous Ballard' about him for one of our concerts.

369

I'll tell you a story, it won't be too long,
So please don't start in to quibble,
About a young fellow – a prisoner of war,
One they call Harry – or Gribble.

In most all respects he was like you and I,
Normal and quite unabashed,
But the only remark he could ever make was
"Has anyone got any gash?"

From first thing in the morning to last thing at night,
He'd be looking for something to nibble,
He wouldn't waste time like you and I might,
In chatting or singing – not Gribble,
But between each mouthful of fish-heads
Which he swallowed by lumps in a flash,
He'd gasp through a gap between his front teeth,
"Has anyone got any gash?"

In fact the food he was missing
So preyed on his mind that one night,
His temperature rose to 200 degrees
And he never got over the fright.
His spirit sank deeper and deeper,
And as they pulled down the Sash
They recorded the words he spoke as he passed,
"Has anyone got any gash?"

He was met at the gate by St. Peter
Who said "The Lord wishes you well,
And as you have never yet stolen
You won't have to go down to Hell.
But we'll have to charge you admission,
The price is five yen, in cash",
Said Harry "I think that's a bargain –
But has anyone got any gash?"

They told him, of course, not to worry
And as he looked harmless and nice,
They gave him a harp and a halo,
Surrounded by bowls full of rice.
And now he is hungry no longer,
With the angels he cuts quite a dash,
And when he passed out on his Trade Test,
He was known to them all as – SAINT GASH.

Harry Gribble cartoon. If something goes wrong as it often did blame it on the (mythical) Harry Gribble. They'll never find him!
Sketch by Derek Clarke

'IT'S FISH' – ANOTHER BOISTEROUS BALLAD

Don't ask me what's for grub tonight
Don't ask me what's for chow,
Don't ask me if it's curry stew,
I hate to tell you now.
But if you really promise
Not to act before you think,
I'll tell you while I'm in the mood,
It's FISH – and does it STINK.

It smells just like a banjo
It doesn't look too clean,
It's either head or else it's tail,
There's nothing in between.
There's maggots crawling in and out,
It's older than the Sphinx.
In other words to make it clear
It's FISH – AND BOY IT STINKS.

INTRODUCING THE BARONS:

In Days of old when Knights were bold
And looting was a pleasure
Many a castle gate was forced
For jewels and other treasure
In '44 with Prisoners of War
Exists a similar state
For many a 'Kaisha' door's been forced
For salmon, 'gluc', or Tate.
And so, within these pages
(Unless he be a rare'un)
You'll find a rhyme or two about
The Great
SHIBAURA BARON.

Author's note:	Kaisha -	Railway freight wagon
	Salmon -	Fish
	'Gluc' -	Glucose
	Tate -	(Tate & Lyle – sugar)

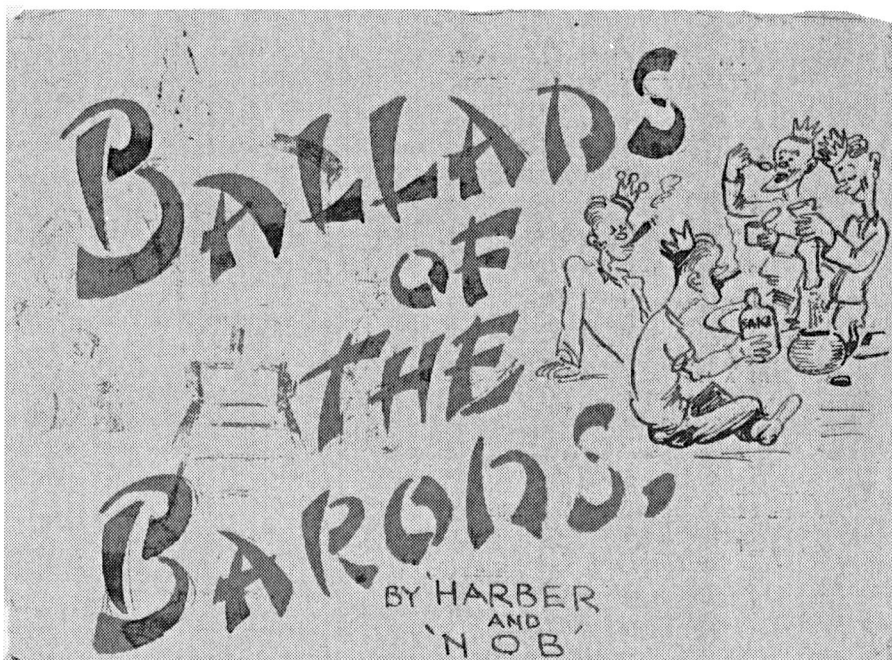

Ballads of the Barons. Cartoons by Derek Clarke.
The "barons" ran the black market in the camps!

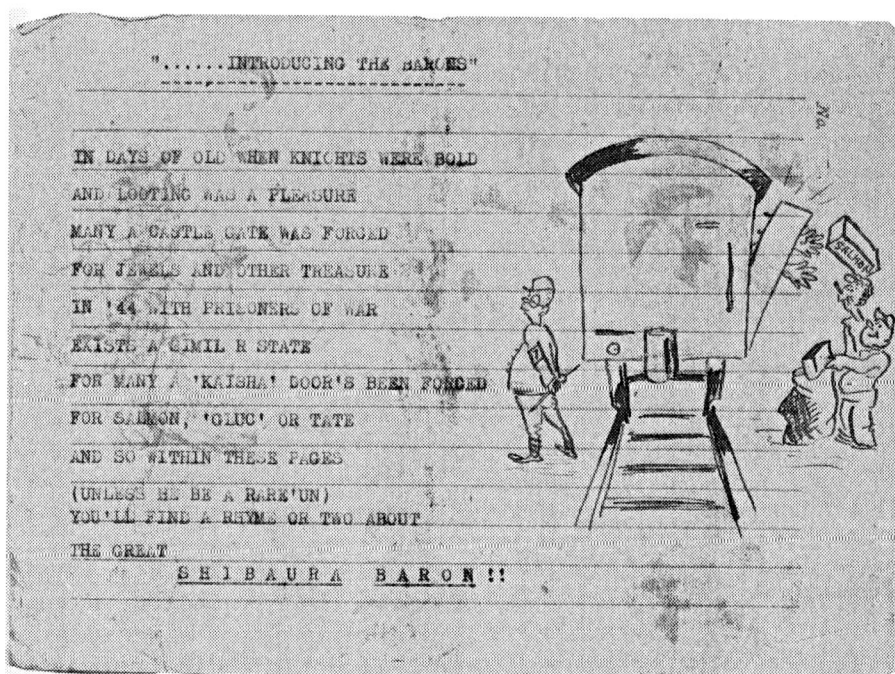

".......INTRODUCING THE BARONS"

IN DAYS OF OLD WHEN KNIGHTS WERE BOLD
AND LOOTING WAS A PLEASURE
MANY A CASTLE GATE WAS FORCED
FOR JEWELS AND OTHER TREASURE
IN '44 WITH PRISONERS OF WAR
EXISTS A SIMILAR STATE
FOR MANY A 'KAISHA' DOOR'S BEEN FORCED
FOR SALMON, 'GLUC' OR TATE
AND SO WITHIN THESE PAGES
(UNLESS HE BE A RARE'UN)
YOU'LL FIND A RHYME OR TWO ABOUT
THE GREAT
        S H I B A U R A   B A R O N !!

THE BARONS (CONT.)

King Topper:
Now Topper was the ruler
Of the Kingdom of Shibaura
He'd let his Barons go so far
So far – and then no farther
And at three o'clock you'd see him
Wearing a furrowed frown
When – going thro' the papers
He'd find the Tonnage DOWN!!

Barons Robinson and Caul:
Barons Robinson and 'Ginty'
Were counsellors of King Topper
They helped to keep the Palace clean
And see that all was proper
And when the Barons entered
With their plunder and their loot
They'd find a feast awaiting them
Of rice – and maybe soup!!

Baron Stocker:
The Mad Baron they called him
Tho' Stocker was his name
But the way he fooled the Yard 'Dick'
He was far from being insane
And whenever the 'Foo' approached
With his armband and his staff
Just like little Audrey
He would laugh and laugh and laugh

Lord McCadden:
Now though he's not a Scotsman
McCadden is his name
He serves under the Dodger flag
And stole his way to fame
He swears he is a Christian
And would have you to believe
That the first two people on this earth
Were McCadden and McEve.

Baron Green:
You've heard, of course, of 'Dodger' Green
And the story that's been told before
Of how, like the famous Oliver Twist
He was always asking for more
But lately he seems to be slipping
And appears to getting quite rash
By asking (when everyone's had quite enough)
"Does anyone want any Gash?"

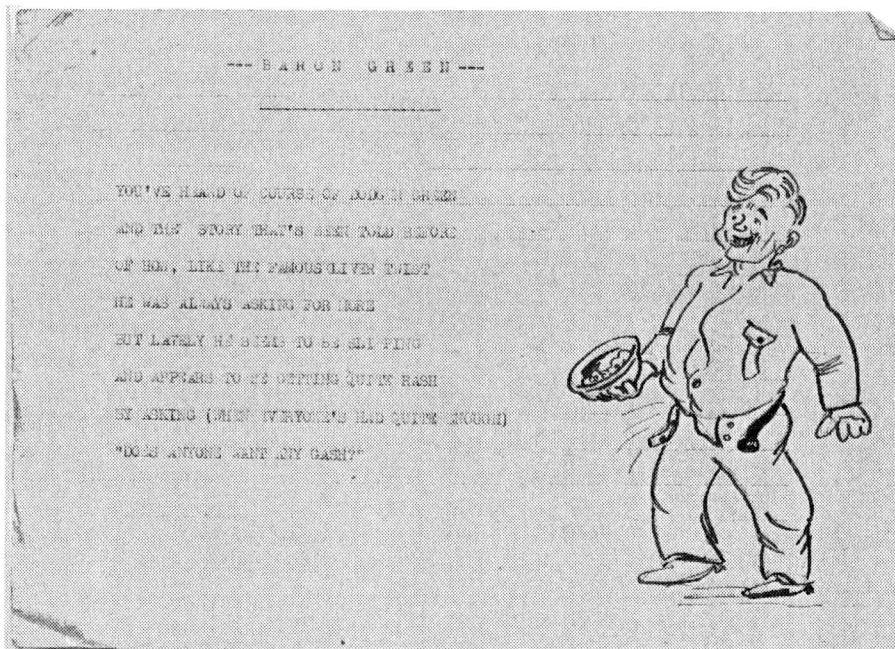

Baron Green Sketch by Derek Clarke

Baron de Josey:
Baron Josey, he was noted
For the largest paunch in camp
Which he used to great advantage
Whilst carrying on his ramp
You've heard, of course, of the Kangaroo
And how she carries her young,
Well that's where Josey keeps the tins
Of Salmon – when caught on the run.

375

Baron Stewart:

Now Stewart was a Baron
With a neck as bold as brass
He could baffle any Yard 'teck'
With his stuck-out chest and arse
But how that man could chatter
And if you cared to hark
You'd hear him talk for hours on end
Of a place called WINDSOR PARK!!

Baron Wags:

One of the new Barons
Is "Wags" – both tall and thin
To look at him you'd wonder
How the hell he'd ever get in
But being tall is handy
And on a really bright day
He'll see the "Tec" at any point
Round Yokohama Bay.

Baron Boo-Boo:

Don't make a sound!
Be careful how you go!
Please whisper very quietly
Don't breathe or even blow
They say there's many a slip can be made
Between the lip and the cup
So for Christ's sake man be careful
Boo-Boo's LOADING UP!!

Baron de Baker:

Doughy was a bright young lad
Who didn't care two figs
His one ambition, so they say
Is to find a Kaisha of WIGS!

Baron Kershaw:

A great romantic Baron
Was Kershaw – Christened Bert
The darling of Shibaura dames
Boy – How that man could flirt.
At any time you'd see him
(If she wasn't on the 'phone)
Standing at the office door

376

Serenading JOAN!!

Barons Mulligan & Mildren:
Mulligan and Mildren
Two wealthy Barons they
Who lived upon the best of food
That came Shibaura way
Any night you'd see them
Going through the range,
Salmon, Jam and Tate and Lyle
Or rice – just for a change.

Baron Fergusson:
Baron Fergy was an Outlaw
A reckless one was he
Who's held up many a Kaisha
For the sake of having sweet tea
And they say it's more than likely
That – when he gets the knack
He'll be walking down the Yama Sen
With the Engine in his sack!!

Baron Tate:
Although his name is Baron Tate
(He knows not Mr. Lyle)
He's noted for his ginger hair
And slightly freckled dial
Now dodger says he's lazy
And if this statement's true
Just offer him a cigarette –
And smoke it for him too!

The Mystery One:
They seek him here
They seek him there
Those Barons seek him everywhere
He's blamed for every unsolved riddle
That damned elusive
HARRY GRIBBLE!!

Christmas shows produced by Glyn Bowen-Jones at Omori prison camp, Tokyo, in 1944 enjoyed by the Japanese.

378

The following was first published in 'The War Illustrated' of October 25th 1945 (Price 6d.)

I WAS A 'GUEST' OF THE JAPS IN TOKYO.

Eleven hundred of us, mainly Artillery, were told we were being sent away from Singapore, and without delay we were carried in lorries, with such kit as we had, to the docks. We presumed we were going to Japan, and although we did not fancy the idea of moving further East and away from the Allied Forces, we did think that physically we should be better off.

"We will be better fed – probably European food," we told each other, "and we shall receive better medical attention." We knew also that Japan's climate was healthier than that of tropical Singapore.

A shock came when we saw our "liner". It couldn't have been more than a 4,000-tonner – an old tramp steamer which the Japs had named, "England Maru".

We did not think it possible they could crowd us all on that small vessel, but they did – plus 1,100 Japs who were going home. Conditions were hellish. There were three holds, each with wooden partitions built in around the sides. The prisoners occupied the bottom of each hold and the Japs the upper "berths".

We had been wise enough to bring along some of the Red Cross food which had reached us in Singapore a few days previously, otherwise we would have starved. There was a small amount of rice, and some greasy stew made with unfresh meat, issued three times a day. This diet naturally made us all very thirsty and it was difficult to get water for drinking; what we did get was salty.

It was not long before many of us became ill with dysentery. For ten days I had nothing to eat except Japanese tea (no sugar or milk). Four men were buried at sea and one of the senior British officers was tied to the mast and whipped because he objected to the terrible conditions. Finally the Japs began to get worried in case their own troops became infected and wirelessed for advice. They were told to put in at Formosa (Taiwan) and were highly pleased about it.

"You have nothing more to worry about," they told the sick. "Directly you dock you will be taken away in ambulances to a nice hospital." The "ambulances" turned out to be one Army lorry, and the "hospital" was our prison camp. It was situated just outside Taikhoku, the Formosan capital, and consisted of seven bamboo huts. Geography books tell us that Formosa has a mild climate, but none of us was ever so cold before as we were during that first winter of captivity. We were not allowed fires and rations were just sufficient to keep us alive. At one time an epidemic of diphtheria struck the camp and two or three prisoners were dying every week.

After three months in "hospital" (on reduced rations because I was not earning my keep by working) I joined my fellow prisoners in making some kind of a park immediately outside the camp; digging holes, putting the soil in a bamboo basket and then dumping it about a hundred yards away. It was extremely monotonous and tiring, and we worked from seven in the morning to five or six in the evening. We all lost three to four stone in weight (I weighed just over 7 stone) and our ribs showed clearly. However, with the approach of summer and the warmer weather we began to feel almost normal and, after our day's work was finished, we set about organizing pastimes.

A concert party began to function and despite interference from the Japs, morale began to soar. After a year of this existence they decided it was time to start splitting us up and interchanging us with prisoners in some of the other camps on the island. One day three of us were told to report to the Japanese Camp Commandant.

"You have been selected," he told us, "for a very special purpose. I cannot tell you what it is now, but you are going to the finest camp in the Japanese Empire. You have nothing more to worry about. You will be well treated and will receive a Red Cross parcel every day."

We had heard similar promises before so we were not impressed and I wondered what it was the Japs had up their confounded sleeves. However, on the following day, November 4th 1943, we started on our journey.

Before we left Formosa we picked up fifteen other POWs from the half-dozen camps, and were then divided into two groups, one of ten and one of eight. The larger group, we were informed, were to be known as the 'Technicians', and the remainder as the 'Cultural Group'.

We were put aboard a convoy (which had just arrived at Takao from Java), already full of Dutch prisoners going to Japan. Conditions were a little better than on the 'England Maru' although we were allowed on deck for only 15 minutes exercise each day.

Before we set sail the Japanese Commandant said he would endeavour to get us safely to Japan, but if we disobeyed orders we would be severely punished.

We reached the port of Moji (Japan) on November 14th. Saying goodbye to the Technicians, we 'Culturals' embarked on a train for Tokyo. We understood now that we were included in this group because of the activity we had taken in camp entertainments.

After a 30 hour journey we reached Omori P.O.W. Camp, Tokyo. At first we were called 'Special Prisoners' and were excused all work and fatigues, but this lasted for only three weeks. We were then interviewed by an English speaking Jap Officer who informed us that they wished to send us to a special Propaganda Camp where we could study Japanese culture. When I was asked, "What do you know about politics and economics?" I answered, "Nothing." Thus I lost my chance of a Red Cross parcel every day!

On December 7th 1943 I started work again. I was amazed at the fitness of the majority of the prisoners in Omori Camp as compared with the fellows I had left behind in Formosa. They were strong strapping fellows and full of life. This was because, working in railway yards and docksides, they managed to steal enough food – even if it were sometimes only rice – to keep them going.

At first I was in no condition to do heavy work. I couldn't carry 70 lbs of rice, and when I saw men with 200 lbs sacks of beans on their backs, walking up and down planks in warehouses, I was in despair. Again the winter for me was a nightmare. I hadn't the strength to lift an empty shovel and I couldn't sleep at night because of the cold. But the climate was far healthier than that of Formosa or Singapore, and after I learned the art of stealing from the Japs I found things a little easier.

On some days quite a variety of foodstuffs was shunted into the railway yard, and despite the vigilance of the armed guards, the vans were often looted by the POWs. At times it became a battle of wits between the British and the Japs. A luxury such as sugar came in only on rare occasions and, knowing that the prisoners would make every effort to obtain some, a special watch was kept. At the end of the day the Japs would be congratulating themselves on their successful vigilance, whilst the prisoners would be secreting socks stuffed with sugar beneath their working clothes. The same thing happened with rice, beans, fish and various tinned foods. In order to fox the few Japs who knew a little English, slang words were used for different commodities.

Sugar was 'Tate & Lyle", rice was 'white mice' and fish was 'tiddlers', and so on. Sometimes it was possible to bribe a Japanese foreman for a percentage of the 'loot'. They were usually quite willing. Despite a search before the ride back to camp it was seldom that anyone was caught, and in spite of repeated warnings of 'severe punishment' hardly a day went by without something being smuggled back. The expert looters lived almost as luxuriously as they would have done in wartime England. They were known as Barons, and could even afford to employ someone to make their beds of an evening and wash their dishes in exchange for a share of their surplus food.

Once again I began to take a share in the camp entertainments. The Japs finally allowed me three days off from work in order to write, produce and rehearse a show – after I had convinced them that it couldn't possibly be done in a few minutes.

It was a tremendous thrill when the Flying Fortresses made their appearance overhead. But also rather frightening.

We were not allowed to stop work during the day raids, and at night chaos was caused when thousands of Tokyo's little wooden buildings were set aflame. It was possible to read a book in the middle of the night by the light of those blazing fires.

Never believing in rumours, it was some time before I was really convinced that the Japanese had surrendered on August 15th 1945.

About a fortnight after this date, the Jap Commandant paraded us and announced the end of hostilities. I took down his speech in shorthand. He had the cheek to say he hoped we would bear no malice as he had always tried to do his best for us.

He has now I believe – and hope – been shot.

On August 29th, at four o'clock in the afternoon, American Marines landed on the beach outside our camp from three landing barges, and by four o'clock the next morning we had all been taken to a hospital ship.

We lucky ones at Omori were the first prisoners to be released from a camp in Japan itself.

Omori P.O.W. Camp from the air 1945

To Freedom at last! Aboard the HMS Speaker.
Harry standing up at the end extreme right

The following article was written on February 17th 1938. Harry Berry, the author, was 21 at the time. It appeared in the London evening newspaper, "The Star". It was the final article in a series called, "Youth Week – What this World Means to Them".

Many years ago (at least so it seems) when I was at school, I was very anxious to write down what I thought and felt of modern life, and how I proposed to cope with the problems that I knew lay before me.

Unfortunately I could never succeed in explaining myself to the English master. I could only vaguely mutter that I wanted to write an essay on Nothing in Particular. But I could never persuade him that I was serious; and my persistent request always afforded a good laugh to the other pupils in the class.

Then I left school; but I never forgot that, at the back of my mind, there was something that I had to put down on paper. Now, over five years later, I have the opportunity of writing what I had so foolishly thought was Nothing in Particular but which I now realise is the self-expression that every young man, at some time or another, longs to set free.

There is so much I wish to write that I have only the slightest idea of where to start, and having once started, of where to end.

Perhaps, in order to break the ice, I can give you a rough idea of my age by disclosing that I was born sometime during the Great War.

Having been brought up during the aftermath of the Great War, when everybody at last realised how futile it had all been and were resolving that it should never happen again, I find myself very bewildered when, in the space of a few years, the world seems to have suddenly gone mad and is finding great delight in playing soldiers.

I cannot accustom myself to the fact that we seem to have slipped back to the childish patriotic days of the last century.

Such phrases as "Keep the Old Flag Flying" and "This Glorious Empire" leave me cold. I should like to kick with studded boots the red-faced diehards who persist in interfering with national affairs. It would give me great pleasure to place them all on a Pacific Island to fight out their petty quarrels among themselves.

I readily admit that I am a coward. I should hate to kill a man, and worse still I should hate to be killed.

But if I am forced to go to the front, if I am forced to march along muddy ditches singing "Tipperary" and "Pack up your Troubles", if I have to shoulder a rifle from which a very patriotic gentleman way back home is making a fortune – then someone is going to suffer for my anger and disgust.

I am quite resigned to the fact that the odds are against me dying a natural death; but, having entered the world during a war I suppose I must console myself with the remarkable coincidence of leaving the same way.

It is the sub-conscious expectation (I will not say fear) of war that makes the young people of today beyond the understanding of their elders.

I intend, now that I have the chance, to do as much as I can, enjoy myself as much as I can, and pay practically no regard to the future.

I like going to parties and dances. I like listening to Swing music, and I like the atmosphere of cigarette smoke and the smell of cocktails.

But do not imagine that I consider myself to be a cheap imitation of a man-about-town. It is just that my motto is to live for the moment and let the future take care of itself.

Alternatively, I like rambling across the countryside in shorts and open-neck shirt. I keep myself fit, not by foolishly losing my beauty sleep in the morning to touch my toes six times, but by walking instead of riding whenever possible, and by insisting on plenty of fresh air.

Although other people of my financial standing cannot seem to afford it, I like running a powerful radio set, I go abroad for my summer holidays, and if I see anything that takes my fancy, I buy it.

The value of money means little to me. I do not save. I once made an attempt when a child, but I was not very successful. Money is made to be spent, and I know I get more out of life than a person who has a substantial amount in the bank and has not the slightest idea of what to do with it; contented to see the week through on a few shillings.

I have no notion of ever wanting to marry. I like girls as companions but detest them as friends. However much money I earned I could not afford to keep a wife; it would mean I should have to save. She would also be a hindrance to the complete freedom of movement which is an essential part of my habits.

For the very same reason I have no close friend either male or female with whom I go out of an evening to cinemas or theatres. I am quite content with my circle of acquaintances who are excellent friends and have no wish to impose on my individuality but are always pleased to welcome my company.

I have, as many young people have, ambition. My ambition is simply to get somewhere. Where, I am not particular, but I want authority to organise and power to act – and I am going to have a good try to get it.

Unfortunately ambition is not usually reached until one is well past youth. This unfair restriction should be crushed.

There are hundreds of young men and women wasting their time pounding typewriters or adding figures all day, when, if it were not for the cussedness of modern times, they should be utilising their brains for the improvement of their business or country.

I know I can make good. I have tried out my pet theories and ideas when holding official posts in social and sports clubs, and I am sure they would be just as successful on a larger scale.

That luck has smiled on me I will not deny. But that luck has given me confidence which I would not exchange for – well, pounds.

One bitter lesson which I have unwittingly learned is that one must sometimes be hard-hearted in the struggle for recognition. I have seen too many people fail because they were always willing to help other people in difficulties but failed to get the same support when they wanted a little help. Tact is a great asset.

I am essentially democratic. I am as good as anybody else, and everybody is as good as I. Consequently I resent both taking orders and having to give them.

I seldom take kindly to other people's advice. That, I suppose, is a common failing.

I hate political parties and financiers. I dislike Mussolini and I do not exactly admire the "haw-haw" attitude of B.B.C. Officials.

I am nervous of doctors and dentists, and I must visit Rio de Janeiro.

This, then, is the overflow of my soul which has been striving for recognition ever since my Nothing in Particular days.

APPENDIX

1.Robert Sinclair's letter (Harry's pre-war boss) Features Editor of "The Star". 1945

2.Gwen's letter to Singapore 2nd March 1942. Never received by Harry.

3. Illustration of Gwen's letter 29th March 1943 "You're alive!"

4.Gwen's letter 22nd August 1945.

5.Gwen's letter 18th September 1945.

6.Obituary of Harry Berry © "The Times" 3rd March 2004.

Robert Sinclair
"The Star" Office,
19, Bouverie Street,
London , E.C. 4.

24th September 1945
My dear Berry,

I don't know whether you'll ever get this, as I hope you'll be travelling home quickly. But everyone is so delighted at the news we've had of you, and we wanted to let you know that we had been thinking about you all the time (much good that did, sez you!) Your batch of five letters reached your wife today, the last only dated ten days ago from Manila. The best news of all was that you were physically A1. You'll be surprised how unchanged the office is and all the old gang. About four months ago it was just as it had been all the war, just grimy and dull. But in the last month or so lots of the chaps have come back. In the tiny Reporters' Staff alone there are three back, big Bernard Murphy, after six years in the RAF, little Tommy Watson, who used to be in the News Room, and who disappeared into the Ack Ack all through the war and never showed himself on a single leave, and Jock Russell, breezy and megaphonic, a little quick on the draw after the Malta and North Russia convoy runs in the Navy. The lads who had been carrying on in the reporters' room through the war and who thought they were old sweats there are shaken when the returned troops get shouting reminiscences across the furniture. Bill Brain, too, who was at Alamein, came in and did a week's reporting during his first leave for 3 years, and has now gone back to Greece - Lord knows what for. And Murphy wrote a funny article the other day about the horrors of working in London again, and how in the service all decisions are made for you but in civvy life you've got to use your elbows all the time, and the women push you off the bus stop, and he can even choose his meals in a restaurant, and oh! How he'd like to be back in uniform again where you just groused and didn't have to plan ahead. So it's cheered up us old stick-in-the-muds to have this little pleasantry from the returning chaps, who pull our legs in that way. I'm sure you'll do the same. Seriously, old chap, it's been an inspiration in the most depressing periods of the war to have your cheerful, hopeful and determined wife popping in at times (at too long intervals, I fear) to tell us the precious news of you, and being so delighted even when a year-old letter turned up. She

389

has been terrific, never thinking of herself, and we shall always remember the way she put a brave face on things. I hear you've done a little composing - or is it a lot? We shall have to have some record of that in the House Magazine when you turn up. Most of the blokes who send us news from the gun-site at Chelmsford are of the Dear-Mum-&-Dad, -Hope-this-finds-you-as-it-leaves-me variety. So a contribution from the Maestro Henry W. Berry will be a change! We have done a lot of physical moving around since you saw us last. The old building where you went in through the swing door is now a hole in the ground for the past 4 or 5 years, and we are installed in the new building (the block where our Feature Room was), while the News Chronicle have cleared out to the super-new building on the other side of the street. So now the main editorial are on the old first floor where the News Chronicle Editorial used to hang out, and the Sport are up in the old restaurant, and you damn near want a white stick and a dog when you want a cutting from the new Library. I don't know how you're coming home or by what route. Most of the chaps from Japan are coming by ship in order, I think, to have medical control of possibly tropical diseases. It may be a troopship, a converted aircraft-carrier or what-have-you. I only know two people out in your part of the world that you may bump into during your journeyings. One is my brother-in-law, who became a prisoner-of-war at Singapore 3½ years ago and who, we heard this week, is now all right. He was a lieut-col in the Indian Medical Service, in charge of a hospital in Singapore, I think, and latterly in a rather bad camp at Changi, near Singapore. The other chap is Capt C. Hughes-Hallett, R.N., captain of the aircraft-carrier Implacable, which the papers say is fitted up to bring home POWs. He is my next-door-neighbour and a very nice chap if you're in a jam about anything. It's great to believe that we shall soon see you in a civvy suit, arguing about swing with old Benson. Here's looking forward to it, and lots of love from all sorts of people whose faces disclosed their relief when I ran around the office telling them you were alive and kicking. All the best!

Yours ever,

(signed 'Sinc')

Robert Sinclair was Features Editor of "The Star", at that time at 19 Bouverie Street, London E.C.4

My Darling husband,

I still haven't received any news since getting your cable from Singapore. I am very anxious about you. I have phoned up but no information has come through yet. You are always in my thoughts darling.

Muriel was up for the week end. She met me from the office Friday. We went along to the Strand corner House to tea. As I sat there I was thinking of that Wednesday when you and I were there together. I could hardly keep the tears out of my eyes. As you were expecting to move and you did the following day; what ages ago that seems to be. I will go back to Tuesday and tell you what I have been doing.

Herbert and Hazel came to the office and had tea with me. Afterwards I walked along to Charing Cross with them. Wednesday and Thursday evening at home doing odd jobs. Friday Muriel home; Saturday my sister Margaret, her boy friend "George", Auntie Bee. Frank and his girl friend Norah were here so there was quite a crowd of us.

Sunday Muriel left at 4.30 pm. I then went on to Mary's. Joe was home. Grandad and Aunt Bertha were there. Mary's son (our nephew) is really a lovely baby.

In case letter 48 has gone astray Mary's son was born the 15th February. His name is going to be "Christopher Seymour". He has blue eyes, fair hair and your mouth darling.

Joe had to get back to Blackpool that night but had missed his train (by 5 minutes) but caught a later one. He is expecting to go overseas soon. I have told you in previous letters he is now an ambulance driver.

Grandad is very fit; also Aunt Bertha. I received a letter from your stepmother "Do" last week; she is better. (I told you in previous letter that she had bad throat again.)

For the last week I have been teaching another girl my work in case I am away at any time, or as my relief when I go on holiday. So many people enquire about you darling. She has suggested I issue a bulletin everyday and pin it up; for instance "Cable received from Singapore 3rd February" No news since.

This girl? (34) working with me is quite jolly; she hopes to be getting married next week. Her fiancé is in the Merchant Navy. So many people when seeing her there at the desk said "You're not leaving us are you? (Thought I might have been going in the Forces but I don't think they will call me up yet.) She wrote a notice out "Cheer up. Mrs. Berry is NOT leaving" and stuck it up by the grill. Thank Goodness darling I am happy (as happy as I can be these days) at my work.

This evening I met Auntie Edie and had tea (or rather a cup of tea and one cake 2/- for two cups of tea and two cakes! Scandalous isn't it darling. But we went in this place as there were queues and queues of people waiting to get in the Corner House and Auntie Edie had to be back by 6.30 pm (Told you in a previous letter she is a telephonist at St James' Club Piccadilly). I arrived home about 7.45 and am now sitting by the fire doing some sewing and will soon be going to bed so Goodnight my darling. I love you.

xxxxxx

Wednesday.... Hello darling. Last night I went to cinema to see "The Little Foxes" Bette David also Charlie Chan in "Rio" quite good programme. This evening I have been doing some sewing again and listening to the radio. I am going to Watford this week-end. Eileen thinks Audrey may be home. There is not very much news to tell you darling. I am keeping fairly fit. How are you keeping these days? Everyday when I arrive home I hope there will be a letter or cable from you, waiting for me. The latest news I have received from you was your cable despatched from Singapore 3rd. February received by me 18th February.

I wonder and wonder what is happening out there, darling. In case my letter 48 has not reached you I will tell you again "London Opinion" has accepted your story and a cheques for £3.3.0 will be sent when it is published. I know you will be pleased. I was very thrilled. Perhaps you will write some more if you have time?
I wonder when it will be published. If possible I will send it out to you. Won't you feel grand to see your name in print again! What a clever husband I have! I don't know when I will be able to send the cash to you, darling. As things are at the moment, I don't know if my letters will find you.

I am now going to read for a little while. Frank is asleep in the chair opposite. It is 9.40. pm. I expect I will be going to bed about 11 pm. I will be saying Goodnight to you later darling xxxx

Friday. Here I am darling sitting by the fire. Nothing to tell you about yesterday, except that I phoned up again to see if any information has come through yet, but no. They told me it wasn't any use sending letters at the moment, as they will only be held up. But I am continuing to write darling and will post as soon as I get an address. It has been bitterly cold today, and snowing. I had a letter from John's mother yesterday. The evening I spent down stairs

393

with Daphne. Tonight I have been listening to radio and sewing. One has to keep things mended these days owing to the coupons for clothes. Big Ben just striking. What news to-night I wonder?

Going to do a little more sewing now darling. I love you darling. xxxxx

Tuesday sitting by the fire 7.15 am will go back to Saturday darling and tell you what I have been doing. I arrived at Watford about 5.30 pm. Eileen very disappointed as Aubrey's leave has been postponed. We didn't go out any where as Eileen has hurt her knee (bumped in the railings in the blackout) we just sat and talked. To bed about 11 pm.

Sunday we were very lazy. We stayed in bed until 10.45 a.m Eileen got up to get a cup of tea about 10 am which we had in bed. Breakfast we had about 11.15 am. After breakfast I thought I would go round to see Mrs. Tucker, but no-one was at home. Being such a lovely morning I thought I would go for a walk before dinner, strolled up the high street up to Town Hall and back thinking darling, of the times when we were together. What a long, long time (ago) it seems.

We had dinner at 2.15 pm About 4 pm I took the dog for a walk through the park. It was a grand afternoon. Sun was shining and the birds singing. (a real Spring Day) I wondered how there could be such a thing as war. I felt darling, you were with me. Although I go out darling and mix with people, I always feel so far away from them. You are always in my thoughts. I pray every night, God will keep you safe. After my walk in the afternoon I did not go out anymore. We had tea and supper combined about 8 o'clock. Went to bed about 10.30 pm lay talking about the

End of the War. It seem so remote at the moment doesn't it darling?

I went back to Watford Monday evening. Going to office from there this morning. I am on my own again at the office. My understudy is having a week off. She hopes to get married. Her fiancé is home.

You knew John Pope didn't you darling? He has been killed; crashed when landing. He was a pilot in the R.A.F.

Mr Grosgrove of the sports enquired after you today. I think this brings my diary up to date, darling. So I must write to John's mother. I love you darling. xxx

After April 6th there will be no white bread sold; so we will have to have brown.

I am now going to sew until fire gets low. I wonder what you are doing darling.

14th March 1942 Saturday. 9.20 pm

Today darling I received a letter from the Royal Artillery Record Office which said:-

"According to the records in this office your husband was serving in Malaya when the garrison of Singapore capitulated on 15th Feb. 1942.

Every endeavour is being made through diplomatic and other channels to obtain information concerning him and it is hoped that he is safe, although he may be a Prisoner of War. Immediately any information is obtained it will be sent to you, but in the meantime it is regretted that it will be necessary to post him as "Missing.""

I am trying to cheer myself up, darling, thinking you will be safer as a Prisoner of War, as there is some very fierce fighting going on out there. I am still going to keep writing and **when** I get an address it will be sent straight away. I am going to write to your father, to "Do" and to granddad. Every moment you are in my thoughts darling and I pray darling, this war will soon be over and we will be together again. I am very lonely without you.

* * * *

Sunday Our nephew was christened. Joe and Mary have asked you and I to be Godparents. So you are a Godfather now, darling.
Monday evening I went to see my friend at Greenford. I cycled there.
Tuesday evening at home.
Wednesday to Hillingdon to see Joe and Mary. Joe has seven days leave. (They have rented two rooms in a house at Hillingdon) Joe by the way has been in hospital for 6 weeks. He is suffering from some nervous trouble. The responsibilities of being a father, I told him. He is returning to hospital after his leave.
Thursday I went over to Finsbury Park to see Dad. Had tea with him. He is, like me, very anxious to get some news of you darling.
Friday I went to cinema" School for Scandal" Rather a ridiculous film.

Saturday 2nd May To Watford for week - end. I cycled there. Arrived about 6 pm.
Sunday Eileen had to go to work in the morning so I went out for a ride. Started at 10.30 am. Arrived home about 1 pm. It was a glorious morning. I went as far as Berkhamstead (if you know where that is, Bucks, near Aylesbury) In the afternoon we sat in the garden. 8 o'clock I cycled back to Ealing.

Monday evening I had an evening at home. I had so many jobs to do.

Tuesday 5th May *have been for a ride to-night darling. Went out about 7.10 pm. arrived home 9.10 pm. Since then I have been bringing this diary up to date I have not been writing every day darling as it is rather doubtful if I will be able to send this lengthy epistle through even when I do get an address to write to. I have written again to the Red Cross and have received a reply. No information at all seems to be coming through. You know darling you are always in my thoughts. It's hard to realize what you are doing and what the conditions are out there, whether you are getting any food other than rice.*

I wonder when all this business will be over and we will be together again darling. I miss you so will say goodnight to you now. All my love, Yours for ever Gwen xxxxx I love you darling. Just think of the day when I will be able to tell you that and not have to write it.

28, Pitshanger Lane
Ealing W5
29 March 1943

My Darling Husband
I can hardly write I
am so excited; today I heard
from the War office. You are
Prisoner of War in Japanese hands
How thankful I am, to know
you are safe. After waiting
fourteen months for news of you.
As you will know by previous
letters I have written to you, I
never lost faith and knew I would
hear oneday. Now I am waiting to
hear from you. I've had a busy
day writing, phoning and writing
letting everyone know, there has
been such excitement in the
office. How pleased they all were
to know you are safe. Now I
am looking forward for the
day when we will be together
again. I hope you are keeping

well. I went up to Library to find out where your Camp is. "Formosa." I will now read about the place. We are all well at home, I have been writing since July 1942. to Tokyo Red Cross & Hope some of my letters have got through. to you. and you will know Joe and Mary have a Son Christopher, now a Year old, Your short story was accepted by London Opinion. Herbert and Hazel are expecting a Son or Daughter in June. Marie and Alf are married, I'm still at the same old firm, and things here are very much the same. You are always in my Thoughts Darling. How I'd long for The Day when you come home to me.
Goodnight my darling
All my Love,
Your ever Loving Wife
Gwen

22nd August 1945
My own darling husband,

It is with great joy and happiness that I write this
letter to you knowing when you receive it, you will
no longer be a P.O.W. but FREE and will soon be
coming home to us all. The Day we have waited for so
long. It cheered us all very much to get your cards
and letters this month dated March 1944, Jan, Feb,
March 1945. To know you were in the best of health
and quite cheerful and that you were getting mail
from home Darling. I do hope you are still very fit. I
feel so thankful darling that all your family and
myself have come safely through these trying times
safe and unharmed. The family are all back at 72 now
and quite well. You will certainly find a change in
Joyce, Ray and Beryl who have all grown. Joe and
Mary have two sons now. I have not seen them for
sometime now. But they are all well and granddad
and Aunt Bertha, Dad, Do and Beryl spent last week
with them. I have not seen them since their return
but hope to pop over one evening next week.

Yes darling the piano is all ready for you. I do not
suppose you had any chance to keep up with your
music out there, did you?

How I am longing for your return darling. I have
missed you so these 4 and a half years. I have had a
grand girlfriend who has helped me through her
husband also being abroad. We have been to
needlework classes: cycling, walking and away for
weekends together. She has been a grand PAL. You
will meet her when you come home I expect. I am

going to my friend at Staines this week-end. All at the office send their best wishes. Mr Sinclair was the first one to phone me to tell me of the surrender of Japan. I've had letters from many people. Things here are very much the same. I still enjoy my work at the office, have really got on very well. I wonder how long it will be before you return to the office. Did you receive the card *Mr. Sinclair wrote to you?

I sent you a radio message which was broadcast 14th July 1945. Did you get it?

Herbert is now a Captain he has been abroad, but is now in England for a while. He is very fit. Muriel is married. Frank is still at home with me. He has been good company. He is engaged but as there is such a shortage of houses they are waiting awhile before they get married.

Darling, won't it be grand when we start planning our home, doing things together again? I love you so much. Every day you have been away, my thoughts and prayers have been for you, that you will come through all the trying times safely. Darling hurry home to me. I am sure we will have our 5th anniversary together. Take care of yourself darling. Love from all the family

All my love, Darling,
Your loving wife,
Gwen.

* Features editor of "The Star," Harry's boss.

18th September 1945
My Darling Harry,

I expect by now you are just beginning to realize it is really true and you ARE FREE:
I try to understand how you must be feeling Darling; after all you must have gone through and your last letters and cards while captive were full of hope. I can see you always looking on the (or for the) brighter-side.

On Sunday I went for a ramble about 16 miles around Amersham it was quite enjoyable. We had a meal out in the evening at a very nice place called 'The Mill Stream'.

Monday evening: Started evening classes, am making a blouse to go with my suit; specially made for you darling.

Tuesday evening: Went over to see my sister Margaret, quite an enjoyable time, stayed the night. TODAY 19 SEPT: VERY HAPPY DARLING AT LAST A LETTER FROM YOU. Frank phoned me up to say there was one: so I left the office straight away. Couldn't get home quickly enough. To hear from you Darling, a real letter, and to know you are, "As fit as a fiddle" in spite of all you have gone through. Gosh you must be tough to carry 200 lbs. I'm longing to hear about the Shows you produced and see the songs you have written. You certainly have plenty of initiative (have I spelt it correctly darling?)

You must have been having a bad time when you weighed 7st 12lbs. As you say, Thank God it's over now:

I too Darling am very much in love with you, all these 4½ years you have been with me in spirit: and I have been very anxious about you. But I always felt that we would both come through this terrible nightmare: Glad my letters got through O.K. I had to repeat much news as I didn't know if they would all get through.

When do you think you will get home Darling? Only very few will be flying so I am not building up hopes that you will be home before four or five weeks. Still I must wait patiently now knowing you are safe and well. I am going over to 72 * this evening to take your letter. How thrilled they will be! Am sending third telegram tonight; longing to get another letter from you, Darling and I think you can write anything now there is no Censorship.

Am writing this in office. All have gone home, but thought I would finish this so you get it soon. Sinclair was very pleased to know I'd had further news from you. "How do you feel about returning to 'Star'?" Just off to 72.

> *All my love for Ever*
> *Your loving wife*
> *Gwen xx*

---

* Harry's father and step-mother's house in Finsbury Park, Islington.

HARRY BERRY

Airport reporter turned PR man who put the BEA into the Beatles

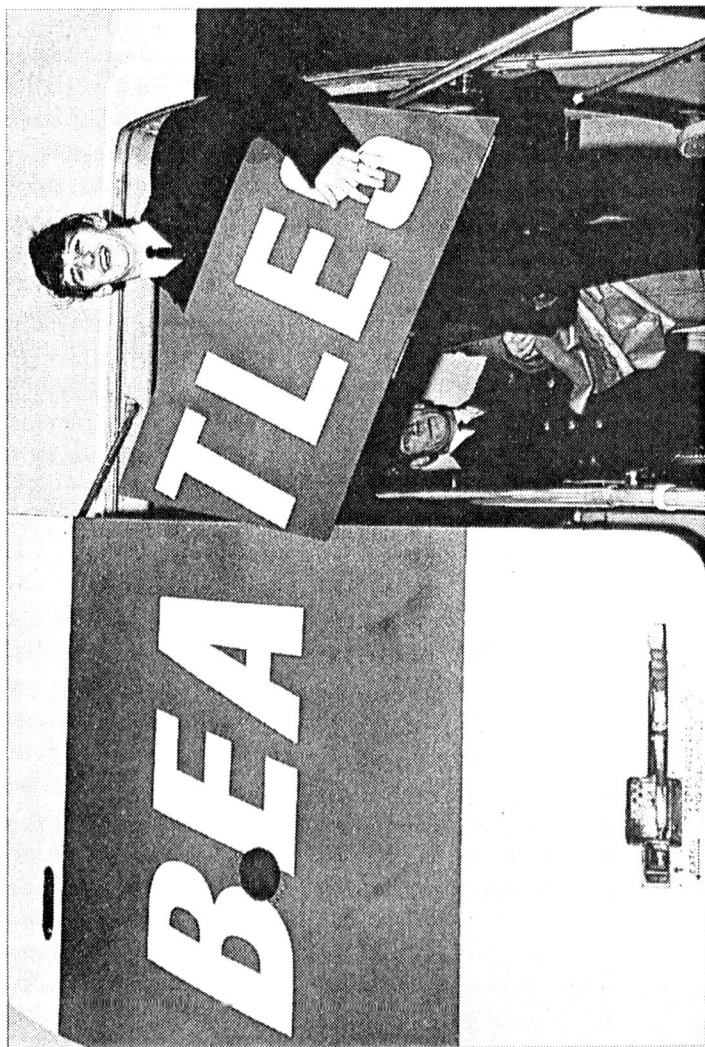

Ringo Starr
boarding a
BEA
Viscount
airliner at
Heathrow
airport in
1963, before
the group's
first
European
tour

© The Times, London (3rd March 2004).

AS PRESS and public relations manager of British European Airways, Harry Berry put the BEA into the Beatles as they boarded a Viscount airliner to set off on their first major European tour in 1963. At the top of the steps to the aircraft he posed Ringo Starr, holding up a board bearing the painted inscription "TIES", which, in conjunction with the airline's BEA logo completed the band's famous name. Berry had invited a throng of press photographers for the occasion, which cannily garnered worldwide free publicity for the airline, as well as for the Beatles themselves. It was a piece with Berry's knack of balancing promotion of the product he represented with a good popular news story.

When, in the early 1970s, BEA and its intercontinental partner, British Overseas Airways Corporation (BOAC), united to become British Airways, Berry continued in post with the new airline. With his nose for the news value attached to the doings of celebrities, he continued his flow of stories along those lines to media airline correspondents. It was something that he had learnt from his postwar days as a reporter for a news agency covering the comings and goings of stars at London's airports.

Harry Berry was born in Islington in 1916 and educated at Tollington Park Central School. He began an apprenticeship in journalism in the mid-1930s, graduating to become a feature writer with the Star, one of London's evening newspapers at the time. A self-taught pianist, he also wrote a jazz column.

When war broke out in 1939 he was called up into the Royal Artillery, serving first in India and then Malaya. At the fall of Singapore in February 1942 he became a prisoner of the Japanese, and with thousands of others was held at first in Changi jail. There, the portable typewriter that was his constant companion remained undetected, and he produced a news sheet for his fellow prisoners.

Later he and others were shipped to Formosa (Taiwan), where his typewriter was confiscated, so he turned to writing songs for camp shows with a fellow prisoner, Sergeant Derek Clarke. Later he and Clarke were sent to the Omori PoW camp just outside Tokyo, the Japanese apparently believing that they could be induced to broadcast favourable propaganda. This they both resolutely declined to do, and they spent the rest of the war working in gangs of British and American PoWs, loading and unloading food supplies in railway marshalling yards.

After being released by the Americans at the end of the war, Berry and his fellow PoWs were repatriated by ship via San Francisco. As they passed under the Golden Gate Bridge and entered San Francisco Bay the former prisoners were greeted by a huge banner suspended from the walls of an island fortress proclaiming "Welcome Home Boys". In the circumstances Berry was amused to learn that the castle was Alcatraz, the notorious maximum-security prison.

Arriving in Southampton in November 1945, Berry at first returned to his old job. In 1947 he applied for a post as a reporter with a news agency which had just been set up to cover the movement of celebrities through the recently opened London (Heathrow) airport. His success at this led to the agency inviting him to set up a similar service at Northolt, which was then the temporary home of BEA and a number of continental airlines.

His output of news stories brought him to the notice of the chief executive of BEA, the future Sir Peter Masefield, who in 1953 invited him to become the airline's spokesman at Heathrow. As poacher turned gamekeeper, Berry used his nose for news to great effect, subtly dividing publicity for the airline with the imperative of providing good stories for journalists. His office frequently became a sanctuary for the many celebrities who passed through the airport. At one time all four Beatles took refuge there to escape the thousands of screaming teenagers who awaited them outside. At other times the comedians Tony Hancock and Bob Monkhouse sought shelter there from the enthusiasm of their fans.

When BEA and BOAC merged as British Airways in 1972 (on paper, at least, BA did not come into being in practice until 1974), Berry continued as press and public relations manager for the new national flag carrier.

Berry retired from BA in 1979 and thereafter enjoyed travelling the world with his wife Gwen. He had married her in December 1940, three months before his departure to the Far East for what was to be a separation of five years. Changi jail was just one of the venues from wartime days that he revisited with her. The voluminous war diaries he wrote are in the Imperial War Museum.

Gwen, whom he nursed through Parkinson's disease, died last year. He is survived by their daughter.

Harry Berry, former press and public relations manager for British European Airways and British Airways, was born on December 1, 1916. He died on January 19, 2004, aged 87.

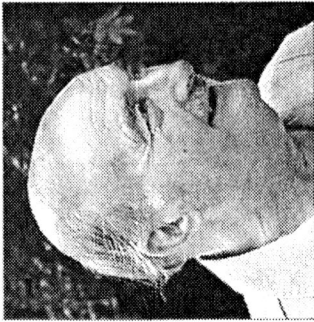

Harry playing the organ at home in the 1970s.

Celebrating 50 years' anniversary of V.J. Day (1995) with family in Bollington, Cheshire. Harry in the centre at the back.

Back row left to right: Harry's brother Ray and his wife Angela Berry, Harry, his daughter Linda and her husband David West.

Front row left to right: Harry's sister Beryl Allen and brother Joe Berry and Harry's wife Gwen Berry.

Finally, brethren,
whatsoever things are true,
whatsoever things are honest,
whatsoever things are just,
whatsoever things are pure,
whatsoever things are lovely,
whatsoever things are of good report;
if there be any virtue, and if there be any praise,
think on these things.

(Philippians Ch 4 v.8)

Printed in the United Kingdom
by Lightning Source UK Ltd.
04059UKS00001B/91-102